CONTEMPORARY
MORAL ISSUES

WADSWORTH CONTINUING
EDUCATION SERIES
Leonard Freedman, General Editor

CONTEMPORARY MORAL ISSUES
edited by Harry K. Girvetz
University of California, Santa Barbara

ISSUES OF THE SIXTIES
edited by Leonard Freedman
University Extension
University of California at Los Angeles
and Cornelius P. Cotter
Stanford University

WADSWORTH
PUBLISHING COMPANY
BELMONT, CALIFORNIA

CONTEMPORARY
MORAL
ISSUES

EDITED BY
HARRY K. GIRVETZ
University of California, Santa Barbara

Second printing, March 1964

L. C. Cat. Card No.: 63-14322
Printed in the United States of America

PREFACE

This book deals with some of the major moral issues of our time. To call them issues is to say that they are not yet resolved, at any rate not among thoughtful and responsible men of good will; or, if they are resolved, the manner of resolution is not one that has decisively affected practice. Admittedly the determination of good will, wisdom, and responsibility involves judgments of value and might be said, therefore, to reflect personal bias. But, quite apart from the quality of the readings and the competence and distinction of their authors, I have employed a principle of selection that should commend itself to reasonable readers of every persuasion. I have chosen authors who might be presumed to encounter dissent without branding it as evidence of malice or stupidity—authors who, in short, claim no monopoly of wisdom and virtue. Presumably these are people who could engage in debate without denouncing each other as knaves or fools.

I have employed another related principle of selection, although obviously with no pretense to infallibility in its application. The authors are, it will be evident, committed people. But they have not, in my judgment, subordinated the pursuit of truth to defense of their commitments; their loyalties, however strong and even passionate, have not blinded them to alternatives.

Such, in addition to evidence of scholarship, are the requirements by which great universities recruit their faculties. The upshot of adherence to such principles is the exclusion of bigots and blind partisans. Their utterances too are of interest, for they often have an impact on history and afford interesting evidence of the extremes to which men may be led by their passions and prejudices, but our concern here is a different one— namely, better understanding of some of the still unsettled moral problems of our day. This is not a project to which fanatics can make a significant contribution. However, such a view does not imply endorsement of what has been called the "ultramiddle"; to reject blind partisanship is not to praise moral timidity or apathy.

The selections in this volume are not concerned with the problems that would occupy a theoretical treatise on ethics. Such a study, although it would do well to deal with specific moral problems and issues, would by

v

necessity go beyond them to an analysis of the concepts of right and good and ought, of moral law and conscience, concepts that most moral controversy takes for granted—as it does the relevance and demonstrability of judgments of moral value. How judgments of value are demonstrated (if indeed they can be demonstrated at all), and the sense in which they may therefore be regarded as meaningful, is a cause of much difference of opinion among professional philosophers. But this is not a question that will concern us here beyond one important comment. Behind the assertions of the writers included in these pages is the assumption that there exists a difference between good and evil that is more than a simple affirmation of preference. The point to moral discourse—unless those who partake of it are in quest of emotional catharsis—is to persuade. Quite obviously, if nothing but preferences were involved, all effort to persuade would founder on the retort that there is no disputing about tastes.

Persuasion is often and most simply accomplished by calling attention to facts concerning the antecedents and consequences of a course of action, or to its consistency or inconsistency with accepted values or standards. One may point out, for example, that the repeal of capital punishment has or has not been followed by an increase of the crimes previously punishable by death, that loyalty oaths have or have not been helpful in exposing Communists or that such oaths are or are not consistent with heretofore accepted standards concerning test oaths. One may cite evidence to indicate the discrepancy between precept and practice in sex conduct, or refer to what psychologists have told us about the causes and consequences of the state of mind that required loincloths to be painted over Michelangelo's nudes in the Sistine Chapel. In all such cases persuasion is accomplished and agreement effected within the framework of a common set of values.

Often, however, the facts do not prevail, and considerations of consistency become hopelessly obscured. When this happens one may conclude that the conflict lies deeper and involves values themselves. It is here, in disputes over standards of value, that our differences are crucial. Can such differences be reconciled?

The question here raised concerns moral suasion in the true sense. When the President of the United States and the president of United States Steel recently disagreed over the respective responsibilities of business management and government concerning the price of steel, they were not merely differing over matters of fact—although many facts were, of course, relevant and in need of clarification. One may assume that Mr. Blough and President Kennedy have different notions concerning what *ought* to be the prevailing pattern of conduct in our society, a basic difference over values that no amount of appeal to verbally identical principles like "the common welfare" or "the public good" can conceal.

The city of Coventry recently completed a cathedral to replace the great Gothic church destroyed by Germany's *Luftwaffe* on the night of November 14, 1940. However, during the years following the war the city council of Coventry refused a building permit for a new cathedral, arguing that there was a prior need for schools, houses, and clinics. The council was overruled, it so happened, by the British Minister of Works, who wrote: "Can we be sure that a cathedral would be so useless? We have never had a greater need for an act of faith." The difference, although perhaps not as acrimonious as the dispute between President Kennedy and Mr. Blough, surely reflects competing sets of values.

Senator Barry Goldwater in *Conscience of a Conservative* condemns liberals because, he contends, their preoccupation with economic security blinds them to the "spiritual" side of man's nature. Clearly, as the Senator suggests in the title of his book, the difference between him and liberals does not arise from questions of fact; it is instead a matter of conscience.

If such differences are to be reconciled and moral suasion is indeed to occur, an *act of will* must take place. This is something more than the act of perception or act of thought required of those who differ because of obscured facts or inconsistent reasoning from accepted moral premises. People must be *willing* (in the double sense of that word) to suspend their prevailing standards of value in order to entertain an alternative—an alternative not envisaged when they first formulated their standards. In the ensuing reevaluation they may reaffirm or revise their heretofore accepted values, but one thing is certain: such values will have new meaning to them by virtue of having been thus tested. Moreover, in this way they may find enhancement that would otherwise have been denied them had they resisted such reappraisal.

What precise circumstances occasion such reevaluations and what occurs as we reappraise our prevailing standards of value are complex questions that must be left to more technical discussions. But this much is clear: bigots and fanatics will not submit their position to reexamination. Neither, for other reasons, will members of preliterate or authoritarian societies, where the individual is so submerged in the group or so submissive that he would not think of challenging the prevailing mores. Reappraisal is possible only for free men conscious of themselves as agents capable of guiding their own development—capable, that is, of an exercise of free will in what is perhaps the only meaningful sense of that term. Such a capacity is not an original endowment, but an achievement laboriously won over the long centuries during which a relatively few men have emancipated themselves from tyranny, whether of law and custom or of their own unrestrained impulses and appetites.

The issues discussed in this volume are arranged into six groupings, although other ways of relating them might be equally appropriate. With each grouping are brief introductory comments, which suggest the main problems in that area and indicate the rationale for that particular grouping. The groupings are subdivided into topics, and accompanying each topic is a brief formulation of the issue. With each selection are comments concerning the author's background. For the most part I have made an attempt to represent important differences in point of view and to emphasize the contributions of living Americans.

I would like to acknowledge the able assistance of Dr. Vernon Nash whose semi-retirement has brought to our community a rare spirit who combines moral fervor with good humor—thereby enabling us to deplore our follies and at the same time smile at them. In addition, I have been helped by my wife, by Sharon McKenna, secretary to the Department of Philosophy, and by the unfailing cooperation of Dr. Leonard Freedman, University of California Extension, Los Angeles, editor of the series to which this volume is a contribution.

CONTENTS

PART ONE

SECURITY
AND ITS
MORAL
IMPLICATIONS

Security of person and property is the first concern of a well-ordered society. Few passages in the literature of political philosophy are more remembered than Thomas Hobbes' observation in the *Leviathan* that in the "war of all against all," there can be "no culture of the earth, no navigation . . . no commodious building . . . no knowledge of the face of the earth . . . no arts; no letters; no society . . ." In Hobbes' famous phrase, life in such circumstances is "solitary, poor, nasty, brutish, and short."

Hobbes lived during a period of prolonged civil strife, and his first concern was with internal order. Today, our first concern is with world order. In such times security takes on new meaning, and nations take special precautions to protect themselves. As a consequence, new moral issues come to the fore—or old issues appear in a new context. In our day the quest for national security is complicated by the threat, posed for the first time, of total destruction from nuclear warfare and by the effect on future generations of the slow contamination of the atmosphere from nuclear testing.

The complications are not only technological; they are also ideological, stemming from the peculiar circumstance that in our present world crisis the division is not primarily between "haves" and "have nots," but between competing ways of ordering the whole scheme of social relationships. The difference could therefore take on a religious character, which is a dangerous possibility because religious wars, as we know from bitter experience, evoke a fanaticism that is heedless of consequences. Fortunately, zealous ideologues rarely achieve high office. Statesmen and politicians are not generally given to religious fervor. They shun holy crusades; and, if the price of the objectives they normally pursue is too high, they content themselves with less—in the present case with coexistence.

The ideological implications of the international crisis, whether these are central or peripheral, bring the problem of defending ourselves from an external threat a great deal closer to the issue of internal security than it would otherwise be. Ideologies are notoriously scornful of national boundaries. Our differences with the Soviet Union have therefore greatly increased concern about Communism at home.

A nation's internal security requires that it protect itself from disloyalty. Such disloyalty may manifest itself in revolutionary activities culminating in efforts to overthrow the government or, where a foreign foe is involved, in sabotage and espionage. Efforts to achieve internal security inevitably come into conflict with individual rights and liberties. The conflict of values thereby generated has sorely tried our national conscience since the loyalty program was first initiated by President Truman in 1947.

Often the conflict appears to be no more than a difference over questions of fact. Is there really a danger of revolution in this country requiring that we take special precautions? Is Communism an authentic revolutionary movement or a conspiracy? In either case does the Communist movement undermine and menace our institutions? Is a given device (for example, loyalty oaths) or a given legal measure (say the McCarran Act or the Smith Act) effective in combating Communism? Here, as usual, one may safely assume that where such questions of fact do not get resolved, differences concerning the facts conceal a more basic difference over values. Spokesmen for the radical right find that Communists inside our country pose an imminent threat even more to be feared than the threat of the Soviet Union. Others would say that this is a preposterous exaggeration. Clearly, more than a difference over questions of fact is involved in this disagreement. The so-called naked facts rarely (in fact) present themselves without raiment; we sometimes forget that they come with a thick cloak of interpretation heavily colored by our interests and values.

Readers of the selections that follow should look for unexpressed or tacit disagreements over values as well as for avowed differences. Often the unavowed difference is the more important one. Thus, the question is rarely raised: is revolution *ever* morally justifiable, and, if so, under what conditions? How far does "loyalty" require that we go in obeying the law of the state? Are we, in fact, obligated to obey a law that we are convinced is morally wrong? The opposite classical answers to this question were made by Socrates and Sophocles' Antigone: by Socrates, who, as the *Crito* reports, refused to escape prison and avoid the death to which an Athenian jury had condemned him; by Antigone, who refused to obey the law of Creon when it decreed that the body of her brother lie unburied. The second position, it has been said, leads to anarchy; the first enabled the men in charge of the Third Reich's extermination camps to plead that they were conforming to the law, which decreed that they obey their superiors. *Ein Befehl ist ein Befehl!* What shall our answer be?

There are other points at which the quest for security raises profound moral issues. We must secure ourselves against thieves, murderers, and the like—against those, that is, who would do violence to us as individuals. Here no political or ideological issues are at stake. Even so, the problems are often similar.

The police are responsible for protecting us from criminals. How far ought they to be allowed to go in ignoring individual rights and invading privacy (for example, with wire-tapping) as they go about the difficult business of detecting crime and catching the culprit? How ought the criminal to be dealt with once he is caught? The crime rate is mounting with alarming rapidity. What can we do to curb crime without flouting accepted moral imperatives? Shall we inflict severer penalties? Many now clamor that we must deal more harshly with the culprit who traffics in narcotics. Shall we say, with the Queen of Hearts, "Off with his head!"? Or is there a more humane and effective way?

Above all, should crime *ever* be punishable by death? Professor Jacques Barzun prefers the term "judicial homicide" to "capital punishment," since the latter designation implies a reason—namely, punishment— to which some who favor the death penalty do not subscribe. In any event, since respect for the sanctity of human life provides the moral basis of our society, the issues raised by the use of the death penalty are fundamental and have therefore occasioned some of our most excruciating moral perplexities.

Such are the diverse and manifold problems raised by the quest for security. Needless to say, they have inspired comparably diverse and manifold solutions.

NATIONAL SECURITY IN THE NUCLEAR AGE: THREE MORAL APPRAISALS

The quest for national security in a nuclear age poses some ancient moral problems as well as a number of radically new ones. Is the position of the pacifist morally justifiable? It often manifests itself nowadays in a slogan that seems more like an appeal to expediency than the invocation of a high moral principle: "Better red than dead!" And it calls for unilateral disarmament if necessary. Is this craven capitulation to the forces of evil, or, as some have argued, is the position supported by moral insights that the critics ignore?

The position of the pacifist does not preclude him from making moral comparisons and from allying himself with one or the other of the parties to the conflict; he simply affirms the futility of armed conflict and opposes the use of force under any circumstances. On the other hand, neutralism, at least in one of its major manifestations, is the view that good and evil in what we call the Cold War are too evenly distributed to justify taking sides. Whether Americans like it or not, morally perceptive men defend such a position. Indeed, the sheer massiveness of neutralist sentiment in the world not only puzzles and disturbs Americans, it presents a potential threat to the bonds that tie us to our allies. Unlike doctrinaire pacifism, which finds few converts and will not be debated in these pages, neutralism is a significant force in the world. Hence, no matter how indignant we may feel, we must examine the neutralist's position. Since there are hardly any influential American neutralists, it has been necessary to find a spokesman from abroad.

At the other extreme are those who challenge our present commitment to a policy of coexistence. Is coexistence morally defensible, or shall we, with Senator Goldwater and the far right, answer the title of his most recent book *Why Not Victory?* with a resounding affirmative? Ironically, the Kremlin, also apparently committed to a policy of coexistence, encounters strikingly similar criticism from its far left—in this instance the Chinese Communists. One may well marvel at the curious trick of circumstances (not to mention the hazards of moral discourse) that has made schismatics of Mao Tse-tung and Barry Goldwater and has them raising the same moral questions. In the selections that follow, three distinguished men—a theologian, a diplomat, and a business executive—provide answers to some of these questions.

NO ANGELS OF DARKNESS AND LIGHT[1]

Karl Barth

> *To many Americans there could be no more disconcerting exponent of the neutralist view than Karl Barth. He is Protestantism's most eminent continental theologian. He has been called "the master theologian of our age" and "the colossus from Basel." President James McCord of Princeton Theological Seminary has said that "he bestrides the theological world like a colossus," and theologian Hans Frei of Yale has called him a "Christ-intoxicated man." Although, as a professor in Germany, he led the fight against Hitlerism, he has refused to take sides against the Russians, even to avoiding open condemnation of the Russian brutalities in Hungary. His advice to us has been to surrender our nuclear weapons—unilaterally if need be. Even so, an American mass-circulation weekly dedicated last year's Easter issue to him, commenting that in this century "no man has been a stronger witness to the continuing significance of Christ's death and Christ's return than the world's ranking Protestant theologian, Swiss-born Karl Barth."[2] Most Americans may not like what Karl Barth says, but they should read him. This need not preclude us from reflecting that if he were to direct similar animadversions at the USSR the Soviets would drown them in vituperation—and from wondering why this has not tempered his impeachment.*

. . . The East-West question has accompanied and shadowed us all since the end of World War II. On this question I cannot agree with the great majority of those around me. Not that I have any inclination toward Eastern communism, in view of the face it presents to the world. I decidedly

---

[1]*The Christian Century,* January 20, 1960, pp. 72 ff. Copyright 1960 Christian Century Foundation. Reprinted by permission from *The Christian Century.*
[2]*Time,* April 20, 1962, p. 59.

prefer not to live within its sphere and do not wish anyone else to be forced to do so. But I do not comprehend how either politics or Christianity require or even permit such a disinclination to lead to the conclusions which the West has drawn with increasing sharpness in the past 15 years. I regard anticommunism as a matter of principle an evil even greater than communism itself. Can one overlook the fact that communism is the unwelcomed yet—in all its belligerence—natural result of Western developments? Has not its total, inhuman compulsion which we complain of so much haunted from remotest times in another form our avowedly free Western societies and states? And was it then something suddenly new and worthy of special horror when communism presented itself as a doctrine of salvation blessing all men and nations and therefore one to be spread over the whole world? Are there not other systems of this kind and tendency? Further, could we really intend to help the peoples governed by communism and the world threatened by it, or even one individual among those suffering under its effects, by proclaiming and seeking to practice toward it a relationship exclusively that of enemies? Have we forgotten that what is at stake in this "absolute enemy" relationship, to which every brave man in the West is now obligated and for which he would give his all, is a typical invention of (and a heritage from) our defunct dictators— and that only the "Hitler in us" can be an anticommunist on principle?

Who in the West has even once taken the trouble to think through from the Eastern and particularly from the Russian standpoint the painful situation which has arisen since 1945? Were we not rather happy, and with good reason, over the Soviet contribution to the conquest of the National Socialist danger? Was it not the leaders of the West who toward the end of the war conceded and guaranteed the Soviet Union a determining influence in eastern Europe? Taking into consideration all that had happened since 1914, was the undoubtedly exaggerated need for security by which the Soviet Union tried to fortify itself and to hold the things offered it so completely incomprehensible? With what right did we begin after 1945 to speak forthwith of a necessary "roll back"? When the communists on their part took measures against such a roll back, was it inevitable to view this as an offensive military threat to the rest of the world?

Did we give the Eastern partner any choice? Did we not provoke him by erecting a massive Western defense alliance, by encircling him with artillery, by establishing the German Federal Republic—which seemed to him like a clenched fist pushed under his nose—and by rearming this republic and equipping it with nuclear missiles? Did we not challenge our former partner to corresponding countermeasures of power display and thus in no small measure strengthen him in his peculiar malice? Did the West finally know no better counsel than to put its trust in its infamous A- and H-bombs? And did it not serve the West right to have to realize that the other side had not remained idle in regard to such weapons? Was there no better diplomacy for the West than the one which now maneuvers the world into what seems a blind alley?

Moreover, what kind of Western philosophy and political ethics—and unfortunately even theology—was it whose wisdom consisted of recasting the Eastern collective man into an angel of darkness and the Western "organization man" into an angel of light? And then with the help of such metaphysics and mythology (the fact of an Eastern counterpart is no excuse!) bestowing on the absurd "cold war" struggle its needed higher consecration? Were we so unsure of the goodness of the Western cause and of the power of resistance of Western man that we could bring ourselves to admit only senselessly unequal alternatives—freedom and the dignity of man as against mutual atomic annihilation—then venture to pass off just this latter alternative as a work of true Christian love?

To the madness (I cannot call it anything else) outlined above I have been unable to accommodate myself in any way in all these years. I think that out of fear of fire we are irresponsibly playing with fire. I think that the West, which should know better, must seek and find a better approach to the necessary confrontation with the power and ideology of the communist East. Possibilities of a worthily, circumspectly and firmly guided policy of coexistence and neutrality were more than once offered to the West in past years. More honor would have accrued to the name of the "free world" had it taken up these possibilities; also, more useful and more promising results would have been achieved than those which stand before us today. In particular I think that the Western press and literature instead of meeting the inhuman with inhumanity should have put to the test the vaunted humanity of the West by quietly observing and understanding Eastern individuals and relationships in their dialectical reality. And I think above all that the Christian churches should have considered it their commission to influence by superior witness to the peace and hope of the kingdom of God both public opinion and the leaders who are politically responsible. The churches have injured the cause of the gospel by the manner, to a great extent thoughtless, in which they have identified the gospel (in this Rome is no better than Geneva and Geneva no better than Rome!) with the badly planned and ineptly guided cause of the West. The cause of the gospel cannot from the human perspective be healed for a long time by even the best ecumenical and missionary efforts. The churches have provided Eastern godlessness with new arguments difficult to overcome instead of refuting it by practical action. . . .

FOREIGN POLICY AND CHRISTIAN CONSCIENCE[1]

George F. Kennan

This selection was presented as a lecture at the Princeton Theological Seminary. George F. Kennan spoke from this forum as a Presbyterian addressing himself to fellow Christians, although he would no doubt be the first to say that his remarks were intended for most other communicants.

Ambassador Kennan is perhaps the outstanding authority in the United States on our relations with the Soviet Union as evidenced by a monumental study, Soviet-American Relations, *the second volume of which appeared in 1958. However, Kennan is no mere specialist and no ordinary student of foreign affairs. As one who has explored the deeper moral implications of conduct, both individual and collective, he has much to contribute to a volume that deals with the moral dilemmas of our time. His theme obviously touches on issues explored in this volume other than those raised by the Cold War.*

Few people are more qualified to discuss the moral implications of the Cold War. Formerly our ambassador to the Soviet Union, he is now our envoy to Yugoslavia, for obvious reasons one of the most sensitive posts to which an American could be assigned. Ambassador Kennan was one of the architects of the policy of containment initiated under the Truman Administration and is today one of the major spokesmen for a policy of coexistence with the USSR. He has condemned what he calls "blind and sterile competition in the ability to wreak indiscriminate destruction." And observing that the Russians breathe the same atmosphere that we breathe, he has said:

> Their idea of peace is, of course, not the same as ours. There will be many things we shall have to discuss with them about the meaning of this term before we can agree on very much else. But I see no reason for believing that there are not, even in Moscow's interpretation of this ambiguous word, elements more helpful to us than all the implications of the weapons race in which we are now caught up. And I refuse to believe that there is no way in which we could combine a search for these elements with a pursuit of a reasonable degree of military security in a world where absolute security has become an outmoded and dangerous dream.[2]

---

[1] *The Atlantic Monthly*, May 1959, pp. 44–49. Reprinted by permission.

[2] *Russia, The Atom and the West* (New York: Harper & Row, Inc., 1957), pp. 92–93.

I should like to say at the outset that questions of method in foreign policy seem to me to be generally a much more fitting subject for Christian concern than questions of purpose. It is very difficult for us to know which of the specific undertakings of government in foreign affairs might have Christian significance and which might not. If there is any one thing that is plain about international statesmanship, it is the extreme difficulty of establishing in advance the relationship between cause and effect—of gauging the likely results of one's own acts.

The English historian Herbert Butterfield has shown us with great brilliance, and so has our own Reinhold Niebuhr, the irony that seems to rest on the relationship between the intentions of statesmen and the results they achieve. I can testify from personal experience that not only can one never know, when one takes a far-reaching decision in foreign policy, precisely what the consequences are going to be, but almost never do these consequences fully coincide with what one intended or expected. This does not absolve the statesman of his responsibility for trying to find the measures most suitable to his purpose, but it does mean that he is best off when he is guided by firm and sound principle instead of depending exclusively on his own farsightedness and powers of calculation. And if he himself finds it hard to judge the consequences of his acts, how can the individual Christian onlooker judge them?

All this is quite different when we come to method. Here, in a sense, one can hardly go wrong. The government cannot fully know what it is doing, but it can always know how it is doing it; and it can be as sure that good methods will be in some way useful as that bad ones will be in some way pernicious. A government can pursue its purpose in a patient and conciliatory and understanding way, respecting the interests of others and infusing its behavior with a high standard of decency and honesty and humanity, or it can show itself petty, exacting, devious, and self-righteous. If it behaves badly, even the most worthy of purposes will be apt to be polluted; whereas sheer good manners will bring some measure of redemption to even the most disastrous undertaking. The Christian citizen will be on sound ground, therefore, in looking sharply to the methods of his government's diplomacy, even when he is uncertain about its purposes.

In the fabric of international life, there are a great many questions that have no certain Christian significance at all. They represent conflicts between those elements of secular motivation which are themselves without apparent Christian meaning: commercial interests, prestige considerations, fears, and what not. I do not think we can conclude that it matters greatly to God whether the free trade area or the Common Market prevails in Europe, whether the British fish or do not fish in Icelandic territorial waters, or even whether Indians or Pakistani run Kashmir. It might matter, but it is hard for us, with our limited vision, to know.

But these are all questions which reflect the normal frictions between peace-loving nations. How about the issues of the cold war? How about colonialism? How about aid to the underdeveloped areas? How about the United Nations as an institution? How about the atom? Are not Christian values involved in our attitude toward these questions?

OUR COMPETITION WITH MOSCOW

In its internal policies, the state can create a decent human atmosphere, in which the individual has the maximum possibility for grappling in a hopeful and constructive way with the moral problems of personal life. Or it can, as we have seen in the examples of Hitler and Stalin and the Chinese Communists, strike out on the most appalling lines of viciousness and cruelty, deliberately fostering a real sickness of the human spirit and inculcating in people's minds, for its own purposes, suspicion, terror, callousness, and the habit of brutality—creating conditions dreadfully adverse to the success of the Christian cause. Christianity cannot be indifferent to the existence of such doctrines and methods; and whatever prevents their spread and their triumph on a world scale serves . . . a Christian purpose.

But I do not think this means that every measure that is damaging to international Communism is necessarily good and every measure that is acceptable to a Communist government is necessarily bad. The world is not that simple. Our competition with Moscow is not the only significant reality of international affairs. Our policies, furthermore, must take into account the interests of the peoples under Communist rule as well as those of their governments. Again, we have the question of method and the fact that not even the greatest conviction of righteousness in our purposes absolves us from the obligation of decency in method. If we allow ourselves to copy our adversary's methods as a means of combating him, we may have lost the battle before we start; for this is, after all, what is most essentially at stake.

Furthermore, we must not make the mistake of regarding international Communism as a static, unchanging quantity in the pattern of world realities. While the full-blown totalitarian state in all its unnatural, nightmarish horror is certainly an abomination in the sight of God, one cannot say this of the conservative authoritarian state which has been the norm of Western society in the Christian era. And we must not forget that it is in this direction that the Soviet government, as distinct from the Chinese Communist government, has been rapidly evolving since Stalin's death. Its gravitation in this direction has not been final or decisive, but it has not been negligible. The mere fact that the most characteristic feature of totalitarian horror, the punishment of whole categories of people for abstract or preventive reasons, has been abolished shows how far the Russians have come since Stalin's day.

Now between democracy and traditional authoritarianism there are still differences, but they are relative and do not present clear-cut issues. The authoritarian regime, despite its origins and its sanctions, often rests on a wide area of popular acceptance and reflects popular aspirations in important degree. In democratic countries, on the other hand, such things as the operations of lobbies and political parties and the inevitable control of nominations by small groups of people tend to reduce the ideal representativeness of government and to make it hard to view the political process as much more than a negative expression of the popular will.

And if you consider, as I do, that the value of a democratic society in the Christian sense depends not just on the fact of its enjoying certain rights and liberties but on the nature of the use made of them, then I think you have to raise questions about our American society of this day. These questions do not need to make us lose hope or hang our heads, but they should cause us to be cautious in drawing conclusions about the merit in God's eyes of any particular form of society.

All these considerations lead me to feel that while Christian values often are involved in the issues of American conflict with Soviet power, we cannot conclude that everything we want automatically reflects the purpose of God and everything the Russians want reflects the purpose of the devil. The pattern is complex, fuzzy, and unstable. We must look sharply at each individual issue before we jump to conclusions. We must bear in mind that there are things we do not know and cannot know. We must concede the possibility that there might be some areas of conflict involved in this cold war which a Divine Power could contemplate only with a sense of pity and disgust for both parties, and others in which He might even consider us to be wrong. . . .

THE UN AS A SYMBOL OF CONSCIENCE

The sovereign national state, to which so much reverent devotion is paid in the various gradations of patriotism and chauvinism that make up national feelings, has no foundation in Christian principle, whatever its secular justification. Nowhere in Christ's teachings was it suggested that mankind ought to be divided into political families of this nature, each a law unto itself, each recognizing no higher authority than its own national ego, each assuming its interest to be more worthy of service than any other with which it might come into conflict. Surely this whole theory is an absurdity from the Christian standpoint. Before we could achieve Christian foreign policy we would have to overcome this unlimited egotism of the sovereign national state and find a higher interest which all of us could recognize and serve.

How about the United Nations? it will be asked. Is this not an institution which, insofar as it represents an endeavor to transcend national sovereignty, deserves our support as a vehicle of the Christian purpose?

The UN represents not a supergovernment, not a separate institutional personality, but one of a number of forums on which governments communicate with one another. It does not, in reality, transcend the barrier of sovereignty. Its members are governments, not peoples, and such slender authority as it sometimes possesses is conferred upon it by these governments, each still acting within the sovereign framework.

There is no particular Christian sanctity lent to decisions taken in the United Nations by the fact that they represent the views of a majority of governments. Little countries are not necessarily more virtuous or more enlightened than big ones; and an international majority does not necessarily reflect the Christian answer, or even the most wise and courageous answer, to anything.

On the other hand, the UN does represent the germ of something immensely necessary and immensely hopeful for this endangered world: namely, a sense of conscience higher than the national one, a sense of the fellowship of fate by which we are all increasingly bound together. I cannot conceive of a satisfactory future for humanity that does not embrace, and draw its strength from, the growth of this consciousness. The present UN is the symbol of it. This symbol is still weak and tender, but it is not insignificant. We must therefore cherish it and guard it, not burdening it beyond its strength, not looking to it for the impossible, but strengthening it where and when we can, above all in our own thoughts and attitudes.

This does not mean that all UN decisions are to be taken as automatically right and good. It does not mean that all diplomatic questions should be uncritically consigned to the UN, whether or not this is a suitable place for their discussion. But it does mean that we should be careful and respectful of the organization as such, remembering that if the idea which it symbolizes is ever allowed to depart from international life, nothing else can stand between us and the horrors of a wholly chaotic world in the atomic age.

THE MORAL IMPLICATIONS OF WAR

This brings me now to the questions on which I think a Christian might, with good conscience, really take a stand. They involve not just the national interests of individual governments but rather the interests of civilization: the question of war, and the atom, and the other weapons of mass destruction.

I am aware that the institution of war has always represented dilemmas for Christian thought to which no fully satisfactory answer has ever been offered. I have, in the past, found myself unable to go along with the

Quakers in their insistence on a sweeping renunciation of power as a factor in international affairs. I do not see the reality of so clear a distinction as they draw between domestic affairs and international affairs. The Communists have taught us that these two things are intimately connected, that civil wars have international implications and that international wars have domestic implications everywhere. I am unable therefore to accept the view which condemns coercion on the international sphere but tolerates it within the national borders.

But that we cannot rule out force completely in international affairs does not seem to me to constitute a reason for being indifferent to the ways in which force is applied—to the moral implications of weapons and their uses. It is true that all distinctions among weapons from the moral standpoint are relative and arbitrary. Gunpowder was once viewed with a horror not much less, I suppose, than are atomic explosives today. But who is to say that relative distinctions are not meaningful? I cannot help feeling that the weapon of indiscriminate mass destruction goes farther than anything the Christian era can properly accept. The older weapons, after all, were discriminate in the sense that they had at least a direct coherent relationship to political aims. They were seen as means of coercing people directly into doing things an enemy government wished them to do: evacuating territory, desisting from given objectives, accepting a given political authority. A distinction was still generally drawn, furthermore, prior to World War I at least, between the armed forces and the civilian population of a hostile country. Efforts were made to see that military action was directed only against those who themselves had weapons in their hands and offered resistance. The law of war did not yet permit the punishment of whole peoples as a means of blackmail against governments.

In all of these respects, the atom offends. So do all the other weapons of mass destruction. So, for that matter, did the conventional bomber of World War II when it was used for area bombing. In taking responsibility for such things as the bombing of Dresden and Hamburg, to say nothing of Nagasaki and Hiroshima, Americans went beyond what it seems to me the dictates of Christian conscience should have allowed (which is not to say that I think their problem was an easy one).

I regret, as an American and as a Christian, that these things were done. I think it should be our aim to do nothing of the sort in any future military encounter. If we must defend our homes, let us defend them as well as we can in the direct sense, but let us have no part in making millions of women and children and noncombatants hostages for the behavior of their own governments.

It will be said to me: This means defeat. To this I can only reply: I am skeptical of the meaning of "victory" and "defeat" in their relations to modern war between great countries. To my mind the defeat is war itself.

In any case it seems to me that there are times when we have no choice but to follow the dictates of our conscience, to throw ourselves on God's mercy, and not to ask too many questions.

ATOMIC TESTING

But this is not the only moral connotation of the atom. There is another in the great controversy that has raged over the question of atomic testing, its effect on the atmosphere, and its consequences for human health. My colleagues in the scientific field advise me to stay away from this subject. They point out that there is a great deal about it which is not yet known; that scientists are themselves in wide disagreement about its seriousness; that I, as a scientific layman, would not even be able to understand the terms in which it is put. All this I readily concede; but even the little that is known to the general public is enough to pose a problem of Christian conscience.

Let us take a random sampling of recent press reports. During the first eight months of 1958, we are told, the fall-out of radioactive strontium on New York City increased by 25 per cent. Readings in Los Angeles are said by the health department of that city to have revealed for limited periods a count of five hundred to one thousand times the normal radioactivity in the atmosphere and double the intensity considered safe for continuous exposure over a lifetime. Only a few weeks ago observations in Sweden showed radioactivity at ten kilometers above sea level to be five times as intense as it was earlier in the year, and individual particles were detected (apparently at ground level), "larger and thought to be more radioactive, than any yet reported except from the immediate area of a test explosion." A similar report has come from Brazil.

All this is only the beginning; a large part of the fall-out from the tests conducted thus far is, we are told, still in the higher atmosphere and will not descend for years. Furthermore, the effect of radioactive substances on human health is cumulative, so that any unnatural exposure presumably reduces the tolerance of exposure from natural causes or for medical purposes.

In the face of these facts, I listen with some amazement to the statements with which some of the scientists endeavor to reassure us about such developments. The damages, they say, have been "negligible" so far. Not *many* deaths, they say, can be expected to ensue from this increase in radioactivity compared with those which occur from natural causes. One scientist, pained and astounded at the concern about the radioactive particles in Sweden, explained that if, for example, 100 people would be killed by the effects of a normal atomic explosion, then only 102 could be expected to die from the effects of the increased radioactivity which Sweden has been experiencing.

But whoever gave us the right, as Christians, to take even one innocent human ilfe, much less 102 or 102,000? I recall no quantitative stipulation in the Sixth Commandment. God did not say through Moses that to take 102,000 lives was wicked but 102 was all right. I fail to see how any of this can be reconciled with the Christian conscience.

I am delighted that our government now shows a serious readiness to work toward the termination of these experiments with atomic explosives. We must go farther and work toward the elimination of the use of atomic weapons in war as well. This cannot be done in a day, and not all that needs to be done can be done by us. But we can at least make a beginning by endeavoring to free ourselves from our unwise dependence on atomic weapons in our own military calculations, from our fateful commitment to the first use of these weapons, whether or not they are used against us.

OUR OBLIGATION TO THE FUTURE

There is a principle involved here which has application beyond just the field of weapons, to a number of other effects in the introduction of modern technology. We of this generation are only the custodians, not the owners, of the earth on which we live. There were others who lived here before, and we hope there will be others who are going to live here afterward. We have an obligation to past generations and to future ones, no less solemn than our obligations to ourselves. I fail to see that we are in any way justified in making, for the safety or convenience of our own generation, alterations in our natural environment which may importantly change the conditions of life for those who come afterward.

The moral laws which we acknowledge predicate the existence of a certain sort of world—a certain sort of natural environment—in which people live. This setting presumably reflects God's purpose. We did not create it; we do not have the right to destroy it. We know the problems which this environment poses for man. We know the nature of the Christian effort to find answers to them. We live by this lore. When we permit this environment to be altered quite basically by things we do today, we are taking upon ourselves a responsibility for which I find no authority in the Christian faith.

Obviously, we do not know what the ultimate effects will be of the atomic weapons tests we have already conducted. I am not sure that we know what will be the ultimate effects of our methods of disposal of radioactive wastes. I doubt that we know what we are doing to the sea through the use of modern detergents and the fouling of its surface with oil. I am not sure that we know what we are doing with modern insecticides, which we employ quite recklessly in agriculture for our immediate purposes, giving little thought to their ultimate effects. We who call ourselves Christians must acknowledge responsibility in these matters, most of which are international in their implications.

We will unavoidably find in the motives and workings of the political process much that is ambiguous in the Christian sense. In approaching the individual conflicts between governments which make up so much of international relations, we must beware of pouring Christian enthusiasm into unsuitable vessels which were at best designed to contain the earthy calculations of the practical politicians. But there are phases of the government's work in which we can look for Christian meaning. We can look for it, first of all, in the methods of our diplomacy, where decency and humanity of spirit can never fail to serve the Christian cause.

Beyond that there loom the truly apocalyptic dangers of our time, the ones that threaten to put an end to the very continuity of history outside which we would have no identity, no face, either in civilization, in culture, or in morals. These dangers represent for us not only political questions but stupendous moral problems, to which we cannot deny the courageous Christian answer. Here our main concern must be to see that man, whose own folly once drove him from the Garden of Eden, does not now commit the blasphemous act of destroying, whether in fear or in anger or in greed, the great and lovely world in which, even in his fallen state, he has been permitted by the grace of God to live.

TURN THE COLD WAR TIDE
IN AMERICA'S FAVOR[1]

David Sarnoff

Brigadier General David Sarnoff (U.S. Army Hon. Reserve) is chairman of the Radio Corporation of America and one of the nation's most prominent business executives. His life is a success story in the Horatio Alger tradition; he began as a messenger boy and wireless operator and rose to the position of general manager and chairman of the board. General Sarnoff was born in Russia and came to the United States at the age of nine. The selection below was one of a series published by the editors of Life *magazine entitled "The National Purpose."*

[1]*Life,* June 6, 1960, pp. 108 ff. Reprinted by permission.

. . . Five years ago I submitted a memorandum to the White House sketching a Program for a Political Offensive against World Communism. "For Moscow," it said, "the real alternative to a nuclear showdown is not 'peace' but political-psychological warfare of a magnitude to weaken, demoralize, chip away and ultimately take over what remains of the free world." The memorandum therefore urged that we renounce all delusions of easy solutions and compromise; that instead we mount a *political counter-strategy* as massive, as intensive and as clear about its ultimate goals as the strategy of the enemy himself.

Events in the intervening years have, if anything, fortified this point of view. The essence of my proposed program, for which I claim no originality, was—and still is—an unequivocal decision to fight the so-called cold war with a will and on a scale for complete victory.

The decision would have to be communicated to the entire world as boldly and energetically as the Communists communicate their intentions. Our message to humankind must be that America has decided, irrevocably, to win the cold war and thereby to cancel out the destructive power of Soviet-based Communism. A national commitment of this scope, I submit, would be consistent with American instincts and experience, a restatement of historic purposes in contemporary terms.

The nature of those purposes . . . is explicit in basic American documents, beginning with the Declaration of Independence. It is implicit in the widespread assertion—presented by some as an accusation—that our foreign policies have been "idealistic." Through the generations Americans have always thought of themselves as being in the vanguard of freedom. They cherished the image of their country as the citadel of democracy and morality and a living defiance to despotism anywhere.

The Rockefeller Brothers Fund Report on U.S. Foreign Policy—prepared by a panel of which I was a member and published last year—put it this way: "The United States at its best has always seen its national life as an experiment in liberty . . . [Americans] have known that the hopes of the world were, in some measure, bound up with their success. . . . Whenever [the United States] has wielded effective power in the world, its ideals and its moral convictions have played a vital part in its decisions. Whenever, on the contrary, the United States has tried to act without moral conviction, or in ways that went counter to its basic beliefs, it has found itself inhibited and has ultimately had to rechart its course. . . . Ideas and ideals are thus to the United States an essential element of reality."

If this is so, why is there such a pervasive skepticism about our historic national purpose and such a widespread search for substitutes? Why the shrinking from lofty goals for all mankind in favor of the safe, the compromising, or mere survival?

The easy answer—that it is all due to the advent of terrible new weapons—will hardly do. The calendar refutes it: the retreat began before those weapons were forged and grew more panicky during the time when America had a monopoly on the atom bomb. It was precisely in the years before Soviet Russia produced the bomb that Communism scored its greatest gains, and it did so almost always by the default of the free world. The Soviet advantages were not military and technological but political and psychological.

The true answer, as I see it, is related to the ever-rising costs of idealism in terms of the sacrifices and the hazards involved. The trouble is not that the older purposes have become irrelevant but that they have become too relevant. I mean that the time when America could serve passively as an example or inspiration to other nations has run out. Today, professions of principle have serious consequences: they must be implemented in policy and action. To say it in slang, the time has come to put up or shut up.

As far as the contest with Communism is concerned we had "shut up," quite literally. We had curbed our tongues for fear of offending the delicate sensibilities of those who daily offend *us*. Few democratic leaders dare to speak as uninhibitedly about the coming doom of the Communist empire as Khrushchev and Mao Tse-tung regularly speak about our impending doom. Our opponents defy, denounce and challenge, while we plead and propitiate. We have left the vocabulary of confidence and victory to the other side, contenting ourselves with such solacing and temporizing words as accommodation, *modus vivendi,* relaxed tensions and coexistence.

This semantic timidity, of course, is merely a symptom and a minor one. The all-encompassing malady is a loss of nerve, marked by depleted self-esteem and purpose. It has impelled us, whenever we have been faced with a choice of interpretations on some aspect of the Communist affliction, to choose the more agreeable one, the one more conducive to complacency and less likely to tax our courage. With rare exceptions the choice has turned out to be the wrong and often the disastrous one, regardless of the political parties in power in this country and in the free world.

Thus in the 1930s we eagerly found assurance in Stalin's talk about "socialism in one country." Later we relaxed in the cozy conviction that the Chinese Communists were simply "agrarian reformers." We prefer to believe in the "evolution" of Communism, though there has not been the slightest revision of ultimate Communist goals. We seek a comforting answer to our prayers in tensions between Moscow and Peking, though these are strictly within the framework of their unshakable alliance against the West, no more significant than Anglo-American tension within our alliance.

A familiar gambit is to list Communism as just one item in a long inventory of problems. But if the Sino-Soviet bloc wins world dominion, the other problems will cease to matter: they will have been solved for the free world in about the way that death solves all bodily ills.

. . . sheer survival, in the elementary physical sense, is not enough. The world has become too small for physical, economic or political isolationism. The polarization of forces dueling for supremacy has gone too far to permit the survival of an island of humanism in a sea of dehumanized totalitarianism. No single nation can survive unless the civilization of which it is part survives.

Our civilization, too, cannot remain isolated, confined to a delimited segment of the earth and indifferent to the humanity beyond those limits. The world cannot be frozen in its present patterns. In this period of great flux and of intermeshed revolutions, static and passive arrangements are doomed to disruption. If the area of freedom is not expanded, then assuredly it will continue to contract.

Despite this, "survival of the free world"—side by side with an unfree world—has been and remains the maximum goal of Western diplomacy. Not the weakening and eventual defeat of Communism but a lasting accommodation seems to mark the farthest reach of hope. It is scarcely a vision to inspire confidence or zeal, and in any case it is utterly utopian, because two parties are needed to make an accommodation.

The best analysis of Communist strategy that I know is in a recent book called *Protracted Conflict* by Dr. Robert Strausz-Hupé of the University of Pennsylvania and three associates. The book's title is a phrase used by Mao Tse-tung. The Communist plan, say the authors, is protracted in time and space and in the limitless variety of its techniques and weapons, and the weapons can even include "the final and total knockout punch." Short of surrender, the authors see for our world no alternative but a many-sided, continuous, long-range counteroffensive.

Such a policy would reject all illusions of an enduring truce, let alone a negotiated division of the globe. The historic contest will be with us for a long, long time. We may delay, maneuver, bargain and compromise, but it will be so much flailing of water unless all such moves become for us—as they have always been for the enemy—calculated holding actions geared to long-range objectives, means not ends, tactics not strategy.

Whatever we do or fail to do in the years and decades ahead, we shall be forced to take great risks and make great sacrifices. These cannot be evaded even by piecemeal surrenders. In fact, if Americans and other free people are to understand and accept these costs and exertions, there must be some rational relation between the magnitude of the goal and the magnitude of the burdens it imposes.

This means that in the conflict with Communism we must become the dynamic challenger rather than remain the inert target of challenge. Only then can freedom regain the initiative. Only then will we have a global goal to match that of Communism, and the incentive to apply the full weight of our brains, energies and resources to its achievement. The great decision, once made and communicated to all concerned, will dictate its appropriate program of policy and action. The strategy will shape the necessary tactics.

Even the things we are now doing and must continue to do will become more relevant and more effective when geared to a conscious ultimate goal. Military and economic aid to our allies, to underdeveloped areas and to neutral nations will cease to be hit-or-miss improvisations. They will be integral elements of an affirmative program. Propaganda, cultural exchanges, diplomatic moves, summit meetings will all acquire for us—as they always have for the Communists—dimensions of purpose beyond their limited immediate effects.

Before the Soviet Union attained its present technological stature, America's paramount problem appeared to be the struggle for men's minds. Today it is dangerous to concentrate on any one facet of the conflict. I think of the image in terms of a table with four legs, military, political, economic and psychological. The significance of the last three is self-evident, since they relate to activities short of all-out war. But the "military leg" must not be underrated.

The present approximate balance of terror presents a false appearance of stability. But it may be upset. And if we relax in this area it will be upset. The enemy is constantly probing our vitality and resolution. Any one of these probes may lead to the brink of war and possibly to war itself. No matter how often we repeat that war is "unthinkable" it remains possible. War may be touched off by accident, or it may come because the Communist high command considers itself ready to deliver the "final and total knockout punch." The maintenance of adequate military power, both offensive and defensive, is therefore of paramount importance. Whether it is ever used or not, moreover, it is the indispensable shield for all other types of action in the protracted conflict.

A strategy for victory in the cold war would, however, begin with a complete reappraisal of present efforts. It would aim to seize the initiative in every possible arena of competition. Not merely the expansion of present projects and the addition of new ones would be considered but how to give each of them a clear role within the framework of the over-all objective.

It would not reject courses of action simply because they are unconventional. We would no longer disdain to use against the enemy some of the weapons used against us. Having finally acknowledged that the struggle is decisive and therefore as real as a "real" war, we would not hesitate to fight fire with fire.

American ingenuity would be called upon to evolve devices and techniques to exploit weaknesses and vulnerabilities in the Communist world, to keep the enemy constantly off balance, to impose upon him problems and crises instead of always waiting to counteract crises of his making. By all the instruments of communication and through the loudspeakers of events, we would aim to saturate the Communist world with reminders that we intend to keep alive the memory of human dignity, the hatred of injustice, the hope of liberation and the courage needed for resistance.

Debates in the United Nations and at diplomatic conferences would be made sounding boards for our views as well as for theirs. No allusions to "colonialism" would be permitted to pass without our throwing the limelight on Red imperialism and on the principles of self-determination.

Thus the Communist world, rather than ours, would tend increasingly to become the principal battlefield of ideological and political conflict. The immunity their world has so long enjoyed would be shattered.

A bill to establish a Freedom Academy for training cold war specialists —what a LIFE editorial called a Political West Point—is before Congress. Whatever the merits or demerits of this particular bill, it is in line with a commitment to victory. Various proposals have been made for setting up a Liberation Force, a volunteer formation drawn largely from among refugees from captive nations and ready to serve in emergencies. That, too, is in line with a strategy for victory. And a new department of Cabinet rank could and should be established to plan and coordinate all cold war activities.

Certainly this new approach would call for substantial sacrifices in material terms. But the notion that it would require a deep cut in American living standards underestimates the wealth and productive genius of our country. The more demanding sacrifices, indeed, would be in the psychological and moral domains. Our people, in short, would have to renounce complacency, euphoria and illusion; they would have to embrace the grim but inspiring realities of our epoch.

The ultimate rise of a world order under law is dictated by the logic of devastating weaponry and modern communications. What remains to be settled is whether it will be an order rooted in freedom or in universal tyranny.

I do not doubt that we have what it takes to assure that it will be an order that we may cherish. The Western concepts of open societies, of liberty under law, of government by the consent of the governed, or the supremacy of the individual rather than the state—these are far closer to the natural aspirations of man than the anthill concepts of Communism. In any equal propaganda contest, what these Western concepts have brought in human well-being will become obvious and irresistible to the majority of mankind. . . .

INTERNAL SECURITY

Civil Disobedience

When a given law or the whole system of laws outrages his conscience, the individual has two recourses: he may abide by the law until such time as he (and others) can change it; or he may refuse to obey. Such disobedience might'take either a peaceful or a violent form. And violent disobedience may be either individual or collective.

In the vocabulary that designates such phenomena, individual violence is called terroristic and is exemplified historically by anarchism of the Bakunin or Kropotkin schools. The Russian Social Revolutionary Party was committed to acts of individual violence—a policy that (contrary to popular assumption) the Russian Communist Party rejected. Disobedience in its terroristic manifestation (it was exemplified by the recent bloodshed in Algeria as well as by that in Czarist Russia) has found hardly any advocates in the United States.

On the other hand, collective disobedience involving the use of force has in the past found us ambivalent: wavering between pride in our revolutionary past and fear of the destructive consequences of revolution. However, there is not now a revolutionary movement in our country nor even a recent revolutionary literature. Although in the 'thirties the American Communist Party reflected and generated some marginal revolutionary sentiments and inspired a considerable literature, it is now virtually moribund as a political movement; and, as Sidney Hook suggests below, its remnants are more aptly described as witting or unwitting agents of a foreign government than as authentic and indigenous revolutionaries. Even so, the moral issues raised by an evaluation of the revolutionary principle are of enduring concern, and some of them are inseparable from a discussion of peaceful resistance, which does have immediate relevance in this country. So much for disobedience committed to the use of force.

Peaceful disobedience, or—as we call it—civil disobedience,[1] like vio-

---

[1]Strictly, one should distinguish between nonresistance to evil and passive resistance. The roots of the former are to be found in Buddha and the Gospels ("whoever shall compel thee to go a mile, go with him twain"), and the intent is to shame the perpetrator of evil and violence.

lent disobedience may be individual or collective. And here Americans are less ambivalent. One particular American's individual act of civil disobedience has indeed become so celebrated that it is almost legendary. Henry Thoreau's refusing to pay his taxes was no mean, penurious evasion of his responsibilities; it was an act of individual defiance against a government that was using his taxes to wage an unjust war against Mexico—and was tolerating slavery besides. He was promptly jailed. "Can there not be a government in which majorities do not virtually decide right and wrong, but conscience? . . . Must the citizen ever for a moment, or in the least degree, resign his conscience to the legislator? Why has every man a conscience, then?" asked Thoreau. He added:

> I think we should be men first and subjects afterward. It is not desirable to cultivate a respect for the law, so much as for the right. . . . Unjust laws exist: shall we be content to obey them, or shall we endeavor to amend them, and obey them until we have succeeded, or shall we transgress at once? Men generally under such a government as this, think they ought to wait until they have persuaded the majority to alter them. They think that, if they should resist, the remedy would be worse than the evil. But it is the fault of the government itself that the remedy *is* worse than the evil. *It* makes it worse. . . . As for adopting the ways the state has provided for remedying the evil, I know not of such ways. They take too much time, and a man's life will be gone. I have other affairs to attend to.[2]

Ghandi read these words. There is a direct link between the collective civil disobedience of India's teeming millions and the solitary American who wrote: "I am not born to be forced. I will breathe after my own fashion." The Reverend Martin Luther King, Jr., who led the Negro boycott of segregated buses in Montgomery, Alabama, also read Thoreau's essay—as one of the articles reprinted below suggests.

However, also echoing in our memories are contrary words such as St. Paul's: "Let every person be subject to the governing authorities. For there is no authority except from God, and those that exist have been instituted by God."[3] Or Luther's: "Even if those in authority are evil or without faith, nevertheless the authority and its power is good and from God."[4]

---

[2] From *On the Duty of Civil Disobedience*.

[3] St. Paul continues: "Therefore he who resists the authorities resists what God has appointed and those who resist will incur judgment. For rulers are not a terror to good conduct but to bad. Would you have no fear of him who is an authority? Then do what is good and you will receive his approval, for he is God's servant for your good." (Rom. 13:1 ff.)

[4] *Römerbrief,* 13:1. Again: "God would prefer to suffer the government to exist no matter how evil, rather than allow the rabble to riot, no matter how justified they are in doing so. . . . A prince should remain a prince no matter how tyrannical he may be. He beheads necessarily only a few since he must have subjects in order to be a ruler."

While many in an age of almost insufferable conformity will applaud the spirit of spontaneous protest that inspired Thoreau, they will also insist on a sober second thought when it comes to trifling with the law, especially in a democracy where men are free—or said to be free—to persuade others to join with them in making changes. They will agree that the freedom to persuade is often too tenuous; and they will concede that the machinery of democracy often works only for "the long run" when, as Lord Keynes once reminded us, we shall all be dead. They will even agree that inert majorities need an occasional act of defiance to jolt them out of their apathy. Even so, they will draw back at the brink of disobedience. Such a man was John Dickinson, whose views on this problem are included below.

Once the universals about sovereignty and law, obedience and disobedience, have been explored, it becomes necessary to test them against particular cases. The critical case immediately before us is the civil resistance of the Negro in the South. With Thoreau, Negroes are saying that the remedy the state provides for their grievances takes too much time. Competing claims to sovereignty by state and federal government complicate the problem. (Civil rights as they pertain to the Negro will be discussed in a later section of this volume.)

In the discussions that follow, the issue will be explored first in broad philosophical terms by two eminent political theorists and then in terms of the crisis over segregation by two spokesmen of the opposing sides.

THE CASE FOR DISOBEDIENCE[1]

Harold Laski
(1893–1950)

Harold Laski will be regarded as one of the foremost political philosophers of our time, even by those who do not share his socialist orientation. In the 'thirties his socialism took on a strong Marxian cast. For many years, until his premature death in 1950, he held England's most prestigious chair in political economy at the London School of Economics. He was at the same time chairman of the executive committee, and generally recognized as the chief theoretician, of the British Labour Party. Professor Laski was as much an authority on the American as on the British system of government. Of his many books [e.g., Authority in the Modern State

[1]From *The State in Theory and Practice* by Harold J. Laski (New York: The Viking Press, Inc., 1935), pp. 65–76. Copyright 1935 by Harold J. Laski, R 1962 by Frida Laski. Reprinted by permission of The Viking Press, Inc.

(1919), A Grammar of Politics (1925), The Rise of Liberalism (1936), The American Presidency (1940), Reflections on the Revolution of Our Time (1943)] *the volume from which the following selection was taken has been perhaps the most influential.*

. . . Neither formal competence . . . nor political power can confer a just title to obedience. With what are we left? Only, I think, with the insistence that law to be ethically valid must conform with the requirements of the system of rights the purposes of which the state exists to maintain. And since law is a command seeking to control my behaviour in some particular way, I must judge that conformity for myself as the test of its ethical adequacy. The roots of valid law, that is, are, and can only be, within the individual conscience. I make law legal, so to say, by giving to its operation the consent of my conscience.

If it is said that such a view, by justifying refusal to obey, opens the door to anarchy, the answer is that the accusation is true. But it is not a serious accusation. In the life of states the door to anarchy is always open because men are never willing to admit the unconditional conference of power. If, further, it be said that the individual conscience is at least as likely to be wrong as the consciences of those who rule the state, the answer, again, is that, while this may be true, the citizen who yields his conviction on the ground that he may be mistaken will soon cease, in any meaning sense, to be a citizen at all. There is no way of making a state active in the fulfilment of its function except the knowledge that men will refuse to obey its commands where they regard them as a violation of that function. That was the truth that Pericles saw when he told the citizens of Athens that the secret of liberty was courage. Unless men are prepared to act by the insights they have, even when these insights are erroneous, they are bound to become no more than the passive recipients of orders to whose moral quality they are indifferent. When they do that, they poison the foundations of the state. For they then cease to be moral beings in any sense of the word that has meaning. They associate truth and justice and right automatically with the possession of physical power. No people prepared in that fashion to abdicate its humanity is likely to be long capable of creative achievement. For so to abdicate the duty of moral judgment is to sell oneself into slavery.

It is said that the individual is powerless, and that he wastes his energy by acting upon his judgment. But there are at least two answers to this view. A moral obligation is not less compelling because it may end in failure. To adopt that canon of effort is to accept the view that justice is the will of the stronger—a doctrine against which, as I have pointed out, the whole history of humanity is a protest. And to argue, secondly, that the individual is powerless is, on the record, quite untrue. He is powerless only when his perceptions are so completely unshared that he fails to arouse any note of response among his fellow-citizens; and he has always to remember that the shift of events may cause them to be shared at a later stage. The early

Christians must have appeared singularly futile to their own generation when they challenged the majesty of Rome; but their steadfastness conquered the Western world. Luther's recalcitrance must have appeared akin to madness to a church which remembered its successful emergence from the stresses of the Conciliar revolt; but he changed the history of the world by his courage. Even so liberal a mind as Emerson could write of the American abolitionists that they were "narrow, self-pleasing, conceited men, and affect us as the insane do"; but it was hardly a generation afterwards that so respectable an observer as Oliver Wendell Holmes, not given to extreme views, could say of his friend's judgment that "it would have taken a long time to get rid of slavery if some of Emerson's teachings in that lecture had been accepted as the whole gospel of liberty."

History, indeed, abounds with such instances. The individual who protests against the law he deems unjust is far less alone than he is likely to imagine. He is acting in a mental climate in which the experience borne in upon him is likely to be shared by others; and the gesture he makes may awaken others to the understanding of their obligations. No one who looks back upon their history can doubt that the suffragettes, who for eight years defied the law, awakened the British government to a sense that their claims were serious in a way that altered the whole perspective of those claims. No one can doubt either that the unbreakable will of Lenin was central to the success of the Bolshevik Revolution in 1917. That we must fight for our philosophy if we believe in it seems to me the inescapable implication of the record.

Against this view two considerations are urged, in both of which there is, unquestionably, considerable force. It is said that to challenge the government is to weaken the authority of all law, and that to do so is to open the floodgates to chaos. It was the sense of this danger which made T. H. Green, who admitted, in the last resort, the right to revolution, insist that we must approach the state in fear and trembling. But it is surely not less important to realize that respect for law must always mean respect for what the law does; and, if the individual, whether alone or in concert with others, judges what the law does to be ethically intolerable, he must act upon the basis of his judgment. To decide otherwise is to argue that the highest duty of the individual is to maintain order, without regard to the quality of the order that is maintained. I do not find this argument compatible with the notion of the individual as a moral being.

It is said, secondly, that this view admits the right of any doctrine to support itself by force, if it can. Men have only to announce that they are moved by some profound conviction to be justified in using violence to attain their ends. Such an attitude, it is argued, is utterly destructive of the foundations of social well-being.

But the answer is surely that no doctrine, however evil, moves to the use of force unless it is rooted in a profound grievance which it sees no other way to remedy. We may believe the Bolshevik Revolution to have been wholly evil; but it is clear that the previous conditions of the Russian state alone account for its origin and methods. We may argue, with the communists, that Hitler has been no more than the agent of finance-capitalism in Germany; but it is also clear that his victory was built upon the profound grievances of millions of Germans who saw no adequate redress for them in the habits of the Weimar republic. The truth is that men in general are so accustomed to obey that their departure from the normal canons of political behaviour is always an index to grave disease in the state. They have, as Burke said, "no interest in disorder; where they do wrong it is their error and not their crime." We need not argue that a doctrine which arms itself is wise or right to do so. But, on the facts, we have to argue that no doctrine ever does successfully arm itself unless the government it attacks has failed to deal with the grievances it expresses in a reasonable way.

That is, I think, apparent in the history of most revolutions. Certainly the student of the English civil wars, of the revolutions of France and of Russia, will note as not the least remarkable of their features the patient efforts of the common people to await reform before they turned to violence. And in any society violence is unlikely if the conviction is widespread that the state is seriously attempting to fulfil its obligations. Violence comes when the facts persuade men to believe that the bona-fides of their rulers are no longer to be trusted. They may be mistaken in that belief. There have certainly been occasions in history when the members of a government which has been overthrown have been well-intentioned men struggling with adverse circumstances it has been impossible to conquer. There have been other occasions, also, when the ends sought by men who resisted the state could not be attained within the framework of existing institutions. The overthrow of Dr. Brüning is, I believe, an instance of the first; the history of the French Revolution is a clear instance of the second.

But, not seldom, the use of violence to defeat the law is the outcome of a clash of values between which compromise is impossible. What is the situation when this arises? No one, at least, can say that the problem is a simple one. It is no answer to it, for example, to argue that the duty of a minority whose values are denied is the simple one of becoming a majority, and so using constitutional processes to obtain power by persuasion. For, in the first place, those constitutional processes may not exist. It is no use telling the citizen of one of the European dictatorships today that he should use the methods of peaceful persuasion to get his views accepted; for, *a priori,* the right, legally, to use those methods has been abrogated. He, at least, has no alternative save revolution if he seeks the realization of his purposes. The German socialist cannot be asked to hope for the peaceful conversion of Hitlerite Germany.

The situation, it is said, is different in a state of which the form is a constitutional democracy. There, at any rate, freedom to criticize exists; and provision is deliberately made for those who differ from the government of the day to take its place if they can persuade a majority of their fellow-citizens to vote with them. There is, I think, a vital truth in this view. In general, it is impossible to condone the use of violence in politics except as a weapon of last resort; it must be shown that all alternative avenues of action have been exhausted before violence is resorted to. But it is, I think, important to realize that even in a constitutional democracy dependence upon reasonable persuasion alone is a function of certain conditions, upon the realization of which the minority concerned must be able to count. First among those conditions is the right to expect the unbiased operation of state-institutions; they must weigh with equal incidence upon all parties to the political equation. In a state even so free as Great Britain that equal incidence does not obtain. For the House of Lords is an instrument in the hands of a single party in the state; and its authority can be deliberately exercised to flout the will of its opponents even when they possess a majority in the electorate. And if it is said that the House of Lords will always give way when the will of the electorate is decisively known (after a general election, for instance, which is fought upon some special issue), the answer surely is that, even if this be the case, it subjects one party in the state to grave disabilities from which its rival is wholly free; and the consequence of those disabilities may render abortive the effort of a party which has won its electoral majority, by reason of the technical conditions under which it may seek to make its purposes effective.

Nor is this all. It is important that the incidence of state-institutions should be unbiased. It is important, also, that those who operate them should be able to assume that the principles of constitutional democracy will be observed by their opponents. It would be facile to argue that this assumption is justified as even approximately an invariable rule. We may say, with some assurance, that in a society long accustomed to those principles departure from them will be less likely than in one where habituation to their exercise is novel. But, even there, it is, I suggest, a reasonable generalization that they will be observed only when the interests which an important minority deems, rightly or wrongly, to be fundamental, are not in jeopardy. . . . Unless, in a constitutional democracy, a government can be certain that its decisions will be respected, one can be certain that the assumptions of such a system will not be long preserved.

It is argued from this that it leads to the obligation, incumbent upon the governments of all such states, not to outrage the fundamental senti-ments of an important minority. There are, that is to say, limits to the rights of a majority whose representatives are exercising the sovereign power. That is a platitude which has not even the merit of being profound.

Anyone can see that, if the King in Parliament prohibited the exercise of the Roman Catholic religion, those who professed it would break the law rather than obey the law. Anyone can see, also, that, if the King in Parliament were foolish enough to declare trade unions illegal organizations, the trade unions would fight rather than give way. No one ever takes the legal right to exercise the powers of sovereignty as equivalent to the moral right to do anything one pleases.

But to say that there are limits to the rights of a majority is not to define those limits; and that, after all, is the real core of the problem. We cannot seriously argue that no government is entitled to take any decision which may outrage the conscience of a significant minority. A significant minority of American opinion was outraged by the decision to abolish slavery; but that did not render unjustifiable the decision to abolish it. A significant minority thought the Reform Act of 1832 an outrage; but, again, we should not attempt to justify a decision to withdraw it on that ground. A significant minority in Great Britain today thinks the "Means Test" in connexion with unemployment insurance outrageous; that is not held to justify its withdrawal. There is hardly, indeed, a single social expedient of any magnitude, adversely affecting an important interest involved, which has not been deemed, at some time or other, "outrageous" by the minority so affected. . . .

Are we then to say that the point at which the limits of majority rule become apparent are defined when the minority proposes to fight rather than to give way? This raises several issues. Does a proposal to fight mean actual conflict in the streets, or is it sufficient that action like a general strike, in which the use of some violence at least is pretty inevitably inherent, should be attempted? But it is impossible to conduct the process of ordered government upon the terms that a majority must not use its power when a minority threatens resistance. In a situation, for instance, like that of Ireland in 1914, the will of the government would have been completely paralysed. For there the Ulster extremists threatened to fight if the Home Rule Bill went into operation, and the Irish nationalists threatened to turn out the government if the bill was withdrawn; and the Asquith solution, which was to enact the bill, but suspend its operation, effectively resulted in a complete victory for the Ulster extremists.

There are, no doubt, occasions when it is wise for a government so threatened to compromise rather than to seek the maintenance of its prestige without regard to the price that may have to be paid for it. . . . But it is certainly not a method which can be made a general rule, for the simple reason that it would make majority government invariably impossible. Normally, a government that is challenged is obliged, so long as it feels confident that it has public opinion behind it, to meet the challenge; for it is the primary thesis of constitutional democracy that it can be overthrown only in ways specifically provided for by law. The limits of majority rule, therefore, cannot really be defined with any precision in terms of principle. They rest upon felt insights rather than exact measurements of what particular situations involve. Certainly a government which estimates their meaning must always remember that any consistent series of surrenders to the clamour of interest will rapidly prevent it from being able to embark upon any measures of serious importance.

What seems to emerge from our historic experience is the lesson that a government can impose its will upon the citizens of a constitutional democracy so long, but only so long, as those citizens are in fundamental agreement about the actual purposes of the state. . . . Valid law, we must affirm, is law judged adequate by men as it seeks for their consent. It has no final title to acceptance because it emanates from the sovereign power. It has no title to acceptance, even, because it presents itself as an effort to realize the right. Its claim to be obeyed is in the decision men make about the legitimacy of its pretensions. It becomes valid law by its power to satisfy the demands they make upon the institutions whose will it represents. . . .

THE CASE AGAINST DISOBEDIENCE[1]

John Dickinson
(1894–1952)

John Dickinson taught at Harvard and Princeton and at the law school of the University of Pennsylvania. He was Assistant U.S. Secretary of Commerce, Assistant U.S. Attorney General, and chief counsel and vice-president of the Pennsylvania Railroad. He wrote Administrative Justice and the Supremacy of Law in the United States (1927). *Like Laski, he is master of a magisterial prose.*

. . . a régime of law in the positive sense, in so far as it is realized at all, prevails only within the limits of each nation-state, and does so only because, and only in so far as, such a state is organized on the principle of sovereignty.

. . . there can be no doubt that a régime of positive law, where it is strictly realized, has its disadvantages as well as its advantages. It empha-

[1]Reprinted from *Political Science Quarterly*, 43, No. 1 (March 1928), 32–59. Reprinted by permission.

sizes order and stability and uniformity, sometimes at the expense of what may be thought to be justice, but almost always at the expense, to some degree, of adaptability and progress. Its mode of operation is to set human conduct into theoretically rigid grooves for the sake of certainty and predictability, and to that extent to put barriers in the way of an experimental quest by private individuals and groups for new and more satisfactory adjustments. Hence arises the familiar and age-old conflict between the claims of order on the one side and of liberty on the other—a conflict which becomes progressively acute when extensive changes in the setting of human life and in the technique of satisfying human wants crowd upon the world and make new adjustments imperative. We are living in the welter of such a period of change today.

At such a time either of two courses seems open to the protagonists of progress. On the one hand they may direct their efforts toward bringing positive law as near as may be into step with the march of the new demands by attempting to so constitute the sovereign organ as to make it more and more delicately responsive to the new impulses within the community. Along this path, and along this path alone, will seriously emerge the challenge to improve the machinery of government, as well as the sole hope and chance of effecting such improvements; for the improvement of government means precisely the difficult task of so altering its machinery as to increase its responsiveness to the needs of the community without impairing its value as an instrument of certainty and order. If we adopt this line of approach, there will be no occasion to question the validity of sovereignty in the sense in which I have sought to describe it. . . .

But of course another method of approach is open. We may take a short cut, and directly challenge sovereignty itself; which, whether we realize it or not, means questioning the value of a régime of positive law as an instrument for the achievement by a community of its internal adjustments. We may be so distrustful lest the sovereign organ fall under the influence of forces which we regard as malign and mischievous that we will refuse to vest any agency with final authority to pronounce what is law, and what is not, as between contending individuals or groups or interests. . . .

The importance of the controversy over sovereignty in its current form hinges precisely on the fact that consciously or unconsciously it is a challenge to choose between these two different attitudes of approach to the disputed issues of political and social reform. Shall we admit that because of the limitations and dangers of positive law, freedom to break through it at the will of the individual who thinks himself right must be erected into a normal working-part of the system of government, available at all times, rather than kept in reserve in the form of an extra-legal power of revolution for use only as an abnormal safety-valve and last resort in exceptional cases of great oppression? This admission is in substance what is demanded by writers who are attacking the concept of sovereignty; they seem to be seeking primarily for a way to regularize and legalize disobedience to existing positive law. Of course this is really to make a régime of positive law impossible; for a law which can be legally broken at the will of the lawbreaker can never be positive law in any intelligible sense. The basic question at stake in the controversy over sovereignty is therefore what our attitude shall be toward breaches of positive law, and so how we shall approach the age-old question of obedience—the question of the *Antigone* and the *Crito*. Shall we regard disobedience as properly a normal, i.e., a *legal* thing, or as only the abnormal, and therefore illegal, though perhaps at times morally justifiable, thing? What concessions to sovereignty are inevitable if we would have the advantages of a legally ordered society? . . .

The capital indictments which so-called political pluralists, as represented by Mr. G. D. H. Cole and Mr. Laski in his earlier books, have brought against the concept of sovereignty seem to be all based on this fundamental confusion between legal considerations on the one hand and moral, social, and factual considerations on the other hand. Thus Mr. Laski has pointed out insistently that the "will" of the so-called sovereign can never be an absolute "will"—that it is almost certain to be controlled by some group, some interest, or combination of interests and forces within or without the community; and that the identity, the nature, of this controlling influence is of major practical consequence. So indeed it is, in connection with all questions of the goodness and badness of laws and forms of government, and with the reform of constitutional machinery; but hardly in connection with the question of the positive legality of a governmental act or pronouncement.

. . . in saying that the sovereign is only sovereign when serving the common good, [Laski] seems to be taking altogether too high and mystical a view of the nature of sovereignty, and of the positive law which proceeds from it. He apparently vests positive law—i.e., a valid pronouncement of the sovereign—with a sanctity so elevated that he is unwilling to admit to it anything that is not in accordance with his own conception of the ultimate philosophical purposes of the state. This is a recurrence of the ancient unwillingness among men to admit that there can ever be discrepancy between law and justice; the unwillingness to vest with the character of law any rule which is not thought to be objectively the one and only best rule for application to the particular circumstances of the case in hand. Now of course positive law ought so far as is humanly possible to conform to the highest ideal standards of justice conceivable at the time and place; if it does not so conform, it is doubtless the civic duty of all members of the community to do their best to bring about such conformity; and if the machinery of government does not readily permit progressive improvement in this direction, it should be overhauled in order that it may do so. But even so, we cannot be purists and insist that until the necessary improvements are brought about, the bad old rule with which we are dissatisfied is not entitled to be considered as law in even the positive sense. Positive law is and must always be a thing of rough and ready adjustments; much of convenience, policy, compromise, doubtful experiment, inevitably enter into its make-up. All the members of the community will by no means be able to agree on what justice in the highest sense is, or on what particular demands it makes in any given situation; meanwhile if they are not to fight out their differences, there must be some rule to settle them by. We can never proceed toward getting the best rule until we first consent that there shall at least be a rule, and we will never consent that there shall be a rule if we insist on having what we privately regard as the best rule, or else on having no rule at all. We must therefore be willing to allow the character of positive law to much that we might well wish were otherwise. . . . Unless we are sheer anarchists, a rule sanctioned by the highest authority in the state is ordinarily preferable to no rule at all, until we can get a better one; and if we feel that because of exceptional circumstances this is not so in a particular case, then we must frankly face in that special case the moral or social issue of revolution, and not hide our heads in the sand by pretending that we are only upholding law when we are resisting the ordinances of the authorized law-declaring organ of the community.

In the second place, the language quoted from Mr. Laski seems to show a certain confusion in refusing to regard as law a rule proclaimed by the sovereign organ whenever such a rule can be thought to result from selfish pressure brought to bear upon the sovereign by contending interests. We get off the track if we proceed to say that such a rule is in reality nothing more than an expression of the "private" will of the strongest special interest, on the ground that the interest exerting the decisive force is really the sovereign. Factually, it may indeed be called the cause of the sovereign's action, but still it must act through the sovereign; and if there were no sovereign through which it had to act, its action might well be quite different. The helm controls the ship no less because some one must give direction to the helm; and the sovereign controls the law no less because some one may give direction to the sovereign. The fact that forces will exert pressure is not the important thing; of course they will; the important thing is the way they must go about exerting it. Now in a community politically organized under sovereignty, they must exert it through the sovereign; in the absence of sovereignty there is no legal obstacle to prevent them from exerting it directly against their opponents to the point of actual intimidation and violence. The difference is not unimportant; it may be only a difference of degree, but still it produces vital differences in both methods and results. It is never quite enough to see in the politically organized community only a pressure of competing interests, as the pluralists so often do.

The competition and the pressure undeniably exist, but there exists also a structure of legal processes which set limits to their action, and often deflect its direction. The kind of competition which goes on between opposing interests within a nation-state is certainly a different kind of competition in enough important particulars from that which goes on between "independent" nation-states to warrant recognizing the differences. . . .

Government, if it performs its function, is simply a great central co-ordinating agency from which these adjustments ultimately emerge . . . But even if government is not well organized, and performs its functions ill, still it sometimes accomplishes one important purpose; even if it habitually favors one group in the community at the expense of others, and advances the interests of the former to the utter disregard of the latter, it may yet afford the advantages, whatever we hold them worth, of peace and order. It at least enables men to know the rules they must live under and the authority to which they must submit if they would be law-abiding. Now there are times, no doubt, when this is not a good thing; there is a peace which is the "bitterest bitterness" and worse than any war; and at such times the anarchy of resistance and civil war may be the only thinkable portal to a fairer and better world. But admitting all this, there is still a truth in the old commonplace that one tyrant is preferable to many; and the age of Augustus, the age of the Medici and of the Tudors, bear witness that as a general rule men appear to find the peace and order even of a despotism a more satisfactory environment wherein to work out their purposes than a continual conflict of authorities, though the latter be shot through with the purest passion for civil or religious liberty of a Brutus or a Becket. . . .

Suppose . . . that we do not accept the doctrine of sovereignty. We will then insist that laws do not derive their validity from the stamp of the sovereign, but that a rule may be validly a law which is directly contrary to the rule which the sovereign is seeking to enforce. But if this is the case, and if we must look not to the sovereign but to some other source to assure us what is the law, where else are we to look? Mr. Laski has suggested the only possible answer—we must look within, each man to his own individual conscience. If we use this method of approach we have no choice but to say that the validity of all law is derived from the conscience of the individual. The question of obedience or resistance then becomes a simple one. All that is involved is for each individual to set side by side and compare the law as promulgated by the sovereign with what his own conscience tells him is the law, and if there is a discrepancy between the two precepts, then he is not merely morally justified, he is legally authorized, to disobey. There are but two factors to be taken into account in solving the problem—the sovereign's pronouncement on the one hand and the individual's own conception of the law—i.e., of what is right—on the other. His career as a member of civil society becomes a continuous process of such comparisons, and he stands at every moment on the brink of disobedience and resistance. "The only ground upon which the individual can give or be asked his support for the state is from the conviction that what it is aiming at is, in each particular action, good. . . . It deserves his allegiance, it should receive it, only where it commands his conscience. . . . Its purpose is at each stage subject to examination." The individual is thus invited to assume habitually what Mr. Laski has elsewhere called the "Athanasius attitude."

The doubt which suggests itself in connection with this attitude is that possibly it may be too naïve—that possibly it may not be sophisticated enough to comprehend the full challenge of civil society. It is the primitive attitude of Antigone, rather than the mature comprehension of Socrates. Its capital defect is that it leaves fundamentally out of account the chief and most difficult factor in the whole problem—the question, namely, of the advantage, not merely to all individuals but to each individual, of having a legally ordered society to live in, and of the price which he must perforce pay for it. This factor is the thing which really causes all the difficulty; and it is the major factor. If there were no question but of a conflict between two opposing wills, the will of the citizen as one individual and the will of the sovereign as another, the problem would be quite easy; the individual could not fairly be expected to surrender his will until convinced intellectually and morally that he was wrong. But so to state the problem is to simplify it out of all recognition. It is not a question of a bare conflict between the individual and the sovereign; the conflict must be regarded as rather between the individual and all that the sovereign stands for. The individual may be convinced and reasonably convinced that the sovereign is wrong, unfairly, brutally wrong; but the deeper question must at once arise of what is involved in disobeying the sovereign.

For sovereignty, as we have seen, is a prerequisite of legal order; a prerequisite, that is, of a condition of affairs where the disputes which will honestly and inevitably arise between man and man, and which will as often be due to a real and involuntary difference in intellectual outlook as to a clash between purely selfish purposes, are settled peaceably by a publicly authorized arbiter, and, so far as possible, by impartial rules, rather than by the rough arbitrament of force and chance. The very essence and meaning of civil society is precisely the fact that the former method rather than the latter is the one which habitually prevails; and this essential method of civil society is just the thing which we strike at whenever we disobey or resist the sovereign. The question of obedience thus raises far more than the mere question of the agreement or disagreement in a particular case between the sovereign's law applying to the case in hand, and what the individual's private conscience tells him the law ought to be; properly approached, it brings dominantly into the foreground the large issue of the desirability of preserving public authority and civil society itself. This is the great truth so clearly put by Socrates, when in answer to Crito's plea for disobedience he represents the City as standing before him and saying, "Tell us, Socrates, what is it you mean to do? Nothing more nor less than to overthrow us by this attempt of yours—to overthrow the laws and the whole commonwealth so far as in you lies. For do you imagine that a city can stand and not be overthrown, when the decisions of the judges have no power, when they are made of no effect and destroyed by private persons?" In other words, something of vastly superior consequence is involved than the essential rightness or wrongness in the given case of any particular exercise of sovereign power; what is involved, fundamentally, is the value and validity of civil society in contrast with the freedom, the flexibility, the experimentalism, of anarchy, whether the latter take the form of benevolent cooperation or of forceful competition. Civil society cannot stand when the decisions of the judges are made of no effect by private persons; and the Athanasius attitude, to be defensible, must balance not particular differences of opinion between the individual conscience and the sovereign will, but the value of the end which conscience has at stake as against the value of civil society.

For there are of course ends which from time to time do validly outweigh the maintenance for the time being of the orderly processes of civil society. Revolution, like war, is no doubt entitled to a place as one of the indispensable ingredients of progress in the existing, and perhaps in any, state of human nature. The only point I am insisting on is that revolution should always be recognized for what it is—a lapse into anarchy. Only so, in any specific case, can the wisdom of taking the plunge be fairly assessed; only so can the full meaning of the alternative between obedience and resistance be grasped in all its awful implications. The chief defect in the doctrine of the denial of sovereignty is that it glosses over with thin sugarcoating this fundamental alternative. The doctrine that there exists somewhere a law above, and independent of, the law of the sovereign, and capable of being discovered for himself by each private individual so as to justify disobedience to the positive law, carries with it the implication that civil society itself exists, and can exist, apart from and independently of obedience to the sovereign; and that therefore resistance by the individual to the sovereign is not necessarily anything like so serious and ultimate a thing as an assault on civil society is readily seen to be. The essential meaning of resistance is obscured, the price which it entails belittled. And at the same time the price that we must pay for civil society itself is belittled. For the demand which civil society makes that private individual will and purpose be always subordinated to the will of the authorized public representative of the society, on no other and no better ground than merely that the one is private and the other public, is by implication denied, if we accept the doctrine that civil society does not depend for its existence and functioning on obedience to its constituted representative. A view of civil society is thus produced which evades the necessity for political organization—which tolerates the claim of separate and discrete groups within the state to be independent of the jurisdiction of, and immune from interference by, the state, and which in pursuance of the same conviction is capable of seeing in an unorganized "society of nations" a substantial substitute for an organized League. The theory seeks to have its cake of order without having to pay the price of organization.

This was the theory that dominated the thought of the Western world throughout the medieval centuries. It is a theory the defectiveness of which is in large part cured if we are able to accept a presupposition which to the mind of the Middle Ages was a commonplace—the presupposition, namely, that there not merely exists a body of law above and independent of human choice, but that the precepts of that law are fixed, definite and capable of being as clearly perceived in identical form by every human intelligence as are the elementary truths of mathematics. Men obviously need no sovereign to exercise a prerogative of choice in order to tell them whether twice two is five or four. If the laws which distinguish right from wrong are equally well defined by "nature," we need no sovereign to tell us whether the issue of watered stock by a corporation is illegal, or whether or not relief by injunction is a lawful remedy to apply in a labor dispute. Men thought, not so long ago, that the one right answer to every such question could be reached by mathematical demonstration. If this were so, there would be no need for a sovereign law-declaring agency. But during the past few centuries there has been growing doubt as to whether it is really so; and the conflict between the faith and the doubt is quaintly reflected in the inconsistency of a central passage of Locke's *Second Treatise of Civil Government:* "In the state of Nature there are many things wanting. Firstly, there wants an established, settled, known law. . . . For though the law of Nature be plain and intelligible to all rational creatures, yet men, being biased by their interest, as well as ignorant for want of study of it, are not apt to allow of it as a law binding to them in the application of it to their particular cases." In other words, the law of nature is there, but we need an authoritative human organ to tell us what it is. "Those who are united into one body and have a common established law and judicature to appeal to . . . are in civil society with one another, but those who have no such common appeal are in the state of nature."

Even, then, if we grant the existence of a "law" that is not of men's making, but recognize that room remains for possible differences of opinion as to its specific precepts, we shall still have to admit the need for political organization, the need for a sovereign to "declare" that law authoritatively; and we shall then be driven forward to face the important practical problems incidental to devising a mechanism of organization best adapted to cause the precepts of the sovereign to conform to the precepts of the "higher" law. But this is a task which the doctrine of resistance minimizes and discourages. If each individual is entitled to search in his own conscience for the precept of the higher law applicable to the case in hand, and then to disobey the sovereign should his inquiry lead to a different conclusion from that which that sovereign has reached, the importance of having a sovereign who will reach the right conclusion in the first place is vastly decreased; for if no law made by the sovereign need be obeyed unless it is a good law, the question of whether the sovereign makes bad laws becomes of relatively secondary consequence. From this point of view, therefore, the real guaranty of good government is the "right" of resistance, not the perfecting of the government machinery adapted to produce the best results under given circumstances. In answer to this theory it should be sufficient to point out that the whole history of progress in the art of government has consisted in the gradual substitution of the latter for the former of these guaranties. Revolution was during long ages the only effective way by which the ordinary acts of government could be corrected; the efforts of many centuries have been spent on devising less wasteful and more orderly methods of control. These efforts have proceeded on the assumption that it is not compatible with the existence of civil society to leave to each individual the protection of his own rights; that so long as the normal conditions of civil order prevail, the sovereign, as the organ of the community, must be entitled to the obedience of the individual precisely because, and for no other reason than because, the sovereign *is* the organ of the community; and that therefore the protection of the individual under normal circumstances must be found not in the "right" of resistance, but in the manner and plan whereby sovereign power is organized and constituted.

The fact that in civil society the individual is thus not entitled to set his own idea of the "higher" precepts which the government should follow against the sovereign's version of them, does not mean that there are no such precepts. Whether they constitute a body of "higher law" or not, is of course a wholly different question; but nothing that has been said implies that there are no canons of morality and justice which the sovereign ought to embody in his positive laws. On the contrary, the institution of sovereignty exists primarily because of the need of an organ to focus and formulate these fundamental, but more or less vague and disputed, canons into precise and uniform rules which on the one hand have the fixity and generality necessary for a rule of law, and which on the other hand represent the moral conceptions that command acceptance among the most influential members of the community rather than views which are held merely by isolated private thinkers. In a realm of ideas where there is so much room for differences of opinion as in connection with the precepts of morality, it is absolutely necessary to have such an authoritative declaration of the rule before there can properly be any thought of enforcing it as a rule of community action. It may, and doubtless often will, result that the rule selected by the sovereign for enforcement, precisely because it will be a rule reflecting the morality of the crowd or the morality of the wealthy or military class, will offend the consciences of the individuals who constitute the most enlightened and morally advanced element of the community. Under such circumstances is not the right of this class to resist essential in order to secure moral progress? As a last resort and in extraordinary situations where the stake is sufficiently high, the answer must certainly be, yes; but always with full recognition of the fact that such resistance constitutes rebellion, and entails for the time being a dissolution of the conditions of civil order. Under a properly adjusted constitution, the necessity should seldom occur, because such a constitution would, on the one hand, provide adequate channels for the views of this class to exert an influence upon the sovereign as far as is compatible with the obvious fact that laws must be made to fit the average rather than the exceptional man; and because, on the other hand, under such a constitution the sovereign would doubtless be wise enough to limit to the narrowest point his interference with those kinds of individual action from which moral improvement can properly be expected to occur. . . .

WHERE DO WE GO FROM HERE?[1]

Martin Luther King, Jr.

Dr. Martin Luther King, Jr., is one of the most articulate and courageous leaders in the battle for integration. The following selection should be read primarily for its bearing on the issue of civil disobedience. However, it will be clear that Dr. King is concerning himself with more than a defense of the duty to disobey an unjust law and with more than a commentary on the technique of nonviolent resistance; included is an examination of such more general moral phenomena as the spiritual invigoration that comes from selfless dedication to a common purpose.

. . . Violence as a way of achieving racial justice is both impractical and immoral. It is impractical because it is a descending spiral ending in destruction for all. The old law of an eye for an eye leaves everybody blind. It is immoral because it seeks to humiliate the opponent rather than win his

---

[1]From *Stride Toward Freedom* by Martin Luther King, Jr. (New York: Harper & Row, Inc., 1958), pp. 213–224. Copyright 1958 by Harper & Row, Publishers, Incorporated. Reprinted by permission.

understanding; it seeks to annihilate rather than to convert. Violence is immoral because it thrives on hatred rather than love. It destroys community and makes brotherhood impossible. It leaves society in monologue rather than dialogue. Violence ends by defeating itself. It creates bitterness in the survivors and brutality in the destroyers. A voice echoes through time saying to every potential Peter, "Put up your sword." History is cluttered with the wreckage of nations that failed to follow this command.

If the American Negro and other victims of oppression succumb to the temptation of using violence in the struggle for freedom, future generations will be the recipients of a desolate night of bitterness, and our chief legacy to them will be an endless reign of meaningless chaos. Violence is not the way.

[Another] way open to oppressed people in their quest for freedom is the way of nonviolent resistance. Like the synthesis in Hegelian philosophy, the principle of nonviolent resistance seeks to reconcile the truths of two opposites—acquiescence and violence—while avoiding the extremes and immoralities of both. The nonviolent resister agrees with the person who acquiesces that one should not be physically aggressive toward his opponent; but he balances the equation by agreeing with the person of violence that evil must be resisted. He avoids the nonresistance of the former and the violent resistance of the latter. With nonviolent resistance, no individual or group need submit to any wrong, nor need anyone resort to violence in order to right a wrong.

It seems to me that this is the method that must guide the actions of the Negro in the present crisis in race relations. Through nonviolent resistance the Negro will be able to rise to the noble height of opposing the unjust system while loving the perpetrators of the system. The Negro must work passionately and unrelentingly for full stature as a citizen, but he must not use inferior methods to gain it. He must never come to terms with falsehood, malice, hate, or destruction.

Nonviolent resistance makes it possible for the Negro to remain in the South and struggle for his rights. The Negro's problem will not be solved by running away. He cannot listen to the glib suggestion of those who would urge him to migrate en masse to other sections of the country. By grasping his great opportunity in the South he can make a lasting contribution to the moral strength of the nation and set a sublime example of courage for generations yet unborn.

By nonviolent resistance, the Negro can also enlist all men of good will in his struggle for equality. The problem is not a purely racial one, with Negroes set against whites. In the end, it is not a struggle between people at all, but a tension between justice and injustice. Nonviolent resistance is not aimed against oppressors but against oppression. Under its banner consciences, not racial groups, are enlisted.

If the Negro is to achieve the goal of integration, he must organize himself into a militant and nonviolent mass movement. All three elements are indispensable. The movement for equality and justice can only be a success if it has both a mass and militant character; the barriers to be overcome require both. Nonviolence is an imperative in order to bring about ultimate community.

A mass movement of a militant quality that is not at the same time committed to nonviolence tends to generate conflict, which in turn breeds anarchy. The support of the participants and the sympathy of the uncommitted are both inhibited by the threat that bloodshed will engulf the community. This reaction in turn encourages the opposition to threaten and resort to force. When, however, the mass movement repudiates violence while moving resolutely toward its goal, its opponents are revealed as the instigators and practitioners of violence if it occurs. Then public support is magnetically attracted to the advocates of nonviolence, while those who employ violence are literally disarmed by overwhelming sentiment against their stand.

Only through a nonviolent approach can the fears of the white community be mitigated. A guilt-ridden white minority lives in fear that if the Negro should ever attain power, he would act without restraint or pity to revenge the injustice and brutality of the years. It is something like a parent who continually mistreats a son. One day that parent raises his hand to strike the son, only to discover that the son is now as tall as he is. The parent is suddenly afraid—fearful that the son will use his new physical power to repay his parent for all the blows of the past.

The Negro, once a helpless child, has now grown up politically, culturally, and economically. Many white men fear retaliation. The job of the Negro is to show them that they have nothing to fear, that the Negro understands and forgives and is ready to forget the past. He must convince the white man that all he seeks is justice, *for both himself and the white man.* A mass movement exercising nonviolence is an object lesson in power under discipline, a demonstration to the white community that if such a movement attained a degree of strength, it would use its power creatively and not vengefully.

Nonviolence can touch men where the law cannot reach them. When the law regulates behavior it plays an indirect part in molding public sentiment. The enforcement of the law is itself a form of peaceful persuasion. But the law needs help. The courts can order desegregation of the public schools. But what can be done to mitigate the fears, to disperse the hatred, violence, and irrationality gathered around school integration, to take the initiative out of the hands of racial demagogues, to release respect for the law? In the end, for laws to be obeyed, men must believe they are right.

Here nonviolence comes in as the ultimate form of persuasion. It is the method which seeks to implement the just law by appealing to the conscience of the great decent majority who through blindness, fear, pride, or irrationality have allowed their consciences to sleep.

The nonviolent resisters can summarize their message in the following simple terms: We will take direct action against injustice without waiting for other agencies to act. We will not obey unjust laws or submit to unjust practices. We will do this peacefully, openly, cheerfully because our aim is to persuade. We adopt the means of nonviolence because our end is a community at peace with itself. We will try to persuade with our words, but if our words fail, we will try to persuade with our acts. We will always be willing to talk and seek fair compromise, but we are ready to suffer when necessary and even risk our lives to become witnesses to the truth as we see it.

The way of nonviolence means a willingness to suffer and sacrifice. It may mean going to jail. If such is the case the resister must be willing to fill the jail houses of the South. It may even mean physical death. But if physical death is the price that a man must pay to free his children and his white brethren from a permanent death of the spirit, then nothing could be more redemptive.

What is the Negro's best defense against acts of violence inflicted upon him? As Dr. Kenneth Clark has said so eloquently, "His only defense is to meet every act of barbarity, illegality, cruelty and injustice toward an individual Negro with the fact that 100 more Negroes will present themselves in his place as potential victims." Every time one Negro school teacher is fired for believing in integration, a thousand others should be ready to take the same stand. If the oppressors bomb the home of one Negro for his protest, they must be made to realize that to press back the rising tide of the Negro's courage they will have to bomb hundreds more, and even then they will fail.

Faced with this dynamic unity, this amazing self-respect, this willingness to suffer, and this refusal to hit back, the oppressor will find, as oppressors have always found, that he is glutted with his own barbarity. Forced to stand before the world and his God splattered with the blood of his brother, he will call an end to his self-defeating massacre.

American Negroes must come to the point where they can say to their white brothers, paraphrasing the words of Gandhi: "We will match your capacity to inflict suffering with our capacity to endure suffering. We will meet your physical force with soul force. We will not hate you, but we cannot in all good conscience obey your unjust laws. Do to us what you will and we will still love you. Bomb our homes and threaten our children; send your hooded perpetrators of violence into our communities and drag us out on some wayside road, beating us and leaving us half dead, and we will still love you. But we will soon wear you down by our capacity to suffer. And in winning our freedom we will so appeal to your heart and conscience that we will win you in the process."

Realism impels me to admit that many Negroes will find it difficult to follow the path of nonviolence. Some will consider it senseless; some will argue that they have neither the strength nor the courage to join in such a mass demonstration of nonviolent action. As E. Franklin Frazier points out in *Black Bourgeoisie,* many Negroes are occupied in a middle-class struggle for status and prestige. They are more concerned about "conspicuous consumption" than about the cause of justice, and are probably not prepared for the ordeals and sacrifices involved in nonviolent action. Fortunately, however, the success of this method is not dependent on its unanimous acceptance. A few Negroes in every community, unswervingly committed to the nonviolent way, can persuade hundreds of others at least to use nonviolence as a technique and serve as the moral force to awaken the slumbering national conscience. Thoreau was thinking of such a creative minority when he said: "I know this well, that if one thousand, if one hundred, if ten men whom I could name—if ten honest men only—aye, if one honest man, in the state of Massachusetts, ceasing to hold slaves, were actually to withdraw from the copartnership, and be locked up in the county jail therefore, it would be the abolition of slavery in America. For it matters not how small the beginning may seem to be, what is once well done is done forever."

Mahatma Gandhi never had more than one hundred persons absolutely committed to his philosophy. But with this small group of devoted followers, he galvanized the whole of India, and through a magnificent feat of nonviolence challenged the might of the British Empire and won freedom for his people.

This method of nonviolence will not work miracles overnight. Men are not easily moved from their mental ruts, their prejudiced and irrational feelings. When the underprivileged demand freedom, the privileged first react with bitterness and resistance. Even when the demands are couched in nonviolent terms, the initial response is the same. Nehru once remarked that the British were never so angry as when the Indians resisted them with nonviolence, that he never saw eyes so full of hate as those of the British troops to whom he turned the other cheek when they beat him with lathis. But nonviolent resistance at least changed the minds and hearts of the Indians, however impervious the British may have appeared. "We cast away our fear," says Nehru. And in the end the British not only granted freedom to India but came to have a new respect for the Indians. Today a mutual friendship based on complete equality exists between these two peoples within the Commonwealth.

In the South too, the initial white reaction to Negro resistance has been bitter. I do not predict that a similar happy ending wi'l come to Montgomery in a few months, because integration is more complicated than independence. But I know that the Negroes of Montgomery are already walking straighter because of the protest. And I expect that this generation of Negro children throughout the United States will grow up stronger and better because of the courage, the dignity, and the suffering of the nine children of Little Rock, and their counterparts in Nashville, Clinton, and Sturges. And I believe that the white people of this country are being affected too, that beneath the surface this nation's conscience is being stirred.

The nonviolent approach does not immediately change the heart of the oppressor. It first does something to the hearts and souls of those committed to it. It gives them new self-respect; it calls up resources of strength and courage that they did not know they had. Finally it reaches the opponent and so stirs his conscience that reconciliation becomes a reality.

I suggest this approach because I think it is the only way to reëstablish the broken community. Court orders and federal enforcement agencies will be of inestimable value in achieving desegregation. But desegregation is only a partial, though necessary, step toward the ultimate goal which we seek to realize. Desegregation will break down the legal barriers, and bring men together physically. But something must happen so to touch the hearts and souls of men that they will come together, not because the law says it, but because it is natural and right. In other words, our ultimate goal is integration which is genuine intergroup and interpersonal living. Only through nonviolence can this goal be attained, for the aftermath of nonviolence is reconciliation and the creation of the beloved community.

It is becoming clear that the Negro is in for a season of suffering. As victories for civil rights mount in the federal courts, angry passions and deep prejudices are further aroused. The mountain of state and local segregation laws still stands. Negro leaders continue to be arrested and harassed under city ordinances, and their homes continue to be bombed. State laws continue to be enacted to circumvent integration. I pray that, recognizing the necessity of suffering, the Negro will make it a virtue. To suffer in a righteous cause is to grow to our humanity's full stature. If only to save himself from bitterness, the Negro needs the vision to see the ordeals of this generation as the opportunity to transfigure himself and American society. If he has to go to jail for the cause of freedom, let him enter it in the fashion Gandhi urged his countrymen, "as the bridegroom enters the bride's chamber"—that is, with a little trepidation but with a great expectation.

Nonviolence is a way of humility and self-restraint. We Negroes talk a great deal about our rights, and rightly so. We proudly proclaim that three-fourths of the people of the world are colored. We have the privilege of watching in our generation the great drama of freedom and independence as it unfolds in Asia and Africa. All of these things are in line with the work of providence. We must be sure, however, that we accept them in the right spirit. In an effort to achieve freedom in America, Asia, and Africa we must not try to leap from a position of disadvantage to one of advantage, thus subverting justice. We must seek democracy and not the substitution of one tyranny for another. Our aim must never be to defeat or humiliate the white man. We must not become victimized with a philosophy of black supremacy. God is not interested merely in the freedom of black men, and brown men, and yellow men; God is interested in the freedom of the whole human race.

The nonviolent approach provides an answer to the long debated question of gradualism *versus* immediacy. On the one hand it prevents one from falling into the sort of patience which is an excuse for do-nothingism and escapism, ending up in standstillism. On the other hand it saves one from the irresponsible words which estrange without reconciling and the hasty judgment which is blind to the necessities of social process. It recognizes the need for moving toward the goal of justice with wise restraint and calm reasonableness. But it also recognizes the immorality of slowing up in the move toward justice and capitulating to the guardians of an unjust status quo. It recognizes that social change cannot come overnight. But it causes one to work as if it were a possibility the next morning.

Through nonviolence we avoid the temptation of taking on the psychology of victors. Thanks largely to the noble and invaluable work of the NAACP, we have won great victories in the federal courts. But we must not be self-satisfied. We must respond to every decision with an understanding of those who have opposed us, and with acceptance of the new adjustments that the court orders pose for them. We must act in such a way that our victories will be triumphs for good will in all men, white and Negro.

Nonviolence is essentially a positive concept. Its corollary must always be growth. On the one hand nonviolence requires noncoöperation with evil; on the other hand it requires coöperation with the constructive forces of good. Without this constructive aspect noncoöperation ends where it begins. Therefore, the Negro must get to work on a program with a broad range of positive goals.

One point in the Negro's program should be a plan to improve his own economic lot. Through the establishment of credit unions, savings and loan associations, and coöperative enterprises the Negro can greatly improve his economic status. He must develop habits of thrift and techniques of wise investment. He must not wait for the end of segregation that lies at the basis of his economic deprivation; he must act now to lift himself up by his own bootstraps.

The constructive program ahead must include a campaign to get Negroes to register and vote. Certainly they face many external barriers.

All types of underhand methods are still being used in the South to prevent the Negroes from voting, and the success of these efforts is not only unjust, it is a real embarrassment to the nation we love and must protect. The advocacy of free elections in Europe by American officials is hypocrisy when free elections are not held in great sections of America.

But external resistance is not the only present barrier to Negro voting. Apathy among the Negroes themselves is.also a factor. Even where the polls are open to all, Negroes have shown themselves too slow to exercise their voting privileges. There must be a concerted effort on the part of Negro leaders to arouse their people from their apathetic indifference to this obligation of citizenship. In the past, apathy was a moral failure. Today, it is a form of moral and political suicide.

The constructive program ahead must include a vigorous attempt to improve the Negro's personal standards. It must be reiterated that the standards of the Negro as a group lag behind not because of an inherent inferiority, but because of the fact that segregation does exist. The "behavior deviants" within the Negro community stem from the economic deprivation, emotional frustration, and social isolation which are the inevitable concomitants of segregation. When the white man argues that segregation should continue because of the Negro's lagging standards, he fails to see that the standards lag because of segregation.

Yet Negroes must be honest enough to admit that our standards do often fall short. One of the sure signs of maturity is the ability to rise to the point of self-criticism. Whenever we are objects of criticism from white men, even though the criticisms are maliciously directed and mixed with half-truths, we must pick out the elements of truth and make them the basis of creative reconstruction. We must not let the fact that we are the victims of injustice lull us into abrogating responsibility for our own lives.

Our crime rate is far too high. Our level of cleanliness is frequently far too low. Too often those of us who are in the middle class live above our means, spend money on nonessentials and frivolities, and fail to give to serious causes, organizations, and educational institutions that so desperately need funds. We are too often loud and boisterous, and spend far too much on drink. Even the most poverty-stricken among us can purchase a ten-cent bar of soap; even the most uneducated among us can have high morals. Through community agencies and religious institutions Negro leaders must develop a positive program through which Negro youth can become adjusted to urban living and improve their general level of behavior. Since crime often grows out of a sense of futility and despair, Negro parents must be urged to give their children the love, attention, and sense of belonging that a segregated society deprives them of. By improving our standards here and now we will go a long way toward breaking down the arguments of the segregationist.

This then must be our present program: Nonviolent resistance to all forms of racial injustice, including state and local laws and practices, even when this means going to jail; and imaginative, bold, constructive action to end the demoralization caused by the legacy of slavery and segregation, inferior schools, slums, and second-class citizenship. The nonviolent struggle, if conducted with the dignity and courage already shown by the people of Montgomery and the children of Little Rock, will in itself help end the demoralization; but a new frontal assault on the poverty, disease, and ignorance of a people too long ignored by America's conscience will make victory more certain.

In short, we must work on two fronts. On the one hand, we must continue to resist the system of segregation which is the basic cause of our lagging standards; on the other hand we must work constructively to improve the standards themselves. There must be a rhythmic alternation between attacking the causes and healing the effects.

This is a great hour for the Negro. The challenge is here. To become the instruments of a great idea is a privilege that history gives only occasionally. Arnold Toynbee says in *A Study of History* that it may be the Negro who will give the new spiritual dynamic to Western civilization that it so desperately needs to survive. I hope this is possible. The spiritual power that the Negro can radiate to the world comes from love, understanding, good will, and nonviolence. It may even be possible for the Negro, through adherence to nonviolence, so to challenge the nations of the world that they will seriously seek an alternative to war and destruction. In a day when Sputniks and Explorers dash through outer space and guided ballistic missiles are carving highways of death through the stratosphere, nobody can win a war. Today the choice is no longer between violence and nonviolence. It is either nonviolence or nonexistence. The Negro may be God's appeal to this age—an age drifting rapidly to its doom. The eternal appeal takes the form of a warning: "All who take the sword will perish by the sword."

WE ARE GOING TO HAVE LAW AND ORDER[1]

LeRoy Collins

LeRoy Collins was governor of Florida from 1955 to 1961 and is a former chairman of the Southern Governors' Conference and the National Governors' Conference. He is now president of the National Association of Broadcasters. Governor Collins is a Southern "moderate." The remarks reprinted below are excerpted from more extended comments delivered without text on March 20, 1960, over a statewide radio and television network in an effort to reduce the rapidly mounting race tensions generated by the "sit-ins."

It was on last October 1 that four Negro college students from a North Carolina college went into a Woolworth store in Greensboro, N.C. They bought some toothpaste or other minor items at one of the counters and turned over to the lunch counter and ordered a cup of coffee.

The waitress said, "I'm sorry. We do not serve Negroes here."

One of the students said, "Why, I have just been served here. I bought a tube of toothpaste over there." She said, "Well, we serve you over there but we do not serve you here."

That was the first of these demonstrations. Many followed there in Greensboro involving hundreds of people. It spread throughout North Carolina on to Virginia, to South Carolina, to all the other states of the South, including Florida.

We've had many throughout our state, and unlike some people assume, not all of these demonstrations were sponsored by students. In fact only a minority have been sponsored by students. But the worst of all has occurred, as I think some of you know, in Tallahassee. And there it was largely sponsored by students from the Florida A.&M. University—our Negro institution—and Florida State University.

There the city of Tallahassee took a rather rigid and punitive position in respect to these demonstrations. And of course, this gave the appearance of partiality or nonobjectivity. And this caused the condition to become

---

[1]From a radio and television address given on March 20, 1960, and reprinted in *The Reporter,* April 14, 1960, p. 26. Copyright 1960 by The Reporter Magazine Company. Reprinted by permission.

aggravated and we finally developed conditions there in Tallahassee of which I am frankly ashamed. Yesterday and the day before there was a tenseness about the atmosphere in Tallahassee that was disgraceful. We had armed patrolmen [on] every street because we had the wildest rumors imaginable . . . about what was going to happen.

But what is the legal situation about these so-called demonstrations? First I want to say this to every one of you: that we are going to have law and order in this state. I don't care who the citizen is, he is going to be protected in pursuing his legal rights in Florida. And that goes for every place in Florida.

Now under our free-enterprise system and under our laws a merchant has the right, the legal right, to select the patrons he serves. And certainly he is going to be protected in that right. The customer has rights, of course, to trade or not to trade with any man he wants to. And of course there is the right to demonstrate. And people should be protected in that right too.

But I want to call to your attention that the right to demonstrate in all cases is limited by the fact if there is any clear and present danger that demonstration will incite public disorder, it is unlawful. And of course a situation of this kind could bring about that kind of condition in one community and not in another.

Now we have applied that rule. I called on our sheriffs to apply it two years ago against the Ku Klux Klan while they were planning a perfectly lawful demonstration under normal circumstances.

The information we had about the way they were going to conduct that, I felt would incite disorder. And so we called upon the sheriffs to prevent demonstrations of that sort. And they did. . . .

I'm amazed at how different people react differently in this particular area. My own mother and father, I found the other day, don't fully agree on how they feel about race relations. I know my own wife and I have disagreements from time to time about race relations.

And so far as I am personally concerned, I don't mind saying that I think if a man has a department store and he invites the public generally to come into his department store and trade, I think then it is unfair and morally wrong to single out one department . . . and say he does not want or will not allow Negroes to patronize that one department.

Now he has the legal right to do that, but I still don't think that he can square that right with moral, simple justice. Now you may not agree with that. . . .

Now none of us have all the answers to this situation. . . . I think all of us are part right and part wrong. We must have more tolerance, more understanding, more Christianity, less words and less demonstrations, I think, if we are going to find the answer ultimately.

I went to church this morning and was amazed that the Scripture—the

Gospel—for the third Sunday in Lent which the minister read includes this:

"These words from the Master. 'But He knowing their thoughts said unto them, Every kingdom divided against itself is brought to desolation; and a house divided against a house falls.' "

How appropriate that Scripture was to me on this day, because I firmly believe, as I hope you will, that every state divided against itself, every city divided against itself is bound to come to desolation.

Now that is true for many reasons, because when there is division there is suspicion, there is fear, there is distrust, and ultimately there is hate. And hate consumes and destroys. . . .

Friends, we've got mobs beginning to form now in this nation, in this Southland, and in this state. The time requires intelligent, careful, thorough study of big problems and the reaching of solutions that are going to be reasonable and sound and that make good sense. We cannot let this matter and these issues be decided by the mob, whether they are made up of white people or whether they are made up of colored people.

And we in this state have this sort of situation. We have extremists on one side and we have extremists on the other. We've got this mob shouting here. We've got mobs shouting there.

But where are the people in the middle? Why aren't they talking? Why aren't they working? They must start efforts that are going to bring about solutions if we are going to get over these problems and these troubles and keep growing as our state should grow. . . .

The Loyalty Program

In no area has the quest for security inspired more bitter controversy than with the loyalty program, in part because those same world tensions that call for reasonable precautions also generate unreasoned fears; in part also because of a tendency in many quarters to identify disagreement with disloyalty.

Many people who are anti-Communist in their orientation are nevertheless profoundly concerned over the measures we have taken to combat Communism. One of these is Alan Barth, who while affirming that Communists are enemies of America and American values and that the American Communist Party is an instrument of Russian foreign policy nevertheless condemns the internal security program somewhat more categorically than does Professor Sidney Hook. Hook characterizes Barth as a "ritualistic liberal."[1] The difference between the two as reflected in the pages that

---

[1] Cf. his "Security and Freedom" in the *New Leader,* June 21, 1954, pp. 8–10.

follow is all the more significant in that both men are liberals and would probably agree on most questions of public policy.

Barth and Hook deal with the universals involved in the quest for internal security. And universals become meaningful when they are illustrated by any of the particulars to which they apply. But they are not thereby made evocative or moving. This is accomplished only in rare instances—sometimes by nature, as when a shattered tree testifies mutely to the force of lightning; or by history, as when the corpse of a tyrant and his mistress dangle grotesquely from meat hooks in a petrol station on Milan's Piazzale Loreta; or, most often, by art: the impersonal brutality of war as when in Remarque's novel a soldier is destroyed as he reaches from his trench for a butterfly, or man's inhumanity to man as recorded in a doomed Jewish child's diary. So, too, the 1957 contempt-of-Congress trial of Arthur Miller, one of America's best playwrights, dramatized the moral complexities, the contradictions, and ambivalences in which the American people have become involved as, seeking internal security, we grope for the meaning of loyalty.

Arthur Miller testified freely before the House Un-American Activities Committee that he had once been a member of the Communist Party. In all respects he was what the Committee calls a "cooperative witness"—in all respects, that is, except one. Miller was asked to identify other writers whom he had known to be Communists. He refused. "I will protect my sense of myself," he said. "I could not use the name of another person and bring trouble on him."

The refusal resulted in his being cited for contempt of Congress and his conviction by a judge who found his motives "commendable," but his action legally indefensible. The problem raised by his refusal to answer must be viewed, of course, as involving much more than possible abuses of Congressional prerogative, or the issue of informing. It raises the supreme question mentioned earlier concerning the relation of law and conscience. The selections below were written before the contempt conviction was reversed.[2]

---

[2]Since 1957 the United States Supreme Court has upset ten convictions for contempt of Congress.

THE CULT OF LOYALTY[1]

Alan Barth

Alan Barth is an editorial writer for the Washington Post, *a former Nieman Fellow at Harvard, and holder of distinguished awards in the field of journalism; he wrote* The Loyalty of Free Men *in 1950 before the eclipse of Senator McCarthy. Perhaps he would write less pessimistically now, although a new wave of radical right-ism might temper his optimism.*

The relation of the individual to the State—or of individual liberty to national security—is the crucial issue of our time. The emphasis in this relation marks the essential distinction between a totalitarian society and a free society. A totalitarian society emphasizes the supremacy of the State, seeking national security through rigid governmental control of individual activity and expression. A free society emphasizes the supremacy of the individual, relying for its national security upon a democratic adjustment of diverse views and interests and upon the freely accorded devotion of its constituents.

The function of national security in a totalitarian society is to preserve the State, while the function of national security in a free society is to preserve freedom. Those who established the American Republic counted freedom among man's "unalienable" or "natural" rights and believed that it was in order to secure these rights that governments are instituted among men. But there is a looseness about freedom that makes it seem hazardous to security. It involves an inescapable element of risk. There have always been men everywhere who viewed it skeptically as a luxury to be enjoyed only within prescribed limits and when the nation is not subject to any external threat. It is commonly in the name of national security that individual liberty is lost.

The purpose here is to show: (1) that we have accepted, without full awareness of their meaning, piecemeal encroachments on personal freedom that threaten to corrupt our richest inheritance; (2) that these encroachments have been accepted as the result of what are in large part groundless

---

and neurotic fears; (3) that, although accepted in the name of national security, they operate, in fact, to impair the security they are intended to protect; and (4) that whether or not individual liberty is, as the founders of the United States believed it to be, an "unalienable" or "natural" right, it serves vital practical purposes and is an affirmative source of national strength.

This is by no means to suggest that national security can be neglected. The institutions of liberty are under attack. They are threatened by an aggressive totalitarianism abroad, and they need the protection of a strong and resolute government. If that government should fall, the institutions of liberty would fall with it. In some measure, too, the institutions are threatened in novel ways by agents of that totalitarianism at home. They are threatened most of all, however, by well-meaning and patriotic but frightened Americans, who have come to think of liberty as a liability rather than an asset.

The error of these men is that they confuse loyalty with orthodoxy. Acting upon this confusion, they tend to suppress diversity and to insist upon a rigid conformity. But loyalty may take as many forms as religious worship. This much about it seems indisputable: like love, it must be freely given. It can be evoked but it cannot be commanded or coerced. Members of a family are loyal to one another, not through any oath or compulsion, but as a result of shared experiences, community of interest, and long mutual dependence. A great aggregation of individuals and families becomes and remains a nation, not through geographical propinquity alone, but rather through much this same process of shared experiences—which is to say, a common history—and, above all, through common acceptance of certain fundamental values. The national loyalty of free men is not so much to their government as to the purposes for which their government was created. . . .

The tolerance on which freedom and opportunity must rest was a necessity of early life in America. Conquest of a continental wilderness fostered a tradition of individualism. The opening of successive frontiers widely different in physical conditions and in the problems of settlement encouraged a variety of political forms. Differences of religion, of social background, of economic interest among the settlers required tolerance of diversity. Out of this necessity the early Americans made a virtue. The idea that they had raised a standard to which the lovers of liberty could repair became a source of tremendous pride to them. "This new world," Thomas Paine boasted in *Common Sense,* "hath been the asylum for the persecuted lovers of civil and religious liberty from *every part* of Europe." . . .

Whatever may have been the vices and weaknesses of this country in the past, want of confidence in itself was not one of them. The nation knew that the American dream would inspire all who had a chance to dream it.

But that sublime self-confidence has now disappeared. Aliens are suspect; there is no longer the old certainty that they will be swept into the mainstream of American life. Prospective immigrants must prove that they are not the bearers of contagious opinions, and even transient visitors are feared. In 1950 the State Department denied visas to the Dean of Canterbury and later to twelve members of the Communist-sponsored World Congress of Partisans for Peace, Pablo Picasso among them, because of their political and economic views. The faith of Americans in their own institutions is apparently no longer considered strong enough to withstand Communist propaganda. Eminent artists have been barred merely because their political sympathies were suspect. The German conductor Wilhelm Furtwängler was kept out because he had collaborated with the Nazis. Later Joseph Krips, the conductor of the Vienna State Opera, was forbidden to fill a summer engagement with the Chicago Symphony Orchestra because he had previously conducted performances at Moscow and Leningrad. Tolerance of diversity and faith in the democratic process are giving way to reliance on the quarantine of hostile doctrines.

Indeed, even those born into the American heritage are now only tentatively trusted; they are obliged to affirm and reaffirm their allegiance. And beyond this ritual of affirmation, in the potency of which there is no longer any confidence, they are commonly required before entering upon any post affecting the national interest to deny disloyalty. Anyone who goes to work for the government of the United States today must swear that he does not advocate its overthrow. In point of fact, Congress thought it necessary in 1940 to make it a penal offense for any citizen to teach or advocate the duty or necessity of overthrowing "any government in the United States by force or violence."

A terrible distrust lies behind this shift to negativism. The country's doubts about the loyalty of its citizens are not unlike the doubts of a husband about the fidelity of his wife. The protestations that answer his doubts are never convincing and are likely to dissipate the mutual confidence that is the essence of a marriage. When men lose faith in one another, they lose the substance of what constitutes a community among them. Thus, to a national community, there is nothing that so dangerously corrupts its integrity as such a loss of faith. As in the case of the suspicious husband, this distrust is the expression of a neurotic insecurity.

Such insecurity is perhaps the most pervasive characteristic of our time. The fear of freedom and the difficulties of realizing its potentialities have been illuminatingly treated by the psychiatrists and the social psychologists. They have contributed invaluable insights of which political theorists have as yet made too little use. The forces that have led great numbers of Europeans and Asiatics to seek the fellowship of disciplined submission to authority as an escape from the responsibilities and isolation of freedom are at work here too. They exhibit themselves in the exertion of powerful pressures, cultural as well as political, toward conformity and in an attitude novel among Americans that they can neither comprehend nor change the awful tides in which they feel themselves engulfed. The consequence is a stultifying tendency to seek unity through uniformity.

"Loyalty" has become a cult, an obsession, in the United States. But even loyalty itself is now defined negatively. It is thought of not so much in terms of an affirmative faith in the great purposes for which the American nation was created as in terms of stereotypes the mere questioning of which is deemed "disloyal." The whole postwar accent is on something called "un-Americanism"—a hyphenated synonym for unorthodoxy. Deviations to the Left are regarded as more suspicious or criminal than deviations to the Right; but the tendency is to question all deviations. "Loyalty" consists today in not being un-American, which is to say, in not being different or individualistic. The very diversity which was the wellspring of loyalty in the past is now distrusted.

The term "disloyalty" as it is commonly used today is nothing more or less than a circumlocution for treason. The authors of the Constitution went to a great deal of trouble in dealing with the subject of treason because they knew from experience how readily the term can be twisted to make discontent or dissent, or mere criticism of the government, a major crime. They took care, therefore, to define treason in the narrowest terms. "Treason against the United States," they declared in Article III, Section 3, of the Constitution, "shall consist only in levying war against them or in adhering to their enemies, giving them aid and comfort." No acts other than those specified in the Constitution can be made treasonable by legislation. Congress can neither extend, nor restrict, nor define the crime. Its power over the subject is limited to prescribing the punishment.

The Constitution is no less exacting as to the means by which conviction of treason may be obtained. "No person shall be convicted of treason," Section 3 continues, "unless on the testimony of two witnesses to the same overt act, or on confession in open court."

James Madison explained in Number 43 of *The Federalist*—that brilliant exegesis of the Constitution characterized by Thomas Jefferson as "the best commentary on the principles of government which ever was written" —the reasons that prompted the Constitutional Convention to define treason so narrowly and to make conviction of it so difficult:

> As treason may be committed against the United States, the authority of the United States ought to be enabled to punish it. But as newfangled and artificial treasons have been the great engines by which violent factions, the natural offspring of free government, have usually wreaked their alternate malignity on each other, the convention have, with great judgment, opposed a barrier to this

peculiar danger, by inserting a constitutional definition of the crime, fixing the proof necessary for conviction of it, and restraining the Congress, even in punishing it, from extending the consequences of guilt beyond the person of its author.

There is a whole lesson in political science in this paragraph—a lesson peculiarly applicable today. The use of "disloyalty" as a "new-fangled and artificial" form of treason has indeed promoted the rise of violent factions and led to a wreaking of "their alternate malignity on each other." There is no way to measure the impairment of national security that has resulted from this disruption of the sense of national community.

Disloyalty, to be sure, has not officially been held to constitute treason. But when a congressional committee or a quasi-judicial government board says that an individual is disloyal—or that he is un-American, or subversive, or a security risk, or ineligible for employment by the United States, or any of the other circumlocutions of the circumlocution—it is saying in not very euphemistic terms, or at least is encouraging the public to believe, that he is a traitor. The difference is that disloyalty is nowhere to be found detailed as a crime upon the statute books, that nowhere has it been defined, that nowhere has a punishment been prescribed for it by law. This ambiguity merely makes the charge more difficult to avoid and a condemnation less difficult to obtain.

Real disloyalty presents a threat to national security. It might find expression in betrayal of the nation—even in espionage or sabotage. Of course these are statutory crimes, clearly defined and punishable through the normal processes of indictment and trial by jury. The law can easily be used to punish any actual spy or saboteur. But the law can no more be used to punish a potential spy or a potential saboteur than it can be used to punish a potential pickpocket or a potential embezzler. The law punishes specifically prohibited antisocial acts. It does not prohibit and cannot punish antisocial ideas or intentions. The distinction has always been considered basic to a free society.

In a period of international tension, however, a potential spy or saboteur is likely to seem very dangerous—so dangerous that there is enormous temptation to deal with him outside the law. The United States, engaged in a world-wide struggle that has led to armed conflict in Asia, has yielded to this temptation to an alarming degree. It has devised an elaborate system and ritual for punishing men—and punishing them most cruelly—for crimes they have not committed but are suspected of desiring to commit. It punishes them by stigmatizing them as disloyal.

Anyone so stigmatized becomes to some degree an outcast. If he retains any friends, he knows himself to be a menace to them. Any association with them may result in their stigmatization too. Wherever he goes he is marked as a man who would be willing to betray his country. He remains at large but is regarded as a menace to society. He is expatriated without being exiled and denied the opportunity to gain a livelihood without the compensation of being maintained in prison at the community's expense. He and his fellows might come, in time, to constitute something new in American life—a caste of untouchables.

The punishment in such cases is something like that in the old story about the Quaker and his dog Tray. " 'Go to,' said the Quaker to poor Tray, 'I will not kill thee, but I will give thee a bad name,' as he turned him into the streets with the cry of 'mad dog,' and somebody else did kill Tray."

Perhaps the punishments meted out on the ground of disloyalty are not too severe for anyone who clearly and demonstrably intends to serve the interest of a foreign government to the detriment of his own countrymen. The fact is, however, that these penalties are meted out without any of the safeguards embodied in the Anglo-American system of justice for the protection of innocent persons against unjust conviction. They are inflicted on the loyal and the disloyal almost without discrimination.

By the simple stratagem of charging a man with disloyalty, instead of with treason or espionage or sabotage, it is possible to evade the constitutional requirements that he be indicted by a grand jury, that he enjoy a speedy and public trial by an impartial petit jury, that he be informed of the nature and cause of the accusation and confronted with the witnesses against him, that he be accorded the benefit of compulsory process to obtain witnesses in his favor. He is indicted and tried and sentenced by congressional committee or administrative tribunal, with the same men acting as prosecutors, judges, and jury. The presumption of innocence supposed to surround him is ignored. The mere charge of disloyalty is treated as evidence of guilt.

     . . . it is the press which executes, so to speak, the sentences passed by congressional committees or by mere individuals speaking under the immunity from suits for slander or libel afforded by Congress. Newspapers especially tend to make headlines out of accusations and to treat denials less prominently. This stems in large measure from the concept of news as sensation and is scarcely less true of those newspapers that strive for objectivity than of those that deliberately use their news pages to serve editorial biases.

The tradition of objectivity, which is the great virtue of the American press, has operated in this context to make the press an instrument of those seeking to inflict punishment by publicity. Allegations which would otherwise be ignored because they would be recognized as groundless and libelous are blown up on front pages and given a significance out of all relation to their intrinsic merit after they have been made before a committee of Congress. Thus, what is one day properly regarded as unpublishable gossip is treated the next day as news of great moment because it has been uttered under official auspices. Refutation, no matter how compelling, never catches up with charges of disloyalty and never erases their imprint. In addition, of course, many newspapers welcome such charges and inflate them for political reasons or for their commercial value in stimulating street sales. . . .

The short-cut to punishment has an effect on society in other ways as well. The knowledge that men may be accused and found guilty of disloyalty in so summary a manner becomes a restraint on the exercise of constitutional rights. It is no longer safe to talk recklessly or foolishly. If the effect of this were no more than to silence recklessness and folly, perhaps the loss would not be great. But the discouragement of reckless and foolish talk tends inescapably to suppress sound and sensible dissent which may seem unpatriotic because it happens to be unpopular.

The trouble with putting any halter upon individual freedom to talk nonsense—even subversive or seditious nonsense—is that it tends to frustrate the democratic process. That process is one in which nonsense cannot be silenced by authority; it can be silenced, or overcome, only by sense. Since it is often not altogether easy to distinguish between the two, silencing of the one cannot help but result in silencing of the other. What happens, of course, is that unorthodox ideas, whether sensible or not, are suppressed in favor of orthodoxy. And consequently the attention of the society is diverted from its real problems, which call for adaptation and change, and focused instead upon a preservation of things as they are.

The situation should not be overstated. There has been, as yet, no formal or statutory suppression of speech in the United States beyond the prohibition of advocacy of violent overthrow of the government and the punitive restrictions of the McCarran Act. Men may, and fortunately a number of them still do, express nonconformist views liable to be termed treasonable. But, as Senator Margaret Chase Smith observed in a speech expressing her revulsion against the name-calling tactics of Senator Joseph McCarthy, "Freedom of speech is not what it used to be in America. It has been so abused by some that it is not exercised by others." Freedom of speech does not mean, to be sure, that a man who says what is unpopular should be protected from the penalties of unpopularity. Heretics and reformers must expect denunciation. The alarming characteristic about what is happening today lies partly in the official source of the denunciation, partly in the easy identification of dissent with disloyalty, partly in the punishment of it by the government itself through extralegal mechanisms.

The cult of loyalty, and its attendant hunt for heresy as a symptom of disloyalty, has generated an intellectually shackled feeling for which terror is too strong a term, but which is marked nevertheless by widespread anxiety. The feeling is most acute, naturally, in Washington, and among government employees. . . . But outside the capital, the pressures for conformity are mounting to a degree never before experienced by the American people. The Committee on Un-American Activities in the national House of Representatives has spawned imitators in state legislatures; some of them, such as the Tenney Committee in California, the Canwell Committee in Washington, the Broyles Commission in Illinois, have rivaled the tactics of the congressional body. In their role of investigators and with the stated object of protecting national security, they have had the effect of penalizing Americans for exercising the fundamental rights of advocacy and association.

Similarly, the Federal Employee-Loyalty Program has been aped and embellished in states and municipalities—where there is far less warrant for such restrictions. Protective measures designed to keep disloyal persons out of jobs that directly affect the national security become merely punitive when applied indiscriminately to all forms of public employment. In many states extremely repressive legislation, of doubtful constitutionality, has been adopted. These laws are aimed at Communists, but their result is to penalize all forms of heterodoxy. Some of the laws deny a place on the ballot to Communists, thereby revealing a distrust of the democratic process. Some, like the Ober Law in Maryland, drastically restrict the right of citizens to join in voluntary associations if the purpose of these associations is officially regarded as subversive. A number of municipalities, especially in the South, have adopted ordinances banning Communists and Communist *sympathizers* from the city limits. Birmingham, Alabama, for instance, announced that it would jail anyone found guilty of "voluntary association" with a Communist. Other cities have undertaken to require the registration of all Communists. The patent invalidity of such edicts from a constitutional point of view has given no apparent pause to local legislative and law-enforcement bodies. In a number of places, police chiefs have intimated that they mean to apply virtual lynch law to political undesirables. Behind all these measures is a fear of freedom and a panicky willingness to disregard the great procedural safeguards that distinguish a free from a totalitarian society.

The hounding of heterodoxy in the name of loyalty takes an especially ugly and mischievous form in connection with schools and universities. The proliferation of loyalty tests and oaths required of teachers inhibits discussion precisely where it should be most free. But perhaps the gravest consequence of the official cult of loyalty is the inflammation of public opinion to a sometimes hysterical pitch. When political disagreement is branded as disloyalty, when neighbor is invited to look with suspicion on neighbor, the bonds of national unity are strained in a way that is directly injurious to national security. Tragic incidents such as the Peekskill riots in the summer of 1949—when war veterans expressed their devotion to American ideals by behaving like Nazi stormtroopers—flow inevitably from official stimulation of intolerance. No matter how wrong-headed Paul Robeson may be, nothing that he might have said or sung at Peekskill could have injured the credit and the peace of the United States as grievously as the silencing of his voice by violence.

The war in Korea gave a tremendous impetus to this intolerance. In the grip of its excitement, many normally rational and gentle people tended to look upon any association with communism, no matter how remote or tenuous, as evidence of disloyalty and to regard a mere charge of such association as incontrovertible proof of guilt. . . .

Censorship in the name of patriotism occurs on an unorganized basis too. Perhaps the most sensitive example of it was provided by a Hollywood motion-picture studio which, after six months of work, shelved plans to produce a film dealing with the life and exploits of Hiawatha, the Onondaga Indian chief immortalized by Longfellow. Hiawatha had succeeded in establishing peace among the warring Five Nations; and it was felt, according to a studio spokesman, that this might cause the film to be regarded as a message for peace and thus as Communist propaganda.

Political discussion has been debased to a species of fishwifery by shrill and redundant accusations of disloyalty. The immunity from suit for slander afforded by the floor of Congress has been abused over and over again to launch extravagant attacks on the good faith of opponents in every issue of policy. . . .

The point is patently illustrated in connection with events in the Far East. The readiness of the China Lobby to impute disloyalty to every realistic appraisal of the collapse of the Chinese Nationalist government has made a rational China policy impossible. The State Department has been forced to cling to a transparent fiction. In other areas as well, mere anti-communism has taken the place of a reasoned evaluation of American interests, allying this country with discredited regimes abroad. Those who dared to protest or dissent were liable to vilification as Communist sympathizers. . . .

The disloyalty of the Americanists [super-patriots] impairs national security more seriously than the comparable disloyalty of the Communists. . . . It is more deeply subversive, strikes more injuriously at the real roots of loyalty and of American strength. It would, in fact, meet the threat of communism by the substitution of Communist techniques for the techniques of freedom. If the relatively impotent Communists aim at overthrowing the government of the United States, the Americanists, whether they are aware of it or not, aim at overthrowing the essential values which that government was instituted to secure.

HERESY, YES—CONSPIRACY, NO![1]

Sidney Hook

Sidney Hook, one of America's foremost philosophers, was fighting Stalinism in the thirties, long before anti-Stalinism became intellectually fashionable. As a spokesman for the Left, his opposition was especially effective, although he may no longer be described as a Marxist. He is the author of From Hegel to Marx *(1936), John* Dewey: An Intellectual Portrait *(1950), The Hero in History (1943), Toward the Understanding of Karl Marx (1933). His now well-known discussion of the difference between heresy and conspiracy is reprinted here.*

The most comprehensive and adequate definition in positive terms of the meaning of liberalism, from Socrates to John Dewey, is suggested by the memorable words of Justice Holmes. It is the belief "in the free trade of ideas—that the test of truth is the power of thought to get itself accepted in the competition of the market." This is not a program of action nor a philosophical theory of truth, but an attitude or temper of mind towards all programs. Liberals may disagree among themselves about everything else; but all of them have this faith in common. It is a faith which marks off liberal from totalitarian culture. Any action which restricts the freedom of ideas to develop or circulate is illiberal.

There are at least two presuppositions of this belief in the free market of ideas. One of them is explicitly drawn by Justice Holmes and already recognized by Jefferson; the other is implicit and perhaps more important, for around it center most of our present difficulties.

The first is that the free expression and circulation of ideas may be checked wherever their likely effects constitute a clear and present danger to public peace or the security of the country. This is a specific application of the principle that no right is absolute when it endangers rights of equal or greater validity. In ordinary affairs, this is a commonplace. The right to inquire is innocent, but not when it leads someone to experiment on a human being to determine how long he can survive torture. The right to free speech is precious, but not when it blasts a reputation by libelous accusation. Truth is sacred, but a person who revealed it knowing that it

---

[1]From *Heresy, Yes—Conspiracy, No!* (New York: John Day Co., Inc., 1953), pp. 19–36. Reprinted by permission.

would be used to destroy his country is a traitor. Freedom to worship God according to one's conscience is one of the historical cornerstones of the structure of American liberties, but it cannot be invoked to protect rituals which require human sacrifice or practices like plural marriages or refusal to submit to vaccination against plagues.

In the context of public affairs, however, there is a certain ambiguity involved in the conception of clear and present danger. Clear to whom? To the public enforcement agencies, to Congress, to the Justices of the Supreme Court (who are notoriously at odds with each other and who, on matters of fact, are less well informed than many laymen)? And how present must a "present danger" be? Must a riot be in progress before an anti-Semitic orator ranting about the forged *Protocols of Zion* is stopped from speaking? Must we await the actual delivery of an atomic bomb by a foreign power, or a formal declaration of war, before the incitements to treason by its fifth columnists in this country are curbed? These are some of the difficulties that attend the clear and present danger formula. They cannot be solved by fiat. In all such questions of "proximity and degree," good judgment is required. The most we can expect is that those who make the judgment will be competently informed and ultimately responsible to the community at large. According to our practice, a clear and present danger exists in the United States when a majority of the Supreme Court says it does; in England, when Parliament says it does.

The second presupposition of the liberal's faith in the free market of ideas is that the competition will be honestly and openly conducted. For unless there are certain rules, so to speak, of honest competition, analogous to those which hold in other domains of testing and inquiry, freedom of choice is an illusion. If the market is rigged by money, power or fraud, what gets accepted is anything but the truth. If ability to withstand honest competition is not a sufficient condition of truth it is at least a necessary one. From the point of view of the liberal, it is not doctrines "fraught with death" which he fears, for his faith in intelligence is such that he is confident that in the open and honest exchange of opinion the majority of men will choose life, not death, and that if they choose death they deserve their fate. Men cannot be compelled to remain free, any more than they can be compelled to love one another. What the liberal fears is the systematic corruption of the free market of ideas by activities which make intelligent choice impossible. In short, what he fears is not heresy but conspiracy.

The failure to recognize the distinction between heresy and conspiracy is fatal to a liberal civilization, for the inescapable consequence of their identification is either self-destruction, when heresies are punished as conspiracies, or destruction at the hands of their enemies, when conspiracies are tolerated as heresies.

A heresy is a set of unpopular ideas or opinions on matters of grave concern to the community. The right to profess publicly a heresy of any character, on any theme, is an essential element of a liberal society. The liberal stands ready to defend the honest heretic no matter what his views against any attempt to curb him. It is enough that the heretic pays the price of unpopularity which he cannot avoid. In some respects each of us is a heretic, but a liberal society can impose no official orthodoxies of *belief*, disagreement with which entails loss of liberty or life.

A conspiracy, as distinct from a heresy, is a secret or underground movement which seeks to attain its ends not by normal political or educational processes but by playing outside the rules of the game. Because it undermines the conditions which are required in order that doctrines may freely compete for acceptance, because where successful it ruthlessly destroys all heretics and dissenters, a conspiracy cannot be tolerated without self-stultification in a liberal society.

A heresy does not shrink from publicity. It welcomes it. Not so a conspiracy. The signs of a conspiracy are secrecy, anonymity, the use of false names and labels, and the calculated lie. It does not offer its wares openly but, by systematic infiltration into all organizations of cultural life, it seeks to capture strategic posts to carry out a policy alien to the purposes of the organization. There is political conspiracy, which is the concern of the state; but there may also be a conspiracy against a labor union, a cultural or professional association, or an educational institution which is not primarily the concern of the state but of its own members. In general, whoever subverts the rules of a democratic organization and seeks to win by chicanery what cannot be fairly won in the process of free discussion is a conspirator.

Communist *ideas* are heresies, and liberals need have no fear of them where they are freely and openly expressed. They should be studied and evaluated in the light of all the relevant evidence. No one should be punished because he holds them. The Communist *movement,* however, is something quite different from a mere heresy, for wherever it exists it operates along the lines laid down by Lenin as guides to Communists of all countries, and perfected in great detail since then. . . .

Under present conditions of political and military warfare, it is not hard to see what immense dangers to the security of liberal institutions is implicit in this strategy of infiltration and deceit. Even a few men in sensitive posts can do incalculable harm. These instructions—and there are many more detailed ones, combined with explicit directives to Communists to transform any war in which their country is involved, except one approved by the Soviet Union, into a civil war against their own government —indicate that members of the Communist party are not so much heretics as conspirators and in actual practice regard themselves as such.

There may be some justification for conspiratorial activity in undemocratic countries where heresies are proscribed, but Lenin . . . makes no exceptions. Since 1917, he maintains, in no country of the world can the revolution be peacefully achieved. . . .

How faithfully the Communist movement pursues the pattern laid down by its authoritative leaders in the political sphere is a matter of historical record. But unfortunately for the peace of mind of liberals, the same tactics are followed in other areas of social and cultural life. The history of American labor is replete with illustrations.

Every large labor organization in the United States has been compelled to take administrative action against Communist party elements not because of their beliefs—their heresies—but because their pattern of conduct made the Communist party, and ultimately the Kremlin, the decisive power in the life of the union, and not the needs and wishes of the membership. President Philip Murray of the CIO exposed the technique in detail when his organization ousted the Mine, Mill and Smelter Workers Union. In all these situations, it is not fear of Communist ideas which has led to disciplinary action. The charge against the Communists is that it is *they* who fear the open and honest confrontation of ideas. They operate through "fronts," the charge continues, because they fear that, given a free choice of honestly labeled alternatives, they will be rejected; once they slip into power, they consolidate their position by terror.

Under existing law punishment is provided for criminal conspiracy, whether this be conspiracy in restraint of trade or conspiracy to overthrow the government by insurrection or to advocate such overthrow in time of clear and present danger. But there are noncriminal conspiracies in sectors of life which are not affected by legislative power. These sectors of life are social and cultural and are regulated by tradition, common standards of propriety or decency in personal relations, and sometimes by explicit rules. The transfer of some of the techniques by which conspirators in the past have seized the state to capturing control of benevolent associations, social, chess, and athletic clubs, literary societies, research groups, professional and trade unions, even philanthropic agencies is unique to modern totalitarian movements. In the past, it was here if anywhere that honest opposition openly declared itself. The elaborate devices adopted by Communists to disguise the nature of their opposition and to prevent others from functioning in opposition to them when they seize control may have been anticipated in earlier times by other groups but they never were previously employed with such fanaticism, rationalized by such body of doctrine, and executed with such lack of scruple.

By now it should be apparent that liberals in the twentieth century are confronted by a situation quite unfamiliar to their forbears. For they must contend not with fearless heretics, indigenous elements of the community who, like the abolitionists and revolutionists of old, scorn concealment, and who make no bones about their hostility to the principles of liberalism. They find themselves in the unique historical predicament of having to deal with native elements who, by secrecy and stratagem, serve the interests of a foreign power which believes itself entitled to speak for all mankind, and whose victory spells the end of all liberal civilization and with it the right to heresy. It is now plain that the Communist regimes of the world have turned out to be the greatest and cruelest heresy-hunters in history, not merely in politics but in every branch of theory and practice. They have even abolished the right to be silent, for on any matter on which the Central Committee of any Communist party has laid down the law, silence is construed as treason.

It is a great pity and a source of much confusion that present-day Communists are often referred to as Marxists, without further qualification. For this overlooks the radical departure from Marx's own position initiated by Lenin and Stalin on the question of conspiracy. Marx was an unconcealed heretic. Even when writing in nondemocratic countries, subject to repression and imprisonment, he scorned the use of conspiratorial techniques and excoriated Bakunin and others for adopting them. The concluding sentence of the *Communist Manifesto* frankly tells the rulers of the nondemocratic countries of Europe: "The Communists disdain to conceal their views and aims. They openly declare that their ends can be attained only by the forcible overthrow of all existing social conditions."

Contrast with this the instructions given to Communists by the Kremlin in democratic countries, to adopt para-military organizational forms, to work underground even when legal work is permitted, and to develop systematic techniques of deception, and we can see the difference between honest and open revolutionists and underground conspirators.

The problems which underground conspiracy creates for a liberal society are of tremendous magnitude. They cannot be dismissed by a quotation from Jefferson. Nor can they be solved by indiscriminately placing the Communist movement and its entire periphery outside the law by special legislation. They require constructive intelligence, the discovery and application of techniques in each field which will meet conspiratorial threats to the proper functioning of liberal institutions without creating still greater ones. Legal outlawry of the Communist Party will not prevent it from reappearing under different names.

Failure to take this approach is characteristic of some current wholesale responses to the problem. The first is that of frightened reactionaries who cannot distinguish between heresy and conspiracy, and identify communism with any decent thing they wish to destroy. By making reckless charges of conspiracy where there is only honest heresy, they prevent intelligent choice. And by labeling all progressive ideas as Communist heresies, they help Communist strategy. For the Communist strategy is to make it appear that Communists are an integral part of the indigenous progressive movement, instead of a cancerous growth upon it, and that any legitimate measure directed against them is actually an attack upon all progressives, and indeed upon the philosophy of liberalism itself. There is nothing new about this unreasoning reaction. It emanates from the same quarters which called the Taft-Ellender Housing Bill "Communist," and plans for national health insurance "un-American."

A second response is made by a small but influential group of men who believe that they can check Communist conspiracy merely by passing laws against it, and that they can protect institutions from subversives by requiring all individuals, particularly teachers, to take loyalty oaths. As if any member of the Communist party regarded any oaths except one to the Communist party and the Soviet Union as binding! This results in foolish legislation like the Feinberg Law in New York and the Ober Law in Maryland, which are potentially dangerous in that they fail to make proper distinctions between conspirators and heretics.

A third group consists of those whom we may call ritualistic, as distinct from realistic, liberals. They ignore or blithely dismiss as comparatively insignificant the mass of evidence concerning the conspiratorial character of the Communist movement in all institutions in which it is active. They regard communism merely as an unpleasant heresy just a little worse than a crotchety theory of disease or finance. They sometimes characterize prosecution of a conspirator for espionage or perjury as persecution of a heretic. Or they condemn as "witch hunting," measures taken to deny access to sensitive posts in government or social institutions to members of the Communist party, who are under explicit instructions to sabotage the purposes of these organizations. The ritualistic liberals would wait until the sabotage has been carried out before proceeding against Communists. This gives a new lease of life to the reactionaries, who now tend to regard the ritualistic liberals as the dupes or accomplices of the Communists, thus confirming the illusions of the ritualistic liberals that there really is no problem of Communist conspiracy.

One of the most ambiguous phrases in current use among ritualistic liberals is "guilt by association.". . . It is or should be now clear that "association" by way of membership in the Communist Party is not innocent or coincidental but is *a form of active\co-operation and collaboration* in carrying out the purposes of a conspiratorial organization. The Communist Party sees to it that all members are instructed about the purposes as soon as they join. Continued membership is possible only in virtue of a series of continued *acts* of obedience to instructions. Those who dub the active co-operation required of all members of the Communist Party "guilt by association" coyly suggest by that phrase the innocuous association of chance or occasional encounters with Communists in social gatherings. They simply ignore the fact that all members of the Communist Party must "associate" by active co-operation with its purposes or be expelled.

Ritualistic liberals legitimately criticize the dangerous nonsense of those who proscribe heresy. But they carry their criticism to a point where they give the impression that the country is in the grip of a deadly reign of terror or hysteria much more dangerous than Communist expansion from without and infiltration from within. Because someone has given a silly characterization of a subversive organization, they imply that there are no subversive organizations. The sad history of recent American liberal movements, however, shows that the instructions given to American Communists by Otto Kuusinen, as Secretary of the Communist International, bore bitter fruit for liberals. Kuusinen advised: "We must create a whole solar system of organizations and smaller committees around the Communist Party, so to speak, smaller organizations working under the influence of the Party." (*American Communist,* May 1931.)

The problem of membership in Communist front organizations which often conceal their purposes is much more difficult. Many innocent people have been ensnared by these organizations. No hard and fast rule can be laid down as a guide. The number of such organizations an individual has joined, the time he joined, his function and activities upon joining—all these, as we shall see, are highly relevant in determining the degree to which an individual is untrustworthy from the point of view of security. Only those exceptional souls who have never made a mistake or have never been fooled can shut the gates of understanding and charity against all members of such groups and pronounce a blanket judgment against them. This troublesome question should not be made a matter of legislation but of judicious administration.

Because some security regulations in government are questionable, and because some blunders have been made, ritualistic liberals intimate that no security regulations are necessary and that the existing laws against treason and criminal conspiracy are sufficient for all purposes. They do not understand that the purpose of the security program is not punishment for acts committed but prevention of acts threatened by those who are under instructions to commit them or whose behavior or habits make them dangerous risks. By artfully collecting instances of foolishness from the press and blowing up their significance, they convey a very misleading picture comparable to what an account of American business would be like if only bankruptcies were reported, or an account of public order that featured only crime stories.

David Lilienthal, a realistic not a ritualistic liberal, has warned us against the "Scare-the-dopes!" method of discussing nuclear energy. There is also a "Scare-the-dopes!" method of discussion of the problem of Communistic conspiracy. It is used by those who employ the term Communist with scandalous looseness as a synonym for any economic or political heresy, and who shout conspiracy where there is only heresy. It is also used by those who do not tell us how to meet the real dangers of Communist conspiracy but shout "Hysteria!" "Fascism!" or "Police State!" when the first faltering efforts are made to cope with dangers hitherto unprecedented in the history of American democracy.

The position of realistic liberalism in three trouble centers of American life in which overt conspiratorial activity of a criminal nature is not involved may be briefly indicated as illustrative of its attitude.

Where government service is concerned, the operating maxim for every sensitive and policy-making post should be a principle enunciated by Roger Baldwin, former head of the American Civil Liberties Union: "A superior loyalty to a foreign government disqualifies a citizen for service to our own." This is not a matter of civil rights but of common sense. Once a policy is adopted by the governing agencies of a liberal society empowered by a democratic consensus to safeguard the public welfare, it is not only its right but its duty to insure its loyal execution. It cannot wait for a major piece of sabotage or leak of information in order to act. Yet this is precisely the procedure advocated by those who urge that once an individual has been appointed and served a probationary period, he should be dismissed only if he is caught engaging in espionage or sabotage. Presumably, even if it had been known that Hiss, Fuchs, Boyer, et al. were members of the Communist Party, once employed they should not have been dismissed until they had carried out their objectives or were on the verge of doing so.

The difficulty lies in determining what constitutes sufficient evidence to warrant the inference that a particular individual is unsafe, for in some cases even past membership in subversive organizations is not conclusive. On the other hand, notoriously bad judgment might bar someone from an important post whose loyalty is not impugned. A fool may sometimes be as dangerous as a rogue. Nor can the principles that apply in a courtroom in determination of *criminal* guilt be applied in these situations. The criteria for establishing "unreliability" must obviously be less stringent than those which lead us to deprive an individual of his life or freedom.

It is not impossible to find knowledgeable individuals who can supervise such a program. Where certain procedural safeguards are adopted and individuals allowed in doubtful cases to resign quietly without prejudice when they do not wish to accept posts in nonsensitive sectors, the likelihood of injustice diminishes. The more fanfare and publicity, however, the greater are the chances of error and injury to reputation. Ritualistic liberals who insist that everything be decided in the public eye, and that a case be made out that can stick in a court of law before an individual is dropped as a security risk, are inviting political circuses and a reaction that will sweep away all administrative safeguards against arbitrary dismissal. It cannot be emphasized too often that there is a difference between legal rules of evidence absolutely essential to our tradition where a man's life or liberty is at stake and rules of evidence that bear only on an individual's qualifications for a position of trust. There is certainly room for criticism of present procedures, but whoever speaks up will be more persuasive if he presents alternative positive proposals which show that he at least recognizes the problem.

In labor organizations, the existence of Communist leaders is extremely dangerous because of their unfailing use of the strike as a political instrument at the behest of the Kremlin. The history of Communist-led trade unions here and abroad is instructive enough. The most effective way of meeting this situation, however, is not by requiring non-Communist oaths on the part of union officers; for this can be circumvented by delegating office to individuals who are faithful but non-cardholding Communists. The most intelligent procedure for labor here is to let labor clean its own house. Free and independent trade unions, which are essential to a democracy, cannot be liberated from the organizational stranglehold of the Communist Party by government intervention. Only an aroused membership together with other labor organizations can do the job.[2]

. . . the question [of freedom and responsibility in the schools] is not primarily political. It does not involve civil rights so much as the ethics of professional conduct. Heresy in the schools—whether in science, economics, or politics—must be protected against any agency which seeks to impose orthodoxy. For the scholar there is no subversive doctrine, but only that which is valid or invalid or not proven in the light of evidence. The primary commitment of the teacher is to the ethics and logic of inquiry. It is not his beliefs, right or wrong—it is not his heresies—which disqualify the Communist Party teacher, but his declaration of intention, as evidenced by official statements, to practice educational fraud. Must one catch him in the act before dismissing him? Not necessarily; any more than we must catch a judge who is a *present* and *active* member of the Ku Klux Klan in the act of discriminating against Negroes or Jews before concluding he is unfit for judicial office. It is amazing to hear from ritualistic liberals that it is a violation of academic freedom to prevent a man from carrying out the professional misconduct which he has pledged himself to engage in by virtue of his membership in an organization whose publicly professed aim is to indoctrinate for the Communist Party in classrooms, enroll students in Communist Youth organizations, rewrite textbooks from the Communist point of view, build cells on campuses, capture departments, and inculcate the Communist Party line that in case of war students should turn their arms against their own government.

This is a matter of ethical hygiene, not of political heresy or of persecution. And because it is, the enforcement of the proper professional standards should rest with the teachers themselves, and not with the state or regents or even boards of trustees. The actual techniques of handling such

---

[2][EDITOR'S NOTE: Professor Hook would undoubtedly agree that since these words were written the trade union movement has done the job.]

issues must be worked out, but the problem cannot be confused with the issue of heresy. If the conspiratorial purposes of Communist Party teachers is glossed over by ritualistic liberals as merely a manifestation of heresy, then all heresy comes under fire. This does not mean that faculties must engage in a hue and cry to rout out the few unfaithful members of the profession who are betraying their trust. But they must not refuse to act whenever evidence of such unfitness is established thus making clear that "not everything gives.". . .

Liberalism in the twentieth century must toughen its fibre, for it is engaged in a fight on many different fronts. It must defend the free market in ideas against the racists, the professional patrioteers, and those spokesmen of the status quo who would freeze the existing inequalities of opportunity and economic power by choking off criticism. It must also be defended against those agents and apologists of Communist totalitarianism who, instead of honestly defending their heresies, resort to conspiratorial methods of anonymity and other techniques of fifth columnists. It will not be taken in by labels like "left" and "right." These terms came into use after the French Revolution, but the legacy of the men who then called themselves "left"—the strategic freedoms of the Bill of Rights—is today everywhere repudiated by those who are euphemistically referred to as "leftists" but who are actually Communists more reactionary than many of those who are conventionally called "rightists."

There is always a danger of excesses being committed when exposure of Communist conspiracy is left to the leadership of reactionaries. When this happens, it testifies to the fact that the liberals have failed to do the necessary job of moral education which is implicit in their dedication to the "free market in ideas." Similarly, they lose by default when, instead of taking the leadership in the struggle against "Know-Nothingism," racial persecution, and cultural repression, they permit Communists to exploit for their own political purposes the idealism of youth and the just resentments of the underprivileged.

Realistic liberalism recognizes that to survive we must solve many hard problems, and that they can be solved only by intelligence, and not by pious rhetoric. Our greatest danger is not fear of ideas but *absence* of ideas—specific ideas, addressed to concrete problems, here and now, problems of such complexity that only the ignorant can claim to know all the answers to them.

Finally, liberalism today conceives life not in terms of bare survival or of peace at any price, but in the light of ideas and ideals without which a life worthy of man cannot be attained. Among them are the strategic freedoms of those American traditions which make the continuous use of intelligence possible. . . .

THE TRIAL OF ARTHUR MILLER[1]

John Steinbeck

The author of such novels as Grapes of Wrath, In Dubious
Battle, *and* Of Mice and Men *would have needed no introduction
even before the award of a Nobel prize brought him greater promi-
nence and world-wide recognition. That same conscience which led
him, in* Grapes of Wrath, *to protest against social injustice brings
him here to the defense of a fellow writer.*

The trial of Arthur Miller for contempt of Congress brings close to all
of us one of the strangest and most frightening dilemmas that a people and
a government has ever faced. It is not the first trial of its kind, nor will it in
all probability be the last. But Arthur Miller is a writer—one of our very
best. What has happened to him could happen to any writer; could
happen to me. We are face to face with a problem by no means easy of
solution. . . .

No man knows what he might do in a given situation, and surely many
men must wonder how they would act if they were in Arthur Miller's shoes.
I wonder what I would do.

Let me suppose that I were going to trial for contempt of Congress as
he is. I might be thinking somewhat as follows:

There is no doubt that Congress has the right, under the law, to ask
me any question it wishes and to punish my refusal to answer with a contempt charge. The Congress has the right to do nearly anything conceivable.
It has only to define a situation or an action as a "clear and present danger"
to public safety, public morals, or public health. The selling or eating of
mince pie could be made a crime if Congress determined that mince pie
was a danger to public health—which it 'probably is. Since many parents
raise their children badly, mother love could be defined as a danger to the
general welfare.

Surely, Congress has the right to ask me anything on any subject. The
question is: Should the Congress take advantage of that right?

Let us say that the Congressional Committee feels that the Communist
Party and many groups which have been linked with it—sometimes arbitrarily—constitute a clear and present danger to the nation. Now actually
it is neither virtue nor good judgment on my part that has kept me from

---

[1]*Esquire*, June 1957, p. 86. Copyright © 1957 by John Steinbeck. Reprinted by
permission of McIntosh and Otis, Inc.

joining things. I am simply not a joiner by nature. Outside of the Boy
Scouts and the Episcopal choir, I have never had an impulse to belong to
things. But suppose I had. And suppose I have admitted my association
with one or more of these groups posted as dangerous. As a writer, I must
have been interested in everything, have felt it part of my profession to
know and understand all kinds of people and groups. Having admitted these
associations, I am now asked by the Committee to name individuals I have
seen at meetings of such groups. I hope my reasoning then would go as
follows:

The people I knew were not and are not, in my estimation, traitors to
the nation. If they were, I would turn them in instantly. If I give names, it
is reasonably certain that the persons named will be called up and questioned. In some cases they will lose their jobs, and in any case their repu-
tations and standing in the community will suffer. And remember that these
are persons who I honestly believe are innocent of any wrongdoing. Perhaps
I do not feel that I have that right; that to name them would not only be
disloyal but actually immoral. The Committee then is asking me to commit
an immorality in the name of public virtue.

If I agree, I have outraged one of our basic codes of conduct, and if I
refuse I am guilty of contempt of Congress, sentenced to prison and fined.
One way outrages my sense of decency and the other brands me as a felon.
And this brand does not fade out.

Now suppose I have children, a little property, a stake in the community. The threat of the contempt charge jeopardizes everything I love. Suppose, from worry or cowardice, I agree to what is asked. My deep and
wounding shame will be with me always.

I cannot be reassured by the past performance of the Committee. I
have read daily for a number of years the testimony of admitted liars and
perjurers whose charges have been used to destroy the peace and happiness
of people I do not know, and many of whom were destroyed without being
tried.

Which path am I to choose? Either way I am caught. It may occur to
me that a man who is disloyal to his friends could not be expected to be
loyal to his country. You can't slice up morals. Our virtues begin at home.
They do not change in a courtroom unless the pressure of fear is put upon us.

But if I am caught between two horrors, so is the Congress caught.
Law, to survive, must be moral. To force personal immorality on a man, to
wound his private virtue, undermines his public virtue. If the Committee
frightens me enough, it is even possible that I may make up things to satisfy
the questioners. This has been known to happen. A law which is immoral
does not survive and a government which condones or fosters immorality
is truly in clear and present danger.

The Congress had a perfect right to pass the Alien and Sedition Act.
This law was repealed because of public revulsion. The Escaped Slave laws

had to be removed because the people of free states found them immoral. The Prohibition laws were so generally flouted that all law suffered as a consequence.

We have seen and been revolted by the Soviet Union's encouragement of spying and telling, children reporting their parents, wives informing on their husbands. In Hitler's Germany, it was considered patriotic to report your friends and relations to the authorities. And we in America have felt safe from and superior to these things. But are we so safe or superior?

The men in Congress must be conscious of their terrible choice. Their legal right is clearly established, but should they not think of their moral responsibility also? In their attempts to save the nation from attack, they could well undermine the deep personal morality which is the nation's final defense. The Congress is truly on trial along with Arthur Miller.

Again let me change places with Arthur Miller. I have refused to name people. I am indicted, convicted, sent to prison. If the charge were murder or theft or extortion I would be subject to punishment, because I and all men know that these things are wrong. But if I am imprisoned for something I have been taught from birth is a good thing, then I go to jail with a deep sense of injustice and the rings of that injustice are bound to spread out like an infection. If I am brave enough to suffer for my principle, rather than to save myself by hurting other people I believe to be innocent, it seems to me that the law suffers more than I, and that contempt of the law and of the Congress is a real contempt rather than a legalistic one.

Under the law, Arthur Miller is guilty. But he seems also to be brave. Congress feels that it must press the charge against him, to keep its prerogative alive. But can we not hope that our representatives will inspect their dilemma? Respect for law can be kept high only if the law is respectable. There is a clear and present danger here, not to Arthur Miller, but to our changing and evolving way of life.

If I were in Arthur Miller's shoes, I do not know what I would do, but I could wish, for myself and for my children, that I would be brave enough to fortify and defend my private morality as he has. I feel profoundly that our country is better served by individual courage and morals than by the safe and public patriotism which Dr. Johnson called "the last refuge of scoundrels."

My father was a great man, as any lucky man's father must be. He taught me rules I do not think are abrogated by our nervous and hysterical times. These laws have not been annulled; these rules of attitudes. He taught me—glory to God, honor to my family, loyalty to my friends, respect for the law, love of country and instant and open revolt against tyranny, whether it come from the bully in the schoolyard, the foreign dictator, or the local demagogue.

And if this be treason, gentlemen, make the most of it.

ARTHUR MILLER'S CONSCIENCE[1]

Richard H. Rovere

Richard Rovere writes the New Yorker's *"Letter from Washington," is American correspondent for* The Spectator, *and co-author with Arthur Schlesinger, Jr., of* The General and the President. *His most recent work is a collection of essays,* The American Establishment and Other Reports, Opinions, and Speculations.

"I will protect my sense of myself," Arthur Miller told the House Committee on Un-American Activities when he refused to identify some writers who had once been Communists. "I could not use the name of another person and bring trouble on him." The refusal brought Miller a conviction for contempt of Congress from a judge who found his motives "commendable" but his action legally indefensible.

A writer's sense of himself is to be projected as well as protected. It becomes, through publication and production, a rather public affair. For this and other reasons, it is fitting that what Miller saw as the testing of his integrity—the challenge to his sense of himself—was a question involving not himself but others. Of himself, he had talked freely, not to say garrulously. He chatted, almost gaily, about his views in the Thirties, his views in the Forties, his views in the Fifties, about Ezra Pound and Elia Kazan and other notables, about the Smith Act and Congressional investigations and all manner of things. . . . His self-esteem was offended only when he was asked to identify others.

Thus, one might say, it was really a social or political ethic that he was defending, while of his sense of himself he gave freely. . . . (It was, of course, a symbolic act, a gesture, for Miller knew very well that the committee knew all about the men he was asked to identify. He could not really shield; he could only assert the shielding principle.) What he was protecting was, in any case, a self-esteem that rested upon a social rule or principle or ethic.

One could almost say that Miller's sense of himself *is* the principle that holds "informing" to be the ultimate in human wickedness. It is certainly a recurrent theme in his writing. In *The Crucible,* his play about the Salem witchcraft trials, his own case is so strikingly paralleled as to lend

---

[1]*New Republic,* June 17, 1957, pp. 13–15. Reprinted by permission.

color—though doubtless not truth—to the view that his performance in Washington was a case of life paying art the sincere flattery of imitation. To save his life, John Proctor, the hero, makes a compromise with the truth. He confesses, falsely, to having trafficked with Satan. "Did you see the Devil?" the prosecutor asks him. "I did," Proctor says. He recognizes the character of his act, but this affects him little. "Good, then—it is evil, and I do it," he says to his wife, who is shocked. He has reasoned that a few more years on earth are worth his betrayal of his sense of himself. (It is not to be concluded that Proctor's concession to the mad conformity of the time parallels Miller's testimony, for Proctor had never in fact seen the devil, whereas Miller had in fact seen Communists.) The prosecutor will not let him off with mere self-incrimination. He wants names; the names of those Proctor has seen with the Devil. Proctor refuses; does not balk at a self-serving lie, but a self-serving lie that involves others will not cross his lips. "I speak my own sins," he says, either metaphorically or hypocritically, since the sins in question are a fiction. "I cannot judge another. I have no tongue for it." He is hanged, a martyr. . . .

Today, in most Western countries, ethics derive mainly from society and almost all values are social. What we do to and with ourselves is thought to be our own affair and thus not, in most circumstances, a matter that involves morality at all. People will be found to say that suicide, for a man or woman with few obligations to others, should not be judged harshly, while the old sanctions on murder remain. Masochism is in one moral category, sadism in another. Masturbation receives a tolerance that fornication does not quite receive. A man's person and his "sense of himself" are disposable assets, provided he choose to see them that way; sin is only possible when we involve others. Thus, Arthur Miller's John Proctor was a modern man when, after lying about his relations with the Devil, he said, "God in heaven, what is John Proctor, what is John Proctor? I think it is honest, I think so. I am no saint.". . . He was speaking for the social ethic which is Arthur Miller's—and he resisted just where Miller did, at "informing."

It is, I think, useful to look rather closely at Miller's social ethic and at what he has been saying about the problems of conscience, for circumstances have conspired to make him the leading symbol of the militant, risk-taking conscience in this period. I do not wish to quarrel with the whole of his morality, for much of it I share—as do, I suppose, most people who have not found it possible to accept any of the revealed religions. Moreover, I believe, as Judge McLaughlin did, that the action Miller took before the committee was a courageous one. Nevertheless, I think that behind the action and behind Miller's defense of it there is a certain amount of moral and political confusion. If I am right, then we ought to set about examining it, lest conscience and political morality come to be seen entirely in terms of "naming names"—a simplification which the House Un-American Activities Committee seems eager to foist upon us and which Miller, too, evidently accepts.

A healthy conscience, Miller seems to be saying, can stand anything but "informing." On the one hand, this seems a meager view of conscience. On the other, it makes little political sense and not a great deal of moral sense. Not all "informing" is bad, and not all of it is despised by the people who invariably speak of it as despicable. The question of guilt is relevant. My wife and I, for example, instruct our children not to tattle on one another. I am fairly certain, though, that if either of us saw a hit-and-run driver knock over a child or even a dog, we would, if we could, take down the man's license number and turn him in to the police. Even in the case of children, we have found it necessary to modify the rule so that we may be quickly advised if anyone is in serious danger of hurting himself or another. (The *social* principle again.) Proctor, I think, was not stating a fact when he said, "I cannot judge another"—nor was Miller when he said substantially the same thing. For the decision *not* to inform involves judging others. "They think to go like saints," Proctor said of those he claimed he could not judge, and Miller must have had something of the sort in mind about the writers he refused to discuss. He reasoned, no doubt, that their impulses were noble and that they had sought to do good in the world. We refuse to inform, I believe, either when we decide that those whose names we are asked to reveal are guilty of no wrong or when we perceive that what they have done is no worse than what we ourselves have often done. Wherever their offenses are clearly worse—as in the case of a hit-and-run driver or a spy or a thief—we drop the ban.

If the position taken by Miller were in all cases right, then it would seem wise to supplement the Fifth Amendment with one holding that no man could be required to incriminate another. If this were done, the whole machinery of law enforcement would collapse; it would be simply impossible to determine the facts about a crime. Of course, Congressional committees are not courts, and it might be held that such a rule would be useful in their proceedings. It would be useful only if we wished to destroy the investigative power. For we live, after all, in a community, in the midst of other people, and all of our problems—certainly all of those with which Congress has a legitimate concern—involve others. It is rarely possible to conduct a serious inquiry of any sort without talking about other people and without running the risk of saying something that would hurt them. We can honor the conscience that says "I speak my own sins. I cannot judge another," but those of us who accept any principle of social organization and certainly those of us who believe that our present social order, whatever changes it may stand in need of, is worth preserving cannot make a universal principle of refusing to inform. If any agency of the community is authorized to undertake a serious investigation of any of our common problems, then the identities of others—*names*—are of great importance. What would be the point of investigating, say, industrial espionage if the labor spies sub-poenaed refused to identify their employers? What would be the point of investigating the Dixon-Yates contract if it were impossible to learn the identity of the businessmen and government officials involved?

The joker, the source of much present confusion, lies in the matter of *seriousness*. Miller and his attorneys have argued that the names of the writers Miller had known were not relevant to the legislation on passports the Committee was supposed to be studying. This would certainly seem to be the case, and one may regret that Judge McLaughlin did not accept this argument and acquit Miller on the strength of it. Nevertheless, the argument really fudges the central issue, which is that the Committee wasn't really investigating passport abuses at all when it called Miller before it. It was only pretending to do so. The rambling talk of its members with Miller was basically frivolous, and the Un-American Activities Committee has almost always lacked seriousness. In this case, as Mary McCarthy has pointed out, the most that it wanted from Miller was to have him agree to its procedure of testing the good faith of witnesses by their willingness to produce names. It was on this that Miller was morally justified in his refusal.

Still, Miller's principle, the social ethic he was defending, cannot be made a universal rule or a political right. For it is one thing to say in *The New Republic* that a committee is frivolous or mischievous and another to assert before the law that such a judgment gives a witness the right to stand mute without being held in contempt. As matters stand today, Miller was plainly in contempt. At one point in *The Crucible,* John Proctor is called to justify his failure to attend the church of the Reverend Mr. Parris and to have his children baptized by that divine. He replies that he disapproves of the clergyman. "I see no light of God in that man," he says. "That is not for you to decide," he is told. "The man is ordained, therefore the light of God is in him." And this, of course, is the way the world is. In a free society, any one of us may arrive at and freely express a judgment about the compe-tence of duly constituted authority. But in an orderly society, no one of us can expect the protection of the law whenever we decide that a particular authority is unworthy of our cooperation. We may stand by the decision, and we may seek the law's protection, but we cannot expect it as a matter of right. There are many courses of action that may have a sanction in morality and none whatever in law.

Yet the law is intended to be, among other things, a codification of morality, and we cannot be pleased with the thought that a man should be penalized for an act of conscience—even when his conscience may seem not as fully informed by reason as it ought to be. In a much more serious matter, war, we excuse from participation those who say their consciences will permit them no part in it. One of the reasons the order of American society seems worth preserving is that it allows, on the whole, a free play to the individual's moral judgment. In recent years, Congressional committees have posed the largest single threat to this freedom. The issues have often been confused by the bad faith of witnesses on the one hand and committee members on the other. Still and all, the problem is a real one, as the Miller case shows. If there is not sufficient latitude for conscience in the law, then there ought to be. It would be unrealistic, I think, simply to permit anyone who chooses to withhold whatever information he chooses. The Fifth Amendment seems to go as far as is generally justified in this direction. Changes in committee procedures have often been urged, but it is doubtful if much clarification of a problem such as this can be written into rules and by-laws. The problem is essentially one of discretion and measurement; it is, in other words, the most difficult sort of problem and one of the kind that has, customarily, been dealt with by the establishment of broad and morally informed judicial doctrines. It is surely to be hoped that in the several cases, including Arthur Miller's, now in one stage or another of review, the courts will find a way of setting forth a realistic and workable charter for the modern conscience.

CRIME AND PUNISHMENT

At the point where other restraints fail to provide security for persons and property from criminal acts, society provides for a penal system. Such a system is intended (a) to deter would-be criminals, (b) to isolate those who have not been deterred, (c) to reform those who are not incorrigible, and (d) to deter them from repeating criminal acts after their release. The purposes of a penal system are thus to deter, to protect where deterrence has failed, to reform or correct. It also serves another purpose, which responsible penologists acknowledge but do not condone: it punishes and thereby vents the wrath of society on those who flout its rules. Although many will argue that an intellectually respectable or morally responsible case for retributive justice can no longer be formulated, in a state like California, where penological practice is quite advanced, responsible office-holders have nevertheless been forced to make concessions to the demand for harsher sentences on dope peddlers.[1] Clearly, the quest for security is inextricably involved with other motives and purposes.

It is almost universally acknowledged that prevailing penal practices are failing to serve as a deterrent. Some 67 percent of federal prisoners have been incarcerated previously. Few—no more than 15 percent—are reformed. The proportions are no doubt similar in state prisons. Most prisoners, when their terms are over, are eventually released into society more hardened and brutalized and potentially more dangerous than they were before. One of our most distinguished jurists, Judge David Bazelon, has said of prisons: "They breed crime. They breed homosexuality. Society is not getting the protection it requires by our present system of punishment, and neither is the prisoner getting the help he needs." Nearly all competent authorities would agree. Why then do we persist in practices that defeat their own purpose? Judge Bazelon's answer is that the community is concerned with *whether* a crime is committed and generally fails to ask *why*.

---

[1]No less an authority than J. Edgar Hoover has testified before the House Appropriations Committee (May 1959) that "reports on youth crimes have indicated a mounting savagery, a senseless brutality, which leaves little doubt that in the interest of self-preservation, it is now time for sterner measures to be taken by the communities and by the courts."

The community does of course take into account such circumstances as extreme youth, the presence of duress, entrapment, and the like in determining guilt; and long ago England reckoned in a formal way with the question of sanity in the now generally accepted M'Naghten rule, by which most American jurisdictions are also bound.

In brief, the M'Naghten rule declares that the perpetrator of an illegal act may not be found guilty if he was unable at the time of the crime to distinguish between right and wrong. In general, it represents—usually supplemented by the "irresistible impulse" test—the limit to which adherents of the retributive justice school are willing to go in reckoning with mental disease or defect.

It is the gravamen of the now famous Durham rule laid down by Judge Bazelon in *Durham* v. *United States* (1954) that the M'Naghten rule is not only unjust but, as he said in his Brandeis Lecture reproduced below, symptomatic of limitations in our approach to criminal conduct that account for the glaring failures of our whole penal system.

Dr. Karl Menninger, whose comments also appear below, has described the Durham opinion as "more revolutionary in its total effect than the Supreme Court decision regarding segregation." If the Durham rule were to win general acceptance it would greatly restrict the area of responsibility on the basis of which we now dispense "justice." The overwhelming weight of scientific opinion is on its side. Why, if nearly all psychologists and penologists favor Durham, does M'Naghten still prevail? In part, of course, because of fear. In part because society is still more interested in punishment than in correction and cure. But most of all because society is still groping for the point at which to draw a line between the area where an individual must be regarded as responsible for his conduct and the area where he is the victim (or beneficiary) of circumstances over which he had no control. It is to this most difficult of all problems in ethics—defining the line between blame and exculpation, a problem involving ultimately the basic issue of freedom and determinism—that M'Naghten and Durham direct attention.

Objections to Judge Bazelon's opinion in the Durham case have been largely limited to frustrated police and prosecuting attorneys, to incensed citizens whose lazy way of achieving a sense of civic responsibility and moral righteousness consists of denouncing crime and demanding severer penalties, and to moralists genuinely concerned about whether the Durham rule hopelessly confounds the meaning of responsibility as a moral category.

In general, psychiatrists have joined with Dr. Menninger and hailed the Bazelon opinion as marking a breakthrough in the treatment of criminals and a new rapprochement between psychiatry and criminology. For this reason a dissent voiced by an able psychiatrist is noteworthy. Dr. Thomas S. Szasz is no apologist for the M'Naghten rule, which he describes elsewhere as based on myths and as "utterly nonsensical." However, he has questioned whether "modern diagnostic notions will serve any better,"[2] and he has argued at length that "the *application* of scientific knowledge about human feelings, motivation, and behavior is not *necessarily* 'beneficial' for the individual or for mankind."[3]

The foregoing considerations come to a dramatic focus on the issue of capital punishment. Two voices separated by an astronomic social distance provide an unusual contrast in the selections appearing below. The first is that of a distinguished scholar and teacher, Jacques Barzun, who defends capital punishment as a means of ridding society of undesirable elements, and the other is that of Caryl Chessman, who was executed on May 9, 1960, twelve years after he was installed in Death Row and shortly after his last reprieve. In retrospect it is difficult to believe that the fate of one individual with a long record of criminal misbehavior could have occasioned the vast uproar that preceded his execution. In the end, the governor would have commuted Chessman's sentence, but under the laws of California he was powerless to do so.[4] In a last-minute effort to alter the outcome, the governor called the state legislature into special session to consider repeal of capital punishment, at least for a trial period. In doing so he jeopardized his political career. Clearly, the execution of Chessman was no routine act of retribution. The great causes célèbres—Dreyfuss, Sacco and Vanzetti, Tom Mooney—had ideological involvements that were completely lacking in the Chessman case. No issue of anti-semitism, radicalism, or the like, was involved in the spontaneous protest against Caryl Chessman's execution. His case was unique because it evoked such worldwide concern over the life of a single person and the moral right of the state to take such a life.

---

[2]"Psychiatric Expert Testimony—Its Covert Meaning and Social Function," *Psychiatry: Journal for the Study of Interpersonal Processes,* August 1957, p. 314.

[3]"Some Observations on the Relationship Between Psychiatry and the Law," *AMA Archives of Neurology and Psychiatry,* March 1956, p. 16.

[4]Chessman was convicted of assault and kidnapping. Assault alone is not a capital crime in California. The kidnapping charge was a strictly "technical" one. The governor may not under California law commute the sentence of a twice-convicted felon without a recommendation from the state supreme court.

THE DILEMMA OF PUNISHMENT[1]

David L. Bazelon

Judge David L. Bazelon, member of the U.S. Court of Appeals, Washington, D.C., has written more than twenty-five opinions on the insanity defense in criminal cases, of which the Durham opinion is the most famous. The American Psychiatric Association has recognized his work by awarding him a certificate of commendation, declaring that "he has removed massive barriers between the psychiatric and legal professions and opened pathways wherein together they may search for better ways of reconciling human values with social safety." The following are selections from his Brandeis Lecture delivered at Brandeis University in 1960.

. . . In the criminal law, where one might expect the assistance of the behavioral sciences and especially psychiatry to be most eagerly solicited—because most obviously relevant—the fact of the matter is that they are not. . . . I will not burden your patience by recounting again the century-old struggle against the exclusionary M'Naghten Rules. These Rules have dominated the administration of the insanity defense in England and most American jurisdictions. It should suffice to remind you of their continued vitality. The M'Naghten formula emphasizes the rational capacity of the mind, and excuses from criminal responsibility only the individual who at the time of the crime "was laboring under such a defect of reason, from disease of the mind, as not to know" what he was doing or that it was wrong. However this test *might* have been interpreted—volumes have been written on the possible meanings of the words—it has in fact worked to exclude medical evidence. I am almost tempted to say that under M'Naghten practice the psychiatrist appears in the proceeding at all only to testify to the irrelevance of psychiatry—that is, to confirm the irrelevance that "the law" has already decided upon. It assigns to the psychiatric expert in court a sacrificial role in a ritual of condemnation. The expert is asked a question which—most leaders of the profession inform us—cannot be answered within the terms of their discipline. And unless the Rules are breached—as they frequently are on the trial level—the psychiatrist is not encouraged or permitted to address himself to the clinical questions which are the only ones he is truly expert in answering.

---

[1]Louis D. Brandeis Memorial Lecture, Brandeis University, March 14, 1960. Reprinted by permission.

That is the scientific expert testifying at the trial level. But on appeal, you may ask, have there been no "Brandeis briefs" setting forth the relevant facts and insights of modern scientific psychiatry? Yes, for example many psychiatric works were referred to in the appellant's brief in the *Durham* case, which, as many of you know, resulted in the adoption in the District of Columbia of a broadened insanity test—a rule designed to relax the rigors of M'Naghten and to welcome genuine psychiatric testimony presented in its own terms. The Durham test simply asks whether the accused was suffering from a mental disease or defect, and inquires as to the relation between any such condition and the criminal act. . . .

In the administration of the criminal law today, we desperately need all the help we can get from modern behavioral scientists—before trial, during trial, and after trial. The law by itself, without these workers, is cast in the hopeless role of a socially isolated, traditional bulwark against the welter of personal, social and economic forces which create today's problem of crime and the so-called criminal population. And in this losing struggle, the law—by which I mean police, judges, lawyers, and prison guards— would have at its disposal a limited set of concepts honored largely by time alone. In brief, the law would have the *lex talionis*—the idea of retributive punishment based on absolute moral principles of purportedly universal application. *By itself,* the law would dispose of both the problem of crime and the criminal himself with the one idea of punishment. The "program" would be: Repress crime and all antisocial behavior by punishment alone; rehabilitate the offender by punishment alone; achieve social understanding of wrong-doing and the wrong-doer by the sole mechanical response— "Punish them—they deserve it!"

If the foregoing remarks seem intemperate, that is of course because they do *not* describe our actual system of criminal law administration. For one thing, stern retributive justice has always been tempered by mercy and forgiveness—by the ubiquitous impulse to afford the transgressor a "second chance." This happens in practice even when it is not allowed by theory. We simply find it too difficult, too non-human to punish, punish, punish—even though we may hold most seriously the moral imperative to punish, and even though our feeling is that we are wrong when we do not. And for another thing, the behavioral scientists—along with their facts, ideas, and methodology—have as a matter of fact intervened increasingly at many stages of the administrative process. Social workers, clinicians, welfare agencies, even the police, as well as many others, attempt to deal constructively with the juvenile delinquent before he is sent to a reformatory to begin his professional training as the criminal of the future. The psychiatrist comes to court and sometimes his presence there *does* have something other than a ritualistic effect on the outcome of the proceeding. . . .

So clearly our criminal system is a very mixed affair—some would say a very *mixed-up* affair. But things are happening, there is agitation and movement, much heat and a certain amount of light. To put it simply, it is a system in transition. We are, painfully and slowly, coming to a clearer understanding of alternatives and necessities. . . .

If our system is in transition, then the question properly arises—Transition from what to what? From M'Naghten to Durham? Hardly. Certainly *from* M'Naghten—but not *just* from that ritualistic phrase, except perhaps symbolically. And Durham—even viewed as a concept, as an approach, which is the way I prefer to view it, rather than nineteen words of a jury instruction—is merely one way of welcoming the psychiatrist into the courtroom. It is a beginning, not an ending—and it relates to the insanity defense, which is only [the] visible one-ninth of the iceberg.

I believe that the deeper part of the iceberg consists of the retributive urge to punish irrespective of effect, and the accompanying intellectual justification of this primitive urge, the so-called theory of deterrence. A deep emotion and a complicated rationalization. . . .

Wherever one turns in an effort at reform in the treatment of offenders, one comes up against this need to punish and its defense by the theory of deterrence. Of course there are many other arguments put forward at various times in justification of the present system, with its great emphasis on punishment for its own sake or punishment as the answer to all problems. For example, both Judge Learned Hand in this country and Lord Justice Denning in England—the first sadly and the latter more firmly—have referred to the *public's* demand that the sinner shall suffer. Judge Hand stated that he did "not share that feeling, which is a vestige . . . of very ancient primitive and irrational beliefs and emotions." Lord Justice Denning spoke more strongly by saying:

> "It is a mistake to consider the objects of punishment as being deterrent or reformative or preventive, and nothing else. . . . The truth is that some crimes are so outrageous that society insists on adequate punishment, because the wrongdoer deserves it, irrespective of whether it is a deterrent or not."

I can assure you that similar views are frequently expressed from the bench in courts throughout our land—and often enough when the crime is no more "outrageous" than juvenile car-theft. Sometimes the court in relieving itself of these sentiments will refer to society's demand for retribution— communicated to the court by some unknown intermediary, or perhaps so obvious as not to require communication. On other occasions a court will abandon that rhetorical flourish and speak directly, saying—"You are going to be punished good and proper because you deserve it, and because too many of you hoodlums have been getting away with it."

So it is still the need to punish that confronts us—although at times not *my* need, but somebody else's. All this, as Judge Hand suggests, is highly irrational. I am sure that we must recognize this irrational need as a social fact, but I cannot see that we must abandon attempts at reform because of it. After all, that public out there that needs to punish also needs to forgive—and it especially needs to be given, for its own protection and well-being, the most rationally effective administration we can devise for it. It is not getting it now. The excessive emphasis on punishment, with the consequent neglect of genuine rehabilitation, is accompanied by a disastrously high level of recidivism. In the relatively progressive Federal Prison System, for example, the rate increased between 1949 and 1958 from 61 percent to 67 percent. In this same period, the number of serious offenders who have had two or more previous commitments has grown from 39 percent to 46 percent. Please realize what these figures mean: In two-thirds of the cases, punishment neither reforms nor deters the individual who has served one sentence. And with those who have served a second sentence, it fails again in nearly half of the cases. . . .

This being the case, why such persistent, irrational emphasis on punishment? I think one thing is the deep childish fear that with any reduction of punishment, multitudes would run amok. It seems to me this fear must be based on exaggerated notions of the role of punishment when we were children. The reasoning is: We are good adults because we were punished when we were bad children; any adult who is bad should get some more of what we got when we were children. *"They"* must be punished to reconfirm our adulthood and our goodness—to distinguish us from them. But most of us who have been good for many years—or at least haven't been caught—have not maintained our high estate because of witnessing frequent public hangings and whippings or stopping to observe a malefactor being drawn-and-quartered on the corner of a busy intersection. Quite the opposite. According to the famous Warden Lawes of Sing Sing Prison, this is especially true of the prosecutors and judges who so zealously take upon themselves the rhetorical burden of carrying out society's need to punish. He sent invitations to the appropriate officers of the law to attend each of the 114 executions carried out at Sing Sing while he was warden. Not one ever found time to attend.

Perhaps one should be encouraged by the fact that the modern urge to punish is no longer so immediately personal. I suppose we should all be pleased by the recent report from Saudi Arabia announcing an important reform in criminal law administration—that hereafter a thief's hand will be cut off by an "expert surgeon" using anesthetics rather than by an amateur with a hatchet. An accompanying reform is that adulteresses will no longer be stoned to death, as in biblical times. As Saudi Arabia enters the modern world, they will now be shot.

So there is something like progress in these matters. I would remind you that not half a century before the M'Naghten Rules were enunciated, more than 200 crimes were punishable by death in England. It is interesting to speculate as to whether England could possibly have become the civilized place it is today if the number of capital crimes had not been reduced. But Lord Justice Denning still believes in punishment for its own sake—or still believes that society believes in it. . . .

. . . what has to be explained—and finally understood—is the really frightening scope of the irrationality of our notions and practices regarding punishment. It seems that we just do not know how to be practical about the matter. For example, most of us, I imagine, have achieved major control over our own aggressive and vindictive impulses. We would be revolted to watch a hanging or a beating, and even more to participate in one. When we are personally called upon to administer punishment or any form of serious deprivation, we take the task as a heavy duty and think very hard to make certain that we do no more and no less than we feel to be necessary and effective in the circumstances. This would be so in the disciplining of our own children or any subordinates. But when it comes to the administration of crime, we hand the whole matter over to a distant bureaucratic machine, and we want to hear no more about it. Our attitude is—"Let the State take care of them."

In other words, our personal resolution of the issue of vindictiveness seems to be achieved at the cost of our human capacity to identify with the offender. Isn't it strange that the criminal law tradition which not so long ago was based on the supposedly deterrent spectacle of public punishment has come full circle and now can be said to be based in effect on the distance and even the secrecy of actual punishment? I wonder how many in this audience have ever seen the inside of a prison? What you would see there can be justified only on the assumption that the prisoners are less than human, and that therefore the obviously de-humanizing process they are undergoing is appropriate for them. Because they have stolen property or committed acts of violence, they are outside the pale of human society, and that is the end of the matter. But of course after having further brutalized them, after having failed to deal with the causes of their behavior, and having failed to effect any serious rehabilitation, we then release them into society where they can experience their second or third or fourth opportunity to fail. As Karl Menninger has said, these people are failures first and "criminals" later. To be a criminal is not strictly speaking merely to have committed a crime—it is a social branding plus penitentiary training, all of which serves only to confirm the initial personal failure which led to the first antisocial act. (As I speak of crime and the criminal tonight, I should emphasize that I am thinking of the delinquent car-thief, the mugger, the amateur burglar and the armed robber, the sex offender, and the man who commits assault and other crimes of violence—my attention is not

directed toward the special problems represented by the criminal elite consisting of competent professionals, the organization men of the syndicates,
or the whole separate area of white-collar crime.)

It is as if society cooperates with certain human beings who are social
failures to create this object called the criminal. Our present system of punishment is an essential part of *this* process, not of any process that can be
called reforming or rehabilitative. Why does society go to all the trouble
and expense of creating this special class of human beings? I think chiefly
because we really do not comprehend what we are doing, because we do not
want to deal with the facts of social failure to begin with, and because we
are not prepared to follow out the logic of our attitude and "dispose" of
these failures outright. There results a sort of half-way house, neither disposal nor rehabilitation, but a new class of human beings to mirror society's
confusion on the profound issue of failure in the educative process—and
reliance on punishment to cure or cover over all such failure.

What I am suggesting is that the criminal serves as a "scapegoat." And
this as much as anything is impeding obvious and sorely needed reform in
the treatment of offenders. I use the word "scapegoat" in the specific sense
in which it has become a key term in the psycho-sociological analysis of
prejudice. That is, a deeply held, unrealistic, projective image of a minority
group indulged by members of a dominant group. The essential fact in this
form of prejudiced perception is that the member of the dominant group
refuses ordinary, human one-to-one identification with representatives of
the minority group, sometimes for lack of opportunity, sometimes because
of a deeper unwillingness. . . .

Another point to be understood about punishment is that it is not a
universal solvent. Different people react differently to it. This is perfectly
obvious with regard to children, and needs no elaboration. Our response to
punishment is like anything else we learn; some learn better than others,
and some learn the same lesson differently than others. In this broad sense,
the criminal is the person who has been miseducated with respect to punishment and the threat of punishment. His re-education must consist of
something in addition to just more of the same, more punishment. To conceive otherwise would be like giving harder and harder lessons in algebra
to a student who has already evidenced his inability to absorb the basic
lessons. Only an incompetent teacher, a man of ill-will or one with very
limited resources, would go about destroying a student in such a fashion.
But that is just what we do with so many people who, if they had had the
proper capacity to respond to punishment, would not have gotten into
trouble in the first place. We do just the wrong thing by confirming all of
their wrong feelings about punishment. And so we create a class of hopelessly recidivistic criminals. . . .

I would not want to leave you with the impression that I am opposed to all measures of punishment, or deprivation. It seems superfluous to state that I recognize their necessity, but perhaps I had better do so because thinking in this field tends to be characterized by an either-or, all-or-nothing attitude. It is just this attitude which I object to and from which I wish to dissociate myself. Let me illustrate its unfortunate effects. When the *Durham* case was decided in the District of Columbia, a great hue and cry was raised that great numbers of vicious criminals would soon be roaming the streets of the city. Nothing could have been more off the mark, as subsequent events have shown. But at the time many people felt that *either* offenders are punished by execution or a penitentiary term, *or* they in effect get off scotfree—that *all* of them must be punished and just punished, or *nothing* would be done to protect society against them. . . . The Court now requires a positive instruction to the effect that the defendant acquitted by reason of insanity will be put in a mental institution until cured and judicially determined to be no longer a danger to himself or others. Such commitments, incidentally, may continue for a longer term than would have been served in a penitentiary for the offense charged. They are clearly a deprivation, a negative sanction—and in this sense a "punishment"—but with the very important difference that it is not retributive, it is no more than may be necessary, and it is punishment subordinate to the purpose of rehabilitation.

. . . Some people seem to feel that whenever trained workers including psychiatric therapists supplement the work of police and prison guards, or play any independent role at all, the offender will be mollycoddled and consequently society's bulwark against crime will crumble. This is nonsense, but the attitude persists. Dr. Melitta Schmideberg of the Association for the Psychiatric Treatment of Offenders is one of the most devoted and distinguished workers in her field. I am not competent to underwrite the validity of her views, but she is a richly experienced therapist in this special and rather neglected area of treatment. She believes in a strongly directive therapy, and in the course thereof gives practical recognition to the fact that the threat of loss of liberty—of going to jail or going back to jail— plays an important part in her work with probationed offenders or repeaters. This threat is an ever-present backdrop to her efforts to help the patient get along with his probation officer, to stop breaking the law, to get a job and hold it, and so on. She feels that—"Fear of punishment and guilt keep normal people in check, but an overdose of anxiety can react in the opposite direction on criminals." She states the problem as follows: "If the therapist condemns the offender out and out, he cannot treat him; if he condones his offense, he cannot change him." This is certainly not a mollycoddling approach. On the other hand, she objects eloquently to the psychological effect on offenders of a period in the usual penitentiary. She feels one of the most imperative uses of therapy is to help the ex-convict overcome the effects of prison! Now does it strike anyone here as sensible to deny early treatment of first offenders, send them to a penitentiary where their dangerous problems will be dangerously augmented, and then end up with an infinitely more difficult problem-personality to deal with later on?

Why do we do it? Why do we treat offenders this way? . . . any satisfactory answer will be found to lie very deep indeed—probably at the core of man's inhumanity to man, in each of us and in the history of all of us. . . .

But when we transcend our emotional urge to punish, and begin to think seriously about crime and the criminal without such undue reliance on the one idea of punishment, we very shortly come right up against an intellectually much more formidable barrier. And that is the ubiquitous theory of deterrence. On the intellectual level, it turns out to be the greatest barrier to progress in the criminal law.

This theory proposes that actual malefactors be punished in order to deter potential malefactors. In its pure form, it is willing to assume arguendo that punishment may not reform and may even damage the particular individual being punished. But this unfortunate person must be sacrified to the common good—he must be punished as an example to all, to keep all the rest of us from committing his crime. Of course the theory is not always stated in this pure form. Indeed, there is a common confusion which you may notice in arguments based on the premise of deterrence—a confusion between deterrence of the person being punished and deterrence of all others. Now clearly the convicted prisoner was not deterred by the prior punishment of others from committing the crime which placed him in prison. And to speak of deterring him from committing another offense later takes us back to the previous discussion of the effectiveness of punishment, and concerns rehabilitation not deterrence. So the theory, properly considered, involves only the justification of punishment because of its show-effect, its supposed effect on others. I need not labor the point that the individual so used is a scapegoat, a sacrificial victim. This is an admitted feature of the theory.

Logically, of course, the more we witness the pains of punishment, the more apt they would be actually to deter us from crime. (That is, if active fear deters.) Originally, this logic was a part of the deterrence theory. But in our day it is not. To illustrate this I would like to quote from the 1953 Report of the Royal Commission on Capital Punishment:

> "In the first half of the nineteenth century executions still took place in public. This indeed was thought to be an essential part of the deterrent value of the death penalty. But public executions, 'though the publicity was deterrent in intention . . . became in practice a degrading form of popular entertainment, which could serve only to deprave the minds of the spectators.' "

Parliament ended the practice in 1868. The Report also suggests that the method of hanging was invented and found favor because of its "advertisement value." But at the hearings before the Commission, "witness after witness" defended hanging because it was the most humane method of execution! The Report notes this "surprising inversion" succinctly as follows:

> "Thus a method of execution whose special merit was formerly thought to be that it was peculiarly degrading is now defended on the ground that it is uniquely humane."

So clearly the deterrence theory is not quite so logical as it used to be. (And just as well!) . . .

A common argument offered in support of deterrence is this: The ordinary citizen would not obey traffic signals if sanctions were not imposed on all drivers for breach of the rules. This argument, please notice, depends for its persuasiveness on a supposed identity between a traffic violation, on the one hand, and murder, assault, and grand theft, on the other—all these being "breach of the rules." Although I suppose they all do come under this category, the empirical differences are more impressive to me than the abstract similarity. But more important, because of the preconditioning of licensing, the persons to whom traffic rules are addressed are a select group to begin with: Those who are incompetent to conform to the rules, for whatever reasons, are weeded out before the sanction system is applied. And that is an important point. Although traffic rules have very little moral force behind them, the system works tolerably well just because reliance is not placed solely on sanctions, but also on the judgment of competence.

I think we all understand that the maintenance of public order must be backed up by a system of sanctions . . . deprivations . . . *punishments,* if you please. Neither law nor morality can sustain itself, from generation to generation, without the threat of some form of punishment. But the difficult point to be comprehended here is that the system requires the *threat* of punishment, not punishment itself. An internal control system generated by our mores and received beliefs keeps most of us from stealing. For those who require external controls, it is the threat of going to jail, not actual time spent there, that keeps them from stealing. Actual sanctions are needed—as far as the system is concerned—only to give substance to the threat, to keep it from being reduced to impotence. The problem really posed by the question of deterrence is, how much actual punishment—and what kind of actual punishment—is required in order to sustain the threat of punishment at an effective level? Or, stated inversely—now looking at the problem from the point of view of the individual rather than the system —how much non-punishment, how much besides punishment, can be allowed in treatment of the individual without inviting a breakdown of the system of sanctions?

I do not propose to solve this problem [now], even stated in such fashion. . . . But I do want to conclude with a few observations about this critical and perplexing question. First of all, I believe that in the absence of decisive empirical data, we should take a developmental approach. That is, we should view the issue historically and not assume that any particular status quo is ultimate and unalterable. I will confess that I am subjectively distrustful of many ponderous proponents of deterrence who answer the question, how much punishment is necessary, with the quick reply, exactly as much as we now have. And those who use the necessity of deterrence to justify the scandal of our prison system, also earn my suspicion.

Some people have argued in favor of the M'Naghten ritual on the grounds of a deterrent effect—that the mentally ill offender should not be recognized as such and treated as such because to do so would encourage crime and perhaps even mental illness. This argument I consider beneath contempt. The M'Naghten Rules were adopted twenty-five years before the English saw fit to do away with public hangings. . . . Why I wonder, are these Rules considered still necessary to deter crime, when public hangings and capital punishment for petty offenses are not? And if M'Naghten is so necessary for this purpose, why do the same people justify it by reminding us that trial courts frequently ignore it?

To sum up briefly: Punishment has a role to play in the education and re-education of the individual. The threat of some form of deprivation is of course essential in the functioning of any moral or legal system—and the threat must have substance. But these basic requirements of the criminal law have been used—I will say misused—to justify the present system which contains a preposterous predominance of senseless punitive elements. The theory of deterrence, as too frequently applied, results in degrading the individual for a purported social purpose—contrary to the democratic ethos and with no convincing evidence that the purpose is promoted. In doing so, in casting the individual offender in the role of a scapegoat, it begs the entire question of justice. And while no socio-legal system can reach a perfect incarnation of justice, none can survive in the hearts of the people which by-passes or does not engage the issue seriously.

If we were not so set on punishing the offender for the sake of punishment, if we did not justify this practice by reference to its deterrent effect, we could understand that rehabilitation lies at the spiritual heart of any vital moral system. The alternative can only be destructiveness. Even the violent corporal punishments of the past were designed to rehabilitate the wrongdoer's soul, which was held to be of much greater concern than his body. In our secular age, we have lost sight of this spiritual truth. But we still punish—without hope of reformation, without belief in saving the soul by damning the earthly body. And our entire moral system necessarily suffers thereby.

Would it really be the end of the world if all jails were turned into hospitals, or "Rehabilitation Centers"? The offender would then—just as the committed mental patient is today—be deprived of his dearest possession, his personal liberty. "Punishment" enough, I should think—to satisfy our punitive urge and to induce a deterrent fear. The offender's purpose in such a Rehabilitation Center would be to change his personality, his very style of responding to life. I would like to suggest, quite seriously, that the effort toward such a personal alteration is the greatest sanction of them all. To make this is indeed the true command of all religion and all morality. And it is the normal law-abiding person's most profound and continuous "punishment." The difference between the offender or the mental patient and the rest of us happily normal citizens, is that "they" have a special problem and need special help in living up to society's expectations. A few of us have had "special problems" in the course of our lives but were lucky enough to get the help we needed, or strong enough to get by on our own. We are entitled to congratulate ourselves on the superiority of our endowment or good fortune—but not, I think, to celebrate our triumphs by degrading our less fortunate neighbors. Is it in any way necessary for our own benefit to perpetuate the shame of our penitentiaries —where a youthful offender, having been processed through the homosexual auction block, will be taught the ways of crime and perversity by a hardened expert? . . .

Among the many serious issues I have not discussed, . . . prominent mention should be made of the current and future limits of that omnibus grouping called the behavioral sciences. How much of their promise is valid hope, how much wishful thinking? We can only find out by trying— by experimenting. Take the question of psychiatric "treatment," for example. It seems clear that new, more sophisticated techniques will have to be developed with more pointed relevance to the problems of offenders. But where are the experimental clinics, where are the budgets to attract competent staff, where is the administrative approach that would welcome and facilitate this urgent work? Blocked, I have suggested, by the belief in punishment. Many critics of the reforming attitude in criminal law administration fear the unknown contours of a future dominated by the experimental ideas of rehabilitation. Reformers may share some of these fears, but they are motivated even more by fear of the consequences of continuing our present practices. For example, I am deeply disturbed by the whole question of the indeterminacy of the period of incarceration, which is a very serious problem today and will undoubtedly grow in importance as reforms favoring rehabilitation are instituted. The image of one class of experts administering the lives of another class of "unfortunates" has some very disquieting aspects. I comfort myself with the thought that images of the future are frequently discomforting, and that early surgery, for example, was probably greeted with the same disquiet. . . .

Perhaps we can take comfort that new problems have a way of begetting new solutions and that, in this instance, solutions may be found which are consonant with our traditional concern for civil liberties. I, for one, have no intention of ushering in permanent incarceration for behavior not seriously dangerous to society. . . .

Crime and criminals belong very much to their particular time and place. They grow out of very specific social settings. Moreover, any system of sanctions and any system of rehabilitation applies to and within a society, it does not substitute for one. And these systems cannot be much better than the society in which they exist. On the other hand, they should not be worse.

THERAPY, NOT PUNISHMENT[1]

Karl Menninger, M.D.

Dr. Karl Menninger is one of America's most distinguished psychiatrists, with headquarters at the famous Menninger Clinic in Topeka, Kansas. His is the psychiatrist's verdict on the principles enunciated by Judge Bazelon in the Durham case. Dr. Menninger has written The Human Mind *(1930),* Man Against Himself *(1938), and* Love Against Hate *(1942).*

. . . On the other hand most lawyers have no really clear idea of the way in which a psychiatrist functions or of the basic concepts to which he adheres. They cannot understand, for example, why there is no such thing (for psychiatrists) as "insanity." Most lawyers have no conception of the meaning or methods of psychiatric case study and diagnosis. They seem to think that psychiatrists can take a quick look at a suspect, listen to a few anecdotes about him, and thereupon be able to say, definitely, that the awful "it"—the dreadful miasma of madness, the loathsome affliction of "insanity"—is present or absent. Because we all like to please, some timid psychiatrists fall in with this fallacy of the lawyers and go through these preposterous antics.

---

[1]*Harper's Magazine*, August 1959, pp. 63–64. © 1959, by Harper & Rowe, Publishers, Incorporated. Reprinted from *Harper's Magazine* by permission of the author.

It is true that almost any offender—like anyone else—when questioned for a short time, even by the most skillful psychiatrist, can make responses and display behavior patterns which will indicate that he is enough like the rest of us to be called "sane." But a barrage of questions is not a psychiatric examination. Modern scientific personality study depends upon various specialists—physical, clinical, and sociological as well as psychological. It takes into consideration not only static and presently observable factors, but dynamic and historical factors, and factors of environmental interaction and change. It also looks into the future for correction, re-education, and prevention.

Hence, the same individuals who appear so normal to superficial observation are frequently discovered in the course of prolonged, intensive scientific study to have tendencies regarded as "deviant," "peculiar," "unhealthy," "sick," "crazy," "senseless," "irrational," "insane."

But now you may ask, "Is it not possible to find such tendencies in any individual if one looks hard enough? And if this is so, if we are all a little crazy or potentially so, what is the essence of your psychiatric distinctions? Who is it that you want excused?"

And here is the crux of it all. We psychiatrists don't want *anyone* excused. In fact, psychiatrists are much more concerned about the protection of the public than are the lawyers. I repeat; psychiatrists don't want anyone excused, certainly not anyone who shows antisocial tendencies. We consider them all responsible, which lawyers do not. And we want the prisoner to take on that responsibility, or else deliver it to someone who will be concerned about the protection of society and about the prisoner, too. We don't want anyone excused, but neither do we want anyone stupidly disposed of, futilely detained, or prematurely released. We don't want them tortured, either sensationally with hot irons or quietly by long-continued and forced idleness. In the psychiatrist's mind nothing should be done in the name of punishment, though he is well aware that the offender may regard either the diagnostic procedure or the treatment or the detention incident to the treatment as punitive. But this is in *his* mind, not in the psychiatrist's mind. And in our opinion it should not be in the public's mind, because it is an illusion.

It is true that we psychiatrists consider that all people have potentialities for antisocial behavior. The law assumes this, too. Most of the time most people control their criminal impulses. But for various reasons and under all kinds of circumstances some individuals become increasingly disorganized or demoralized, and then they begin to be socially offensive. The man who does criminal things is less convincingly disorganized than the patient who "looks" sick, because the former more nearly resembles the rest of us, and seems to be indulging in acts that we have struggled with and controlled. So we get hot under the collar about the one and we call him "criminal" whereas we pityingly forgive the other and call him "lunatic." But a surgeon uses the same principles of surgery whether he is dealing with a "clean" case, say some cosmetic surgery on a face, or a "dirty" case which is foul-smelling and offensive. What we are after is results and the emotions of the operator must be under control. Words like "criminal" and "insane" have no place in the scientific vocabulary any more than pejorative adjectives like "vicious," "psychopathic," "bloodthirsty," etc. The need is to find all the *descriptive* adjectives that apply to the case, and this is a scientific job—not a popular exercise in name-calling. Nobody's insides are very beautiful; and in the cases that require social control there has been a great wound and some of the insides are showing.

Intelligent judges all over the country are increasingly surrendering the onerous responsibility of deciding in advance what a man's conduct will be in a prison and how rapidly his wicked impulses will evaporate there. With more use of the indeterminate sentence and the establishment of scientific diagnostic centers, we shall be in a position to make progress in the science of *treating* antisocial trends. Furthermore, we shall get away from the present legal smog that hangs over the prisons, which lets us detain with heartbreaking futility some prisoners fully rehabilitated while others, whom the prison officials know full well to be dangerous and unemployable, must be released, *against our judgment,* because a judge far away (who has by this time forgotten all about it) said that five years was enough. In my frequent visits to prisons I am always astonished at how rarely the judges who have prescribed the "treatment" come to see whether or not it is effective. What if doctors who sent their seriously ill patients to hospital never called to see them!

As more states adopt diagnostic centers directed toward getting the prisoners *out* of jail and back to work, under modern, well-structured parole systems, the taboo on jail and prison, like that on state hospitals, will begin to diminish. Once it was a lifelong disgrace to have been in either. Lunatics, as they were cruelly called, were feared and avoided. Today only the ignorant retain this phobia. Cancer was then considered a *shameful* thing to have, and victims of it were afraid to mention it, or have it correctly treated, because they did not want to be disgraced. The time will come when offenders, much as we disapprove of their offenses, will no longer be unemployable untouchables.

To a physician discussing the wiser treatment of our fellow men it seems hardly necessary to add that under no circumstances should we kill them. It was never considered right for doctors to kill their patients, no matter how hopeless their condition. True, some patients in state institutions have undoubtedly been executed without benefit of sentence. They were a nuisance, expensive to keep and dangerous to release. Various people took it upon themselves to put an end to the matter, and I have even heard them boast of it. The Hitler regime had the same philosophy.

But in most civilized countries today we have a higher opinion of the rights of the individual and the limits to the state's power. We know, too, that for the most part the death penalty is inflicted upon obscure, impoverished, defective, and friendless individuals. We know that it intimidates juries in their efforts to determine guilt without prejudice. We know that it is being eliminated in one state after another, most recently Delaware.[1] We know that in practice it has almost disappeared—for over seven thousand capital crimes last year there were less than one hundred executions. But vast sums of money are still being spent—let us say wasted—in legal contests to determine whether or not an individual, even one known to have been mentally ill, is now healthy enough for the state to hang him. (I am informed that such a case has recently cost the State of California $400,000!)

Most of all, we know that no state employees—except perhaps some that ought to be patients themselves—want a job on the killing squad, and few wardens can stomach this piece of medievalism in their own prisons. For example, two officials I know recently quarreled because each wished to have the hanging of a prisoner carried out on the other's premises.

Capital punishment is, in my opinion, morally wrong. It has a bad effect on everyone, especially those involved in it. It gives a false sense of security to the public. It is vastly expensive. Worst of all it beclouds the entire issue of motivation in crime, which is so importantly relevant to the question of what to do for and with the criminal that will be most constructive to society as a whole. Punishing—and even killing—criminals may yield a kind of grim gratification; let us all admit that there are times when we are so shocked at the depredations of an offender that we persuade ourselves that this is a man the Creator didn't intend to create, and that we had better help correct the mistake. But playing God in this way has no conceivable moral or scientific justification. . . .

We, the agents of society, must move to end the game of tit-for-tat and blow-for-blow in which the offender has foolishly and futilely engaged himself and us. We are not driven, as he is, to wild and impulsive actions. With knowledge comes power, and with power there is no need for the frightened vengeance of the old penology. In its place should go a quiet, dignified, therapeutic program for the rehabilitation of the disorganized one, if possible, the protection of society during his treatment period, and his guided return to useful citizenship, as soon as this can be effected.

[1]Editor's note: Although Delaware abolished the death penalty for all crimes in 1958, it reintroduced the death penalty for murder in 1961.

A PSYCHIATRIST DISSENTS
FROM DURHAM[1]

Thomas S. Szasz, M.D.

Dr. Szasz was a staff member of the Institute for Psychoanaly-
sis, Chicago, and when the following article was written, a member
of the Department of Psychiatry, State University of New York.

The following brief comments are intended to call attention to what I believe are inroads of serious import which organized psychiatry is making into the area of civil liberties. The significance of this encroachment transcends the specialized interests of psychiatry and jurisprudence, for it involves the most basic value of Anglo-American democracy, namely, the worth of the individual's autonomy and dignity. Cast in the context of current political and social events, it would seem that what the Western democracies can put against the claims of opposing ideologies is not a high standard of living; nor is it the abstract notions of free enterprise, capitalism, or even the Christian ethic. What democracies, and *only* democracies, possess, and what can not be imitated by other ideologies—without themselves becoming democracies—is respect for the dignity and autonomy of the individual. Stripped of proud adjectives, this simply means that people must be taken seriously for what they do; and this implies holding them accountable for their actions.

Having argued elsewhere that psychiatric testimony concerning mental illness (as presently conceived) is distracting to judicial proceedings, and that acquittal from a criminal charge by reason of insanity followed by commitment to a mental hospital constitutes a serious infringement of a person's civil liberties, I shall turn, without further comment, to a recent case to illustrate and add to the points made previously.

The case is that of Miss Edith L. Hough. The following are the salient facts, as abstracted from the records of her appeal to the U.S. Court of Appeals for the District of Columbia Circuit. On May 30, 1957, Miss Hough shot and killed a male friend who came to call on her to express his

[1]*The Journal of Nervous and Mental Disease,* July 1960, pp. 58–63. Copyright ©, 1960, The Williams & Wilkins Co., Baltimore 2, Md., U.S.A. Reprinted by permission.

sympathy over the recent death of her father. The next day she was ordered to St. Elizabeths Hospital for determination of her competency to stand trial. She was subsequently found incompetent to stand trial and was committed to the hospital until restoration of her competency. In May, 1958, she was declared competent. She was tried for her offense—first degree murder—on July 10, 1958, and was acquitted by reason of insanity. She was then committed to St. Elizabeths Hospital.

On October 20, 1958, the Superintendent of St. Elizabeths Hospital filed in the District Court a certificate stating in part:

> "Miss Hough has now recovered sufficiently to be granted her conditional release from Saint Elizabeths Hospital pursuant to section 927 (e) of Public Law 313."

The District Court denied conditional release, whereupon the "patient" appealed to a higher court seeking reversal of this decision. The U.S. Court of Appeals for the District of Columbia Circuit heard the case and, on September 14, 1959, affirmed the decision of the lower court. In hearing the appeal, psychiatric testimony was obtained from Doctors Benjamin Karpman and Winfred Overholser, and judicial opinions were rendered by Judges David Bazelon and Wilbur K. Miller. In the context of decision-making in an actual, real-life situation, the opinions and actions of the various participants become clearer than any statement, concerning psychiatry and law, that could be made in the abstract. My comments will be based on testimony and opinion recorded in the transcript of the decision rendered by the Appellate Court.

The first point on which I shall comment is the problem of acquitting a person of a crime and then committing him. Once he is acquitted, he must be considered (legally) innocent. If he is not so considered, the word "acquittal" and the deed it designates will lose their customary meanings.

Commitment of the insane—a complex, and in my opinion, highly questionable procedure as presently practiced—must now be scrutinized. Courts are legally empowered to commit people to mental hospitals, provided that certain conditions obtain. Illustrative is the case of a person who manifests such behavior as is considered patently deranged in our culture. A young man, for example, may become increasingly withdrawn and uncommunicative; he may stop eating and start masturbating in the presence of others. Sooner or later in the course of these events, the patient's family would very likely seek the aid of a physician (who may or may not be a psychiatrist). The latter would then make out the necessary papers *certifying* that the patient is in need of involuntary hospitalization. Finally, the judge under whose jurisdiction this matter falls would, in the ordinary course of events, order the patient *committed*.

Another type of situation in which people might be committed as mentally ill has traditionally been associated with the general area of criminal behavior. Without entering into the complexities of this matter, I wish to note only that according to the Durham Rule and its implementations, persons charged with offenses but acquitted by reason of insanity are committed to St. Elizabeths Hospital. If this practice were to be carried out *seriously* such persons would have to be treated as if they were *bona fide innocent.* This is required by the fact that they have been tried and have been pronounced "*not guilty* (by reason of insanity)." While the court has the right to order commitment, once a patient has been committed he comes under the jurisdiction of the hospital authorities. Hospital psychiatrists should be able to release the patient should they wish to do so. In cases of ordinary civil commitment, the court has no jurisdiction over the actions of the hospital staff vis-à-vis patients. To be more exact, the courts do have a say concerning hospital-patient relationships even in such cases, but this is essentially limited to giving the patient freedom. In other words, if the patient wishes to be released from the hospital over the opposition of the psychiatrists, he can, by availing himself of the appropriate legal safeguards, *e.g., habeas corpus,* enlist the aid of the court to gain his freedom. The reverse of this does not obtain! Should the hospital wish to release the patient, the court cannot interfere and keep the patient confined. It can not do this simply because commitment is legally justified—and this shows how poor this justification really is—by the psychiatric testimony of the physicians involved. Hence, if they (*i.e.,* the state hospital physicians) testify that the patient is sane, how can the court commit?

In the present case, it is to be noted that the court had the power not only to commit but also to regulate the patient's movements in and out of the hospital. This was in accord with a statute of the District of Columbia (D.C. Code #24–301 (e) Supp. VII, 1959). This meant, in effect, that the hospital functioned as an arm of the court. It had no real autonomy, but was merely a subordinate body to the superordinate power of the courts. If a hospital superintendent and his staff can not discharge a patient from their "hospital" when they wish, then, I submit, they are but the functionaries of those who do have the power to make this decision.

All this points to the fact that hospitals functioning in such a fashion are, in fact, jails. But we can go further than this, for jails have a high degree of regulatory autonomy over their inmates. Parole boards, for example, can decide—within certain legally set limits—when prisoners may be released. The courts, once having passed sentence, can not interfere in this process. The regulations governing the release of mental patients from St. Elizabeths Hospital thus give the staff of this institution *less* jurisdiction over (some of) its "patients" than have jails over their prisoners.

We must infer from this that the courts, after having relinquished their responsibility to the psychiatrists for judging and sentencing criminals, have turned around and have arrogated to themselves the responsibilities of physicians and psychiatrists. This conclusion must be drawn from the fact that the courts take it upon themselves to decide when a person—officially designated a "patient," and one who has been acquitted of a criminal charge in a duly conducted trial, and is therefore "innocent"—may or may not be released from a place called "hospital." As matters now stand, psychiatric testimony in criminal trials—to the effect that the accused is mentally ill —makes it virtually unnecessary to have juries and judges, for acquittal follows almost automatically. Similarly, judicial authority of the type considered makes it virtually unnecessary, for patients of *this type* at least, to have psychiatrists and psychotherapists in mental hospitals—for it is the court, in the last analysis, that will decide when the "patient" is well enough to be released. The tragi-comedy that has been called "psychiatric testimony" has traversed a full circle: The psychiatrists who displaced the legal authorities (the latter having abdicated their responsibilities for decision-making of this type) have, in their turn, been displaced by the legal authorities, who now function in the guise of psychiatrists and social therapists.

All this leads finally and inevitably to the psychiatrist's surrender of his professional responsibility. For, if a psychiatrist in charge of a patient— who is *not* a convicted criminal!—regards him, in his own best judgment, as ready to leave a hospital and assume the duties of a job, how can he, in his professional conscience, let a court tell him that this he can not do? What is the psychiatrist "treating" the patient for, anyway? To make him a good "prisoner"? The farcical, were it not tragic, character of the notion of mental illness is well illustrated by these impossible dilemmas into which psychiatrists and lawyers place themselves, each other, their patients, and their clients.

The peculiar legal condition of a person such as Miss Hough has not escaped the participants in this difficult affair. Judge Bazelon expressly affirmed that such a person is a "patient," not a "prisoner." The facts of the matter, however, vitiate the practical meaning of these terms. Judge Bazelon's words illustrate the crux of the problem:

> "Nothing in the history of the statute—and nothing in its language—indicates that an individual committed to a mental hospital after acquittal of a crime by reason of insanity is other than a patient. The individual is confined in the hospital for the purpose of treatment, not punishment; and the length of confinement is governed solely by considerations of his condition *and* the public safety. Any preoccupation by the District Court with the need of punishment for crime is out of place in dealing with an individual who has been acquitted of the crime charged."
> It does not follow, however, that the hospital authorities are free to allow such a patient to leave the hospital without supervision.

> We readily grant that periodic freedom may be valuable therapy.
> So, we suppose, may outright release sometimes be. But the statute
> makes one in appellant's situation a member of 'an exceptional class
> of people.' It provides generally, that the District Court have a voice
> in any termination of her confinement, whether unconditional or
> conditional."

There is an attempt here to circumvent the problem by creating the
somewhat mystical entity of "an exceptional class of people." What is
meant by this? Are these people who are "legally innocent but really
guilty"? Or are these people who, by virtue of their actions, shall henceforth
and forever after be considered second-class citizens? Does this mean that
we shall have two sets of laws, one for ordinary citizens and ordinary
criminals, and another for the "mentally ill"? If these questions are answered
in the affirmative—as they seem to be in this case—then surely we ought
to ask: Is this in accord with the spirit and the letter of our Constitution,
our Bill of Rights, and with the ethics of democracy?

Before bringing this discussion to an end, I wish to comment briefly on
two other items found in this record. One is an opinion by Judge Wilbur K.
Miller, stating:

> "It is, of course, much easier to believe that a sane person will
> not in the reasonable future be dangerous to himself or others than
> to believe that an insane person will not be."

Here is an ancient view, equating violence and insanity, dressed in
slightly more modern garb. What is being asserted here, if anything? Both
"insanity" and "dangerousness" are such vague terms that it is impossible to
know what is being asserted by such a statement. But not only is this statement
vague, worse, it is tautologous, for we habitually infer a condition
of "insanity" from acts of violence. This was precisely the case in the present
instance, for Miss Hough was considered legally sane until after she
committed a murder. But if we infer insanity from violence, naturally we
shall always expect violence when we speak of insanity, even though, in
everyday life, the latter term is often used quite independently of whether
or not a person is considered "dangerous."

In this connection, we must also note that the common-sense formulation
of "insanity" propounded by Judge Miller seems to serve the function
of enabling the observer—and this means all of us, and especially juries
and judges—to wrestle with the problem of a person's so-called possible
future dangerousness. At the very least, by codifying acts of violence as
expressions of "mental illness" and some sort of irrationality (which, according
to *certain* criteria, they might well be), we neatly rid ourselves of the
task of dealing with criminal offenses as rational, goal-directed acts in principle
no different from other forms of conduct.

Finally, I wish to call attention to a portion of Doctor Overholser's testimony. Being challenged by the attorney for the appellee to show reason why the patient should be released from the hospital, he was asked this question:

> "Now, if this woman, who has this major mental disease, were released conditionally into the community and met a great number of frustrations in adjusting herself in getting along, isn't there a probability or possibility that she might explode, so to speak, and even do harm to herself or to others?"

His answer was:

> "Well, there is that possibility with a great many people, some of whom have never been in mental hospitals. I can't make any guarantee about permanence, or even about the conduct."

Here, it seems to me, Doctor Overholser spoke as a psychiatric scientist. As such, he could not predict with certainty, and surely could not guarantee, that this woman would not kill again. But if this is true, how can psychiatrists justify hospitalizing and "psychiatrically treating" someone whose "illness" appears to be mainly that she killed someone. Is being a murderer an illness? And if psychiatric treatment still leaves open the possibility of future crime, as obviously it must, then why use it as a *substitute* for legally codified imprisonment?

Does all this not mean that a logically simpler, and legally and psychiatrically clearer approach to a problem such as this might lie in treating persons in Miss Hough's predicament with the same dignity and firmness as we treat others confronted by serious problems? Why could she not be found guilty of a crime she obviously committed? Why could she not be imprisoned for a given term and, if necessary, given psychiatric help in jail? Is it not a truism that in a democracy, imprisonment (or loss of liberty) is justified only by conviction for a crime? But Miss Hough, and others in similar positions, were never convicted of a crime, but are, nevertheless, deprived of their liberty. This is clearly done as a *preventive measure*! Herein lies, I think, the worst and most dangerous feature of this procedure: it establishes legal precedent, and hence a measure of sanction, for prophylactic imprisonment! Let us not forget that this social act has, and with good reason, been regarded as the hallmark of the totalitarian state. The legal restraint of a person justified by *what he might do* (in the future) is there used with the explicit aim of social reform. Although not explicitly formulated, and perhaps only as an unwitting and undesired side-effect, this tactic of preventive restraint seems to be implicit in the operations of the Durham Rule and its subsequent modifications and applications.

The merits and risks of preventive imprisonment—even if some choose to call it "hospitalization"—are well worth the attention of every informed and intelligent person. This was my reason for stating at the outset that many problems of psychiatry and law transcend the boundaries of these disciplines and rightly concern all the people of the land. Let us at least entertain the possibility that by engaging in certain modifications of social living—for this is what we are doing—we run the risk of squandering the greatest asset of our Nation and its distinctive form of government, namely, the autonomy, integrity, responsibility, and freedom of the individual.

A recent decision rendered by the United States Court of Appeals for the District of Columbia Circuit was examined for the light it threw on some problems concerning crimes, psychiatry, and civil liberties. It was shown that acquittal by reason of insanity, followed by automatic commitment, seems to lead by easy steps to preventive jailing (hospitalization) of persons because of their alleged future dangerousness.

Increased psychiatric participation in the disposition of criminals seems to invite its corollary, namely, increased legal participation in psychiatric operations. We might raise the question: Do the questionable benefits of the Durham Rule (and its implementation) justify the risks of this "social therapy"? Could it be, perchance, that the cure, in this case, is worse than the disease? In other words, are the political and ethical risks of preventive jailing (preventive mental hospitalization) worth running, even if the psychiatric value of this measure were firmly established? (The psychiatric-scientific rationale of this procedure is hardly clear-cut or well established.) Personally, I hold that the value of formal psychiatric therapy for "criminals"—under present medico-legal conditions—is, at best, highly questionable. But beyond this, I believe that even if this psychiatric-legal procedure could be shown to be highly efficacious in restoring offenders of a certain type to useful social existence (which is the most that even its proponents claim for it), I would doubt that, *in a hierarchy of values,* such therapy of a small group could be justified *if* its results could be achieved *only* at the cost of a significant reduction in the autonomy and dignity of the majority of the people. In any case, the problem of crime and "mental illness" should be cast in a much broader context, and should be scrutinized by many more people, than it is at present.

IN FAVOR OF CAPITAL PUNISHMENT[1]

Jacques Barzun

*Jacques Barzun is a well-known historian and critic and Dean
of Faculties and provost of Columbia University. His most recent
books are* Classic, Romantic and Modern *and* The House of Intellect. *Professor Barzun's defense of capital punishment is all the
more interesting in that it comes from an unexpected quarter.*

. . . I readily concede at the outset that present ways of dealing out
capital punishment are as revolting as Mr. Koestler says in his harrowing
volume, *Hanged by the Neck*. Like many of our prisons, our modes of execution should change. But this objection to barbarity does not mean that
capital punishment—or rather, judicial homicide—should not go on. The
illicit jump we find here, on the threshold of the inquiry, is characteristic of
the abolitionist and must be disallowed at every point. Let us bear in mind
the possibility of devising a painless, sudden and dignified death, and see
whether its administration is justifiable.

The four main arguments advanced against the death penalty are: (1)
punishment for crime is a primitive idea rooted in revenge; (2) capital
punishment does not deter; (3) judicial error being possible, taking life is
an appalling risk; (4) a civilized state, to deserve its name, must uphold,
not violate, the sanctity of human life.

I entirely agree with the first pair of propositions, which is why . . .
I replace the term capital punishment with "judicial homicide." The un-
controllable brute whom I want put out of the way is not to be punished
for his misdeeds, nor used as an example or a warning; he is to be killed
for the protection of others, like the wolf that escaped not long ago in a
Connecticut suburb. No anger, vindictiveness or moral conceit need preside
over the removal of such dangers. But a man's inability to control his violent impulses or to imagine the fatal consequences of his acts should be a
presumptive reason for his elimination from society. This generality covers
drunken driving and teen-age racing on public highways, as well as incurable obsessive violence; it might be extended (as I shall suggest later) to
other acts that destroy, precisely, the moral basis of civilization.

[1]Reprinted from *The American Scholar,* 31, No. 2 (Spring 1962), 182–191. Copyright © 1962 by the United Chapters of Phi Beta Kappa. By permission of the publishers.

But why kill? I am ready to believe the statistics tending to show that the prospect of his own death does not stop the murderer. For one thing he is often a blind egotist, who cannot conceive the possibility of his own death. For another, detection would have to be infallible to deter the more imaginative who, although afraid, think they can escape discovery. Lastly, as Shaw long ago pointed out, hanging the wrong man will deter as effectively as hanging the right one. So, once again, why kill? If I agree that moral progress means an increasing respect for human life, how can I opposite abolition?

I do so because on this subject of human life, which is to me the heart of the controversy, I find the abolitionist inconsistent, narrow or blind. The propaganda for abolition speaks in hushed tones of the sanctity of human life, as if the mere statement of it as an absolute should silence all opponents who have any moral sense. But most of the abolitionists belong to nations that spend half their annual income on weapons of war and that honor research to perfect means of killing. These good people vote without a qualm for the political parties that quite sensibly arm their country to the teeth. The West today does not seem to be the time or place to invoke the absolute sanctity of human life. As for the clergymen in the movement, we may be sure from the experience of two previous world wars that they will bless our arms and pray for victory when called upon, the sixth commandment notwithstanding.

"Oh, but we mean the sanctity of life *within* the nation!" Very well: is the movement then campaigning also against the principle of self-defense? Absolute sanctity means letting the cutthroat have his sweet will of you, even if you have a poker handy to bash him with, for you might kill. And again, do we hear any protest against the police firing at criminals on the street—mere bank robbers usually—and doing this, often enough, with an excited marksmanship that misses the artist and hits the bystander? The absolute sanctity of human life is, for the abolitionist, a slogan rather than a considered proposition.

Yet it deserves examination, for upon our acceptance or rejection of it depend such other highly civilized possibilities as euthanasia and seemly suicide. The inquiring mind also wants to know, why the sanctity of *human* life alone? My tastes do not run to household pets, but I find something less than admirable in the uses to which we put animals—in zoos, laboratories and space machines—without the excuse of the ancient law, "Eat or be eaten."

It should moreover be borne in mind that this argument about sanctity applies—or would apply—to about ten persons a year in Great Britain and to between fifty and seventy-five in the United States. These are the average numbers of those executed in recent years. The count by itself should not, of course, affect our judgment of the principle: one life spared or forfeited is as important, morally, as a hundred thousand. But it should inspire a comparative judgment: there are hundreds and indeed thousands whom, in our concern with the horrors of execution, we forget: on the one hand, the victims of violence; on the other, the prisoners in our jails.

The victims are easy to forget. Social science tends steadily to mark a preference for the troubled, the abnormal, the problem case. Whether it is poverty, mental disorder, delinquency or crime, the "patient material" monopolizes the interest of increasing groups of people among the most generous and learned. Psychiatry and moral liberalism go together; the application of law as we have known it is thus coming to be regarded as an historic prelude to social work, which may replace it entirely. Modern literature makes the most of this same outlook, caring only for the disturbed spirit, scorning as bourgeois those who pay their way and do *not* stab their friends. All the while the determinism of natural science reinforces the assumption that society causes its own evils. A French jurist, for example, says that in order to understand crime we must first brush aside all ideas of Responsibility. He means the criminal's and takes for granted that of society. The murderer kills because reared in a broken home or, conversely, because at an early age he witnessed his parents making love. Out of such cases, which make pathetic reading in the literature of modern criminology, is born the abolitionist's state of mind: we dare not kill those we are beginning to understand so well.

If, moreover, we turn to the accounts of the crimes committed by these unfortunates, who are the victims? Only dull ordinary people going about their business. We are sorry, of course, but they do not interest science on its march. Balancing, for example, the sixty to seventy criminals executed annually in the United States, there were the seventy to eighty housewives whom George Cvek robbed, raped and usually killed during the months of a career devoted to proving his virility. "It is too bad." Cvek alone seems instructive, even though one of the law officers who helped track him down quietly remarks: "As to the extent that his villainies disturbed family relationships, or how many women are still haunted by the specter of an experience they have never disclosed to another living soul, these questions can only lend themselves to sterile conjecture."

The remote results are beyond our ken, but it is not idle to speculate about those whose death by violence fills the daily two inches at the back of respectable newspapers—the old man sunning himself on a park bench and beaten to death by four hoodlums, the small children abused and strangled, the middle-aged ladies on a hike assaulted and killed, the family terrorized by a released or escaped lunatic, the half-dozen working people massacred by the sudden maniac, the boatload of persons dispatched by the skipper, the mindless assaults upon schoolteachers and shopkeepers by the increasing hordes of dedicated killers in our great cities. Where does the sanctity of life begin?

It is all very well to say that many of these killers are themselves "children," that is, minors. Doubtless a nine-year-old mind is housed in that 150 pounds of unguided muscle. Grant, for argument's sake, that the misdeed is "the fault of society," trot out the broken home and the slum environment. The question then is, What shall we do, not in the Utopian city of tomorrow, but here and now? The "scientific" means of cure are more than uncertain. The apparatus of detention only increases the killer's antisocial animus. Reformatories and mental hospitals are full and have an understandable bias toward discharging their inmates. Some of these are indeed "cured"—so long as they stay under a rule. The stress of the social free-for-all throws them back on their violent modes of self-expression. At that point I agree that society has failed—twice: it has twice failed the victims, whatever may be its guilt toward the killer.

As in all great questions, the moralist must choose, and choosing has a price. I happen to think that if a person of adult body has not been endowed with adequate controls against irrationally taking the life of another, that person must be judicially, painlessly, regretfully killed before that mindless body's horrible automation repeats.

I say "irrationally" taking life, because it is often possible to feel great sympathy with a murderer. Certain *crimes passionnels* can be forgiven without being condoned. Blackmailers invite direct retribution. Long provocation can be an excuse, as in that engaging case of some years ago, in which a respectable carpenter of seventy found he could no longer stand the incessant nagging of his wife. While she excoriated him from her throne in the kitchen—a daily exercise for fifty years—the husband went to his bench and came back with a hammer in each hand to settle the score. The testimony to his character, coupled with the sincerity implied by the two hammers, was enough to have him sent into quiet and brief seclusion.

But what are we to say of the type of motive disclosed in a journal published by the inmates of one of our Federal penitentiaries? The author is a bank robber who confesses that money is not his object:

> My mania for power, socially, sexually, and otherwise can feel no degree of satisfaction until I feel sure I have struck the ultimate of submission and terror in the minds and bodies of my victims. . . . It's very difficult to explain all the queer fascinating sensations pounding and surging through me while I'm holding a gun on a victim, watching his body tremble and sweat. . . . This is the moment when all the rationalized hypocrisies of civilization are suddenly swept away and two men stand there facing each other morally and ethically naked, and right and wrong are the absolute commands of the man behind the gun.

This confused echo of modern literature and modern science defines the choice before us. Anything deserving the name of cure for such a man presupposes not only a laborious individual psychoanalysis, with the means to conduct and to sustain it, socially and economically, but also a re-education of the mind, so as to throw into correct perspective the garbled ideas of Freud and Nietzsche, Gide and Dostoevski, which this power-seeker and his fellows have derived from the culture and temper of our times. Ideas are tenacious and give continuity to emotion. Failing a second birth of heart and mind, we must ask: How soon will this sufferer sacrifice a bank clerk in the interests of making civilization less hypocritical? And we must certainly question the wisdom of affording him more than one chance. The abolitionists' advocacy of an unconditional "let live" is in truth part of the same cultural tendency that animates the killer. The Western peoples' revulsion from power in domestic and foreign policy has made of the state a sort of counterpart of the bank robber: both having power and neither knowing how to use it. Both waste lives because hypnotized by irrelevant ideas and crippled by contradictory emotions. If psychiatry were sure of its ground in diagnosing the individual case, a philosopher might consider whether such dangerous obsessions should not be guarded against by judicial homicide *before* the shooting starts.

I raise the question not indeed to recommend the prophylactic execution of potential murderers, but to introduce the last two perplexities that the abolitionists dwarf or obscure by their concentration on changing an isolated penalty. One of these is the scale by which to judge the offenses society wants to repress. I can for example imagine a truly democratic state in which it would be deemed a form of treason punishable by death to create a disturbance in any court or deliberative assembly. The aim would be to recognize the sanctity of orderly discourse in arriving at justice, assessing criticism and defining policy. Under such a law, a natural selection would operate to remove permanently from the scene persons who, let us say, neglect argument in favor of banging on the desk with their shoe. Similarly, a bullying minority in a diet, Parliament or skupshtina would be prosecuted for treason to the most sacred institutions when fists or flying inkwells replace rhetoric. That the mere suggestion of such a law sounds ludicrous shows how remote we are from civilized institutions, and hence how gradual should be our departure from the severity of judicial homicide.

I say gradual and I do not mean standing still. For there is one form of barbarity in our law that I want to see mitigated before any other. I mean imprisonment. The enemies of capital punishment—and liberals generally—seem to be satisfied with any legal outcome so long as they themselves avoid the vicarious guilt of shedding blood. They speak of the sanctity of life, but have no concern with its quality. They give no impression of ever having read what it is certain they have read, from Wilde's *De Profundis* to the latest account of prison life by a convicted homosexual. Despite the infamy of concentration camps, despite Mr. Charles Burney's remarkable work, *Solitary Confinement,* despite riots in prisons, despite the round of escape, recapture and return in chains, the abolitionists' imagination tells them nothing about the reality of being caged. They read without a qualm, indeed they read with rejoicing, the hideous irony of "Killer Gets Life"; they sigh with relief instead of horror. They do not see and suffer the cell, the drill, the clothes, the stench, the food; they do not feel the sexual racking of young and old bodies, the hateful promiscuity, the insane monotony, the mass degradation, the impotent hatred. They do not remember from Silvio Pellico that only a strong political faith, with a hope of final victory, can steel a man to endure long detention. They forget that Joan of Arc, when offered "life," preferred burning at the stake. Quite of another mind, the abolitionists point with pride to the "model prisoners" that murderers often turn out to be. As if a model prisoner were not, first, a contradiction in terms, and second an exemplar of what a free society should not want.

I said a moment ago that the happy advocates of the life sentence appear not to have understood what we know they have read. No more do they appear to read what they themselves write. In the preface to his useful volume of cases, *Hanged in Error,* Mr. Leslie Hale, M.P., refers to the tardy recognition of a minor miscarriage of justice—one year in jail: "The prisoner emerged to find that his wife had died and that his children and his aged parents had been removed to the workhouse. By the time a small payment had been assessed as 'compensation' the victim was incurably insane." So far we are as indignant with the law as Mr. Hale. But what comes next? He cites the famous Evans case, in which it is very probable that the wrong man was hanged, and he exclaims: "While such mistakes are possible, should society impose an irrevocable sentence?" Does Mr. Hale really ask us to believe that the sentence passed on the first man, whose wife died and who went insane, was in any sense *revocable*? Would not any man rather be Evans dead than that other wretch "emerging" with his small compensation and his reasons for living gone?

Nothing is revocable here below, imprisonment least of all. The agony of a trial itself is punishment, and acquittal wipes out nothing. Read the heart-rending diary of William Wallace, accused quite implausibly of having murdered his wife and "saved" by the Court of Criminal Appeals—but saved for what? Brutish ostracism by everyone and a few years of solitary despair. The cases of Adolf Beck, of Oscar Slater, of the unhappy Brooklyn bank teller who vaguely resembled a forger and spent eight years in Sing Sing only to "emerge" a broken, friendless, useless, "compensated" man— all these, if the dignity of the individual has any meaning, had better have been dead before the prison door ever opened for them. This is what counsel always says to the jury in the course of a murder trial and counsel is right: far better hang this man than "give him life." For my part, I would choose death without hesitation. If that option is abolished, a demand will one day be heard to claim it as a privilege in the name of human dignity. I shall believe in the abolitionist's present views only after he has emerged from twelve months in a convict cell.

The detached observer may want to interrupt here and say that the argument has now passed from reasoning to emotional preference. Whereas the objector to capital punishment *feels* that death is the greatest of evils, I *feel* that imprisonment is worse than death. A moment's thought will show that feeling is the appropriate arbiter. All reasoning about what is right, civilized and moral rests upon sentiment, like mathematics. Only, in trying to persuade others, it is important to single out the fundamental feeling, the prime intuition, and from it to reason justly. In my view, to profess respect for human life and be willing to see it spent in a penitentiary is to entertain liberal feelings frivolously. To oppose the death penalty because, unlike a prison term, it is irrevocable is to argue fallaciously.

In the propaganda for abolishing the death sentence the recital of numerous miscarriages of justice commits the same error and implies the same callousness: what is at fault in our present system is not the sentence but the fallible procedure. Capital cases being one in a thousand or more, who can be cheerful at the thought of all the "revocable" errors? What the miscarriages point to is the need for reforming the jury system, the rules of evidence, the customs of prosecution, the machinery of appeal. The failure to see that this is the great task reflects the sentimentality I spoke of earlier, that which responds chiefly to the excitement of the unusual. A writer on Death and the Supreme Court is at pains to point out that when that tribunal reviews a capital case, the judges are particularly anxious and careful. What a left-handed compliment to the highest judicial conscience of the country! Fortunately, some of the champions of the misjudged see the issue more clearly. Many of those who are thought wrongly convicted now languish in jail because the jury was uncertain or because a doubting governor commuted the death sentence. Thus Dr. Samuel H. Sheppard, Jr., convicted of his wife's murder in the second degree is serving a sentence that is supposed to run for the term of his natural life. The story of his numerous trials, as told by Mr. Paul Holmes, suggests that police incompetence, newspaper demagogy, public envy of affluence and the mischances of legal procedure fashioned the result. But Dr. Sheppard's vindicator is under no illusion as to the conditions that this "lucky" evader of the electric chair will face if he is granted parole after ten years: "It will carry with it no right to resume his life as a physician. His privilege to practice medicine was blotted out with his conviction. He must all his life bear the stigma of a parolee, subject to unceremonious return to confinement for life for the slightest misstep. More than this, he must live out his life as a convicted murderer."

What does the moral conscience of today think it is doing? If such a man is a dangerous repeater of violent acts, what right has the state to let him loose after ten years? What is, in fact, the meaning of a "life sentence" that peters out long before life? Paroling looks suspiciously like an expression of social remorse for the pain of incarceration, coupled with a wish to avoid "unfavorable publicity" by freeing a suspect. The man is let out when the fuss has died down; which would mean that he was not under lock and key for our protection at all. He *was* being punished, just a little —for so prison seems in the abolitionist's distorted view, and in the jury's and the prosecutor's, whose "second-degree" murder suggests killing someone "just a little."[2]

If, on the other hand, execution and life imprisonment are judged too severe and the accused is expected to be harmless hereafter—punishment being ruled out as illiberal—what has society gained by wrecking his life and damaging that of his family?

What we accept, and what the abolitionist will clamp upon us all the more firmly if he succeeds, is an incoherence which is not remedied by the belief that second-degree murder merits a kind of second-degree death; that a doubt as to the identity of a killer is resolved by commuting real death into intolerable life; and that our ignorance whether a maniac will strike again can be hedged against by measuring "good behavior" within the gates and then releasing the subject upon the public in the true spirit of experimentation.

These are some of the thoughts I find I cannot escape when I read and reflect upon this grave subject. If, as I think, they are relevant to any discussion of change and reform, resting as they do on the direct and concrete perception of what happens, then the simple meliorists who expect to breathe a purer air by abolishing the death penalty are deceiving themselves and us. The issue is for the public to judge; but I for one shall not sleep easier for knowing that in England and America and the West generally a hundred more human beings are kept alive in degrading conditions to face a hopeless future; while others—possibly less conscious, certainly less controlled—benefit from a premature freedom dangerous alike to themselves and society. In short, I derive no comfort from the illusion that in giving up one manifest protection of the law-abiding, we who might well be in any of these three roles—victim, prisoner, licensed killer—have struck a blow for the sanctity of human life.

---

[2]The British Homicide Act of 1957, Section 2, implies the same reasoning in its definition of "diminished responsibility" for certain forms of mental abnormality. The whole question of irrationality and crime is in utter confusion, on both sides of the Atlantic.

A LETTER TO THE GOVERNOR[1]

Caryl Chessman

(1922–1960)

The voice of Caryl Chessman is stilled. The words of Chessman, in a letter written to the Governor after his reprieve and not previously available to readers in the form presented here, survive as a remarkable commentary on the moral implications of capital punishment.

Name: Caryl Chessman
             Box 66565, San Quentin, Calif.
Date: February 26, 1960

The Hon. Edmund G. Brown
Governor of the State of California
State Capitol
Sacramento, California

Dear Governor Brown:

As you know, at approximately 4:45 P.M. on Thursday, February 18, 1960, I was removed from the Death Row Unit located on the fifth floor of the North Block here at San Quentin and locked in the small holding cell, just a few feet from the State's lethal gas chamber, where California's condemned spend their last night on earth. The death watch began. So far as I knew, I would be put to death at ten o'clock in the morning.

I was permitted to see an early edition of a Friday newspaper. Its headlines were large and black: CHESSMAN MUST DIE, BROWN SAYS. Again, only an hour earlier, the members of the California Supreme Court had voted 4 to 3 against a recommendation to you for clemency. Thus, by a simple vote, you were foreclosed from exercising your commutation powers. The court had made its order "final forthwith." I had been notified

---

[1] Unpublished correspondence.

of that action a few hours before being taken downstairs to the holding cell. In anticipation of it, I had put my affairs in order and executed a new will. . . .

And death appeared inevitable. I held out no feverish, desperate hope for a life-sparing miracle. On the contrary, what sustained me, what made it possible for me to await the morning and oblivion with a detached, almost clinical calm was hope of an entirely different sort: the burning hope that my execution would lead to an objective reappraisal of the social validity or invalidity of capital punishment, and that such a reexamination would lead, in turn, to an awareness on the part of all Californians that Death Rows, and death chambers and executioners were unworthy of our society, that the former, in fact, were gross obscenities, solving nothing but rather confounding solution.

The minutes passed, the hours. The prison's Catholic Chaplain, Father Edward Dingberg, visited me. Associate Wardens Walter D. Achuff and Louis S. Nelson saw me for a few minutes. Dr. David G. Schmidt, San Quentin's chief psychiatrist, came in. Attorney George Davis conferred with me hurriedly, intending to return later. Warden Fred R. Dickson dropped by for a talk.

Contrary to published accounts that I consumed the condemned man's traditional hearty meal of "fried chicken, French fried potatoes, vegetable salad, coffee and two kinds of pie—apple and chocolate cream," I am compelled to confess these reports, seemingly attesting to my capacity as a trencherman, are somewhat exaggerated. Actually, my wants were more modest. I had a hamburger and a coke about 7:30, and during the course of the evening I drank three cups of coffee. I also puffed on a cigar, although I normally do not smoke.

I waited. Midnight came. All my visitors had left but Warden Dickson. Then the telephone rang mutedly, and one of the death watch officers said, "It's for you, Warden." I watched Mr. Dickson disappear around a bend in the hallway. I paced the floor, my steps reduced to almost soundlessness by the cloth slippers. The radio outside the cell played quietly. Over it I had listened to a succession of newscasts. The news was all negative. One commentator reported Miss Asher[2] had been unable to see you but, in vain, had talked with two members of your staff. A second commentator solemnly quoted you as having said, "Only an act of God can save Caryl Chessman now."

My eyes fell on the newspaper I had been allowed whose stark headline I quoted above. One of its front-paged lead paragraphs read: "The world was disturbed last night as the hour for Caryl Chessman's execution drew near. Protests echoed from continent to continent." This San Fran-

---

[2][EDITOR'S NOTE: Chessman's attorney.]

cisco daily also reported: "There was little question that the Governor . . . was undergoing great emotional stress as Chessman's last hours ticked away," and: "The mail—most of it running about three to one for clemency —continued to pour in. So did the telegrams and the zero-hour telephone calls. . . ."

On page two were pictures of the gas chamber and this account of how I would die in less than ten hours:

". . . He'll get a physical examination from the prison's chief physician, Dr. Herman H. Gross, at 9 A.M. and undoubtedly will once again be found to be in perfect condition.

"At 9:45 A.M. come the last, formal visits from Warden Dickson and his aide to hear any last requests. Once again the chaplains will wait silently.

"Over a carpeted floor, his stockinged feet should take the last walk at 10 A.M. on the dot.

"There have been 164 people in the gas chamber before him, and experience gives the prison staff an almost split-second foretelling of the rest.

"By 10:01 A.M. he should be in one of the two death chairs—chair B. in his case.

"Two straps for each arm and leg, one across the chest and another for the waist. That, and the final slamming of the great iron door—less than three minutes.

"At 10:03½, by schedule, Warden Dickson would nod at a guard and a lever will send the cyanide pellets into the sulphuric acid basins."

I smiled, grimly, I'm sure. I knew how it felt to be a dead man. Only the ritualized formalities of physically extinguishing my life with hydrocyanic acid gas remained.

"Has the Warden gone?" I asked one of the death watch. "No," I was told, "he's still on the phone."

I gave no thought to the significance of the call. Then, audibly, I heard Warden Dickson say, "All right, Governor." A few seconds later the Warden reappeared. I'd glanced up from the paper I was reading. As he approached the cell, the Warden's face was a thoughtful mask.

"I have some news for you, Caryl." Mr. Dickson paused. "Oh?" I responded. He nodded, smiled. "The Governor has just granted you a 60-day reprieve."

The words had been spoken softly—but they crashed and reverberated in my mind like thunder in an echo chamber. Except possibly in a mocking, sadistic nightmare, they were words I truly never had expected to hear up to the instant of their utterance. I had been prepared to die; now I must be ready to go on living, I realized, for at least another 60 days.

I drew a deep breath as my thoughts raced. My words have been reported in the press: "Thank you. This is a great surprise. I really didn't expect it. Tell the Governor I thank him. I am surprised and grateful."

The Warden said he would see me again later in the morning. We said goodnight. Swiftly I was taken back upstairs in the elevator to Death Row. Swiftly, in the office, I changed into my regular clothing. Accompanied by the officers, I was passed through the "Bird Cage"—with its double doors and multiplicity of bolts and bars and locks—into the Row proper. From most of the occupied cells, yellow light spilled out into the corridor. The condemned were awake, listening to their earphones, silent, waiting—for what? Somehow, even better than I, they had sensed their fate was tied to mine, and mine to a pressing social issue of far greater significance than what might, individually or collectively, happen to any or all of us. They had heard me say repeatedly that obviously the greatest hope for abolition of the death penalty lay with my death. They—even the tortured and troubled ones—knew this to be true. Their obvious course was to accept this fact and hope it might lead them out from the cold shadow of the gas chamber. But, as I later learned, they had sent you a telegram, urging your intercession in my behalf. They had refused to believe that death—even another's—was a solution. I don't know whether that telegram ever came to your attention in the flood of messages you were receiving. I do know it had a profound effect on me. . . .

I continued along the corridor, stopping for a moment or two to speak to the occupant of each cell. The reaction was the same. Here was a genuine and spontaneous expression of brotherhood, commingled for them with a miracle. And make no mistake, Governor, I was for my doomed fellows no arrogant, swaggering hero returned after breathing defiance into the teeth of the cosmos. On the contrary, since they had come to know the man rather than the counterfeit black criminal legend, I was a flesh and blood human being whose appointment with man-imposed death had come to symbolize the critical and yet unresolved basic struggle of social man to rise above wrath and vengeance, to trust not the executioner, but their—mankind's—own reason and humanity in building a saner world for their children and their children's children. These men had been accused and convicted of homicidal violence, and so, better than any, they knew the futility of such violence. Now, after a bitter contest, life in my case had claimed at least a temporary victory. . . .

We got the word [that] you had granted the reprieve because, since the people of California were sharply divided on the issue, you wanted "to give the people . . . an opportunity, through the Legislature, to express themselves once more on capital punishment.". . .

And then, as well as in the hectic days to come, before there were calmer reflections and clearer analysis, the paradoxical evidence mounted: While the Chessman case had made evident the urgent need for a calm, careful and objective reexamination of the question whether capital punishment should not be discarded as a barbarous anachronism, productive finally of nothing but division and uneasy doubt among us, my continued existence, if only for another few weeks, and the fearful Chessman legend, which portrayed me as a cunning, fiendish, Cataline-like mocker of justice, threatened to throttle such a reexamination and reevaluation at the outset.

I remain haunted by that paradox. Beyond the descriptive power of words, these have been troubled and difficult days for me. I do not resort to hyperbole when I say they have been hell, even more than the past 11½ years have been hell. I cannot escape the fact I owe you my life for whatever days remain to me. I cannot forget that literally millions of people from nations around the world spoke out for me. In terms of the larger social good that is your goal, my obligation is a heavy one, and I refuse to try to rationalize it away. Over and over I have asked myself the questions. What possibly can I do, if anything, to divorce the ugly, emotion-inflaming image of Caryl Chessman from the grave social issue of capital punishment? What can I say—and mean, and demonstrate?

. . . I decided I can and I do, without theatrics, offer them my life. If the hysteria and the mob wrath that surrounds the problem only can be propitiated by my death and if otherwise they agree that the death penalty should be abolished, then I earnestly urge the members of our Legislature to frame their bill in such a way as to exclude me. This can be done readily —for example, by a declaration in the law that anyone convicted of a capital offense during or subsequent to the year 1950, whose sentence of death remains in force and unexecuted, shall be treated as though serving a sentence of life imprisonment. I give my solemn word before the world that I will never challenge such a law in the courts and I will disavow any attempt by any attorney purporting to act in my behalf.

. . . If the legislators do not necessarily demand my death but do believe the final question of my fate, under the California Constitution, should be resolved by yourself and the majority opinion of the State Supreme Court, then I urge them so to indicate. This way, by the passage of the type of bill mentioned above, they can sever the two problems. . . .

Except for the days I was out to court, I have occupied a death cell continuously since Saturday morning, July 3, 1948. I have had eight dates for execution in California's lethal gas chamber fixed and then canceled, some in the very last hours. A ninth date soon will be set. Ninety-odd men have taken that last, grim walk by my cell to their deaths since I came to Death Row. If it gives them any satisfaction, Californians may be assured my prolonged half-life in the shadow of the gas chamber has been an indescribably punishing ordeal. The shock of it, I think, has brought me to maturity; it has forced upon me keen social awareness of the problem that, in exaggerated form, I am said to typify.

I am now 38 years of age. I was 26 when arrested. Behind me is a long record of arrest. I am a graduate of California reform schools and prisons. I have been called a "criminal psychopath." Certainly, as a young man, I was a violent, rebellious, monumental damn fool. I was at odds with my society; I resisted authority. I am ashamed of that past but I cannot change it. However, with my writings, I have tried to salvage something of larger social significance from it. Without shifting responsibility for my conduct, I endeavored in my first book to tell the story of my life and hence to explain how young men like myself got that way. I realized that Death Rows made sense only because people like Caryl Chessman didn't.

After being brought to the death house, the change in me and my outlook came slowly and painfully. Defiantly, I stood and fought in the courts for survival, asking no quarter and expecting none. But, ironically, to have any chance for survival, I had to turn to the law; I had to invoke the protections of the Constitution; I had to study, often as much as 18 to 20 hours a day; I had to learn to impose upon myself a harsh self-discipline; I had to think and to be ruthlessly honest with myself; in time, I forced myself to admit, "Chessman, you have been, and to some degree still are, an irrational, impossible fool. What are you going to do about it?"

At that juncture, the traditional thing, the conventional response almost certainly would have been for me to confess my past folly and to beg for mercy. But I hesitated, not out of pride or false pride. I couldn't escape the fact that such a response on my part would, in practical effect, amount to affirmation that gas chambers and a system of justice ultimately based upon retribution possessed a genuine—rather than a mistakenly conceived and defended—social validity. I knew they did not possess such a validity. Without mock heroics, I became aware then that the greatest contribution I could make was to cause people, all people, to become angrily aware of places like Death Row and the administration of criminal justice in general. This, in my own way, I did: by continued total resistance. I was told I could not write another line for publication and I wrote anyway. When concerted efforts were made to suppress my manuscripts, I found a way to smuggle them from the prison. I intensified my court fight, winning some battles, losing others. Vituperation was heaped upon me. I became known as a mocker of justice. Editorial writers and public officials roundly denounced me. The public clamored for "this cunning fiend's" execution. Often I was half-mad with doubt; often I was ready to collapse with a brutal fatigue; often I sardonically sneered at myself and my goal. But I kept on somehow. A remorseless voice within told me, "This is your penance, fool —to be reviled and hated. This, if you call yourself a man, is the price you must pay."

I had certain advantages, and almost impossible handicaps. Among others, I had been convicted of unsavory sex offenses, sordid acts that, when recounted, inflamed the mind of the listener. They had inflamed the judge, the prosecutor, the jury. A Red Light Bandit—so-called because the bandit had operated, according to trial testimony, with a car equipped with a red spotlight such as those on police cars. He had accosted couples in lonely lovers' lanes. Armed with a gun, he would sometimes rob the couples, if they had any money. On two occasions testified to at my trial, he took the woman to his car. In one of these instances, under threat of death, he compelled her, the victim, to commit an unnatural sex act before letting her out and driving off. On a second occasion, he drove off with a 17-year-old girl to another secluded area, compelled her, too, to commit a perverted sexual act and attempted to rape her. Then he let her off near her home. (This tragic young woman, who had a history of serious mental disturbance, was committed to a mental hospital some 19 months after her traumatic experience. "Today," the wire services have quoted her mother as saying, "she just sits and stares"—lost in the withdrawn unreal world of the schizophrenic.)

It is no wonder, then, that the Red Light Bandit crimes so aroused judge, jury and prosecutor and antagonized them against the man accused of their commission. They angered and outraged me to an equal or greater degree, to an extent where in a red haze of emotion, I was unable to defend myself as effectively as otherwise I might. Stupidly and stubbornly, as well, I had withheld certain vital facts about my involvement in a violent internecine struggle for control of an illegal but police protected bookmaking syndicate. The convict's code said I shouldn't talk, or name names. I didn't. Then, not by myself, other critical evidence got suppressed. Witnesses disappeared. And a damning net was drawn around me. The jury returned verdicts of guilty, doomed me. I was brought to Death Row, twice sentenced to death and to 15 consecutive prison terms. The question of guilt or innocence was closed unless I could convince an appellate court I had been convicted illegally. Otherwise, branded a loathsome sex predator, I would die. I would have no chance to establish California had convicted the wrong man. It would make no difference that the description furnished the police of the bandit didn't remotely fit me; that the 17-year-old girl said her attacker had been "shorter than the usual man" and had weighed nearly 50 pounds less than the evidence showed I did, while I was six feet tall; or that she said the bandit had spoken with a slight accent, had appeared to be Italian and had a linear cut scar extending back from his right ear; or that this bandit usually gave his victims a look at his face before pulling up a handkerchief mask, while I just had been released from prison on parole and knew that my photographs almost certainly would be the first shown robbery victims; or that I had absolutely no history as a sex offender; or that I had been refused the right to produce witnesses at the trial who would testify to my reputation for sexual normality as well as to produce expert psychiatric evidence that I did not possess the psychological disposition to commit sexual crimes, particularly those involving force or violence, and that I was not a sexual psychopath.

All this made no difference. In the eyes of the law, I was guilty and would remain guilty unless I could win a new trial and acquittal. This galled but it also drove and sustained me. . . .

I wait to die. I remain locked in a death cell. More than 12 years have passed since my arrest. The State has spent nearly a million dollars in trying to kill me.

Now, in a few days, the California Legislature will be called into special session to consider abolition of capital punishment. Disturbed that a vote against the death penalty will be a vote for me, the man they believe has embarrassed their State and made a mockery of their laws, many legislators have vowed publicly to see that capital punishment is retained. I do not presume to tell them what to do; I do pray they will reconsider and reevaluate. . . . I am more than willing that they separate me decisively from the greater issue. I am quite willing to die if that will bring about this desperately needed social reform. I do suggest that if our positions were reversed and they had found themselves occupying a death cell under the conditions I have they too, and honorably, would have done as I have done, even though it meant bringing the wrath of the State down upon them. Happily, they will never know what it means to be doomed, to be within hours and minutes of execution, to feel the full, terrible impact of mob wrath, to have a claim of innocence brushed impatiently aside, to be called a "monster" and vilified, to seek redemption, not through hypocritical groveling, but by a harder, perhaps impossible road, to win friends and want desperately to justify their friendship and their faith, to want to live and to believe, humbly, that within them is a gift for words that can enrich our literature and, their own case aside, contribute significantly to the pressing social problems of our day.

I do not overstate when I say I gladly would die ten thousand gas chamber deaths if that would bring these truths into the hearts and minds of those who make our laws: A vote for either abolition or a moratorium is not an indication of approval of murder or other capital crimes, for the death penalty does not deter; it does not protect society. On the contrary, it leaves it defenseless, since as long as we have an executioner and a gas chamber, we will be content to believe that we can bury the problem with the offender. We will think that revenge is enough. It isn't. We must find why men kill and we must learn to prevent killing. We must become as intensely concerned with tomorrow's prospective victims as yesterday's actual ones. We must learn how to save lives and to salvage lives.

As long as the death penalty is on our statute books, there will be too much emotionality and circus atmosphere tainting our administration of justice. And for those who doubt this, there is a ready and rational test at hand: Let a moratorium be ordered on the supreme penalty for a period of, say, five years. I am certain during that period there will be no rise in the per capita crimes. Rather, I am convinced the crime rate will drop appreciably, and that justice will function in a far more even-handed and fair way. The sensationalism inevitably attending capital cases will vanish. The citizen will be reassured. He will know that the man who has killed has been isolated. The accused is more likely, if he is guilty, to plead guilty. Our courts thus will be able to perform their duties more efficiently. And if an innocent man is later found to have been mistakenly convicted, it will not be too late to correct the error.

Unfortunately, as investigation will confirm, too often it is the friendless and the fundless upon whom the death penalty is imposed. The man with means or who knows the angles does not come to Death Row. As well, under our outmoded tests for legal sanity or insanity, too often the man who is executed is one who, while not legally insane, suffers from some serious mental disability. It needlessly demeans our society to engage in killing the mentally ill. Still further, among this group, as psychiatrists and penologists will attest, is the type of personality who is inflamed by the thought and threat of the gas chamber. His response to it, his overt expression of defiance, is to strike out homicidally. In effect, he gets his revenge in advance, and we in turn get ours after the tragedy.

That is why so many thoughtful citizens advocate abolition or a moratorium. They feel, as I do, a sense of guilty responsibility at a lethal act that is both more than futile and less than futile when the State takes a life. They want their laws to express humanity's ideal of nobility, compassion, understanding and social awareness. They know that our laws can do so without endangering the citizens of California. The basis for their opposition to man's government killing man is thus, in the highest sense, ethical, social, practical and religious. They do not want to see their society needlessly degraded, their system of justice compromised.

I must close, and in closing I again earnestly urge you to ask the Legislature to consider the question of capital punishment apart from Caryl Chessman and the Chessman case. I urge you to request that they consider framing their bill as suggested above, to exclude me. You can do this honorably by taking my life back into your hands alone. You can let me die. Indeed, as the matter now stands, you are powerless to do otherwise because of the present 4–3 vote against me in the California Supreme Court. But, at the same time, you can give your proposal to the Legislature a chance.

It deserves that chance. It deserves your forceful leadership. You are right in the position you have taken. It is time to speak out, for too seldom does unlightened humanity in this age of fear and awesome nuclear devices have a spokesman with the courage to advocate that death and hate are not and never can be an answer to the problems that beset our civilization. Mankind and future generations ever will remain in your debt and ever will honor your name.

Yours respectfully,

/s/ Caryl Chessman

PART TWO

THE VALUES
OF A
BUSINESS
SOCIETY

"The business of America is business." Thus did Calvin Coolidge, a man not given to prolixity, sum up America's ideals and aspirations. In this he seemed to confirm Dickens' harsh impeachment of Americans in *Martin Chuzzlewit:* "All their cares, hopes, joys, affections, virtues, and associations, seemed to be melted down into dollars. . . . Men were weighed by their dollars; life was auctioneered, appraised, put up and knocked down for its dollars."

The image of Americans and America that such statements perpetuate is of a materialist civilization exclusively preoccupied with the accumulation of wealth and physical goods,[1] an image inspired these days, one suspects, as much by secret envy of our wealth as by an accurate estimate of the difference in taste and refinement between Europeans and Americans. Our European cousins are prone to such an appraisal of us, and they have succeeded in converting some American intellectuals to the same view. In truth, now that prosperity has come to the West Europeans, they generally display that same regard for mechanical gadgets that overwhelmed many of us;[2] they pursue wealth just as avidly, and, if public benefactions and tax avoidance are measures, their capitalists are far more grasping.

We often find in others the faults that are most conspicuous in ourselves—the psychological mechanism involved may aptly be called a disowning projection—and the European in stigmatizing Americans as materialistic may well be guilty of this rationalization. The libel is compounded when critics ignore the growing concern in America for scholarship and the fine arts. However, once all this is said and we have expressed our righteous indignation over what is an unfair caricature of American culture, the ques-

---

[1] For some, Coca-Cola has unaccountably become the symbol of our degradation. Thus, in a letter to the editor of *The New York Times* (June 14, 1962) a prominent British historian, A. R. Burns, refers to the "Coca-Cola-vization of the American way of life" and adds that "if the only way to keep Europe from Communism were to have it completely Americanized, I should have my doubts about the merits of the bargain." It is reassuring to learn in the same letter that some of historian Burns' best friends are Americans.

[2] Peter Viereck's comment is surely apt: "Old world disdainers of us soulless American vulgarians still engage in heated debates about the rival aesthetics of the 'Cinquecents' and 'Seicents.' These two Italian labels, however, no longer refer to Renaissance art but to Fiat automobiles. Soon it may be necessary for left-bank sensitive plants to flee from modern, rootless, gadget-giddy Europe to ancient, medieval, traditionalist America." (*The Unadjusted Man*, p. 69.)

tion may well be raised: ought not our concern for the arts and letters and sciences to be greater? Is it not true that, however overstated by unfair critics, profoundly important values are overshadowed and obscured by the emphasis in our society on the pursuit of wealth? Is it not the case that the motives of the marketplace invade the church, the school, government, the professions, the arts, deflecting them from their proper mission? In particular, how has the profit motive affected the quality of the so-called mass media to which we give so many of our leisure hours? May it not be said that business monopolizes too much of our lives? Many years ago De Tocqueville, most perceptive of foreign observers of American life, spoke of "the business-like qualities" of the Americans and of their "trading passions." The question is, have we carried these passions too far?

There is another aspect to the problem. A society that emphasizes pecuniary motives is organized about the satisfaction of *individual* needs and interests. Must this result in a neglect of national or community goals and purposes? Our cities, for example, have been called by Lewis Mumford a "crystallization of chaos." The rich and moderately well-to-do of the most affluent country in all history are engaged in an ignominious evacuation of their cities, leaving them—except for well-guarded islands of high commerce and plush living—to ethnic minorities, to marginal members of the majority group, and to the superannuated. In the past this occurred because there was an invader at the gates; today it occurs because our cities are less and less viable as communities. Does this suggest, as many have charged, that in our quest for consumer goods we have starved our social services, neglected public amenities, ignored national goals?

A major reason for our preoccupation with consumer goods is that the talents and energies of a great many able people are concentrated on promotion and salesmanship, which in effect bias the outlay we make as a people in favor of consumption to the neglect of such social needs as urban redevelopment, education, recreation, and conservation. Quite apart from the fact that supersalesmanship may—by persuading people to buy what they would not in ordinary circumstances want—lead to such neglect and to a misdirection of resources, how are we morally to evaluate the main manifestation of such promotion in the form of advertising? Is the effect desirable? Without reference to the tastelessness of the average commercial message on television or radio, or the influence of advertisers on newspaper or program content, how shall we morally assess the deception that characterizes most advertising? Is it discounted by the listener or viewer and therefore innocuous and morally irrelevant, or are we so institutionalizing mendacity that we dull our capacity to be morally discriminating?

Such a line of inquiry leads to two issues of increasing concern to responsible business leaders and to the community at large. Both issues concern the ethics of the business community. Industry in this country, according to a number of its most distinguished leaders, is facing a moral crisis. The issue quite simply is honesty—honesty as commonly defined and understood. To what extent are businessmen honest with each other, honest with their government, honest with the public? The same question may of course be put to labor leaders. But businessmen are leaders of the larger community as well as of their own enterprises in a sense in which labor leaders are not. An answer to this question as directed to them is therefore crucially important. Quite probably if businessmen are dishonest—the reference here is not to marginal businessmen or even to an occasional Billie Sol Estes, but to the respected and established businessman—we as a people will be dishonest, with ourselves and with others.

The second question is more difficult and the answer more controversial. It involves much more than considerations of simple honesty. What are the responsibilities of the business community to the larger community of which it is a part? In recent years we have heard much of "corporate citizenship." It is said by many that the robber-baron days are over and that business executives have a new sense of the larger social responsibilities of the corporations over which they preside. Large-scale financial aid to colleges and universities is often cited as an example. Others will argue that the stewardship of private ownership and management has degraded our mass media, that the action of management in the steel industry's recent effort to raise steel prices indicated an obliviousness to the impact such action would have on the nation's economy, that—in sum—the ideal of corporate citizenship is a veneer and a pretense. Clearly, such questions are of profound interest to every American.

It is all too easy to come up with simple answers and sweeping generalizations. All of them, including many of the adverse judgments implied above, must be weighed against the achievements of an open society that, uniquely in man's history, has made vast strides towards banishing want and suffering and in which—to borrow from Pericles—"Although only a few may originate a policy, we are all able to judge it." Such a judgment is made in the challenging comments that follow.

THE ACQUISITIVE IDEAL

The acquisitive impulse is as old as man and has manifested itself wherever men have lived, but what R. H. Tawney has called the Acquisitive Society hardly antedates the third quarter of the eighteenth century. For a large part of this period its ambit was limited to England, the United States, and a small part of the continent of Europe. Max Weber was referring to a period not too long before the eighteenth century, when he wrote: "That anyone should be able to make it the sole purpose of his life-work, to sink into the grave weighed down with a great material load of money and goods, seems to him [pre-capitalist man] explicable only as the product of a perverse instinct, the *aura sacra fames*."[1]

The acquisitive society institutionalized the profit motive, gave it a central role, made it the driving force that transformed the static and stable economies of an earlier era. This was, as Tawney has said, its "whole tendency and interest and preoccupation."[2] An acquisitive society is one in which the means of production are privately owned and in which the motives of the market, that is to say, the calculated interests of buyers and sellers, determine the allocation of productive resources and the distribution of incomes. Such a society, as Joseph Schumpeter has written, "has been cast in a purely economic mold: its foundations, beams and beacons are all made of economic material. The building faces toward the economic side of life. Prizes and penalties are measured in pecuniary terms. Going up and down means making and losing money."[3]

For a long time such a society felt no need to examine its basic premises, including its economic bias and the central place it accorded economic man—viewed always, in Veblen's famous phrase, as a "lightening calculator." In recent years, however, such a review has been going on. Not only did the acquisitive society develop unexpected weaknesses; it had to meet

---

[1] *The Protestant Ethic and the Spirit of Capitalism,* translated by Talcott Parsons (London: George Allen & Unwin, Ltd., 1930), pp. 71–72.

[2] *The Acquisitive Society* (New York: Harcourt, Brace and World, Inc.), p. 29.

[3] *Capitalism, Socialism, and Democracy* (New York: Harper & Row, Inc., 1942), p. 73.

the challenge of competing systems and ideologies. The resulting reexamination has gone far beyond economic analysis to a reappraisal of the basic values of a good society. If the society emerging from appraisals such as those that follow would be unrecognizable to Mr. Gladstone or Mr. Coolidge, there is good reason to believe that it will prove more durable in the end.

THE HOUSE DIVIDED AGAINST ITSELF[1]

John Dewey

(1859–1952)

Although it is fashionable in some quarters to denigrate him, John Dewey remains the towering eminence of American philosophy. In 1952, when he died at the age of 93, he left behind him a prodigious legacy of provocative and important books and articles such as few other men have encompassed in a lifetime. It is safe to say that he influenced our thinking more than any other American. His greatest works in the field of general philosophy are Experience and Nature *and* Quest for Certainty. *In ethical theory he waged a long war not only against absolutism, but against the kind of relativism which asserts that judgments of value are not, like judgments of fact, demonstrable and are therefore merely "emotive." Dewey believed that judgments of value are susceptible of validation and hence meaningful, even though this is not accomplished by referring them to or deriving them from moral absolutes. Much of what he said on this subject is intended for the professional philosopher, but his* Ethics *(especially Part II, which he wrote without his collaborator, James Tufts) will reward the general reader, as will* Human Nature and Conduct *and* Reconstruction in Philosophy.*

Dewey was an ardent social reformer. In this sense he was a philosophe *as well as a philosopher, if we agree with Carl Becker's view of the former as interested not only in ideas but in the impact of ideas on events. Dewey's interest was a logical outcome of his "instrumentalism," to use the term he preferred for his version of the pragmatic philosophy of which he was the leading exponent. But it was also an outcome of his recoil as an individual from what he regarded as the less wholesome features of a pecuniary culture.* Individualism, Old and New *appeared in 1930. It is a severe impeachment of patterns of conduct prevalent at that time. We need to ask ourselves to what extent they still prevail.*

---

[1]*Individualism, Old and New* (New York: Minton, Balch and Company, Inc., 1930), pp. 9–56. Reprinted by permission.

. . . Anthropologically speaking, we are living in a money culture. Its cult and rites dominate. "The money medium of exchange and the cluster of activities associated with its acquisition drastically condition the other activities of the people." This, of course, is as it should be; people have to make a living, do they not? And for what should they work if not for money, and how should they get goods and enjoyments if not by buying them with money—thus enabling someone else to make more money, and in the end to start shops and factories to give employment to still others, so that they can make more money to enable other people to make more money by selling goods—and so on indefinitely. So far, all is for the best in the best of all possible cultures: our rugged—or is it ragged?—individualism.

And if the culture pattern works out so that society is divided into two classes, the working group and the business (including professional) group, with two and a half times as many in the former as in the latter, and with the chief ambition of parents in the former class that their children should climb into the latter, that is doubtless because American life offers such unparalleled opportunities for each individual to prosper according to his virtues. If few workers know what they are making or the meaning of what they do, and still fewer know what becomes of the work of their hands . . . this is doubtless because we have so perfected our system of distribution that the whole country is one. And if the mass of workers live in constant fear of loss of their jobs, this is doubtless because our spirit of progress, manifest in change of fashions, invention of new machines and power of overproduction, keeps everything on the move. Our reward of industry and thrift is so accurately adjusted to individual ability that it is natural and proper that the workers should look forward with dread to the age of fifty or fifty-five, when they will be laid on the shelf.

All this we take for granted; it is treated as an inevitable part of our social system. To dwell on the dark side of it is to blaspheme against our religion of prosperity. But it is a system that calls for a hard and strenuous philosophy. If one looks at what we do and what happens, and then expects to find a theory of life that harmonizes with the actual situation, he will be shocked by the contradiction he comes upon. For the situation calls for assertion of complete economic determinism. We live as if economic forces determined the growth and decay of institutions and settled the fate of individuals. Liberty becomes a well-nigh obsolete term; we start, go, and stop at the signal of a vast industrial machine. Again, the actual system would seem to imply a pretty definitely materialistic scheme of value. Worth is measured by ability to hold one's own or to get ahead in a competitive pecuniary race. . . . The philosophy appropriate to such a situation is that of struggle for existence and survival of the economically fit. One would expect the current theory of life, if it reflects the actual situation, to be the most drastic Darwinism. And, finally, one would anticipate that the personal traits most prized would be clear-sighted vision of personal advantage and resolute ambition to secure it at any human cost. Sentiment and sympathy would be at the lowest discount.

It is unnecessary to say that the current view of life in Middletown, in Anytown, is nothing of this sort. Nothing gives us Americans the horrors more than to hear that some misguided creature in some low part of the earth preaches what we practice—and practice much more efficiently than anyone else—namely, economic determinism. Our whole theory is that man plans and uses machines for his own humane and moral purposes, instead of being borne wherever the machine carries him. Instead of materialism, our idealism is probably the loudest and most frequently professed philosophy the world has ever heard. We praise even our most successful men, not for their ruthless and self-centered energy in getting ahead, but because of their love of flowers, children, and dogs, or their kindness to aged relatives. Anyone who frankly urges a selfish creed of life is everywhere frowned upon. Along with the disappearance of the home, and the multiplication of divorce in one generation by six hundred per cent, there is the most abundant and most sentimental glorification of the sacredness of home and the beauties of constant love that history can record. We are surcharged with altruism and bursting with the desire to "serve" others.

These are only a few of the obvious contradictions between our institutions and practice on one hand, and our creeds and theories on the other, contradictions which a survey of any of our Middletowns reveals. It is not surprising that the inhabitants of these towns are bewildered, uneasy, restless, always seeking something new and different, only to find, as a rule, the same old thing in a new dress. It may all be summed up, perhaps, by saying that nowhere in the world at any time has religion been so thoroughly respectable as with us, and so nearly totally disconnected from life. . . .

. . . the whole story is told in brief when one contrasts what is actually happening to family life and the complete secularization of daily activities with a statement from the pulpit that "the three notable words in the English language are mother, home and heaven," a remark that would certainly pass unquestioned in any representative American audience.

It makes little difference whether one selects important or trivial aspects of the contradiction between our life as we outwardly live it and our thoughts and feelings—or what we at least say are our beliefs and sentiments. The significant question is: What is the cause of this split and contradiction? . . . It is evident enough that the rapid industrialization of our civilization took us unawares. Being mentally and morally unprepared, our older creeds have become ingrowing; the more we depart from them in fact, the more loudly we proclaim them. In effect we treat them as magic formulae. By repeating them often enough we hope to ward off the evils of the new situation, or at least to prevent ourselves from seeing them— and this latter function is ably performed by our nominal beliefs.

With an enormous command of instrumentalities, with possession of a secure technology, we glorify the past, and legalize and idealize the *status quo,* instead of seriously asking how we are to employ the means at our disposal so as to form an equitable and stable society. This is our great abdication. It explains how and why we are a house divided against itself. Our tradition, our heritage, is itself double. It contains in itself the ideal of equality of opportunity and of freedom for all, without regard to birth and status, as a condition for the effective realization of that equality. This ideal and endeavor in its behalf once constituted our essential Americanism; that which was prized as the note of a new world. It is the genuinely spiritual element of our tradition. No one can truthfully say that it has entirely disappeared. But its promise of a new moral and religious outlook has not been attained. It has not become the well-spring of a new intellectual consensus; it is not (even unconsciously) the vital source of any distinctive and shared philosophy. It directs our politics only spasmodically, and while it has generously provided schools it does not control their aims or their methods.

Meanwhile our institutions embody another and older tradition. Industry and business conducted for money profit are nothing new; they are not the product of our own age and culture; they come to us from a long past. But the invention of the machine has given them a power and scope they never had in the past from which they derive. Our law and politics and the incidents of human association depend upon a novel combination of the machine and money, and the result is the pecuniary culture characteristic of our civilization. The spiritual factor of our tradition, equal opportunity and free association and intercommunication, is obscured and crowded out. Instead of the development of individualities which is prophetically set forth, there is a perversion of the whole idea of individualism to conform to the practices of a pecuniary culture. It has become the source and justification of inequalities and oppressions. Hence our compromises, and the conflicts in which aims and standards are confused beyond recognition. . . .

The marks and signs of [the] "impersonalization" of the human soul are quantification of life, with its attendant disregard of quality; its mechanization and the almost universal habit of esteeming technique as an end, not as a means, so that organic and intellectual life is also "rationalized"; and, finally, standardization. Differences and distinctions are ignored and overridden; agreement, similarity, is the ideal. There is not only absence of social discrimination but of intellectual; critical thinking is conspicuous by its absence. Our pronounced trait is mass suggestibility. The adaptability and flexibility that we display in our practical intelligence when dealing with external conditions have found their way into our souls. Homogeneity of thought and emotion has become an ideal.

Quantification, mechanization and standardization: these are then the marks of the Americanization that is conquering the world. They have their good side; external conditions and the standard of living are undoubtedly improved. But their effects are not limited to these matters; they have invaded mind and character, and subdued the soul to their own dye. The criticism is familiar; it is so much the burden of our own critics that one is never quite sure how much of the picture of foreign critics is drawn from direct observation and how much from native novels and essays that are not complacent with the American scene. This fact does not detract from the force of the indictment; it rather adds to it, and raises the more insistently the question of what our life means.

. . . we are still in an early stage of transition. Anything that is at most a hundred years old has hardly had time to disclose its meaning in the slow secular processes of human history.

. . . the impoverishment of the individual is accompanied, even now, by an enrichment of community resources. Collectively, present society . . . is marked by a power over nature and by intellectual resource and power exceeding that of the classic Athenian and the man of the Renaissance. Why is it that this collective enrichment does not operate to elevate correspondingly the life of the individual? . . . Failure to consider [this question] constitutes to my mind the chief failure of critics whether foreign or native. Our materialism, our devotion to money making and to having a good time, are not things by themselves. They are the product of the fact that we live in a money culture; of the fact that our technique and technology are controlled by interest in private profit. There lies the serious and fundamental defect of our civilization, the source of the secondary and induced evils to which so much attention is given. Critics are dealing with symptoms and effects. The evasion of fundamental economic causes by critics both foreign and native seems to me to be an indication of the prevalence of the old European tradition, with its disregard for the body, material things, and practical concerns. The development of the American type, in the sense of the critics, is an expression of the fact that we have retained this tradition and the economic system of private gain on which it is based, while at the same time we have made an independent development of industry and technology that is nothing short of revolutionary. When our critics deal with this issue instead of avoiding it there will be something really doing.

Until the issue is met, the confusion of a civilization divided against itself will persist. The mass development, which our European critics tell us has submerged individuality, *is* the product of a machine age; in some form it will follow in all countries from the extension of a machine technology. Its immediate effect has been, without doubt, a subjection of certain types of individuality. As far as individuality is associated with aristocracy of the historic type, the extension of the machine age will presumably be hostile to individuality in its traditional sense all over the world. . . . The problem of constructing a new individuality consonant with the objective conditions under which we live is the deepest problem of our times. . . .

Assured and integrated individuality is the product of definite social relationships and publicly acknowledged functions. Judged by this standard, even those who seem to be in control and to carry the expression of their special individual abilities to a high pitch, are submerged. They may be captains of finance and industry, but until there is some consensus of belief as to the meaning of finance and industry in civilization as a whole, they cannot be captains of their own souls—their beliefs and aims. They exercise leadership surreptitiously and, as it were, absentmindedly. They lead, but it is under cover of impersonal and socially undirected economic forces. Their reward is found not in what they do, in their social office and function, but in a deflection of social consequences to private gain. They receive the acclaim and command the envy and admiration of the crowd, but the crowd is also composed of private individuals who are equally lost to a sense of social bearings and uses.

The explanation is found in the fact that while the actions promote corporate and collective results, these results are outside their intent and irrelevant to that reward of satisfaction which comes from a sense of social fulfillment. To themselves and to others, their business is private and its outcome is private profit. No complete satisfaction is possible where such a split exists. Hence the absence of a sense of social value is made up for by an exacerbated acceleration of the activities that increase private advantage and power. One cannot look into the inner consciousness of his fellows; but if there is any general degree of inner contentment on the part of those who form our pecuniary oligarchy, the evidence is sadly lacking. As for the many, they are impelled hither and yon by forces beyond their control. . . .

The unrest, impatience, irritation and hurry that are so marked in American life are inevitable accompaniments of a situation in which individuals do not find support and contentment in the fact that they are sustaining and sustained members of a social whole. They are evidence, psychologically, of abnormality, and it is as idle to seek for their explanation within the deliberate intent of individuals as it is futile to think that they can be got rid of by hortatory moral appeal. Only an acute maladjustment between individuals and the social conditions under which they live can account for such widespread pathological phenomena. Feverish love of anything as long as it is a change which is distracting, impatience, unsettlement, nervous discontentment, and desire for excitement, are not native to human nature. They are so abnormal as to demand explanation in some deep-seated cause.

I should explain a seeming hypocrisy on the same ground. We are not consciously insincere in our professions of devotion to ideals of "service"; they mean something. Neither the Rotarian nor the big business enterprise uses the term merely as a cloak for "putting something over" which makes for pecuniary gain. But the lady doth protest too much. The wide currency of such professions testifies to a sense of a social function of business which is expressed in words because it is so lacking in fact, and yet which is felt to be rightfully there. If our external combinations in industrial activity were reflected in organic integrations of the desires, purposes and satisfactions of individuals, the verbal protestations would disappear, because social utility would be a matter of course.

CAPITALIST ECONOMY AND
BUSINESS CIVILIZATION[1]

Max Lerner

Max Lerner is one of the most discerning observers of the American scene. He makes his views known in the college classroom, through a daily column in the New York Post, *and in books and essays that invariably provide new insights into the American character. Among these are his* It's Later Than You Think *(1943),* Ideas Are Weapons *(1939),* The Mind and Faith of Justice Holmes *(1943) and, most recently, the two-volume work from which the following selection is taken. Although no apologist for things as they are, Lerner is much less severe with the culture of a business society than was Dewey.*

. . . The reach of the commercial spirit penetrates into every area of American culture. The business principle has sometimes been confused with the machine principle. The latter is used to dispense with human labor and make possible standardized and large-scale production, while the business

[1]*America as a Civilization* (New York: Simon and Schuster, Inc., 1957), pp. 311–317. Reprinted by permission of Simon and Schuster, Inc.

principle focuses on market sale for profit. It puts the making of money ahead of other craft and civilization values, gives primacy to the cultural and personal traits which lead to that end, and tends to apply money values even to the human personality.

America has often been called a business civilization, but the term is too sweeping. One cannot say that the business principle is the only one operating in American culture. In some areas—religion, education, the arts, the family—it exerts only an incipient influence. But even where it has not become decisive, there has been a creeping imperialism of business over the other domains of life.

The business principle has given a synthetic cohesion to the far-flung diversity of American life. Before the Civil War it could genuinely be said that American culture was a loose collection of principalities—those of politics, of farming and industry, of religion, of literature and art and the press—tied together mainly by a pride of pioneering and a sense of the emerging national strength, and some belief in the democratic idea. The advance of business power and values weakened the hold of the democratic idea, while translating both the pioneering sense and the nationalist pride into the boom terms of growing industrial power and profit. . . .

In America, as everywhere, politics has been vulnerable to bribery. Yet it is a paradox of a business civilization that there has been notably less political corruption in America than in many precapitalist societies such as in Asia, the Middle East, and South America, or even some of the Latin societies of Europe. Perhaps this is exactly because of the importance of business: for those to whom money is all-important there are in America (as in no other culture) more direct channels open to the money-making energies than through the circuitous routes of the political career and political power. Political corruption is most rampant in the cultures where for many men it is the only road to wealth and status; in America it is only one of many.

Yet the business spirit, which directly carries along in its torrential course so many of the talents and energies of men into money-making, also breaks down some of the moral barriers that had been built into the conscience for generations. The big temptation in the era of the expanding frontier was land speculation. In the era of an expanding capitalism the temptations lie less in speculation than in the sale of political influence to businessmen intent on getting some of the Big Money, by crucially placed governmental subalterns who don't see why they too should not get their cut. As in the post-Civil War days of Grant and Conkling, or the post-World War days of Harding and Daugherty, the torrents of fresh business energy which open new opportunities for big profits also carry away with them much of the terrain of social conscience. In this sense it is not the periods of business decay but the periods of business expansion and vitality which play havoc with moral principles, because they fix men's aims at the attainable goals of the Big Money. . . .

Until recently, at least, the appeal of business has been as a way of making money, not as a way of life. Sensitive people have rejected the way of life but then been lured by the money; hence the split in the American attitude toward business, which has been most marked where the tradition of an educated elite has been strongest. The Adams family, for example, showed both a cultivated understanding and a cultivated fear of the new and pushing type of business activity. Writing in *The Education,* Henry Adams expressed the melancholy sense that for all the processes of civilization that had gone to make him, he was unfit to survive in the world that business values were fashioning. Brooks Adams, living as a *rentier* from corporate securities, was able to dissect pitilessly the social sources of his income, all the time ransacking history to explain the emergence of this new form of centralized power to which he owed the leisure he had for ransacking history. The third brother, Charles Francis Adams, was a railroad president who wrote with shriveling contempt for the narrowness of outlook and the niggardliness of spirit of business as a way of life. Henry James, for all his preoccupation with money and what it could buy, always pushed the question of its sources into the background and felt slightly soiled by them. He was most at home with a businessman like the hero of *The Golden Bowl,* spending in Europe the fortune he had made in America, a Maecenas who knew what he wanted and went after it with the practiced assurance that betokened the habitual conqueror. The secret that Sir Joseph Duveen discovered about American businessmen, which made his fortune as an art salesman, was that they gloried in their power over the things that money commanded but hungered for the symbols of the life values that went beyond money. Throughout the history of the business spirit, the monied men have used business first as a way of making the Big Kill, then turned to philanthropy or the life of the patron, travel, or hobbies as a way of making a life.

The business spirit, then, has not in itself been regarded as a nourishing one but as a means to bring a good life within reach. For that reason perhaps it has exerted an attraction for the young men of talent who in other civilizations might have gone into government, the Army, or the priesthood, into literature or the arts or the study of philosophy, into science or the professions. Even those in government service have, when successful, been tempted to turn their knowledge to the service of the corporation: if they have worked in the Treasury Department on taxes, or as economists in government bureaus, they can command good salaries as consultants or executives in business. If they have been good newspapermen they are eagerly recruited for public-relations jobs in the corporate world. And the corporations have learned to go directly to the colleges in recruiting young men of talent who are rarely able to resist the offer of an immediate job as against the uncertainties of a career in the arts or professions.

Even for those who stay outside business, there is a strong drive to conduct themselves in a "businesslike" way. The trade-union movement in America has been largely, as Hoxie first described it, "business unionism," expressing the competing claims to income of the corporate employees as part of the larger structure of the business economy itself. In education the school administrator and the university president have tended to act as corporate executives. Even in the churches the temptation is to be "practical" in administering vast properties rather than unworldly in pursuing the values of the spirit. In the newspaper and magazine fields the pressure is toward building big power aggregates that can command writing talent and the reader market and get a big share of national advertising: the magazine or big newspaper is likely to make its more blatant public boasts not so much about its newsgathering or its crusading spirit as about its circulation and advertising gains. In radio and television the art forms are subsidiary to the selling of time to the business sponsors. In moviemaking, the final art product has to run the gantlet of box-office appeal, and the Hollywood values of inflated salaries and skyrocketing careers are a kind of caricature of the corporate executives. In literature the emphasis has shifted to the products that can be marketed to a mass audience, notably crime and detection thrillers.

In fact, it may turn out that the business spirit will leave its most enduring imprint on the adjoining provinces of literature and entertainment, government and opinion: for these are the areas in which capital investment counts least and personality and talent still can carve out empires. They are the last Klondikes of venture skills, which are even more important in the history of business than venture capital. The lure of the acquisitive impulse, wedded to talent and ideas, produces a powerful amalgam.

It is customary to speak of this as the "commercializing" of art and opinion. But the process is more complex. The crux of it is that the dominant activity of any civilization colors the prevailing notions of what is effective or futile in the exercise of men's talents. In a business civilization the stamp of effectiveness is placed on whatever can be exchanged in the personality market for money and success; the stamp of ineffectuality is placed on whatever talent is not vendible, whatever cannot move to a maximum degree into the channels where it is capitalized and reaches a mass market with all the accruing rewards. Thus the business spirit, itself incapable of yielding nourishing life values, has become for Americans the prime gateway to a way of life, with few questions asked about what you find when you have gone through the gates.

When one inquires what may account for the "domination effect" of the business spirit, the answer lies partly in the attractiveness of the big rewards and the big market, partly in the admiration felt for the men who have shown that they can run things best, partly in the pragmatic strain of a culture which accepts whatever is practical and successful as the valid and pays it the flattery of mimicry.

The final tribute to the domination effect of the business spirit is the extent to which the phases of the human personality are measured in its terms. In a seminal analysis of types of character structure that bear aptly on American life, Fromm has spoken of the "marketing orientation" as one that is crowding out much else in the business society. There is little question that the marketable personality is becoming the dominant one, even in areas outside business. Courtesy and charm come to be valued not for themselves but because they pay off in salesmanship; clothes must be worn well to make an impression on a prospective customer or employer; the "dreamer type" of person is dangerous because he will estrange those who seek alertness. America itself, in the impact it makes on other peoples in the struggle for world leadership, must "sell" itself and its ideas; and the clinching argument used even by liberal intellectuals against the denial of civil rights of Negroes and other minority groups is that it will interfere with such international "selling" and acceptance.

This then is what seems to have happened in the American business economy. The more strictly technical problems of production and scarcity, of income distribution, of bigness in the sense distinct from monopoly, even of the business cycle, are fairly on the way to being resolved. But the bureaucratization of life through the new managerial structures in business, the trade-union, the government, and the corrupting reach of marketing values and the money spirit are being extended through the whole culture. The real problems of the business culture are thus less the technical and strictly economic problems than the moral and psychological ones.

Yet, to say, as some foreign observers and American critics have said, that only money talks in America is to vulgarize the impact of the business spirit. Other values than the acquisitive find a place in American life, and often they triumph; and other qualities than the money-making qualities blossom. But even when they do triumph, it is only after they have been measured and defended against the money values and the vendible qualities. That they survive is the final tribute to their hardihood, and when they do survive—in literature and the arts, in human relations, in religion and education and government, in the armed services, in the professions, perhaps even in business itself—they have a greater strength than in those cultures where they do not have to measure themselves so searchingly against the domination effect of the business spirit.

THE CASH-NEXUS[1]

Peter Viereck

The selection that follows is an evaluation of the business spirit from the point of view of a conservative who is not himself a member of the business community.

Peter Viereck teaches history at Mount Holyoke College and was an eloquent spokesman for the conservative point of view even during the 'thirties, when conservatism found few intellectual adherents. However, many of those who call themselves conservatives today will derive meager comfort from his views. Viereck regards the current crop of right-wing nationalists as spurious conservatives devoid of generous social impulses and disposes of them as "rootless, counter-revolutionary doctrinaires."[2]

Besides the volume from which the present selection is taken, he has written such works as Metapolitics: From the Romantics to Hitler (1941), Conservatism Re-Visited (1949), *and* Shame and Glory of the Intellectuals (1953).

The conservative philosophy developed partly as an ethical reaction against the value-dissolving huckster-materialism accompanying the industrial revolution in the early 1800's. Though founded earlier by Burke as an answer to the French Revolution, the conservative philosophy gained its depth-psychology only under the agony of industrialism. The main impact of industrialism on western man was not economic but psychological: the trauma it inflicted on the traditional value-heritage. The post-Burkean depth-psychology of conservatism derived not from politicians but from sensitive creative artists like Coleridge, Matthew Arnold, Cardinal Newman in England; Baudelaire, Dostoyevsky, Nietzsche, Burckhardt on the continent; Melville, Hawthorne, Poe, Henry Adams, Faulkner in America. Melville was the one to state the most succinctly the attitude they all shared:

> The spider in the laurel spins,
> The weed exiles the flower;
> And, flung to kiln, Apollo's bust
> Makes lime for Mammon's tower.

[1]*The Unadjusted Man* (Boston: Beacon Press, 1956), pp. 87–96. Reprinted by permission of the Beacon Press, copyright © 1956 by the Beacon Press.
[2]"The New Conservatism," *New Republic,* September 24, 1962, p. 18.

Such literary or religious value-conservers could not endure the dissolving of society's aesthetic, ethical, and religious ties by the arid cash-nexus. Its dissolution of these traditional ties was opposed, long before Marx, by Tory spirits like Donoso Cortés, Metternich, Disraeli. Therefore, most (not all) new conservatives have actively opposed that last Indian summer of hucksterdom which flowered in America after the Republican victory of 1952.

But unlike socialists, with their class-determinism, new conservatives do not indiscriminately equate most businessmen with a huckster-mentality. It is a kind of Aryan racism of economics to brand classes instead of individuals. A mentality characterizing more individual businessmen in the McKinley context of yesteryear may, under a new context, characterize more individual trade-unionists, rustics, grand dukes, or professors. Such a mentality should no more be attributed permanently to a party than to a class. The cash-nexus Old Guard is not the whole Republican party, did not represent it in Lincoln's day, need not represent it tomorrow.

It is mere romanticism to ignore the reality of industrialism and flee into some never-existent idealization of the Middle Ages. What is deadly is not the industrial gadgetry itself nor the material prosperity itself but the overadjusted smugness, self-sufficiency, and betrayal of spiritual traditions that accompany this gadgetry, this prosperity unless these become servants, not tyrants of man. In their different ways, the starting point 150 years ago of both aristocratic conservatism and democratic socialism was their shared fear that the middleclass *laissez faire* liberalism was allowing industrial mechanization to become not the servant but the tyrant of man. In their historical and European origins, conservatism and socialism are both psychological reactions against the intolerable cash-nexus mentality of the nineteenth-century burgher.

In twentieth-century America, that same capitalism has achieved (in contrast with the high-priced, low-production capitalism of Europe) miraculous economic benefits for all, benefits which its socialist-proletarian and conservative-aristocratic opponents never dreamed of in Europe and in the nineteenth century. The diffusion of these benefits among workers has rendered out of date most of the socialist attacks on capitalism, insofar as these attacks were mainly economic and material. But these admittedly attractive benefits have not rendered out of date the traditional conservative attacks on middleclass capitalism, attacks which were not economic but spiritual (Coleridge, Carlyle, Newman, Ruskin, Arnold, Melville). Nor have these material benefits of modern American capitalism rendered out of date that minority within socialist thinkers who represent not materialism but Christian ethics.

The benefits of American capitalism, its admirable flexibility, its ability to reform its own weaknesses via free parliamentary channels, its wide diffusion of private property (which Henry Maine in *Popular Government,* 1885, showed to be indispensable to full personal liberty), and the greatest material well-being in history—all these benefits, while refuting and out-dating the Marxist predictions of ever greater poverty and inequality under capitalism, have neither outdated nor solved the problem of the Over-adjusted Man. That is, the problem of mass-mechanization leading to an economically delicious but stereotyping prosperity. There is, therefore, no need to abandon smugly those attacks on the cash-nexus which character-ized almost all the greatest religious, philosophical, and literary figures of America's past. Today and tomorrow those attacks must continue on cul-tural, ethical, or religious levels—the three proper levels of conservatism in contemporary America—even though those attacks on capitalism have been outdated on the economic level, the proper level of socialist ma-terialists.

In Europe socialism and conservatism both had a social base, a party, a class: proletariat or landed aristocracy. In America, where the whole country is diffused with middleclass psychology, the two anti-middleclass movements cannot play a role in terms of political parties or economic classes. This obvious lack of a class base for either socialism or conserva-tism in America has led to their being scorned as having no role to play in America. What their scorners forget is that attitudes can work through diffusion as well as through a movement. Both conservatism and socialism work in America as a whole, equally in all parties and classes, as an un-labeled and unconscious diffusion, not as a movement. When they become a movement, they become small, comical splinter-groups. They become cranks who imagine nostalgically a non-existent class of feudal southern landowners or class-conscious proletarians, as the case may be. To make this statement is not to minimize the important role of conservative and socialist thought. Diffusion can be more influential than any localized move-ment or party. But that important intellectual influence will be jeopardized if New Conservatives should make the mistake of trying to localize their essentially cultural and ethical thought into one particular party or into apologetics for one particular American class, whether that class be the no-longer-existent agrarian nobles of the Middle Ages and the feudal south or the all-too-existent urban hucksters.

In the case of Europe, conservatism and socialism differ in their class base, their economic base, and their general historical base. In the case of America, neither has inherited any class base from history, and neither is identified with any political party (except for irrelevant splinter-groups, our parties are neither aristocratic nor proletarian but middleclass). Therefore, in the case of America, conservatism and socialism are not only weaker than in Europe (except for diffusion under other labels) but differ far less from each other than they do in Europe. What unites them in America is their distrust of the commercialism prevailing ever since the defeat of the Civil War of the agrarian south as well as the subsequent defeat of the Lincolnian non-commercial idealists inside the north.

In America, ever since the death of the truly conservative Federalist party, we must speak (except for rootless, doctrinaire fringes) not of socialist or conservative ideologies, parties, movements but of diffused and unlabeled conservative or socialist attitudes, at their most effective when least labeled and at their least effective when articulate and conscious. Despite their close kinship in America as fellow anti-commercialists, there is one important area where conservative and socialist attitudes do differ from each other, even in America, with an unbridgeable gap. That area is their view of human nature. Socialism shares with Jeffersonian liberals a faith in human nature, the masses, the natural goodness of man; sometimes it also shares with Progressives and Populists of the Paine heritage a faith in direct democracy. In contrast, the conservative view of human nature takes into account its complexity, its tragic tensions between incompatible impulses, and therefore its inability to plan the long-range rational blueprints desired by socialists. Historically the conservative view of human nature is a secularization of the Christian doctrine of original sin. At the same time the conservative view of human nature is close to the discoveries of the Freudians about the subconscious and about stifled impulses, discoveries that Coleridge and Nietzsche so uncanilly anticipated.

The usual capitalist defense of private property against socialists sounds appalling, especially in the ears of idealistic artists and scholars, because of its grubby materialist basis. If the issue is debated on that basis alone, then trade-unions of Europe and the majority of the intellectuals of Asia and Europe are justified in strongly sympathizing with the socialists, who at least have a generous breadth of vision. Yet it is the socialists who are wrong, the American kind of capitalists who are right about the need for a widely-diffused possession of unmolested private property. The capitalists are right, not in sloganizing about a maximum *laissez faire* (which they themselves fail to practice whenever they can get tariffs and state subsidies) but in insisting upon some minimum level of property beyond which not even the kindliest state may intervene. However, the proper argument for their excellent case is not their profit-motive but the fact that capitalist private property has also a non-material, moral function. It educates its possessor in the moral qualities of sturdy independence, sense of responsibility, and the training of judgment and character brought whenever free choice is exercised in any field, including the economic field. It is these moral qualities, not the gluttonous material ones that have historically associated the rise of personal liberty with the rise of personal property. To recognize this concrete historical fact about property and liberty is not, be it added, the same as abstracting that fact into a vast, rigid ideology of Manchester liberalism or into an imagination-stifling cash-nexus.

Most socialists are anti-communists. The horrible example of Soviet terrorist dictatorship, which socialists like George Orwell and Norman Thomas opposed more effectively than most capitalists, has forced most socialists to reconsider their frequent earlier minimizing of the danger of statism to their own lofty ideals. The best socialist thought today, independent and non-sectarian, is ably engaged in trying to work out a formula preserving personal choice in all non-economic spheres at the same time as having centralized economic planning. To a distruster of the abstract, the flaw in even the best of these socialist theories lies not in their sincerity, intellect, and good will (often superior in those three qualities to their detractors). Their flaw lies in their assumption that society can be understood or perfected by over-all formulas in the first place. Thomas I. Cook has defined the new conservatism as the rediscovery that liberty depends on concrete traditions and is menaced by "excessive reliance on human reason, functioning deductively and *a priori* on a foundation of abstract principle.

The proper corollary to the able socialist indictments of Soviet Russia is not to contrive some new and shinier formula to replace the discredited old one but to stop seeing salvation in any brand of over-all formula. The proper corollary is to begin seeing history as the darkly growing relationship of concrete to concrete. No kind of socialist over-all explanation and chart, no pedantic, top-of-the-brain ideology (whether it calls itself socialist, liberal, or conservative), can ever systematize or control the rich, helter-skelter plenitude of man.

The latest thought of certain socialists and of certain *laissez faire* capitalists is producing insights no conservative can neglect without being the loser. A number of those writers are far removed from being the usual grubby caricatures of materialism. And yet, even when one leans over backward to consider their writings without prejudice, how many others turn out to be just that. And how much such big-business materialists and socialist materialists resemble each other! They differ on the non-essentials: on economic theory, on the boring wrangle about whether the fat swine or the lean swine of materialism should hog a bit more of the economic trough. But they agree on certain essentials: a mechanistic view of life, utilitarianism, the unpleasant duty of dutiful pleasure-seeking, faith in bigger and better progress, in sterile efficiency, in doctrinaire apriorism. To these goals both sacrifice what the conservative cherishes: all that is warm, concrete, human in human nature, everything precarious, diversified, unpredictable, unorganized, unadjusted. . . .

Industrialism is still a young force, a post-1789 force, a force still unpatterned and experimental. If its strutting, success-intoxicated children will subordinate the raw material energies of that new force to the old, legitimizing pattern of the Christian-Judaic ethic, then American democratic capitalism will increasingly evolve a non-huckster, non-philistine businessman, just as America has already amazed continental Europe by evolving a non-Marxist workingman. Then the new legitimism of a more deeply-rooted, ethic-centered west can transcend the false choice between plutocratic and Marxist materialism. Such transcendence can still save America from a warning of Emerson that ought especially to haunt an atomic age. "Things are in the saddle and ride mankind."

THE PROFIT MOTIVE[1]

Peter Drucker

Peter Drucker is a well-known authority on the corporation as a social institution. A teacher and management consultant, he is the author of a number of widely read books, including The End of Economic Man *(1939),* The Future of Industrial Man *(1941),* The New Society *(1950), and* Landmarks of Tomorrow *(1959). For eighteen months he served as outside consultant to General Motors Corporation, which had asked him to study and report on its managerial policies and organization. The volume from which the following selection is taken is a result of this study. While rejecting the hedonistic preconceptions of orthodox economics as a basis on which to plead that the profit motive is inherent in human nature, he argues that the profit motive is nevertheless indispensible to a viable economy and a free society.*

Profit and profitability are objective criteria of economic action. They have nothing to do with the beliefs of a given society or with particular institutions but apply to any society however organized. Essentially profit and profitability are nothing but reformulations of the law of the conservation of energy in economic terms.

The "profit motive" on the other hand pertains to man's actions and reactions. In capitalist society, moreover, it is institutionalized in special institutions, and behavior according to the "profit motive" receives social sanctions and rewards. It is this "profit motive," the socially sanctioned behavior of the individual to obtain the maximum material gain, which is under attack as "unnatural" and "antisocial." And since the corporation

---

[1]*The Concept of the Corporation* by Peter F. Drucker (New York: John Day Company, Inc., 1946), pp. 236–245. Copyright © 1946 by Peter F. Drucker. By permission of The John Day Company, Inc., publisher.

in a free-enterprise economy is directed by, and dedicated to, the satisfaction of this "profit motive," the question arises whether the "profit motive" is indeed incompatible with a stable, functioning and good society.

The attack on the profit motive as "unnatural" and conflicting with socially and individually more beneficial and more fundamental human motives is, like the attack on profitability, partly the result of an excessive reaction against the wrong psychology of the utilitarian economists. They had proclaimed that man has a natural instinct to "truck and bargain," and they deduced from this instinct the laws of classical economics. We know today that there is no such thing as a natural instinct to "truck and bargain." If we ever needed proof of the fallacy of the utilitarian concept, it has been abundantly supplied by modern cultural anthropology and modern psychology. We also know that in most human activities, motives are thoroughly mixed, and that we will never find anybody acting on the basis of that "simple and clear calculation" of possible gain against possible effort on which the classical economists based their theories of economic behavior. Finally, we know that the orthodox economists were completely mistaken when they used the utilitarian "pleasure-pain calculus" to equate "work" with "pain." The psychological and social ravages of unemployment have certainly shown that idleness, far from being pleasing, is destructive, and that work, far from being disagreeable, is a necessity of human existence and self-respect and in itself a source of pride and satisfaction. There is little left today of that psychology from which the profit motive emerged as the controller of human destinies and as the natural law of human behavior.

To say that the profit motive is not inborn in man and the expression of his true nature is, however, something very different from asserting that it is vicious, unnatural and socially undesirable. This assertion rests on two beliefs which are both as untenable and as fallacious psychologically as the dogma of the preordained profit motive which they tried to replace. The first of these is the belief that man's "creative instinct" is not only good in itself but alone sufficient to make man socially constructive—the belief which is expressed in Veblen's famous juxtaposition of "industry" and "business." The second of these beliefs asserts that, but for the profit motive, human society would be one of equality and peace, and that all drive for power and privilege, all conflict and all inequality are the result of the lust for gain. In other words, both beliefs see in the profit motive the one, or at least the main, obstacle to the millenium.

It cannot be said too emphatically that no society can be based on man's "creative instincts." In order to make social life possible there must always be a principle of organization which reduces individual fulfillment and individual drive to a social purpose. Otherwise that co-ordinated human effort on which social life rests becomes impossible. If we do not use profit and profitability as the reduction gear, we would have to work out some other social mechanism to convert the subjective drive of the individual into the objective performance of society.

If we take, for instance, the people employed in the production of an automobile, we shall find that the "instinct of workmanship" leads in totally different directions, depending upon whether we look at the engineer, the production man or the sales manager. For the engineer the highest standard of achievement and craftsmanship lies in the most functional and most up-to-date car embodying the best and newest in engineering research, in materials and in design. He may be inclined to regard as alien and as in conflict with his ideas of workmanship such considerations as cheapness and ease of production, habits of automobile users, their comfort, etc.; and he would want to change his design all the time in order to incorporate the latest engineering improvements. The standards by which the production man will measure his workmanship and achievement would be above all cheapness, speed and ease of production. His ideal is an engineering design that will never change. His attitude towards the consumer's preference and desires was summed up perfectly in the epigram attributed to that prince of production men, Henry Ford, when he said that "the customer can have any color as long as it's black." The sales manager finally—or anybody whose business it is to distribute cars—sees maximum achievement in the most salable car, a cheap car that "looks like a million dollars" and satisfies the consumer's desire to keep up with the Joneses—however unreasonable this may appear to the engineer or to the production man. Each has "instincts of workmanship" which are creative. But the instinct of the one can find free rein only at the expense of the instinct of another. If society wants automobiles, it must be able to subordinate the instincts of each man to an objective principle of social satisfaction. However much such an objective principle "violates" individual integrity—a point mooted since the dawn of history—society must have it.

The profit motive may not be the best reduction gear. It certainly is not the only possible one. But to denounce it because it is a reduction gear—Veblen's procedure—begs the question. What we have to answer is not whether the profit motive is good or bad, but whether it is efficient or inefficient as a principle of social integration of individual motives and desires.

In a society which accepts economic advancement and economic goals as socially efficient and as socially desirable the profit motive is socially the most efficient device. In any other society, it is not an efficient mechanism. In the Middle Ages, for instance, the profit motive was clearly socially inefficient from the point of view of an order which regarded economic goals—beyond mere physical survival—as socially irrelevant and as morally suspect. In a society which believes in the desirability of economic progress, as has ours for the last two hundred years, the profit motive is an efficient mechanism of integration, because it relates individual motives and drives directly to accepted social purposes. Obviously, this creates problems in those spheres of social life to which economic rationality is not applicable, such as the arts. But these problems are no greater than those faced by the Middle Ages in applying their noneconomic objective principle of social integration to the economic sphere with its necessarily economic rationality. In other words, while no society and no principle of social integration can be perfect or automatic, the profit motive is the most efficient and the simplest mechanism for the conversion of individual drives into social purpose and action under the given conditions and beliefs of *our* society. It is, perhaps, the best commentary on this conclusion that the Soviet Union has gone as far as any capitalist country—and further—in using economic rewards and incentives in industry. For, however different its social tenets and institutions, Russia shares with the West the belief in economic goals.

What about the second count in the popular indictment of the profit motive: that it is the cause of the lust for power and dominance and the sole or main obstacle to peace and equality? Certainly the "profit motive" is not necessarily inherent in human nature. But inherent in human nature there is a drive for power and distinction of which the profit motive is only one possible form. If we eliminate the profit motive, the result will not be the equal and peaceful society of the millennium but the emergence of some other outlet for men's basic lust for power.

The weakness of the traditional argument is beautifully illustrated by the first great sermon on the profit motive as the original sin, and on its abolition as the key to the earthly paradise—Thomas More's *Utopia*. More's ideal society is perfect, peaceful, free of strife and ambition simply because property and gain have been eliminated. At the same time—almost on the same page—More proposes an elaborate system of honors and preferments as the basis for social power and political rulership. And he never sees the obvious: that the competition for these honors and preferments would at once bring back the ambition, the strife, the factionalism and the lust for power and prestige which he had just driven out by banishing the profit motive. Plato—and More was a Platonist—knew better. But his proposal in the *Republic* not to admit anyone to rulership until he be old enough to be past ambition is hardly more realistic; is there an age limit on ambition and pride? Wherever in history a man was kept out of power until very late, his lust for power, his ambition, his dominance and factiousness increased, often to the point of pathological exaggeration.

If I may again point to the findings of modern anthropology: the sentimental concept of "primitive equality" popularized by Rousseau and Marx has been exploded completely. There are many primitive tribes which do not know individual property in the sense in which we use the term.

There are however no examples of real communism among primitive tribes; communism is far too complicated a social arrangement to be attainable for a primitive society. And in every single culture we know of, there is a socially accepted motive of advancement to power and prestige around which the social organization is built.

Actually, we should not have needed anthropology to teach us that society is based on man's innate drive for power and social recognition. We have known for thousands of years that Pride is an essentially human quality. We may, with the ancient Greeks and the Renaissance, accept Pride as a virtue. Or we may with the Christian doctrine regard Pride as both cause and result of man's fall from grace and as the center of his corruption. But we can never hope to have a society without it. The statesman may, as a Christian, deplore the weakness of man and strive to overcome it in himself. As a statesman, however, he has to accept the fact that Pride and its manifestations are both the reason for the existence of society, and a constant in any social organization. The problem of the statesman is not to suppress or to overcome the drive for power; that is the concern of philosopher and saint. The political problem is how to direct the drive for power into the socially most constructive or least destructive channels.

To say, as is customary, that the profit motive is bad because all drive for power is bad, evades the issue; it may be good theology but it certainly is not relevant to politics. To say that the profit motive is bad because without it there would be no drive for power, is not even bad theology; it is nonsense. The only relevant and meaningful question is whether the profit motive is the socially most efficient one of the available directions in which the drive for power can be channeled.

I do not think that anyone can give a dogmatic answer; the absolutely best lies in the field of religion or philosophy, not in that of politics or social organization. But we can say that of the channels available and known to us, the profit motive has a very high, if not the highest, social efficiency. All the other known forms in which the lust for power can be expressed, offer satisfaction by giving the ambitious man direct power and domination over his fellow man. The profit motive alone gives fulfillment through power over things. It is an old truth that the richest and most overbearing millionaire in a capitalist society has less power over the individual worker than the worst paid official in a collectivist state, who can grant or withhold a license to do business or a work card. Certainly there is the danger that the power over things may develop into a power over men. But it is not an inevitable danger, and it can be checked by social action. . . .

The profit motive is the one way known to us to divert ambition from the socially destructive goal of power over men, into a socially constructive channel, that of economic production. This, though not by itself sufficient, is a protection against the danger that the lives and the livelihood of the individual citizen will become pawns in the game of human ambition and fair prey for the drive for power. It is no accident that the great villains of history are not found among the "economic royalists" but among the "incorruptibles," whose aim was power and power alone. Neither Robespierre nor Hitler could have been bought off by money; they lacked economic acquisitiveness entirely. But this hardly made them any more beneficial for mankind; their indifference to anything but naked power over men only heightened their inhumanity. . . .

To have a free society we must make it possible for man to act and to live in society without destroying himself or enslaving his fellow men. We must harness the lust for power to a social purpose. This, in a society accepting economic goals, the profit motive can do.

We do not have to regard the drive for gain as noble or as the best man is capable of. But noble or base, it directs the drive for power into the least dangerous channel. Of course the profit motive does not bring about a free society; the identification of capitalism with democracy, so current today, is utterly superficial and is the result of a truly shocking confusion. But while the profit motive by itself leads to a free society as little as any other human drive, it is more compatible with it than the other forms in which the lust for power may manifest itself socially. A free society is not based on man's drive but on his reason; it always has to guard against the danger of its perversion by the drive for power or by any other drive. The profit motive contains potential threats like all other manifestations of human pride. But unlike the other forms in which the drive for power may become socially effective, the profit motive of a free-enterprise society also contains powerful safeguards against the politically most dangerous consequence of human pride, the tyranny of the power-drunk.

THE PROBLEM OF PRIORITIES

The foregoing discussions have dealt in general terms with the way in which the profit motive has shaped our culture and influenced our ideals and aspirations as a people. Traditionally in our country the profit motive operates through the market and ours is known as a "market economy." The alternative to a market economy is some form of planning, either private or public, partial or total. In truth, ours is a "mixed economy" in which private planning and public planning combine with the conventional forces of the market to determine the way in which we allocate our human and physical resources. Even so, the movements of the market are influenced primarily by the decisions of those who own or manage the private sector of the economy. In recent times the beneficence of this influence on our scale of preferences as these are reflected in public and private expenditures has become a subject of much controversy. It will become evident that the problem of priorities, as we have come to know it, is a special one, touched upon, to be sure, in the preceding selections but not in its own terms.

Thus, if an individual were to spend a disproportionate amount of his income on luxuries—flashy automobiles, sports, liquor, etc.—at the same time that his family was badly housed and without adequate medical care, and his children inadequately educated, our moral appraisal of him would be a severe one. The contention is that collectively as a people we dispose of our resources in some analogous fashion.

The disposition of our resources, to repeat, is determined either by the market or by government. In our folklore, if not in fact, the market is thought to reflect the multitudinous decisions of individuals, each one the best judge of his own interest and each choosing freely and rationally[1] within the limitations of his income and thereby guiding the flow of resources into one use or other. Government is generally thought of as consisting of potentially tyrannous individuals arbitrarily imposing their judg-

---

[1]To be rational in this sense is to know what one wants and to choose the means most likely to get it and least likely to interfere with the satisfaction of stronger wants.

ment on others. Is this an accurate description of the alternatives? And does the kind of market economy that prevails in the United States bias the allocation of resources in favor of frivolous expenditures to the neglect of fundamental needs? The question has come increasingly into the forefront of our thinking. Although it is generally discussed in economic and political terms, moral issues are clearly involved.

Many would say that, except at the margins, we need not stumble over distinguishing between what is extravagant and frivolous and what is basic and fundamental. Oversized cars, rapid changes of fashion in attire, and built-in obsolescence would appear to fall into the first category; water purification, housing, medical care, and education, into the latter. Even so, some will ask who is to determine what is good or bad in the way we spend our money? Others will answer that the consumer should, but under conditions that enable him to exercise his best judgment. This, then, is the problem of priorities: Do our economic institutions as they now operate make for a wise or foolish allocation of our resources? Two contrasting views are presented in the selections that appear below.

THE THEORY OF SOCIAL BALANCE[1]

John Kenneth Galbraith

> *John Kenneth Galbraith, until President Kennedy appointed him ambassador to India, was Professor of Economics at Harvard. As an economist he has generally preferred novel and arresting insights and generalizations to detailed statistical analyses, a preference no doubt abetted by a biting epigrammatic style that has been lacking in the literature of political economy since the days of England's R. H. Tawney and America's Thorstein Veblen. More than any recent book, Galbraith's volume from which the following selection is taken focused attention on the contrast between what he has called "private opulence and public squalor." He has also written* Modern Competition and Business Policy *(1938),* American Capitalism: The Concept of Countervailing Power *(1952), and, more recently,* The Liberal Hour *(1960).*

The final problem of the productive society is what it produces. This manifests itself in an implacable tendency to provide an opulent supply of some things and a niggardly yield of others. This disparity carries to the

---

[1] *The Affluent Society* (Boston: Houghton Mifflin Company, 1958), pp. 251–269. Reprinted by permission.

point where it is a cause of social discomfort and social unhealth. The line which divides our area of wealth from our area of poverty is roughly that which divides privately produced and marketed goods and services from publicly rendered services. Our wealth in the first is not only in startling contrast with the meagerness of the latter, but our wealth in privately produced goods is, to a marked degree, the cause of crisis in the supply of public services. For we have failed to see the importance, indeed the urgent need, of maintaining a balance between the two.

This disparity between our flow of private and public goods and services is no matter of subjective judgment. On the contrary, it is the source of the most extensive comment which only stops short of the direct contrast being made here. In the years following World War II, the papers of any major city—those of New York were an excellent example—told daily of the shortages and shortcomings in the elementary municipal and metropolitan services. The schools were old and overcrowded. The police force was under strength and underpaid. The parks and playgrounds were insufficient. Streets and empty lots were filthy, and the sanitation staff was under-equipped and in need of men. Access to the city by those who work there was uncertain and painful and becoming more so. Internal transportation was overcrowded, unhealthful, and dirty. So was the air. Parking on the streets had to be prohibited, and there was no place elsewhere. The deficiencies were not in new and novel services but in old and established ones. Cities have long swept their streets, helped their people move around, educated them, kept order, and provided horse rails for vehicles which sought to pause. That their residents should have a nontoxic supply of air suggests no revolutionary dalliance with socialism.

The discussion of this public poverty competed, on the whole successfully, with the stories of ever-increasing opulence in privately produced goods. The Gross National Product was rising. So were retail sales. So was personal income. Labor productivity had also advanced. The automobiles that could not be parked were being produced at an expanded rate. The children, though without schools, subject in the playgrounds to the affectionate interest of adults with odd tastes, and disposed to increasingly imaginative forms of delinquency, were admirably equipped with television sets. We had difficulty finding storage space for the great surpluses of food despite a national disposition to obesity. Food was grown and packaged under private auspices. The care and refreshment of the mind, in contrast with the stomach, was principally in the public domain. Our colleges and universities were severely overcrowded and underprovided, and the same was true of the mental hospitals.

The contrast was and remains evident not alone to those who read. The family which takes its mauve and cerise, air-conditioned, power-steered, and power-braked automobile out for a tour passes through cities that are badly paved, made hideous by litter, blighted buildings, billboards, and posts for wires that should long since have been put underground. They pass on into a countryside that has been rendered largely invisible by commercial art. (The goods which the latter advertise have an absolute priority in our value system. Such aesthetic considerations as a view of the countryside accordingly come second. On such matters we are consistent.) They picnic on exquisitely packaged food from a portable icebox by a polluted stream and go on to spend the night at a park which is a menace to public health and morals. Just before dozing off on an air mattress, beneath a nylon tent, amid the stench of decaying refuse, they may reflect vaguely on the curious unevenness of their blessings. Is this, indeed, the American genius?

In the production of goods within the private economy it has long been recognized that a tolerably close relationship must be maintained between the production of various kinds of products. The output of steel and oil and machine tools is related to the production of automobiles. Investment in transportation must keep abreast of the output of goods to be transported. The supply of power must be abreast of the growth of industries requiring it. The existence of these relationships—coefficients to the economist—has made possible the construction of the input-output table which shows how changes in the production in one industry will increase or diminish the demands on other industries. To this table, and more especially to its ingenious author, Professor Wassily Leontief, the world is indebted for one of its most important of modern insights into economic relationships. If expansion in one part of the economy were not matched by the requisite expansion in other parts—were the need for balance not respected—then bottlenecks and shortages, speculative hoarding of scarce supplies, and sharply increasing costs would ensue. Fortunately in peacetime the market system operates easily and effectively to maintain this balance, and this, together with the existence of stocks and some flexibility in the coefficients as a result of substitution, insures that no serious difficulties will arise. We are reminded of the existence of the problem only by noticing how serious it is for those countries—Poland or, in a somewhat different form, India—which seek to solve the problem by planned measures and with a much smaller supply of resources.

Just as there must be balance in what a community produces, so there must also be balance in what the community consumes. An increase in the use of one product creates, ineluctably, a requirement for others. If we are to consume more automobiles, we must have more gasoline. There must be more insurance as well as more space on which to operate them. Beyond a certain point more and better food appears to mean increased need for medical services. This is the certain result of the increased consumption of tobacco and alcohol. More vacations require more hotels and more fishing rods. And so forth. With rare exceptions—shortages of doctors are an exception which suggests the rule—this balance is also maintained quite effortlessly so far as goods for private sale and consumption are concerned. The price system plus a rounded condition of opulence is again the agency.

However, the relationships we are here discussing are not confined to the private economy. They operate comprehensively over the whole span of private and public services. As surely as an increase in the output of automobiles puts new demands on the steel industry so, also, it places new demands on public services. Similarly, every increase in the consumption of private goods will normally mean some facilitating or protective step by the state. In all cases if these services are not forthcoming, the consequences will be in some degree ill. It will be convenient to have a term which suggests a satisfactory relationship between the supply of privately produced goods and services and those of the state, and we may call it social balance.

The problem of social balance is ubiquitous, and frequently it is obtrusive. As noted, an increase in the consumption of automobiles requires a facilitating supply of streets, highways, traffic control, and parking space. The protective services of the police and the highway patrols must also be available, as must those of the hospitals. Although the need for balance here is extraordinarily clear, our use of privately produced vehicles has, on occasion, got far out of line with the supply of the related public services. The result has been hideous road congestion, an annual massacre of impressive proportions, and chronic colitis in the cities. As on the ground, so also in the air. Planes collide with disquieting consequences for those within when the public provision for air traffic control fails to keep pace with private use of the airways.

But the auto and the airplane, versus the space to use them, are merely an exceptionally visible example of a requirement that is pervasive. The more goods people procure, the more packages they discard and the more trash that must be carried away. If the appropriate sanitation services are not provided, the counterpart of increasing opulence will be deepening filth. The greater the wealth the thicker will be the dirt. This indubitably describes a tendency of our time. As more goods are produced and owned, the greater are the opportunities for fraud and the more property that must be protected. If the provision of public law enforcement services do not keep pace, the counterpart of increased well-being will, we may be certain, be increased crime.

The city of Los Angeles, in modern times, is a near-classic study in the problem of social balance. Magnificently efficient factories and oil refineries, a lavish supply of automobiles, a vast consumption of handsomely packaged products, coupled with the absence of a municipal trash collection service which forced the use of home incinerators, made the air nearly unbreathable for an appreciable part of each year. Air pollution could be controlled only by a complex and highly developed set of public services—by better knowledge stemming from more research, better policing, a municipal trash collection service, and possibly the assertion of the priority of clean air over the production of goods. These were long in coming. The agony of a city without usable air was the result.

The issue of social balance can be identified in many other current problems. Thus an aspect of increasing private production is the appearance of an extraordinary number of things which lay claim to the interest of the young. Motion pictures, television, automobiles, and the vast opportunities which go with the mobility, together with such less enchanting merchandise as narcotics, comic books, and pornographia, are all included in an advancing gross national product. The child of a less opulent as well as a technologically more primitive age had far fewer such diversions. The red schoolhouse is remembered mainly because it had a paramount position in the lives of those who attended it that no modern school can hope to attain.

In a well-run and well-regulated community, with a sound school system, good recreational opportunities, and a good police force—in short a community where public services have kept pace with private production— the diversionary forces operating on the modern juvenile may do no great damage. Television and the violent mores of Hollywood and Madison Avenue must contend with the intellectual discipline of the school. The social, athletic, dramatic, and like attractions of the school also claim the attention of the child. These, together with the other recreational opportunities of the community, minimize the tendency to delinquency. Experiments with violence and immorality are checked by an effective law enforcement system before they become epidemic.

In a community where public services have failed to keep abreast of private consumption things are very different. Here, in an atmosphere of private opulence and public squalor, the private goods have full sway. Schools do not compete with television and the movies. The dubious heroes of the latter, not Miss Jones, become the idols of the young. The hot rod and the wild ride take the place of more sedentary sports for which there are inadequate facilities or provision. Comic books, alcohol, narcotics, and switchblade knives are, as noted, part of the increased flow of goods, and there is nothing to dispute their enjoyment. There is an ample supply of private wealth to be appropriated and not much to be feared from the police. An austere community is free from temptation. It can be austere in its public services. Not so a rich one.

Moreover, in a society which sets large store by production, and which has highly effective machinery for synthesizing private wants, there are strong pressures to have as many wage earners in the family as possible. As always all social behavior is part of a piece. If both parents are engaged in private production, the burden on the public services is further increased. Children, in effect, become the charge of the community for an appreciable part of the time. If the services of the community do not keep pace, this will be another source of disorder.

Residential housing also illustrates the problem of the social balance, although in a somewhat complex form. Few would wish to contend that, in the lower or even the middle income brackets, Americans are munificently supplied with housing. A great many families would like better located or merely more houseroom, and no advertising is necessary to persuade them of their wish. And the provision of housing is in the private domain. At first glance at least, the line we draw between private and public seems not to be preventing a satisfactory allocation of resources to housing.

On closer examination, however, the problem turns out to be not greatly different from that of education. It is improbable that the housing industry is greatly more incompetent or inefficient in the United States than in those countries—Scandinavia, Holland, or (for the most part) England —where slums have been largely eliminated and where *minimum* standards of cleanliness and comfort are well above our own. As the experience of these countries shows, and as we have also been learning, the housing industry functions well only in combination with a large, complex, and costly array of public services. These include land purchase and clearance for redevelopment; good neighborhood and city planning, and effective and well-enforced zoning; a variety of financing and other aids to the housebuilder and owner; publicly supported research and architectural services for an industry which, by its nature, is equipped to do little on its own; and a considerable amount of direct or assisted public construction for families in the lowest income brackets. The quality of the housing depends not on the industry, which is given, but on what is invested in these supplements and supports.

The case for social balance has, so far, been put negatively. Failure to keep public services in minimal relation to private production and use of goods is a cause of social disorder or impairs economic performance. The matter may now be put affirmatively. By failing to exploit the opportunity to expand public production we are missing opportunities for enjoyment which otherwise we might have had. Presumably a community can be as well rewarded by buying better schools or better parks as by buying bigger automobiles. By concentrating on the latter rather than the former it is failing to maximize its satisfactions. As with schools in the community, so with public services over the country at large. It is scarcely sensible that we should satisfy our wants in private goods with reckless abundance, while in the case of public goods, on the evidence of the eye, we practice extreme self-denial. So, far from systematically exploiting the opportunities to derive use and pleasure from these services, we do not supply what would keep us out of trouble.

The conventional wisdom holds that the community, large or small, makes a decision as to how much it will devote to its public services. This decision is arrived at by democratic process. Subject to the imperfections and uncertainties of democracy, people decide how much of their private income and goods they will surrender in order to have public services of which they are in greater need. Thus there is a balance, however rough, in the enjoyments to be had from private goods and services and those rendered by public authority.

It will be obvious, however, that this view depends on the notion of independently determined consumer wants. In such a world one could with some reason defend the doctrine that the consumer, as a voter, makes an independent choice between public and private goods. But given the dependence effect—given that consumer wants are created by the process by which they are satisfied—the consumer makes no such choice. He is subject to the forces of advertising and emulation by which production creates its own demand. Advertising operates exclusively, and emulation mainly, on behalf of privately produced goods and services. Since management and emulative effects operate on behalf of private production, public services will have an inherent tendency to lag behind. Automobile demand which is expensively synthesized will inevitably have a much larger claim on income than parks or public health or even roads where no such influence operates. The engines of mass communication, in their highest state of development, assail the eyes and ears of the community on behalf of more beer but not of more schools. Even in the conventional wisdom it will scarcely be contended that this leads to an equal choice between the two.

The competition is especially unequal for new products and services. Every corner of the public psyche is canvassed by some of the nation's most talented citizens to see if the desire for some merchantable product can be cultivated. No similar process operates on behalf of the nonmerchantable services of the state. Indeed, while we take the cultivation of new private wants for granted we would be measurably shocked to see it applied to public services. The scientist or engineer or advertising man who devotes himself to developing a new carburetor, cleanser, or depilatory for which the public recognizes no need and will feel none until an advertising campaign arouses it, is one of the valued members of our society. A politician or a public servant who dreams up a new public service is a wastrel. Few public offenses are more reprehensible.

So much for the influences which operate on the decision between public and private production. The calm decision between public and private consumption pictured by the conventional wisdom is, in fact, a remarkable example of the error which arises from viewing social behavior out of context. The inherent tendency will always be for public services to fall behind private production. . . .

Social balance is also the victim of . . . the truce on inequality . . . With rare exceptions such as the post office, public services do not carry a price ticket to be paid for by the individual user. By their nature they must, ordinarily, be available to all. As a result, when they are improved or new services are initiated, there is the ancient and troublesome question of who is to pay. This, in turn, provokes to life the collateral but irrelevant debate over inequality. As with the use of taxation as an instrument of fiscal policy, the truce on inequality is broken. Liberals are obliged to argue that the services be paid for by progressive taxation which will reduce inequality. Committed as they are to the urgency of goods . . . they must oppose sales and excise taxes. Conservatives rally to the defense of inequality—although without ever quite committing themselves in such uncouth terms—and oppose the use of income taxes. They, in effect, oppose the expenditure not on the merits of the service but on the demerits of the tax system. Since the debate over inequality cannot be resolved, the money is frequently not appropriated and the services not performed. . . .

In practice matters are better as well as worse than this statement of the basic forces suggests. Given the tax structure, the revenues of all levels of government grow with the growth of the economy. Services can be maintained and sometimes even improved out of this automatic accretion.

However, this effect is highly unequal. The revenues of the federal government, because of its heavy reliance on income taxes, increase more than proportionately with private economic growth. In addition, although the conventional wisdom greatly deplores the fact, federal appropriations have only an indirect bearing on taxation. Public services are considered and voted on in accordance with their seeming urgency. Initiation or improvement of a particular service is rarely, except for purposes of oratory, set against the specific effect on taxes. Tax policy, in turn, is decided on the basis of the level of economic activity, the resulting revenues, expediency, and other considerations. Among these the total of the thousands of individually considered appropriations is but one factor. In this process the ultimate tax consequence of any individual appropriation is *de minimus,* and the tendency to ignore it reflects the simple mathematics of the situation. Thus it is possible for the Congress to make decisions affecting the social balance without invoking the question of inequality.

Things are made worse, however, by the fact that a large proportion of the federal revenues are pre-empted by defense. The increase in defense costs has also tended to absorb a large share of the normal increase in tax revenues. The position of the federal government for improving the social balance has also been weakened since World War II by the strong, although receding, conviction that its taxes were at artificial wartime levels and that a tacit commitment exists to reduce taxes at the earliest opportunity.

In the states and localities the problem of social balance is much more severe. Here tax revenues—this is especially true of the General Property Tax—increase less than proportionately with increased private production.

Budgeting too is far more closely circumscribed than in the case of the federal government—only the monetary authority enjoys the pleasant privilege of underwriting its own loans. Because of this, increased services for states and localities regularly pose the question of more revenues and more taxes. And here, with great regularity, the question of social balance is lost in the debate over equality and social equity.

Thus we currently find by far the most serious social imbalance in the services performed by local governments. The F.B.I. comes much more easily by funds than the city police force. The Department of Agriculture can more easily keeps its pest control abreast of expanding agricultural output than the average city health service can keep up with the needs of an expanding industrial population. One consequence is that the federal government remains under constant pressure to use its superior revenue position to help redress the balance at the lower levels of government. . . .

A feature of the years immediately following World War II was a remarkable attack on the notion of expanding and improving public services. During the depression years such services had been elaborated and improved partly in order to fill some small part of the vacuum left by the shrinkage of private production. During the war years the role of government was vastly expanded. After that came the reaction. Much of it, unquestionably, was motivated by a desire to rehabilitate the prestige of private production and therewith of producers. No doubt some who joined the attack hoped, at least tacitly, that it might be possible to sidestep the truce on taxation vis-à-vis equality by having less taxation of all kinds. For a time the notion that our public services had somehow become inflated and excessive was all but axiomatic. Even liberal politicians did not seriously protest. They found it necessary to aver that they were in favor of public economy too.

In this discussion a certain mystique was attributed to the satisfaction of privately supplied wants. A community decision to have a new school means that the individual surrenders the necessary amount, willy-nilly, in his taxes. But if he is left with that income, he is a free man. He can decide between a better car or a television set. This was advanced with some solemnity as an argument for the TV set. The difficulty is that this argument leaves the community with no way of preferring the school. All private wants, where the individual can choose, are inherently superior to all public desires which must be paid for by taxation and with an inevitable component of compulsion.

The cost of public services was also held to be a desolating burden on private production, although this was at a time when the private production was burgeoning. Urgent warnings were issued of the unfavorable effects of taxation on investment—"I don't know of a surer way of killing off the incentive to investment than by imposing taxes which are regarded by people as punitive." This was at a time when the inflationary effect of a very high level of investment was causing concern. The same individuals who were warning about the inimical effects of taxes were strongly advocating a monetary policy designed to reduce investment. However, an understanding of our economic discourse requires an appreciation of one of its basic rules: men of high position are allowed, by a special act of grace, to accommodate their reasoning to the answer they need. Logic is only required in those of lesser rank.

Finally it was argued, with no little vigor, that expanding government posed a grave threat to individual liberties. "Where distinction and rank is achieved almost exclusively by becoming a civil servant of the state . . . it is too much to expect that many will long prefer freedom to security."

With time this attack on public services has somewhat subsided. The disorder associated with social imbalance has become visible even if the need for balance between private and public services is still imperfectly appreciated.

Freedom also seemed to be surviving. Perhaps it was realized that all organized activity requires concessions by the individual to the group. This is true of the policeman who joins the police force, the teacher who gets a job at the high school, and the executive who makes his way up the heirarchy of Du Pont. If there are differences between public and private organizations, they are of kind rather than of degree. As this is written the pendulum has in fact swung back. Our liberties are now menaced by the conformity exacted by the large corporation and its impulse to create, for its own purposes, the organization man. This danger we may also survive.

Nonetheless, the postwar onslaught on the public services left a lasting imprint. To suggest that we canvass our public wants to see where happiness can be improved by more and better services has a sharply radical tone. Even public services to avoid disorder must be defended. By contrast the man who devises a nostrum for a nonexistent need and then successfully promotes both remains one of nature's noblemen.

PRIVATE VS. PUBLIC[1]

Henry E. Wallich

Henry E. Wallich is one of the diminished number of academic economists who might be described as belonging to the "conservative" school. He is Professor of Economics at Yale and author of Mainsprings of the German Revival (1955) *and a recent book,* The Cost of Freedom: A New Look at Capitalism. *He was a member of President Eisenhower's Council of Economic Advisers between 1959 and 1961.*

. . . It is one thing to be irritated by certain manifestations of our contemporary civilization—the gadgets, the chrome, the tailfins, and the activities that go with them. It is quite another—and something of a *non sequitur*—to conclude from this that the only alternative to foolish private spending is public spending. Better private spending is just as much of a possibility. My contention here will be that to talk in terms of "public vs. private" is to confuse the issue. More than that, it is to confuse means and ends. The choice between public and private money is primarily a choice of means. The sensible approach for those who are dissatisfied with some of the ends to which private money is being spent, is to specify first what other ends are important and why. Having determined the ends, the next step is to look to the means. That is the order in which I propose to proceed here.

One may share the irritation of the new social critics as they look upon some of the fluff and the floss on our standard of living. My personal feelings can be characterized by noting that I have a 1951 car and no TV. The critics may want to bear in mind, however, that not all the money in this country is spent by people for whom life begins at $25,000. The median family income is $5,600. Would these critics of the affluent society want to try living on much less than that? When Galbraith inveighs eloquently against switchblades, narcotics, and other phases of juvenile delinquency, he deserves the support of all right-thinking representatives of what he calls the "conventional wisdom." But are the sources of these aberrations more intimately tied to affluence or to poverty? The exponents of the new social criticism may also want to remember the outcome of that "noble experi-

---

[1]*Harper's Magazine*, October 1961, pp. 12–25. Reprinted by permission.

ment," Prohibition. It should have taught us that it is futile to become our brother's dietitian. I hope that it has also imbued us with wholesome doubt about the moral right of some members of the community to regulate the lives of the rest.

Irritation with the poor judgment of other people who fail to appreciate one's own more advanced tastes is not new. It was a familiar situation during the 1920s. The critics then quoted T. S. Eliot's *The Waste Land,* and some went off to Paris in search of greener cultural pastures. The feeling behind the new social criticism is not dissimilar. Hence one might suppose that the reaction would likewise turn in a cultural direction. One might expect the critics of contemporary materialism to plead for more intensive preoccupation with things of the mind. Some fits and starts in that direction there have been, to be sure. But they have not been in the main stream of the movement. The principal alternative to private materialism that has been offered to us has been public materialism.

Obviously, the quality of our culture could be greatly improved by public expenditures for education and support of the arts. The sales of good paperbacks and LPs are encouraging signs. But if contemporary materialism is to be leavened by such pursuits, it will be principally because large numbers of individuals make private decisions to that end. Social criticism is constructive if it helps precipitate these decisions. It obstructs a desirable evolution if it suggests that public creature comforts are the only alternative to private.

But while emphasis on nonmaterial ends seems sadly lacking in the new social criticism, the critics are right in pointing out that new material needs also have been carried to the fore by social and economic evolution—even though they mislabel them as public needs. In the good old days, when this was still a nation of farmers, most people had no serious retirement worries, there was no industrial unemployment problem, good jobs could be had without a college degree, most diseases were still incurable—in short, social security, education, and health care found primitive and natural solutions within the family and among the resources of the neighborhood. Today, these solutions are neither adequate nor usually even possible.

Meanwhile mounting wealth and advancing technology have brought within reach the means of meeting these needs. We can afford to live better in every way—more creature comforts, more leisure, more attention to matters of the mind and the spirit. At the same time we can take better care of retirement, of unemployment, of illness, of education, of the possibilities opened by research, than ever before.

There are indeed new needs. The citizen-taxpayer has his choice of meeting them, as well as all his other needs, in one of two ways. He can buy the goods or services he wants privately, for cash or credit. Or he can buy them from the government, for taxes.

The nation as a whole pays taxes to buy public services as it pays grocery bills to buy groceries. The tax burden may be heavier for some individuals than for others. But the nation as a whole has no more reason to complain about the "burden" of taxes than about the "burden" of grocery bills—and no more reason to hope for relief.

Of the two stores, the private store today still is much the bigger. The public store is smaller, but it is growing faster.

Each store has some exclusive items. The private store sells most of the necessities and all of the luxuries of life, and in most of these has no competition from the government side. The public store has some specialties of its own: defense, public order and justice, and numerous local services that the private organization has not found profitable. But there is a wide range of items featured by both stores: provision for old age, health services, education, housing, development of natural resources.

The bulk of the new needs are in this competitive area. The fashionable notion is to claim them all for the public store and to label them public needs. The statistics say otherwise. They say in fact two things: First, the supply of this group of goods and services has expanded very rapidly in recent years; and second, they are being offered, in varying degrees, both by the private and the public suppliers. Let us run down the list.

Provision for old age is predominantly private. The average American family, realizing that while old age may be a burden, it is the only known way to achieve a long life, takes care of the matter in three ways: (1) by private individual savings—home ownership, savings deposits, securities; (2) by private collective savings—life insurance, corporate pension funds; and (3) by public collective savings through social security. Statisticians report that the two collective forms are advancing faster than the individual. The increases far exceed the rise in the Gross National Product of almost 80 per cent (in current prices) over the past ten years; they do not indicate either that these needs are neglected or that they are necessarily public in character.

Education: the bulk of it is public; but a good part, particularly of higher education, is private. Total expenditures for all education have advanced in the last ten years from $9.3 billion to $24.6 billion ($19.3 billion of it public). Education's share in the national income has advanced from 3.8 per cent to 5.8 per cent. The silly story that we spend more on advertising than on education is a canard, though with its gross of over $10 billion, advertising does take a lot of money.

Health expenditures are still mainly private. At considerable expense, it is now possible to live longer and be sick less frequently or at least less dangerously. In the past, most people paid their own doctors' bills, although health care for the indigent has always been provided by public action or private philanthropy. Since the war, the proliferation of health insurance has given some form of collective but private insurance to three-quarters of our 182 million people. This has greatly reduced pressure for a national health service along British lines. For the aging, whose health-care needs stand in inverse proportion to their capacity to pay or insure, public insurance has finally been initiated and needs to be expanded. The total annual expenditure on health is estimated at over $25 billion, a little more than on education. Of this, about $6 billion is public.

So much for the allegation that the "new needs" are all public needs. Now for some further statistics on the public store, which is said to have been neglected. Some of them could make an investor in private growth stocks envious. Research expenditures (mainly for defense and atomic energy) have gone from about $1 billion to over $8 billion in the last ten years. Federal grants to the states have advanced from $2.2 billion to $7 billion during the same period. Social-security benefits rose from $1 billion to over $10 billion. All in all, public cash outlays (federal and state) advanced from $61 billion to $134 billion over ten years, 57 per cent faster than the GNP.

For those who feel about public spending the way Mark Twain felt about whiskey, these figures may still look slim. (Mark Twain thought that while too much of anything was bad, too much whiskey was barely enough.) To others, the data may suggest that the advocates of more public spending have already had their way. Could their present discontent be the result of a not keeping their statistics up-to-date? In one of his recent pamphlets, Arthur M. Schlesinger, Jr. claims that the sum of the many neglects he observes (including defense) could be mended by raising public expenditures by $10 to $12 billion. That is well below the increase in public cash outlays that actually did take place in one single fiscal year, from $118.2 billion in 1958 to $132.7 billion in 1959. In the three fiscal years 1957–59, these outlays went up more than $31 billion, though the advance slowed down in 1960. More facts and less indignation might help to attain better perspective.

Some parts of federal, state, and local budgets have expanded less rapidly than those cited—in many cases fortunately. The massive buildup in defense expenditures from the late 'forties to the 'fifties has squeezed other programs. Unfortunately, on the other hand, some programs that both political parties have favored—including aid to education, to depressed areas, for urban renewal—have been delayed unduly by the vicissitudes of politics. But the figures as a whole lend little support to the thesis that politicians don't spend enough, and that the government store is not expanding fast enough.

The two stores—private and public—work very hard these days to capture the business of the citizen-taxpayer. Here is what he hears as he walks into the private store.

"The principal advantage of this store," the private businessman says, "is that you can shop around and buy exactly what you want. If I don't have it I'll order it. You, the consumer, are the boss here. To be sure, I'm not in business for charity but for profit. But my profit comes from giving you what you want. And with competition as fierce as it is, you can be sure the profit won't be excessive."

If the proprietor has been to Harvard Business School, he will perhaps remember to add something about the invisible hand which in a free economy causes the self-seeking of competitors to work for the common good. He will also, even without benefit of business school, remember to drop a word about the danger of letting the public store across the street get too big. It might endanger freedom.

As the citizen turns this sales talk over in his mind, several points occur to him. Without denying the broad validity of the argument, he will note that quite often he has been induced to buy things he did not really need, and possibly to neglect other, more serious needs. Snob appeal and built-in obsolescence promoted by expensive advertising don't seem to him to fit in with the notion that the consumer is king. Looking at the brand names and patents and trademarks, he wonders whether most products are produced and priced competitively instead of under monopoly conditions. The invisible hand at times seems to be invisible mainly because it is so deep in his pocket.

Bothered by these doubts, the citizen walks across the street and enters the public store.

"Let me explain to you," says the politician who runs it—with the aid of a horde of hard-working bureaucrats doing the chores. "The principles on which this store is run are known as the political process, and if you happen to be familiar with private merchandising they may seem unusual, but I assure you they work. First of all, almost everything in this store is free. We simply assess our customers a lump sum in the form of taxes. These, however, are based largely on each customer's ability to pay, rather than on what he gets from the store. We have a show of hands from the customers once a year, and the majority decides what merchandise the store is to have in stock. The majority, incidentally, also decides how much everybody, including particularly the minority, is to be assessed in taxes.

"You will observe," the politician continues, "that this store is not run for profit. It is like a co-operative, run for the welfare of the members. I myself, to be sure, am not in politics for charity, but for re-election. But that means that I must be interested in your needs, or you would not vote for me. Moreover, there are some useful things that only I can do, with the help of the political process, and in which you and every citizen have an interest. For instance, everybody ought to go to school. I can make them go. Everybody ought to have old-age insurance. I can make that compulsory too. And because I don't charge the full cost of the service, I can help even up a little the inequalities of life.

"By the way," the politician concludes, "if there is any special little thing you want, I may be able to get it for you, and of course it won't cost you a nickel."

The citizen has some fault to find with the political process too. He notes that there is not even a theoretical claim to the benefits of an invisible hand. Majority rule may produce benefits for the majority, but how about the other 49 per cent? Nor is there the discipline of competition, or the need for profits, to test economy of operation. There is no way, in the public store, of adjusting individual costs and benefits. And the promise to get him some small favor, while tempting, worries him, because he wonders what the politician may have promised to others. The political process, he is led to suspect, may be a little haphazard.

He asks himself how political decisions get to be made. Sometimes, obviously, it is not the majority that really makes a decision, but a small pressure group that is getting away with something. He will remember that —after payments for major national security and public debt interest—the largest single expenditure in the federal budget is for agriculture, and the next for veterans. He may also recall that one of the first budgetary actions of the new Administration was to increase funds for agriculture by $3 billion.

Next, the citizen might consider the paralyzing "balance-of-forces" effect that often blocks a desirable reshuffling of expenditures. The allocation of public funds reflects the bargaining power of their sponsors, inside or outside the government. A classical example was the division of funds that prevailed in the Defense Department during the late 'forties. Army, Navy, and Air Force were to share in total resources in a way that would maximize military potential. By some strange coincidence, maximum potential was always achieved by giving each service the same amount of money. It took the Korean War to break this stalemate.

What is the consequence of the balance-of-forces effect? If the proponents of one kind of expenditure want to get more money for their projects, they must concede an increase also to the advocates of others. More education means more highways, instead of less; more air power means more ground forces. To increase a budget in one direction only is as difficult as letting out one's belt only on one side. The expansion tends to go all around. What this comes down to is that politicians are not very good at setting priorities. Increases in good expenditures are burdened with a political surcharge of less good ones.

The last-ditch survival power of federal programs is a specially illuminating instance of the balance of forces. If a monument were built in Washington in memory of each major federal program that has been discontinued, the appearance of the city would not be greatly altered. In contrast, when the Edsel doesn't sell, production stops. But the government is still reclaiming land to raise more farm surpluses and training fishermen to enter an occupation that needs subsidies to keep alive. Old federal programs never die, they don't even fade away—they just go on.

The citizen will remember also the ancient and honorable practice of logrolling. The unhappy fate of the Area Development bill illustrates it admirably. As originally proposed, the bill sought to aid a limited number of industrial areas where new jobs were badly needed. It got nowhere in the Congress. Only when it was extended to a large number of areas with less urgent or quite different problems were enough legislators brought aboard to pass it. Because of the heavy political surcharge with which it had become loaded, President Eisenhower vetoed the bill. A bill was finally enacted early this year, long after aid should have been brought to the areas that needed it.

Finally, the citizen might discover in some dark corner of his mind a nagging thought: Any particular government program may be a blessing, but could their cumulative effect be a threat to freedom? He has heard businessmen say this so often that he has almost ceased to pay attention to it. He rather resents businessmen acting the dog in the manger, trying to stop useful things from being done unless they can do them. He is irritated when he hears a man talk about freedom who obviously is thinking about profit. And yet—is there any conclusive rebuttal?

The citizen would be quite wrong, however, if he blamed the politician for the defects of the political process. The fault lies with the process, or better with the way in which the process, the politician, and the citizen interact. The citizen therefore would do well to examine some of his own reactions and attitudes.

First, when he thinks about taxes, he tends to think of them as a burden instead of as a price he pays for a service. As a body, the nation's taxpayers are like a group of neighbors who decide to establish a fire department. Because none is quite sure how much good it will do him, and because each hopes to benefit from the contribution of the rest, all are prudent in their contributions. In the end they are likely to wind up with a bucket brigade.

But when it comes to accepting benefits, the citizen-taxpayers act like a group of men who sit down at a restaurant table knowing that they will split the check evenly. In this situation everybody orders generously; it adds little to one's own share of the bill, and for the extravagance of his friends he will have to pay anyhow. What happens at the restaurant table explains —though it does not excuse—what happens at the public trough.

Finally, in his reaction to public or free services, the citizen takes a great deal for granted, and seldom thinks of the cost. Public beaches mistreated, unmetered parking space permanently occupied, veterans' adjustment benefits continued without need—as well as abuses of unemployment compensation and public assistance—are some examples. This applies also, of course, to privately offered benefits, under health insurance, for instance. The kindly nurse in the hospital—"Why don't you stay another day, dearie, it won't cost you anything, it's all paid for by Blue Cross"—makes the point.

By removing the link between costs and benefits, the political process also reduces the citizen's interest in earning money. The citizen works to live. If some of his living comes to him without working, he would be less than rational if he did not respond with a demand for shorter hours. If these public benefits increase his tax burden so that his over-all standard of living remains unchanged, the higher taxes will reduce his work incentive. Why work hard, if much of it is for the government?

These various defects of the political process add up to an obvious conclusion: the dollar spent by even the most honest and scrupulous of politicians is not always a full-bodied dollar. It often is subject to a discount. It buys less than it should because of the attrition it suffers as it goes through the process, and so may be worth only 90 cents or 80 cents and sometimes perhaps less. The private dollar, in too many cases, may also be worth less than 100 per cent. But here each man can form his own judgment, can pick and choose or refuse altogether. In the political process, all he can do is say Yes or No once a year in November.

The discount on the public dollar may be compensated by the other advantages of government—its ability to compel, to subsidize, to do things on a big scale and at a low interest cost. Whether that is the case needs to be studied in each instance. Where these advantages do not apply, the private market will give better service than the political process. For many services, there is at least some leeway for choice between the private and public store—health and retirement, housing, research, higher education, natural-resource development. Defense, on the other hand, as well as public administration, public works of all kinds, and the great bulk of education —while perhaps made rather expensive by the political process—leave no realistic alternative to public action.

The argument I have offered is no plea to spend more or less on any particular function. It is a plea for doing whatever we do in the most effective way.

CORPORATE "CITIZENSHIP"

Private ownership of the means of production in a highly industrialized economy has produced the modern corporation, through which the financial resources of large numbers of people are pooled, ownership and management are separated, and vast enterprises launched and operated. Given the central place of the private corporation in our institutional life, the ideals and standards of management, in particular management's conception of the social obligations of the corporation, will have a great deal to do with the kind of society in which we live. In recent times, the strategic place of the corporation has presented management with a new problem: whether to construe the role of the corporation narrowly as a strictly amoral business enterprise organized to maximize profits, or to accept a broader, socially oriented interpretation of the responsibilities of the corporation that would include the welfare of the community. Inseparably related to the solution of the moral problem are complex economic and political issues that are not explored here, especially the question of managerial power and its control.[1]

THE TRADITIONAL CORPORATION[2]

Richard Eells

Richard Eells is Public Policy Research Consultant for the General Electric Company and Adjunct Professor in Business of the Graduate School of Business, Columbia University. He has collaborated recently with Dean Clarence Walton of that school on a volume entitled Conceptual Foundations of Business.

[1]Cf. my *Evolution of Liberalism,* Collier Books, 1963, Ch. XII.
[2]*The Meaning of Modern Business* (New York: Columbia University Press, 1960), pp. 38–49. Reprinted by permission.

*Mr. Eells offers a contrast between the "traditional" corpora-
tion and what he calls the "metrocorporation." These are presented
as heuristic models on the assumption that all actual corporations
fall at some point in between.*

In the traditional corporation there is a simple answer to the basic
ethical question that confronts every director and every executive officer.
The central question—what is my station and what are its duties?—has an
answer that is fortified by law and custom: to serve the property interests
of the company's stockholders. There are secondary responsibilities to
creditors, to employees, to customers, and others; but the primary responsibility is to the group of persons who are investors in the enterprise. . . .

One seeks in vain in contemporary corporate statutes for any theory of
corporate social responsibility that places the shareowner interest in a subordinate role, as though the use of the corporate form required them to
transform a private business operation into a quasi-public agency. . . .

Corporation law, in short, is mainly designed to carry out the purpose
of the traditional corporation—a business instrument of its owners—with
only such restraints on managerial freedom as appear to be necessary to
protect the owners' interests and those of certain other contributors of
factors of production.

But the theory of the traditional corporation by no means rests on such
legalistic grounds alone. The philosophy which corporation statutes reflect
is a far more pervasive one. It is at once an economic and a political philosophy. On the economic side it is a philosophy that relies heavily on the
market mechanism as the chief means of making the optimum use of a
society's resources. On the political side, it is a philosophy that circum-
scribes the authority of public government or of any private collectivity to
meddle with this self-regulating mechanism. And since it is presumed to be
an automatic process, the market mechanism when left relatively free is
expected to achieve the beneficent results in public welfare that "socially
responsible" corporations would erroneously try to achieve by making the
business corporation a quasi-public instrumentality.

Thus the model of the traditional corporation rests essentially on a
social theory that has variously been described as economic liberalism, "the
conventional wisdom," and the doctrine of "intact" or "old-style capitalism."
The managers of the traditional corporation think of their business as an
entrepreneurial unit. . . .

"Business is business" for managers of the traditional corporation, and
this does not include any such objective as the promotion of the general
welfare. That the general welfare of society will be advanced by those who
pursue the profit motive is certainly one of the articles of faith of the American business creed. But by this view the general welfare is held to be the

automatic net result of the system as a whole and not the motivating force that impels the individual businessman to do what he does as a business-man. There is, in fact, a general suspicion that when he dilutes business with altruism the net result for all concerned will be neither businesslike nor altruistic. And the business corporation, under this traditional theory, is but the businessman writ large. It is simply a specialized instrument for the kind of competitive drive that has presumably brought our way of life to the high level of affluence of which we are so proud. . . .

But it is sometimes held that the theory of social responsibility is re-flected in corporate practice, particularly with reference to corporate giving, better community relations, employee benefit programs, plant safety pro-grams, the new emphasis in management techniques on "human relations," the lending of selected personnel to educational institutions and public serv-ice, and the development of a "corporate conscience."

It is equally arguable that social responsibility stops at the pocketbook. The figures for total corporate giving in the United States would tend to support this view, for while they are large in dollars they are minuscule in percentages of corporate net income. . . .

If one studies the usual statements on behalf of the new doctrine of social responsibility, it is found that its justification generally lies in the *quid pro quo* argument: social responsibility pays off, even if the pay-off has to be long-run rather than of immediate advantage to the corporation. There are exceptions. But it is fair to say that for most advocates of the socially responsible corporation their rationale is hardly more than a gloss on the theory of the traditional corporation, despite statements which might seem to indicate otherwise.

Language that proclaims the doctrine of social responsibility is usually little more than a verbal commitment to abstract principles of justice. In the traditional corporation one is especially careful not to specify concrete applications, particularly as to who has responsibility for what and to whom, and how these responsibilities are to be implemented in practice. . . .

The traditional corporation as a model tends to its owners' business and its managers are not diverted by irrelevant activities. They function in the strictly limited role of profit makers and subordinate every functional kind of work within the organization to the goal of profitability for stock-holders, who are entitled to one hundred percent of net earnings after taxes. . . .

The traditional corporation clearly has no general *public* responsibility. As to its wage policies, for example, it is argued that neither industry nor labor should be expected to "exercise voluntary restraint" in the public interest. Labor unions and traditional corporations are, by function, the stewards of special interests; their obligation is to their own organizations; and their duty is to face the community in the name of their members and not their members in the name of the community. The argument in the case of labor-management relations is said to apply with equal force to all market operations of the corporation. Each must look out for his own; and when a leader of business (or of labor) goes over to the "public interest" his associates may suspect that he ceases to function in accordance with the ground rules of a free, capitalist society. . . .

The traditional corporation, with its single-minded devotion to profit, has been maligned as amoral or even immoral. But its proponents are certainly moralists in their own right and their ethical principles are directly related to their economic theory. It is a liberal theory in the classical sense of that term, emphasizing liberty above equality and fraternity, and liberty not for the group but for the man.

The proponents of the traditional corporation would keep the corporation to its strictly economic functions within a free and competitive market economy, not because they defend profit seeking as the Ultimate Good, but because they believe this to be a necessary condition for the preservation of human freedom. The traditional corporation, under this view, will make no pretense of being a true "society" that serves the "whole man." Nor will any other private group, for that matter. The only true society that can serve the whole man is a political community that includes special-function organizations of many kinds: economic, educational, religious, and so on. When any of these special-function organizations try to make the enormous claim that their Organization Men should be wholly absorbed in the affairs of these enclaved groups, the result can be devisive and ruinous to the health of the community as a whole. Such absorption is avoidable so long as every private organization, corporation included, limits its functions to a reasonable division of effort.

But managers of the traditional corporation feel no compunction to exercise voluntary restraint on such matters as wage and price policy, guided by zealous concern for the public interest. In the austere view, managers are responsible for the operation of a competitive enterprise and will not, in this role, concern themselves unduly with "the general welfare." As citizens and as members of associations devoted to social melioration, they can and should be concerned with advancing the public interest. But they will insist that the business corporation is not designed for such a task. Rather, they would say, the traditional corporation is designed to supply goods and services to those who assert a market demand for them, and to supply these only at a profit to the risk taker. . . .

THE METROCORPORATION[1]

Richard Eells

One response to a crescendo of demand for more "socially responsible" business enterprises has been the conception of a business corporation that is far more socially oriented, more gregarious, more civic-minded and more cosmopolitan than the austere traditional corporation. We shall call this conceptualized model of a nascent corporate form the *metrocorporation,* thereby underlining its maternal concern for a numerous brood.

As a heuristic model, the metrocorporation is more difficult to describe than the traditional corporation, and not merely because it is still an inchoate form of business organization. The traditional corporation is better known in legal and economic theory. Since we are outlining only the most simplified models, it will be conceded that there are many variations on the traditional type; but it stands in decided contrast, even with modification, to the idea of a metrocorporation.

In this search for a new pattern of corporate behavior that avoids the extremes of privatization and statization, business leaders have tried to preserve a high degree of corporate autonomy while at the same time steering the corporate ship into the main streams of public policy. Privatization—or acute withdrawal into the corporate shell—is characteristic of corporate behavior in the traditional corporation. Statization—or surrender of business decision making to public government—is the other extreme, and one of grave danger to individual liberty as well as to freedom of enterprise for the businessman. To steer a course between these treacherous shoals has been a matter of concern not only for the corporate executive but for the public policy maker as well. The metrocorporate idea is one answer to this problem.

The metrocorporation lays emphasis upon the rights and duties of the corporation as a citizen and upon its relationships to society. Its managers undertake a dual role as individual citizens in their political communities and as representatives of the "corporate citizen." The metrocorporation is more a quasi-public than a private association as indicated by the general use of the term "public corporation" to designate a company with widely dispersed stockholding. Technically, it is a private corporation with constitutional protections not available to public corporations such as munici-

---

[1]*The Meaning of Modern Business,* pp. 50–67. Reprinted by permission.

palities and government corporations. It is also clearly a part of the private sector of the economy and not within the public sector as an administrative unit of public government. It has a private or, at the most, a quasi-public polity or government system of its own with a considerable degree of autonomy vis-à-vis the public governmental system and other private polities. . . .

The metrocorporation, as a model, is premised more on the similarity of Government and Business than on their disparity. The range of corporate policy is not so narrowly defined as to exclude large issues of public policy. The strategic decision areas of corporate policy in the metrocorporation are not limited to its own economic problems. It has concern for the larger economic problems of the economy as a whole, as well as for those problems that concern managers of single enterprises which must perform as efficient and profitable producers of goods and services.

But the metrocorporation also has many noneconomic goals. It tends to become a society in microcosm, with concern about human relations and human aspirations, not only among those immediately associated with the enterprise but among its neighboring social groups.

Its critics deplore this tendency because they assert that it is feudalistic and retrogressive. The metrocorporation is charged with egregious attempts to claim the whole man, giving him protection and security in return for lifetime loyalty to the Organization. It is further charged with retrogressing from a society characterized by division of labor into a centralized, collectivized, and bureaucratic institution with overweening ambitions to become a lesser society in its own right.

Seen in a more favorable light, the metrocorporation is highminded, philanthropic, and socially responsible. It strives to avoid the labels of excessive materialism, of cynical disregard for moral and religious standards, and of undemocratic values. With this ethical perspective there is a strong tendency to develop a theory of corporate governance consistent with the ideals of a democratic society. . . .

The metrocorporation . . . does not confine its activities to business purposes in any narrowly defined sense. It has broad social goals and assumes large social responsibilities. It holds itself accountable to many different sectors of society. Its managers regard themselves as arbiters, adjusters, or balancers of many interests. With such heavy and extensive responsibilities it would be natural to expect the organization to claim and to wield large powers. . . .

The traditional corporation conscientiously avoids any general involvement in political action at any level—local, state, national, or international. On occasion it will intervene in the government process by lobbying or giving direct testimony before congressional committees charged with writing new legislation of direct business concern. Behind the scenes, it will use protective measures against governmental encroachments. The metrocorporation, on the other hand, will systematically, actively, and openly involve itself in political affairs at all levels and in all branches of public government. It will consider that its moral obligation is to maintain a free and open pluralistic society by giving the corporation a political voice in the governance of society. The metrocorporation represents a significant private sector with its own system of private government; but it also assumes a right—and a responsibility to its own constituencies—to help shape the economic, social, and political environment to its own ends, as well as to what it considers to be society's ends. . . . This subtler type of relationship with external polities raises problems of strategic significance in corporate policy and can be illustrated in the field of labor relations.

Labor relations are more than internal employee relations; they involve external relations with unions. For the traditional corporation the problem of labor is statable as a problem of business management: the efficient use of labor as a factor of profitable production. But for the metrocorporation it has larger dimensions. . . .

During the past few decades the whole conception of industrial employment has undergone dramatic change. Labor is no longer regarded as a commodity. In place of the commodity concept there is the more recent "welfare concept" of employment, especially in the case of large industrial organizations, though not limited to them. All large organizations become increasingly responsible for the welfare of their personnel. A persistently expressed goal is security for all workers in the organization. Without pursuing an ostensibly paternalistic labor policy, the metrocorporation could embrace this trend with alacrity. . . .

In sum, the metrocorporation, even with its wide range of social responsibilities that are alien to the traditional, austere corporation, is engaged in business as its major objective. But its meaning of "business" is vastly different from many that would be acceptable in the traditional corporation. Business becomes a socially definable term and the corporate environment widens.

The business of the metrocorporation is more than profitability for the share owners. Metrocorporate managers see numbers of contributor-claimant groups, including the general public, to which they owe obligations in return for special kinds of contributions. These obligations are the corporation's "social responsibilities." Like the managers of the traditional corporation they insist upon the privateness of the sectors of business. But it becomes more and more difficult for them to draw the line between public and private affairs precisely because the metrocorporation has so many "publics" to serve.

With so many interests converging upon the corporate enterprise, it ceases to be the private domain of its stockholders. It looks more and more like a public polity. When the manager of the traditional corporation asks himself, "What is my station and what are its duties?" his answer is fairly clear. He is responsible to the property-owners who put up the risk capital; he is the guardian of a specific property interest. But the manager of the metrocorporation has no such clear-cut answer. He acts in a representative capacity in relation to many different groups of interests, but he has no theory of representation to guide him.

As a result, the corporate polity inherited from the pattern of the traditional corporation will not suffice. The ethics of the metrocorporation seem to require new patterns of corporate polity, new conceptions of corporate relations with public governments, and new forms of labor relations. . . .

HONESTY IN BUSINESS

The issue of honesty is related to, yet nevertheless distinct from, a discussion of the social obligations of the business community. The area of social responsibility embraces much terra incognita: should business acknowledge responsibility (as few businesses have) for the employment of workers during slack periods and off-seasons; should a large corporation shut down a marginal plant in a community completely dependent on its operation; should a plant foul a nearby stream or incur added costs in disposing of pollutants; should corporations (as distinguished from individuals) give aid to churches and institutions of higher learning; should the steel industry reckon with the impact of its pricing policies on the economy as a whole? The nature of obligation, as indicated earlier, is not clearly defined in these areas, and standards are in flux.

On the other hand, the question of honesty involves no comparable perplexities, not even in certain practices not banned by law. Normal people generally know when they are dishonest. At issue here is adherence to precepts that the business community itself accepts. Quite simply, honesty is opposed to lying, cheating, or stealing. Also, it involves practicing what we preach, especially when we preach with moral fervor.

Are incidents like the illegal conduct for which Westinghouse and General Electric executives were recently jailed, the padding of expense accounts, profiteering without business risk on the government's stockpiling program by high-placed advocates of government economy, and the purchase of political influence isolated and unrepresentative, or do they indicate the presence of widespread dishonesty and moral obtuseness in the business community?[1] In the General Electric case, the defense pleaded in

---

[1] For example, last year a federal judge upheld the conviction of eleven major oil firms on gasoline price-fixing charges. As this is written (October 29, 1962) five steel corporations were fined a total of $44,000 on their plea of no contest to charges of conspiracy to fix prices and rig bids in steel sales. There are indications of more to come. For another example, shipments of General Foods' Maxwell House instant coffee were seized recently by the Food and Drug Administration because the giant "economy" size was costing the consumer more per ounce than the small jar. Instances can be multiplied.

extenuation that the violations were part of a "prevailing business morality."
Was counsel exaggerating to save his client or describing a true state of
affairs?

Again, the business community affirms its dedication to the ideal of
consumer "sovereignty" with moral fervor and great vigor.[2] Yet the "Truth
in Lending" bill, authored by Senator Paul H. Douglas, which would require disclosure of simple annual interest rates and the actual cost in dollars
of buying on the installment plan has been almost universally opposed by
retailers and lenders, and is at this writing going down to almost certain
defeat. Quite apart from the ethics of calling a 14 percent interest rate 7
percent, is it honest to call the consumer sovereign while energetically opposing a measure intended to let him know what he is doing? Only a few
such questions can be answered here. But they will be raised more and
more persistently until the business community comes up with a satisfactory
answer.

As we appraise the answer we must, of course, be on guard against
regarding dishonesty as an exclusive monopoly of the business community.
We are helped in this by the Teamsters' Union and similarly managed labor
organizations, by the refusal of congress to pass a "conflict of interest" law
applicable to its own members, and by the precautions that must be taken
even in the rarified atmosphere of a college campus against cheating on
examinations and book thefts. In a more inclusive survey these would deserve close attention. Even so, one may still ask whether such evidences of
widespread dishonesty suggest an inherent depravity in human nature or
reflect the influence of the acquisitive ideal in our society.

---

[2]"Within the market society the working of the price mechanism makes the consumer supreme. . . . In that endless rotating mechanism the entrepreneurs and capitalists are servants of the consumer. The consumers are the masters. . . . The market
is a democracy in which every penny gives a right to vote . . ." Ludwig Von Mises,
Omnipotent Government (New Haven: Yale University Press, 1944), pp. 49–50. So,
too, John Chamberlain, whose book *The Roots of Capitalism* is one of a series designed to promote understanding of prevailing business practices, writes: "The test
of an economic system lies in the choices it offers. . . ." In a free system such as ours
"the consumer directs production, forcing or luring energy, brains, and capital to obey
his will" (New York: D. Van Nostrand Co., 1959), p. 165. If there is need for reform here, Mr. Chamberlain is powerless since, in the title of an earlier book, he bade
Farewell to Reform.

A NEW CODE OF BUSINESS ETHICS[1]

Clarence B. Randall

Clarence B. Randall has occupied a rare vantage point from which to view business morality. He is former president and chairman of the board of Inland Steel Company, which he joined in 1925, and has served three administrations as an expert on foreign economic policy. He is the author of The Folklore of Management *(1959). It is unlikely that management, whatever its prevailing practice, would dissent from his criticism. Disagreement is likely to come from those who believe that the kinds of practices he castigates are built into the "business system."*

. . . Industry in this country is facing a moral crisis. The American people are taking a new, hard look at us and are asking themselves whether by any chance the whole lot of us are dishonest.

They demand urgently to know whether we operate behind a pious façade, whether our public posture is a fraud, whether deep down inside we are completely antisocial in our purposes. We are not yet convicted in the public mind, but a heavy cloud of suspicion surrounds us.

We must face this issue squarely . . . In my opinion, we must at once do one of two things. If our ethical practices are in fact shameful, we must change them forthwith, and make it clear that we have done so. If conscience tells us that they are completely above reproach, we must offer a new declaration of faith to the American people, and then by our conduct demonstrate the complete integrity of our purposes.

No man of senior years, like myself, can fail to sense that the moral climate in industry today is greatly improved over what we knew in earlier years, but this is partly because it was so bad in the period when we first went to work. We remember all too vividly practices which prevailed then, and which we would now like to forget.

For example, in the steel industry, I knew a time when it was common for one company to endeavor continuously by subversive means to steal the research secrets of its competitors. This was done in many ways, with all the stealth of a Communist agent. Technicians in other laboratories would be suborned and for a fixed payment per month, delivered in rolls of bills at

[1]*The New York Times Magazine,* April 8, 1962, pp. 24 ff. Reprinted by permission.

secret rendezvous, would turn over copies of blueprints or duplicates of new formulae. A second and even more effective way was simply to hire away the chief chemist or other research officer by doubling his pay, on condition that he would bring his secrets with him.

During the Great Depression, these methods were applied to sales. The vice-president of a company whose pay had been severely cut was an easy mark for the competitor who offered a big increase. When he changed jobs, he brought his little black book with him, and revealed the secret rebates which he had been giving customers. The trouble was that his aroused former employer often hired him back at the end of the first year, and when he returned he crossed up his new employer and took his new little black book with him.

There was another kind of venality—a betrayal of trust within a company for a cold cash payment. I was once trapped in the midst of one such nasty situation where, for every carload of steel scrap shipped to the steel plant, the inspector was paid handsomely for not looking beneath the top layer. Nor was that enough. A further shocker was in store for me, because I found that the shipper who had bought the inspector had also bought the court.

Bribery of public officials, the crude buying of legislators, was also widely practiced in earlier days. The notorious black bag was not a fiction in my day but reality, and devious indeed were the mental processes by which otherwise high-minded men justified the practice. For example, I knew a company which for years secretly put a particular member of the legislature on its payroll for $400 a month (that was real money then) with the justification that he was making a great personal sacrifice in accepting the office. I do not recall, however, that he ever voted for a measure of which the company disapproved.

And I knew another corporation in which the officer who handled the taxes was directed by the president to get the assessment reduced, and not to report back. He did in fact get the assessment down. He did it by meeting the assessor in a hotel room. And he did not tell the boss what he had done —but he did tell me.

Now most of those crude and crass practices have disappeared from American business practices—most, but not all. For example, the large-scale pirating of trade secrets in big industry is no longer resorted to. In steel, at least, technical information is now openly and freely exchanged. Advances based upon research by one company become available to all. Competitors have learned that they gain more that way than they lose. Nevertheless, in new industries which depend heavily on design factors and advanced technology, or in fields where only a few large companies carry on research programs, I suspect that the stealing still goes on.

Graft, unhappily, is still practiced by many at the municipal level, in such cases as buying off an alderman for an alley permit and this is very wrong. Though undoubtedly rare, money may still sometimes actually pass to a member of a state legislature, or of Congress, to influence his attitude.

I regret, too, that in all candor I must record the unsavory fact that there is a related area of business endeavor where the state of morality is very low indeed, and where there is a stain on the conscience of industry which needs to be removed soon. I mean the bribery of officials in the governments of new countries in the underdeveloped parts of the world.

In the course of my government service, I visited many of these areas. I know whereof I speak, and I say that there are many otherwise respectable companies which still buy their way in when it comes to securing a mineral concession or establishing an operation in a remote part of the world.

This must stop, and it can only be accomplished by self-discipline. Surprisingly enough, I happen to have grave doubt whether it is a violation of any present Federal law for an American citizen to corrupt an officer of a foreign government, but that fact merely highlights the challenge to our business leadership. I reject the argument that other nations are doing it, and therefore we must if we are to compete. Better to lose the business than to deny our heritage. The entire prestige of our country, and its ability to preserve our way of life in the world, is at stake. Those precious values must not be jeopardized by individual dishonor.

In the host countries, someone always knows the facts. What could be more tragic than for us to lose an air base that is vital to our national security because of moral turpitude on the part of American business? What will be our position when some demagogue from the desert calls his people to arms with the cry "Drive the filthy Americans into the sea. We have been robbed of our ancient heritage"?

Either we have a code of morals, or we do not. If we do, it is for universal application, and must be adhered to in all circumstances, regardless of the impact on earnings. This is the acid test of our integrity.

That was the moral point at issue in the investigations of the electrical industry—setting artificially high prices to keep profits up. It is perhaps unfair to pass judgment upon those cases without personal knowledge of the facts, but who among us can avoid it, when so much is at stake?

For myself, there is no doubt whatever that serious mistakes were made. Things were done which have prejudiced the continuing development of the private-enterprise system, and this is bad for all of us. How could this have come to pass? How may one explain these incredible circumstances? All that an outsider may do is to speculate.

Conceivably, for example, these were mistakes of the head, and not of the heart, committed by overzealous executives. It might be argued that here were men who in their daily lives were decent, law-abiding citizens, and who responded to the highest loyalty they knew, the desire to advance the interests of their companies. In other words, it is possible that they put corporate welfare above that of their country merely because they knew no better. It is possible that they simply did not understand the vital function of a free market in a democratic society.

If this were the answer, it would still be bad. To hold the confidence of our public, we in industry must not only have the moral courage to do the right, but sufficient insight to know the right. Our minds must be clear, as well as our consciences.

This hypothesis does not ring true, however. These executives were men of long years of service and broad experience, and it is hard to believe that they did not know that they were violating the law. Our moral crisis is there, either way.

But beyond these proved and punished aberrations there are large, new, somewhat peripheral areas of moral problems, of such comparatively recent origin that the issues have not yet been sharply defined, nor full corrective measures taken. Here the impeccable conduct of the many is being placed in jeopardy by the rascality of the few.

This is a partial list:

(1) *Lack of truth in advertising.* There is still an occasional business buccaneer who misrepresents the quality of the product, or who understates the price by concealing the fact that there are indispensable accessories which will also be required.

(2) *The credit racket.* There are still unscrupulous vendors who overpersuade the unwary buyer of modest means by the no-payment-down, take-all-the-time-you-need pitch. The true interest charge on the deferred balance is not revealed, and the seller makes his money out of the financing of the debt rather than as legitimate profit on the merchandise.

(3) *The union agent racket.* There are still evil-minded employers who cross the palm of the organizer, and buy exemption from legitimate worker grievances, thus cheating the employes, and rejecting the responsibilities of orderly collective bargaining.

(4) *Denial of promotion on merit to minority groups.* There are still those who give lip service in public to the doctrine of fair opportunity for all workers, regardless of creed or color, but who deny it in actual practice.

(5) *Expense account cheating.* No well-informed observer can doubt for a moment that the Federal Government is still being deprived of large

sums of revenue by the unscrupulous padding of income-tax deductions claimed as business expenses. The honest citizen pays more than his share of the tax load when the man who cheats pays less.

In listing this catalogue of corporate sins one must, in fairness, point out that industry is not alone in having its moral lapses. The commercial world has no monopoly on character weakness. There are newspaper reporters who state as fact that for which they have no documentation; there are clergymen whose conduct is such that they have to be unfrocked; there are scholars who must be dismissed from faculties; there are surgeons who split fees, and lawyers who are disbarred.

But the human frailty of others can never justify moral turpitude in business. The American people are entitled to expect the very best from us at all times. We have no present alternative other than to submit forthwith all our practices to the most intensive re-examination, done in an atmosphere of heart-searching humility, and thereafter we must have the fortitude to do the right, wherever that may take us. We can and must set off a moral and spiritual reawakening which will touch every segment of American life.

Here is a unique challenge for our trade associations. Let our two great groups, the National Association of Manufacturers and the United States Chamber of Commerce, seize the initiative in denouncing obvious misconduct and in proclaiming new codes of ethical conduct. Then let the trade groups, industry by industry, promote the doing of the right as zealously as they now promote the sale of the product.

Above all, let each corporate officer determine in his own heart that never again will he put expediency above principle, never again let a chance for a quick profit stifle the dictates of his conscience.

Only thus can the survival of private enterprise in this troubled world be assured.

TELEVISION ON TRIAL

The effects of the free enterprise system or, as Max Lerner calls it, the "business spirit" or, to use Viereck's term, the "cash-nexus" are on full display in television broadcasting, which—whether we like it or not—provides a kind of showcase for our society. Most television stations depend on advertising revenue and are run as a private enterprise for a profit. How does this affect the quality or value of their contribution to the community? Here the business spirit has operated with nearly unrestrained exuberance; have its effects on the culture been good or bad? Here great corporations have an opportunity to display citizenship in a highly sensitive area; do they? Here a bewildering variety of skills is enlisted to influence our scale of preferences; quite apart from the question whether we have been bored or entertained, is the outcome a people whose tastes and values have been vulgarized or elevated? The statements which follow represent opposing answers to these questions by two highly qualified spokesmen.

THE BROADCASTERS ARE
PUBLIC TRUSTEES[1]

Newton N. Minow

Newton N. Minow, 36, a law partner of Adlai Stevenson, was appointed chairman of the Federal Communications Commission by President Kennedy. It would not be an overstatement to say that this, his maiden address, had a traumatic effect on the television industry. In commenting that Minow "has exercised greater influ-

---

[1]Address delivered to the 39th Annual Convention of the National Association of Broadcasters in Washington, D.C., May 9, 1961, and reprinted in *Vital Speeches of the Day,* June 15, 1961, pp. 533 ff. Reprinted by permission.

ence over broadcasting than the FCC has ever shown before" and that he "could justifiably take credit that his campaign . . . had forced the TV industry to think a little more about its responsibility to its audience," Time magazine probably reflects the verdict of most students of the television industry. Some, however, will have recourse to an old French proverb: "Plus cela change, plus c'est la même chose."

It may . . . come as a surprise to some of you, but I want you to know that you have my admiration and respect. Yours is a most honorable profession. Anyone who is in the broadcasting business has a tough row to hoe. You earn your bread by using public property. When you work in broadcasting you volunteer for public service, public pressure, and public regulation. You must compete with other attractions and other investments, and the only way you can do it is to prove to us every three years that you should have been in business in the first place.

I can think of easier ways to make a living.

But I cannot think of more satisfying ways.

I admire your courage—but that doesn't mean I would make life any easier for you. Your license lets you use the public's airwaves as Trustees for 180,000,000 Americans. The public is your beneficiary. If you want to stay on as Trustees, you must deliver a decent return to the public—not only to your stockholders. So, as a representative of the public, your health and your product are among my chief concerns.

As to your health: let's talk only of television today. 1960 gross broadcast revenues of the television industry were over $1,268,000,000; profit before taxes was $243,900,000, an average return on revenue of 19.2%. Compared with 1959, gross broadcast revenues were $1,163,900,000, and profit before taxes was $222,300,000, an average return on revenue of 19.1%. So, the percentage increase of total revenues from 1959 to 1960 was 9%, and the percentage increase of profit was 9.7%. This, despite a recession. For your investors, the price has indeed been right.

I have confidence in your health.

But not in your product.

It is with this and much more in mind that I come before you today.

One editorialist in the trade press wrote that "the FCC of the New Frontier is going to be one of the toughest FCC's in the history of broadcast regulation." If he meant that we intend to enforce the law in the public interest, let me make it perfectly clear that he is right—we do.

If he meant that we intend to muzzle or censor broadcasting, he is dead wrong.

It would not surprise me if some of you had expected me to come here today and say in effect, "Clean up your own house or the government will do it for you."

Well, in a limited sense, you would be right—I've just said it.

But I want to say to you earnestly that it is not in that spirit that I come before you today, nor is it in that spirit that I intend to serve the FCC.

I am in Washington to help broadcasting, not to harm it; to strengthen it, not weaken it; to reward it, not punish it; to encourage it, not threaten it; to stimulate it, not censor it.

Above all, I am here to uphold and protect the public interest.

What do we mean by "the public interest"? Some say the public interest is merely what interests the public.

I disagree.

So does your distinguished president, Governor Collins. In a recent speech he said, "Broadcasting to serve the public interest must have a soul and a conscience, a burning desire to excel, as well as to sell; the urge to build the character, citizenship and intellectual stature of people, as well as to expand the gross national product. . . . By no means do I imply that broadcasters disregard the public interest . . . But a much better job can be done, and should be done."

I could not agree more.

And I would add that in today's world, with chaos in Laos and the Congo aflame, with Communist tyranny on our Caribbean doorstep and relentless pressure on our Atlantic alliance, with social and economic problems at home of the gravest nature, yes, and with technological knowledge that makes it possible, as our President has said, not only to destroy our world but to destroy poverty around the world—in a time of peril and opportunity, the old complacent, unbalanced fare of Action-Adventure and Situation Comedies is simply not good enough.

Your industry possesses the most powerful voice in America. It has an inescapable duty to make that voice ring with intelligence and with leadership. In a few years, this exciting industry has grown from a novelty to an instrument of overwhelming impact on the American people. It should be making ready for the kind of leadership that newspapers and magazines assumed years ago, to make our people aware of their world.

Ours has been called the jet age, the atomic age, the space age. It is also, I submit, the television age. And just as history will decide whether the leaders of today's world employed the atom to destroy the world or rebuild it for mankind's benefit, so will history decide whether today's broadcasters employed their powerful voice to enrich the people or debase them.

If I seem to address myself chiefly to the problems of television, I don't want any of you radio broadcasters to think we've gone to sleep at your switch—we haven't. We still listen. But in recent years most of the controversies and cross-currents in broadcast programming have swirled around television. And so my subject today is the television industry and the public interest.[2]

Like everybody, I wear more than one hat. I am the Chairman of the FCC. I am also a television viewer and the husband and father of other television viewers. I have seen a great many television programs that seemed to me eminently worthwhile, and I am not talking about the much bemoaned good old days of Playhouse 90 and Studio One.

I am talking about this past season. Some were wonderfully entertaining, such as The Fabulous Fifties, the Fred Astaire Show, and the Bing Crosby Special; some were dramatic and moving, such as Conrad's Victory and Twilight Zone; some were marvelously informative, such as The Nation's Future, CBS Reports, and The Valiant Years. I could list many more —programs that I am sure everyone here felt enriched his own life and that of his family. When television is good, nothing—not the theatre, not the magazines or newspapers—nothing is better.

But when television is bad, nothing is worse. I invite you to sit down in front of your television set when your station goes on the air and stay there without a book, magazine, newspaper, profit and loss sheet or rating book to distract you—and keep your eyes glued to that set until the station signs off. I can assure you that you will observe a vast wasteland.

You will see a procession of game shows, violence, audience participation shows, formula comedies about totally unbelievable families, blood and thunder, mayhem, violence, sadism, murder, western badmen, western good men, private eyes, gangsters, more violence, and cartoons. And, endlessly, commercials—many screaming, cajoling, and offending. And most of all, boredom. True, you will see a few things you will enjoy. But they will be very, very few. And if you think I exaggerate, try it.

Is there one person in this room [who] claims that broadcasting can't do better?

Well, a glance at next season's proposed programming can give us little heart. Of 73½ hours of prime evening time, the networks have tentatively scheduled 59 hours to categories of "action-adventure," situation comedy, variety, quiz, and movies.

Is there one network president in this room who claims he can't do better?

Gentlemen, your trust accounting with your beneficiaries is overdue.

---

[2][EDITOR'S NOTE: A year later, addressing the same audience, Minow turned his attention to radio. Noting that there are three times as many radio stations now as there were at the end of World War II, he added with some astringency: "In too many communities to twist the radio dial today is to be shoved through a bazaar, a clamorous casbah of pitchmen and commercials which plead, bleat, pressure, whistle, groan and shout. Too many stations have turned themselves into publicly franchised jukeboxes." He added: "Moreover, radio stations do not fade away, they just multiply."]

Never have so few owed so much to so many.

Why is so much of television so bad? I have read many answers: demands of your advertisers; competition for ever higher ratings; the need always to attract a mass audience; the high cost of television programs; the insatiable appetite for programming material—these are some of them. Unquestionably, these are tough problems not susceptible to easy answers.

But I am not convinced that you have tried hard enough to solve them.

I do not accept the idea that the present over-all programming is aimed accurately at the public taste. The ratings tell us only that some people have their television sets turned on and of that number, so many are tuned to one channel and so many to another. They don't tell us what the public might watch if they were offered half a dozen additional choices. A rating, at best, is an indication of how many people saw what you gave them. Unfortunately, it does not reveal the depth of the penetration, or the intensity of reaction, and it never reveals what the acceptance would have been if what you gave them had been better—if all the forces of art and creativity and daring and imagination had been unleashed. I believe in the people's good sense and good taste, and I am not convinced that the people's taste is as low as you assume.

My concern with the rating services is not with their accuracy. Perhaps they are accurate. I really don't know. What, then, is wrong with the ratings? It's not been their accuracy—it's been their use.

Certainly, I hope you will agree that ratings should have little influence where children are concerned. The best estimates indicate that during the hours of 5 to 6 P.M. 60% of your audience is composed of children under 12. And most young children today, believe it or not, spend as much time watching television as they do in the schoolroom. I repeat—let that sink in —most young children today spend as much time watching television as they do in the schoolroom. It used to be said that there were three great influences on a child: home, school, and church. Today, there is a fourth great influence, and you ladies and gentlemen control it.

If parents, teachers, and ministers conducted their responsibilities by following the ratings, children would have a steady diet of ice cream, school holidays, and no Sunday School. What about your responsibilities? Is there no room on television to teach, to inform, to uplift, to stretch, to enlarge the capacities of our children? Is there no room for programs deepening their understanding of children in other lands? Is there no room for a children's news show explaining something about the world to them at their level of understanding? Is there no room for reading the great literature of the past, teaching them the great traditions of freedom? There are some fine children's shows, but they are drowned out in the massive doses of cartoons, violence, and more violence. Must these be your trademarks? Search your consciences and see if you cannot offer more to your beneficiaries whose future you guide so many hours each and every day.

What about adult programming and ratings? You know, newspaper publishers take popularity ratings too. The answers are pretty clear: it is almost always the comics, followed by the advice to the lovelorn columns. But, ladies and gentlemen, the news is still on the front page of all newspapers, the editorials are not replaced by more comics, the newspapers have not become one long collection of advice to the lovelorn. Yet newspapers do not need a license from the government to be in business—they do not use public property. But in television—where your responsibilities as public trustees are so plain, the moment that the ratings indicate that westerns are popular there are new imitations of westerns on the air faster than the old coaxial cable could take us from Hollywood to New York. Broadcasting cannot continue to live by the numbers. Ratings ought to be the slave of the broadcaster, not his master. And you and I both know that the rating services themselves would agree.

Let me make clear that what I am talking about is balance. I believe that the public interest is made up of many interests. There are many people in this great country and you must serve all of us. You will get no argument from me if you say that, given a choice between a western and a symphony, more people will watch the western. I like westerns and private eyes too— but a steady diet for the whole country is obviously not in the public interest. We all know that people would more often prefer to be entertained than stimulated or informed. But your obligations are not satisfied if you look only to popularity as a test of what to broadcast. You are not only in show business; you are free to communicate ideas as well as relaxation. You must provide a wider range of choices, more diversity, more alternatives. It is not enough to cater to the nation's whims—you must also serve the nation's needs.

And I would add this—that if some of you persist in a relentless search for the highest rating and the lowest common denominator, you may very well lose your audience. Because, to paraphrase a great American who was recently my law partner, the people are wise, wiser than some of the broadcasters—and politicians—think.

As you may have gathered, I would like to see television improved. But how is this to be brought about? By voluntary action by the broadcasters themselves? By direct government intervention? Or how?

Let me address myself now to my role not as a viewer but as Chairman of the FCC. I could not, if I would, chart for you this afternoon in detail all of the actions I contemplate. Instead, I want to make clear some of the fundamental principles which guide me.

First: the people own the air. They own it as much in prime evening time as they do at 6 o'clock Sunday morning. For every hour that the people give you—you owe them something. I intend to see that your debt is paid with service.

Second: I think it would be foolish and wasteful for us to continue any worn-out wrangle over the problems of payola, rigged quiz shows, and other mistakes of the past. There are laws on the books which we will enforce. But there is no chip on my shoulder. We live together in perilous, uncertain times; we face together staggering problems; and we must not waste much time now by re-hashing the clichés of past controversy. To quarrel over the past is to lose the future.

Third: I believe in the free enterprise system. I want to see broadcasting improved and I want you to do the job. I am proud to champion your cause. It is not rare for American businessmen to serve a public trust. Yours is a special trust because it is imposed by law.

Fourth: I will do all I can to help educational television. There are still not enough educational stations, and major centers of the country still lack usable educational channels. If there were a limited number of printing presses in this country, you may be sure that a fair proportion of them would be put to educational use. Educational television has an enormous contribution to make to the future, and I intend to give it a hand along the way. If there is not a nation-wide educational television system in this country, it will not be the fault of the FCC.

Fifth: I am unalterably opposed to governmental censorship. There will be no suppression of programming which does not meet with bureaucratic tastes. Censorship strikes at the tap root of our free society.

Sixth: I did not come to Washington to idly observe the squandering of the public's airwaves. The squandering of our airwaves is no less important than the lavish waste of any precious natural resource. I intend to take the job of Chairman of the FCC very seriously. I believe in the gravity of my own particular sector of the New Frontier. There will be times perhaps when you will consider that I take myself or my job *too* seriously. Frankly, I don't care if you do. For I am convinced that either one takes this job seriously—or one can be seriously taken.

Now, how will these principles be applied? Clearly, at the heart of the FCC's authority lies its power to license, to renew or fail to renew, or to revoke a license. As you know, when your license comes up for renewal, your performance is compared with your promises. I understand that many people feel that in the past licenses were often renewed *pro forma*. I say to you now: renewal will not be *pro forma* in the future. There is nothing permanent or sacred about a broadcast license.

But simply matching promises and performance is not enough. I intend to do more. I intend to find out whether the people care. I intend to find out whether the community which each broadcaster serves believes he has been serving the public interest. When a renewal is set down for hearing, I intend—wherever possible—to hold a well-advertised public hearing, right in the community you have promised to serve. I want the people who own the air and the homes that television enters to tell you and the FCC what's been going on. I want the people—if they are truly interested in the service you give them—to make notes, document cases, tell us the facts. For those few of you who really believe that the public interest is merely what interests the public—I hope that these hearings will arouse no little interest.

The FCC has a fine reserve of monitors—almost 180 million Americans gathered around 56 million sets. If you want those monitors to be your friends at court—it's up to you.

Some of you may say—"Yes, but I still do not know where the line is between a grant of a renewal and the hearing you just spoke of." My answer is: Why should you want to know how close you can come to the edge of the cliff? What the Commission asks of you is to make a conscientious, good faith effort to serve the public interest. Every one of you serves a community in which the people would benefit by educational, religious, instructive or other public service programming. Every one of you serves an area which has local needs—as to local elections, controversial issues, local news, local talent. Make a serious, genuine effort to put on that programming. When you do, you will not be playing brinkmanship with the public interest.

What I've been saying applies to broadcast stations. Now a station break for the networks:

You know your importance in this great industry. Today, more than one-half of all hours of television station programming comes from the networks; in prime time, this rises to more than three-fourths of the available hours.

You know that the FCC has been studying network operations for some time. I intend to press this to a speedy conclusion with useful results. I can tell you right now, however, that I am deeply concerned with concentration of power in the hands of the networks. As a result, too many local stations have foregone any efforts at local programming, with little use of live talent and local service. Too many local stations operate with one hand on the network switch and the other on a projector loaded with old movies. We want the individual stations to be free to meet their legal responsibilities to serve their communities.

I join Governor Collins in his views so well expressed to the advertisers who use the public air. I urge the networks to join him and undertake a very special mission on behalf of this industry: you can tell your advertisers, "This is the high quality we are going to serve—take it or other people will. If you think you can find a better place to move automobiles, cigarettes and soap—go ahead and try."

Tell your sponsors to be less concerned with costs per thousand and more concerned with understanding per millions. And remind your stockholders that an investment in broadcasting is buying a share in public responsibility.

The networks can start this industry on the road to freedom from the dictatorship of numbers.

But there is more to the problem than network influences on stations or advertiser influences on networks. I know the problems networks face in trying to clear some of their best programs—the informational programs that exemplify public service. They are your finest hours—whether sustaining or commercial, whether regularly scheduled or special—these are the signs that broadcasting knows the way to leadership. They make the public's trust in you a wise choice.

They should be seen. As you know, we are readying for use new forms by which broadcast stations will report their programming to the Commission. You probably also know that special attention will be paid in these reports to public service programming. I believe that stations taking network service should also be required to report the extent of the local clearance of network public service programming, and when they fail to clear them, they should explain why. If it is to put on some outstanding local program, this is one reason. But, if it is simply to carry some old movie, that is an entirely different matter. The Commission should consider such clearance reports carefully when making up its mind about the licensee's over-all programming.

We intend to move—and as you know, indeed the FCC was rapidly moving in other new areas before the new administration arrived in Washington. And I want to pay my public respects to my very able predecessor, Fred Ford, and my colleagues on the Commission who have welcomed me to the FCC with warmth and cooperation.

We have approved an experiment with pay TV, and in New York we are testing the potential of UHF broadcasting. Either or both of these may revolutionize television. Only a foolish prophet would venture to guess the direction they will take, and their effect. But we intend that they shall be explored fully—for they are part of broadcasting's New Frontier.

The questions surrounding pay TV are largely economic. The questions surrounding UHF are largely technological. We are going to give the infant pay TV a chance to prove whether it can offer a useful service; we are going to protect it from those who would strangle it in its crib.

As for UHF, I'm sure you know about our test in the canyons of New York City. We will take every possible positive step to break through the allocations barrier into UHF. We will put this sleeping giant to use and in the years ahead we may have twice as many channels operating in cities where now there are only two or three. We may have a half dozen networks instead of three.

I have told you that I believe in the free enterprise system. I believe that most of television's problems stem from lack of competition. This is the importance of UHF to me: with more channels on the air, we will be able to provide every community with enough stations to offer service to all parts of the public. Programs with a mass market appeal required by mass product advertisers certainly will still be available. But other stations will recognize the need to appeal to more limited markets and to special tastes. In this way, we can all have a much wider range of programs.

Television should thrive on this competition—and the country should benefit from alternative sources of service to the public. And—Governor Collins—I hope the NAB will benefit from many new members.

Another and perhaps the most important frontier: television will rapidly join the parade into space. International television will be with us soon. No one knows how long it will be until a broadcast from a studio in New York will be viewed in India as well as in Indiana, will be seen in the Congo as it is seen in Chicago. But as surely as we are meeting here today, that day will come—and once again our world will shrink.

What will the people of other countries think of us when they see our western badmen and good men punching each other in the jaw in between the shooting? What will the Latin American or African child learn of America from our great communications industry? We cannot permit television in its present form to be our voice overseas.

There is your challenge to leadership. You must reexamine some fundamentals of your industry. You must open your minds and open your hearts to the limitless horizons of tomorrow.

I can suggest some words that should serve to guide you:

"Television and all who participate in it are jointly accountable to the American public for respect for the special needs of children, for community responsibility, for the advancement of education and culture, for the acceptability of the program materials chosen, for decency and decorum in production, and for propriety in advertising. This responsibility cannot be discharged by any given group of programs, but can be discharged only through the highest standards of respect for the American home, applied to every moment of every program presented by television.

"Program materials should enlarge the horizons of the viewer, provide him with wholesome entertainment, afford helpful stimulation, and remind him of the responsibilities which the citizen has towards his society."

These words are not mine. They are yours. They are taken literally from your own Television Code. They reflect the leadership and aspirations of your own great industry. I urge you to respect them as I do. And I urge you to respect the intelligent and farsighted leadership of Governor LeRoy Collins, and to make this meeting a creative act. I urge you at this meeting and, after you leave, back home, at your stations and your networks, to strive ceaselessly to improve your product and to better serve your viewers, the American people.

I hope that we at the FCC will not allow ourselves to become so bogged down in the mountain of papers, hearings, memoranda, orders, and the daily routine that we close our eyes to the wider view of the public interest. And I hope that you broadcasters will not permit yourselves to become so absorbed in the chase for ratings, sales, and profits that you lose this wider view. Now more than ever before in broadcasting's history the times demand the best of all of us.

We need imagination in programming, not sterility; creativity, not imitation; experimentation, not conformity; excellence, not mediocrity. Television is filled with creative, imaginative people. You must strive to set them free.

Television in its young life has had many hours of greatness—its Victory at Sea, its Army-McCarthy hearings, its Peter Pan, its Kraft Theaters, its See It Now, its Project 20, the World Series, its political conventions and campaigns, The Great Debates—and it has had its endless hours of mediocrity and its moments of public disgrace. There are estimates that today the average viewer spends about 200 minutes daily with television, while the average reader spends 38 minutes with magazines and 40 minutes with newspapers. Television has grown faster than a teen-ager, and now it is time to grow up.

What you gentlemen broadcast through the people's air affects the people's taste, their knowledge, their opinions, their understanding of themselves and of their world, and their future.

The power of instantaneous sight and sound is without precedent in mankind's history. This is an awesome power. It has limitless capabilities for good—and for evil. And it carries with it awesome responsibilities, responsibilities which you and I cannot escape.

IN DEFENSE OF TELEVISION[1]

Frank Stanton

Frank Stanton is president of Columbia Broadcasting Company. He and General Sarnoff may be regarded as the two chief spokesmen for the television industry. In effect, his is the television industry's response to Mr. Minow's "wasteland" speech and the criticism of program content that Mr. Minow was voicing.

---

[1]Benjamin Franklin Lecture, University of Pennsylvania, December 7, 1961. Reprinted by permission.

Television . . . is a medium bringing the sights and sounds of every area of life into ninety per cent of America's 52 million homes. Here is a medium obliged, by its nature, to provide something for everybody in a heterogeneous nation of 185 million people. Here is a medium calling for resources of untold millions of dollars, unprecedented in communications, to support it. Here is a medium as fraught with the public interest as printing was in Franklin's day, and to which freedom is as vital. Here is a medium on the verge of directly linking together all the continents of a troubled and divided world. . . .

Today television is very nearly at the beginning of its international era. It has, I think, an enormous potential contribution to make towards world order. But American television faces that era with many unresolved problems. It is, of course, inevitable that a medium that has grown so fast should create unique problems just as it has presented unique opportunities.

Some of them are transitory in nature. Some are fundamental. In an impatient society, hard pressed with the ugly potentials of a cold war, these fundamental problems can invite dangerously precipitous solutions, superficially attractive perhaps but full of land mines.

Chief among these fundamental problems is the arrival at standards for programming. Whose standards should they be? How should they be determined? Can you trust the people to know what is good for them? Or must they be told by some authority? I want to discuss this problem against the total context—social, cultural, economic and political—in which television must function, and against the background of a free society that has been particularly alert to abridgments of the freedom of communications —whether of the press, of speech, of assembly, or of any extension of these that technical developments since the Bill of Rights have made possible.

The volume and variety of programming produced by the three television networks are, I think, wholly without precedent in the history of communications. In the month of November, for example, the three networks provided their affiliates with over a thousand hours of programming. This consisted chiefly of 99½ hours of actual news events and straight news broadcasts, 23¾ hours of documentary news, 19 hours of discussion, 45 hours of education and religion, 77 hours of sports, 63¼ hours of general drama, 8 hours of panel shows, 84 hours of situation comedy, 42½ hours of variety, 84¾ hours of serial drama, and 74¾ hours of children's programs. Of the total, 56 hours were mysteries and 60½ hours were Westerns—a combined total of 11 per cent of all the programming.

The range of subjects and material that appeared on the three networks in November was extremely wide. There were biographical studies of such diverse men as U. S. Grant and Vincent Van Gogh, Al Smith and Sinclair Lewis. There were several special half-hour biographies of Speaker Sam Rayburn. There were long reports on such countries as Germany,

Spain, Yugoslavia, and France. There were interviews with men repre-
senting a provocative cross section of the world today: Prime Minister
Nehru, Igor Stravinsky, Hugh Gaitskell, John Kenneth Galbraith, Bertrand
Russell. Full-length dramatic productions included Hans Conried and Jane
Wyatt in *Little Lost Sheep,* Julie Harris in *Victoria Regina,* and Fred Astaire
in *Moment of Decision.*

It is true, of course, that much of the television fare of the month was
light. But most fiction published every month is light reading. It is relevant
to remember, too, that of the hundreds of popular magazines published in
this country, only four are news magazines and only four more are of generally serious editorial content. And many Sunday newspapers, with from
sixteen to eighteen pages devoted to sports and amusements, have a single
page devoted to editorials and a single column to education.

The press in this country, nevertheless, is carrying out its responsibilities far better than that of any other country and better than it ever has
before, given the economic and social context in which it must function.
Newspapers and magazines must attract and hold their readers. They must
attract and hold their advertisers. They have arrived at patterns of content
after a good deal of tough trial and error. They are not, of course, an exact
parallel to television, for they are not subject to licensing; most publications, however, are objects of partial government subsidy through advan-
tageous postal rates.

Like the magazines and newspapers, television fills a dual role of entertaining and informing, diverting and instructing, relaxing and stimulating.
There are those, I am sure, who would have television exclusively informative and instructive. There are those, too, who would have it exclusively
entertaining and diverting. But the economic demands of the medium and
the capacities and interests of human beings require it to be both. Despite
this diversity of taste, somebody has to set standards. Broadcasters have
turned to the general public. In the absence of the kind of physical circulation that publications have to measure their public acceptance, there is a
nationwide rating service to provide the networks with means of determining
public acceptance of programs. This does not mean that no network would
broadcast a program that does not attract a high rating. This is obviously
not so, since year after year many important broadcasts, particularly of an
informational character, do go on the air in spite of consistently low
ratings.

In October, for example, the CBS Television Network broadcast the
first of a series of three hour-long interviews with General Eisenhower on
the problems of the Presidency. The first was universally acclaimed by the
critics. It was on the air in prime evening time. Its rating indicated that
some six million people saw the broadcast as compared to 21 million who
tuned to the suspense drama and 26 million to the popular song program
that were on the air at the same time on the other two networks.

Now there are several ways that you can look at that figure, six million. Compared to the audience of a popular entertainment television show, it is small. Compared to the audience of a best selling book, whether informative or escape fiction, it is gigantic. Compared to the largest metropolitan newspapers, it ranges from three to ten times their daily circulation. Now consider what an hour-long discussion is equal to in terms of the written word. It is about nine thousand words—twenty-seven typed pages. So the real gauge of public interest in what General Eisenhower had to say on the problems he faced as President can be judged by the fact that more people, by many times over, were exposed to twenty-seven pages of comment on serious matters than read any newspapers, or any best seller. We broadcast a second conversation with General Eisenhower on Thanksgiving night, and we are scheduled to broadcast another early in 1962.

On December first, the CBS Television Network broadcast a Young People's Concert of the New York Philharmonic in prime evening time. Although we knew that this concert would interest fewer viewers than RAWHIDE, which it displaced that evening, we believed that there was enough following of good serious music in America to justify the experiment of making such a distinguished orchestra available to the family in prime time. As it turned out, 40 times as many people heard the Philharmonic that night as heard it during the entire season at Carnegie Hall last year. But we were certainly not under any illusion that there would be more than sing along with Mitch every week.

This illustrates, I think, the kind of perplexing questions that are evoked by the phrase "meeting the standards set by the people." Should we meet the standards set by *most* of the people *all* of the time? I think that the answer to that is clearly No. We must be constantly aware that ours is a most varied population, with a wide range of degrees of sophistication, of education, of interest, of tastes. We must make an effort to accommodate that endless variety. But we must do it with some sort of scale and balance in mind. For the second perplexing question is: At what point should a mass medium stop moving towards the interests of a relative few? How few is the "relative few"?

I think that it would be a misuse of the air waves, for example, to carry very esoteric, avant-garde material that experienced observers know would be meaningless to all but a handful of the initiated. On the other hand, there is a great and restless potential in the American people to broaden their cultural horizons. Television can, and does, play an enormous role in stimulating that potential. I don't think, however, that these stirrings are visited upon all of the people, or even most of them, at the same time. And so we have to experiment. We know pretty clearly, after a reasonable trial, when a program of popular entertainment registers with the people. We assume that if it does, they are entitled to see it and we ought to continue it. We assume that if a vast majority of the people vote against it, we ought to discontinue it and try something else. . . .

I don't know any satisfactory or democratic alternative to letting the people set the standards of programming by the simple act of accepting or rejecting what is offered. It has been said that the public is getting no choice of kinds of television fare, but with rare exceptions in the schedules this is simply not the case. It has also been said—contradictory as it may sound —that television is ruled by two tyrannies: the tyranny of the majority, and the tyranny of the mercantilists; that, on the one hand, its sole purpose is to drug the great mass of citizens and, on the other hand, it is the tool exclusively of greedy men who will foist anything on the public if it will serve their purpose in selling things that nobody wants. . . .

The tyranny of the majority is, of course, a classical dilemma of the democratic state. It has been asserted from ancient times that it leads to a rule of mediocrity, or even of the lowest common denominator. It seems to me that the American political experience—and I believe also the American social and cultural experiences—have minimized this danger by a widely respected recognition of the rights and interests of minorities. . . .

The unique problem in this respect with regard to television is that, both because of the technical limitations on the number of channels and because of the economic demands of the medium, it is impossible to have separate channels to serve every worthwhile minority whatever its size.[2] . . .

Television is concerned with the relative size of cultural minorities, because television has a primary responsibility to serve more than quantitatively minute minorities. It is unlikely that we will do anything to stimulate discussion of the use of classical images in early eighteenth century poetry—although I am quite sure that somewhere there are several passionately dedicated students of the subject. But we would do something about the general subject of art in American life, even though an overwhelming share of the audience is not interested. . . .

We all know that many . . . programs will not attract a large share of the viewers watching television at the time that they are on the air. They . . . are broadcast because the interest of significant minorities are recognized by broadcasters. But the broadcasters are thoroughly justified, under any principles of cultural democracy, in basing such recognition to some extent on reasonable assurance that the program is not so specialized as virtually to black out the station. In fact, responsible programming should

---

[2][EDITOR'S NOTE: Developments are under way that, by addition of ultra-high-frequency (UHF) bands, will greatly increase the number of available channels. It may be noted also that all major cities in the United States (with the temporary exception of Los Angeles) have educational TV stations.]

have the opposite effect and invite the many to come in with the interested few—and get something out of it.

The blanket charge that the trouble with television is that it permits the tyrannizing of the public by the manufacturers of consumer goods and their advertising agencies—in league with the broadcasters and in contempt of any except mercantile values—seems to me to impede any useful discussion. We live in a mercantile society, and our material life is based on the sale and purchase of goods and services. This is not unique to our century or to our land. The development of mercantilism has coincided in modern history with the development of democracy—not because it was a philosophic ideal but because it worked best, even if imperfectly, with democratic institutions. The reason, of course, is that, for all its faults, mercantilism is not categorical, not authoritative. It is open-ended and gives room to move around economically; and, without that, political democracy would be meaningless in practical life.

. . . the advertiser has no immunity from the verdict of the public. Every time his program is on the air, it is submitted to the viewer's vote. If it lost or never attained that vote, it would go off the air with absolute inevitability. And so again we get back to the fundamental question: Should it be the public or should it be some authority—whether in the government or a czar in the industry or some independent commission—that makes the verdict?

The public verdict is, I have no doubt, the safest and surest, the most valid and most enduring, one. But it has its price. It is less swift and less efficient, but it shares such limitations with all other procedural aspects of the democratic life. We in America have over and over again faced that particular dilemma, and we have refused to put a premium on speed and efficiency at any cost. . . .

A decade from now, if the public verdict prevails, television will be unrecognizable from what we have today. The medium will change because there is a constant, slow but inevitable upward movement in the standards and interests and capacities of a free people. If this were not so, the American experience would be meaningless, for life consists in growth. If we say that it is not so, if we start making exceptions, we are losing faith in the democratic dynamic. If we liken the mass of people and their ability to make their own decisions to unsupervised children and their desire for a constant diet of sweets, we are striking at the heart of what a democracy is all about —that the people, whatever their temporary errors or inadequacies, are, in the long run, the best judges of their own interests, and that they will make themselves heard.

In a pluralistic society like ours there are a great many additional built-in safeguards against persistent excesses. These are far more effective over the long haul than paternal authority. The variety of pressures that make themselves felt in such a society—civic organizations, academic groups, churches, the newspapers, articulate and forceful individuals—are the indirect influences that set the pace for the evolution of culture in a democracy. The important thing is that essential freedom remains—there is freedom to yield to pressures or to resist them, to respect those that seem enlightened and to ignore those that seem self-serving, to make mistakes, to take risks. All this takes time, and all this involves the chance of error. But there is no finality about it. And *that* is the rub with any pressure stemming from authority. The pressures normal in a democracy say, "You should." The pressure of authority says, "You shall."

We have also on the side of the public verdict the continued rise in the educational level of the people: they are better qualified each year to make the verdict. Isn't this—and not salvation by authority—our real, in fact our only, hope?

The material available on the television networks pretty much parallels, in kind, the material that characterizes such other mass media as the paperback book—the rise of which chronologically has matched that of television and which now sells 294 million copies annually. Reassuring as it is to know that you can get Plato's dialogues or Trevelyan's histories in inexpensive editions at Liggett's, it is still not surprising that Mickey Spillane remains the all-time best seller. Or that, of the 248 new titles in paperback fiction in the present fall season, 92, or 37 per cent, are Westerns, adventures and mysteries. Or even that the majority of the other titles are obviously light romances and other escape fiction.

But I would think that a literary critic would be something less than perceptive if he picked up the first fifty titles and used them as a base for a report on the achievement of the American novel. I would question also the judgment of an historian who concluded that a sound basis for appraising the role of the magazine in American life was to read indiscriminately every magazine that he found on the first shelf of his neighborhood newsstand. Such a method would be considered an aberration in critical methodology and its results could not be taken seriously.

But isn't this exactly what has happened in the case of television? The process by which it was concluded that television programming was "a vast wasteland" was described in these words: ". . . sit down in front of your television set when your station goes on the air . . . and keep your eyes glued to that set until the station signs off." A writer in a series for a magazine with a long history of Westerns and mysteries, began with the same specious approach: ". . . arose at five-thirty . . . turned the family television set to Channel 5, sat down in front of it and stayed there until Channel 5 went off the air twenty hours later."

The danger of this kind of sensationalized and oversimplified approach, with its broad brush conclusions, is not only that it grotesquely distorts the situation as it is, a clear perception of which is necessary to improvement, but also that it invites impulsive measures directed at making fundamental changes on the ground that any change is a change for the better. Actually, the only change that I have seen suggested is that the government supervise programming by use of its licensing power and by regulating a major program source, the networks.

How much improvement can either of these really bring about? If government authority sets standards, qualitative or quantitative, for television programming, whose standards are they going to be? The chairman of a commission? A majority of a commission? A Congressional committee?

You would have authoritative standards that would stifle creativity. You would have a rigidity that would discourage experimentation. You would have the subjective judgment of a small group imposed on the many. And you would have the constant danger of the misuse of the medium for political purposes.

Television does need improving. So do private colleges and charitable organizations. So do motion pictures and magazines. So do typewriters and cameras. All these have improved immeasurably over the years, and they will improve further. But they did not improve because some central authority said they must. They improved because they had elbow room to move forward in response to the demands put upon them and the new opportunities that new conditions brought them. Are we so bereft of that trust in the people . . . that we must now turn over the substance of the most promising medium we have to the control of government because the people do not know what is good for them? I think not.

THE ETHICS OF PERSUASION

The question of business and morality and corporate citizenship is hardly separable from the more specific issue of how private enterprise conducts one of its two most important activities. As every commercial on television reminds us, it is engaged in *selling* as well as producing—and this involves making representations to the buying public. Are these representations, whether through advertisements, labels, or simple statements concerning the rate of interest charged for a loan, honest or dishonest? This question should focus not on marginal practices that are illegal, or universally characterized as shady even by those who engage in them, but on the more or less general conduct of selling as it prevails in our economy.

THE ARTS OF SELLING[1]

Aldous Huxley

Aldous Huxley is one of the great humanists of our time. Novelist, essayist, poet, dramatist, he is also justly called a humanist because he is interested in people and what happens to them. This interest extends from (quite literally) improving their sight (The Art of Seeing) *to improving their vision* (The Perennial Philosophy). *Of his many works the best known are no doubt* Point Counter Point *and* Brave New World. *In* Brave New World, *written in 1931, he prophesied for the sixth or seventh century "A.F. (After Ford)" the coming of a completely organized society with, in his summary words, a "scientific caste system, the abolition of free will by methodical conditioning, servitude made acceptable by regular*

[1]From *Brave New World Revisited* by Aldous Huxley (New York: Harper & Row, Inc., 1958), pp. 58–71. Copyright © 1958 by Aldous Huxley. Reprinted by permission of Harper & Row, Publishers.

doses of chemically induced happiness, . . . orthodoxies drummed in by nightly courses of sleep-teaching. . . ." The depression-ridden world of the 1930's was, he says, "a nightmare of too little order," the world of the seventh century, A.F., of too much. He had hoped that during the long interval in between the more fortunate third of the human race would make the best of both worlds. He is no longer so sure, and in Brave New World Revisited, *from which the selection below is taken, he tells us why. Among the uncontrolled impersonal forces that he finds accelerating the speed with which his depressing prophecies are being brought to pass is modern advertising.*

The survival of democracy depends on the ability of large numbers of people to make realistic choices in the light of adequate information. A dictatorship, on the other hand, maintains itself by censoring or distorting the facts, and by appealing, not to reason, not to enlightened self-interest, but to passion and prejudice, to the powerful "hidden forces," as Hitler called them, present in the unconscious depths of every human mind.

In the West, democratic principles are proclaimed and many able and conscientious publicists do their best to supply electors with adequate information and to persuade them, by rational argument, to make realistic choices in the light of that information. All this is greatly to the good. But unfortunately propaganda in the Western democracies, above all in America, has two faces and a divided personality. In charge of the editorial department there is often a democratic Dr. Jekyll—a propagandist who would be very happy to prove that John Dewey had been right about the ability of human nature to respond to truth and reason. But this worthy man controls only a part of the machinery of mass communication. In charge of advertising we find an anti-democratic, because anti-rational, Mr. Hyde— or rather a Dr. Hyde, for Hyde is now a Ph.D. in psychology and has a master's degree as well in the social sciences. This Dr. Hyde would be very unhappy indeed if everybody always lived up to John Dewey's faith in human nature. Truth and reason are Jekyll's affair, not his. Hyde is a motivation analyst, and his business is to study human weaknesses and failings, to investigate those unconscious desires and fears by which so much of men's conscious thinking and overt doing is determined. And he does this, not in the spirit of the moralist who would like to make people better, or of the physician who would like to improve their health, but simply in order to find out the best way to take advantage of their ignorance and to exploit their irrationality for the pecuniary benefit of his employers. But after all, it may be argued, "capitalism is dead, consumerism is king"—and consumerism requires the services of expert salesmen versed in all the arts (including the more insidious arts) of persuasion. Under a free enterprise system commercial propaganda by any and every means is absolutely indispensable. But the indispensable is not necessarily the desirable. What is demonstrably good in the sphere of economics may be far from good for men and women as voters or even as human beings. An earlier, more moralistic generation would have been profoundly shocked by the bland cynicism of the motivation analysts. Today we read a book like Mr. Vance Packard's *The Hidden Persuaders,* and are more amazed than horrified, more resigned than indignant. Given Freud, given Behaviorism, given the mass producer's chronically desperate need for mass consumption, this is the sort of thing that is only to be expected. But what, we may ask, is the sort of thing that is to be expected in the future? Are Hyde's activities compatible in the long run with Jekyll's? Can a campaign in favor of rationality be successful in the teeth of another and even more vigorous campaign in favor of irrationality? These are questions which, for the moment, I shall not attempt to answer, but shall leave hanging, so to speak, as a backdrop to our discussion of the methods of mass persuasion in a technologically advanced democratic society.

The task of the commercial propagandist in a democracy is in some ways easier and in some ways more difficult than that of a political propagandist employed by an established dictator or a dictator in the making. It is easier inasmuch as almost everyone starts out with a prejudice in favor of beer, cigarettes and iceboxes, whereas almost nobody starts out with a prejudice in favor of tyrants. It is more difficult inasmuch as the commercial propagandist is not permitted, by the rules of his particular game, to appeal to the more savage instincts of his public. The advertiser of dairy products would dearly love to tell his readers and listeners that all their troubles are caused by the machinations of a gang of godless international margarine manufacturers, and that it is their patriotic duty to march out and burn the oppressors' factories. This sort of thing, however, is ruled out, and he must be content with a milder approach. But the mild approach is less exciting than the approach through verbal or physical violence. In the long run, anger and hatred are self-defeating emotions. But in the short run they pay high dividends in the form of psychological and even (since they release large quantities of adrenalin and noradrenalin) physiological satisfaction. People may start out with an initial prejudice against tyrants; but when tyrants or would-be tyrants treat them to adrenalin-releasing propaganda about the wickedness of their enemies—particularly of enemies weak enough to be persecuted—they are ready to follow him with enthusiasm. In his speeches Hitler kept repeating such words as "hatred," "force," "ruthless," "crush," "smash"; and he would accompany these violent words with even more violent gestures. He would yell, he would scream, his veins would swell, his face would turn purple. Strong emotion (as every actor and dramatist knows) is in the highest degree contagious. Infected by the malignant frenzy of the orator, the audience would groan and sob and scream in an orgy of uninhibited passion. And these orgies were so enjoyable that most of those who had experienced them eagerly came back for more. Almost all of us long for peace and freedom; but very few of us have much enthusiasm for the thoughts, feelings and actions that make for peace and freedom. Conversely almost nobody wants war or tyranny; but a great many people find an intense pleasure in the thoughts, feelings and actions that make for war and tyranny. These thoughts, feelings and actions are too dangerous to be exploited for commercial purposes. Accepting this handicap, the advertising man must do the best he can with the less intoxicating emotions, the quieter forms of irrationality.

Effective rational propaganda becomes possible only when there is a clear understanding, on the part of all concerned, of the nature of symbols and of their relations to the things and events symbolized. Irrational propaganda depends for its effectiveness on a general failure to understand the nature of symbols. Simple-minded people tend to equate the symbol with what it stands for, to attribute to things and events some of the qualities expressed by the words in terms of which the propagandist has chosen, for his own purposes, to talk about them. Consider a simple example. Most cosmetics are made of lanolin, which is a mixture of purified wool fat and water beaten up into an emulsion. This emulsion has many valuable properties: it penetrates the skin, it does not become rancid, it is mildly antiseptic and so forth. But the commercial propagandists do not speak about the genuine virtues of the emulsion. They give it some picturesquely voluptuous name, talk ecstatically and misleadingly about feminine beauty and show pictures of gorgeous blondes nourishing their tissues with skin food. "The cosmetic manufacturers," one of their number has written, "are not selling lanolin, they are selling hope." For this hope, this fraudulent implication of a promise that they will be transfigured, women will pay ten or twenty times the value of the emulsion which the propagandists have so skilfully related, by means of misleading symbols, to a deep-seated and almost universal feminine wish—the wish to be more attractive to members of the opposite sex. The principles underlying this kind of propaganda are extremely simple. Find some common desire, some widespread unconscious fear or anxiety; think out some way to relate this wish or fear to the product you have to sell; then build a bridge of verbal or pictorial symbols over which your customer can pass from fact to compensatory dream, and from the dream to the illusion that your product, when purchased, will make the dream come true. "We no longer buy oranges, we buy vitality. We do not buy just an auto, we buy prestige." And so with all the rest. In toothpaste, for example, we buy, not a mere cleanser and antiseptic, but release from the fear of being sexually repulsive. In vodka and whisky we are not buying a protoplasmic poison which, in small doses, may depress the nervous system in a psychologically valuable way; we are buying friendliness and good fellowship, the warmth of Dingley Dell and the brilliance of the

Mermaid Tavern. With our laxatives we buy the health of a Greek god, the radiance of one of Diana's nymphs. With the monthly best seller we acquire culture, the envy of our less literate neighbors and the respect of the sophisticated. In every case the motivation analyst has found some deep-seated wish or fear, whose energy can be used to move the consumer to part with cash and so, indirectly, to turn the wheels of industry. Stored in the minds and bodies of countless individuals, this potential energy is released by, and transmitted along, a line of symbols carefully laid out so as to bypass rationality and obscure the real issue.

Sometimes the symbols take effect by being disproportionately impressive, haunting and fascinating in their own right. Of this kind are the rites and pomps of religion. These "beauties of holiness" strengthen faith where it already exists and, where there is no faith, contribute to conversion. Appealing, as they do, only to the aesthetic sense, they guarantee neither the truth nor the ethical value of the doctrines with which they have been, quite arbitrarily, associated. As a matter of plain historical fact, the beauties of holiness have often been matched and indeed surpassed by the beauties of unholiness. Under Hitler, for example, the yearly Nuremberg rallies were masterpieces of ritual and theatrical art. "I had spent six years in St. Petersburg before the war in the best days of the old Russian ballet," writes Sir Nevile Henderson, the British ambassador to Hitler's Germany, "but for grandiose beauty I have never seen any ballet to compare with the Nuremberg rally." One thinks of Keats—"beauty is truth, truth beauty." Alas, the identity exists only on some ultimate, supramundane level. On the levels of politics and theology, beauty is perfectly compatible with nonsense and tyranny. Which is very fortunate; for if beauty were incompatible with nonsense and tyranny, there would be precious little art in the world. The masterpieces of painting, sculpture and architecture were produced as religious or political propaganda, for the greater glory of a god, a government or a priesthood. But most kings and priests have been despotic and all religions have been riddled with superstition. Genius has been the servant of tyranny and art has advertised the merits of the local cult. Time, as it passes, separates the good art from the bad metaphysics. Can we learn to make this separation, not after the event, but while it is actually taking place? That is the question.

In commercial propaganda the principle of the disproportionately fascinating symbol is clearly understood. Every propagandist has his Art Department, and attempts are constantly being made to beautify the billboards with striking posters, the advertising pages of magazines with lively drawings and photographs. There are no masterpieces; for masterpieces appeal only to a limited audience, and the commercial propagandist is out to captivate the majority. For him, the ideal is a moderate excellence. Those who like this not too good, but sufficiently striking, art may be expected to like the products with which it has been associated and for which it symbolically stands.

Another disproportionately fascinating symbol is the Singing Commercial. Singing Commercials are a recent invention; but the Singing Theological and the Singing Devotional—the hymn and the psalm—are as old as religion itself. Singing Militaries, or marching songs, are coeval with war, and Singing Patriotics, the precursors of our national anthems, were doubtless used to promote group solidarity, to emphasize the distinction between "us" and "them," by the wandering bands of paleolithic hunters and food gatherers. To most people music is intrinsically attractive. Moreover, melodies tend to ingrain themselves in the listener's mind. A tune will haunt the memory during 'the whole of a lifetime. Here, for example, is a quite uninteresting statement or value judgment. As it stands nobody will pay attention to it. But now set the words to a catchy and easily remembered tune. Immediately they become words of power. Moreover, the words will tend automatically to repeat themselves every time the melody is heard or spontaneously remembered. Orpheus has entered into an alliance with Pavlov— the power of sound with the conditioned reflex. For the commercial propagandist, as for his colleagues in the fields of politics and religion, music possesses yet another advantage. Nonsense which it would be shameful for a reasonable being to write, speak or hear spoken can be sung or listened to by that same rational being with pleasure and even with a kind of intellectual conviction. Can we learn to separate the pleasure of singing or of listening to song from the all too human tendency to believe in the propaganda which the song is putting over? That again is the question.

Thanks to compulsory education and the rotary press, the propagandist has been able, for many years past, to convey his messages to virtually every adult in every civilized country. Today, thanks to radio and television, he is in the happy position of being able to communicate even with unschooled adults and not yet literate children.

Children, as might be expected, are highly susceptible to propaganda. They are ignorant of the world and its ways, and therefore completely unsuspecting. Their critical faculties are undeveloped. The youngest of them have not yet reached the age of reason and the older ones lack the experience on which their new-found rationality can effectively work. In Europe, conscripts used to be playfully referred to as "cannon fodder." Their little brothers and sisters have now become radio fodder and television fodder. In my childhood we were taught to sing nursery rhymes and, in pious households, hymns. Today the little ones warble the Singing Commercials. Which is better—"Rheingold is my beer, the dry beer," or "Hey diddle-diddle, the cat and the fiddle"? "Abide with me" or "You'll wonder where the yellow went, when you brush your teeth with Pepsodent"? Who knows?

"I don't say that children should be forced to harass their parents into buying products they've seen advertised on television, but at the same time I cannot close my eyes to the fact that it's being done every day." So writes the star of one of the many programs beamed to a juvenile audience. "Children," he adds, "are living, talking records of what we tell them every day." And in due course these living, talking records of television commercials will grow up, earn money and buy the products of industry. "Think," writes Mr. Clyde Miller ecstatically, "think of what it can mean to your firm in profits if you can condition a million or ten million children, who will grow up into adults trained to buy your product, as soldiers are trained in advance when they hear the trigger words, Forward March!" Yes, just think of it! And at the same time remember that the dictators and the would-be dictators have been thinking about this sort of thing for years, and that millions, tens of millions, hundreds of millions of children are in process of growing up to buy the local despot's ideological product and, like well-trained soldiers, to respond with appropriate behavior to the trigger words implanted in those young minds by the despot's propagandists.

Self-government is in inverse ratio to numbers. The larger the constituency, the less the value of any particular vote. When he is merely one of millions, the individual elector feels himself to be impotent, a negligible quantity. The candidates he has voted into office are far away, at the top of the pyramid of power. Theoretically they are the servants of the people; but in fact it is the servants who give orders and the people, far off at the base of the great pyramid, who must obey. Increasing population and advancing technology have resulted in an increase in the number and complexity of organizations, an increase in the amount of power concentrated in the hands of officials and a corresponding decrease in the amount of control exercised by electors, coupled with a decrease in the public's regard for democratic procedures. Already weakened by the vast impersonal forces at work in the modern world, democratic institutions are now being undermined from within by the politicians and their propagandists.

Human beings act in a great variety of irrational ways, but all of them seem to be capable, if given a fair chance, of making a reasonable choice in the light of available evidence. Democratic institutions can be made to work only if all concerned do their best to impart knowledge and to encourage rationality. But today, in the world's most powerful democracy, the politicians and their propagandists prefer to make nonsense of democratic procedures by appealing almost exclusively to the ignorance and irrationality of the electors. "Both parties," we were told in 1956 by the editor of a leading business journal, "will merchandise their candidates and issues by the same methods that business has developed to sell goods. These include scientific selection of appeals and planned repetition. . . . Radio spot announcements and ads will repeat phrases with a planned intensity. Billboards will push slogans of proven power. . . . Candidates need, in addition to rich voices and good diction, to be able to look 'sincerely' at the TV camera."

The political merchandisers appeal only to the weaknesses of voters, never to their potential strength. They make no attempt to educate the masses into becoming fit for self-government; they are content merely to manipulate and exploit them. For this purpose all the resources of psychology and the social sciences are mobilized and set to work. Carefully selected samples of the electorate are given "interviews in depth." These interviews in depth reveal the unconscious fears and wishes most prevalent in a given society at the time of an election. Phrases and images aimed at allaying or, if necessary, enhancing these fears, at satisfying these wishes, at least symbolically, are then chosen by the experts, tried out on readers and audiences, changed or improved in the light of the information thus obtained. After which the political campaign is ready for the mass communicators. All that is now needed is money and a candidate who can be coached to look "sincere." Under the new dispensation, political principles and plans for specific action have come to lose most of their importance. The personality of the candidate and the way he is projected by the advertising experts are the things that really matter.

In one way or another, as vigorous he-man or kindly father, the candidate must be glamorous. He must also be an entertainer who never bores his audience. Inured to television and radio, that audience is accustomed to being distracted and does not like to be asked to concentrate or make a prolonged intellectual effort. All speeches by the entertainer-candidate must therefore be short and snappy. The great issues of the day must be dealt with in five minutes at the most—and preferably (since the audience will be eager to pass on to something a little livelier than inflation or the H-bomb) in sixty seconds flat. The nature of oratory is such that there has always been a tendency among politicians and clergymen to over-simplify complex issues. From a pulpit or a platform even the most conscientious of speakers finds it very difficult to tell the whole truth. The methods now being used to merchandise the political candidate as though he were a deodorant positively guarantee the electorate against ever hearing the truth about anything.

WANTED:
RESPONSIBLE ADVERTISING CRITICS[1]

James Webb Young

James Webb Young is regarded as one of the elder statesmen of the advertising industry. He helped build the world's largest advertising agency and now serves as an advertising consultant. He has taught business history and advertising at the University of Chicago.

I learned my trade as a writer of advertisements in a religious publishing house, selling books by mail to Methodist ministers. My first big success was with a book called "Personal Evangelism," which had the worthy purpose of telling these ministers how to increase the membership of their church and, as the saying had it, to "bring more souls to Christ."

In such an activity I had no suspicion that I was entering upon what—much later—President Angell of Yale told me was a *déclassé* profession." And I dare say the present writer of an effective series of advertisements, now being published by the Knights of Columbus for the Catholic faith, would have been as astonished as I was when I heard this.

My first warning on the status of the advertising man came on another campus. Early in the 1920s, in the midst of a busy advertising life, I had undertaken to get a solid physiological base for the study of psychology. And the famous Anton J. Carlson at the University of Chicago had agreed personally to give it to me in his laboratory.

One day Dr. Carlson introduced me to the late C. Judson Herrick, notable for his researches on the brain and nervous system, whose latest book I had been given to study. I said: "Dr. Herrick, it may surprise you to know that an advertising man is finding your new book on the brain of the greatest interest." Said Dr. Herrick, looking at me sourly over his glasses: "I am not only surprised; I am chagrined. As far as I can see there is no connection between brains and advertising."

Since then, through the years, in my notes on many kinds of human behavior, I have recorded other equally sweeping generalizations about advertising, made by faculty members of Harvard, Columbia, Princeton, Cornell, Wisconsin, Johns Hopkins, and McGill.

---

[1]*Saturday Revew,* April 23, 1960, pp. 35 ff. Reprinted by permission.

But sweeping generalizations about advertising are not confined to the academic groves, nor to recent times. A notable piece on the subject came from the pen of Dr. Samuel Johnson, in the mid-eighteenth century. And currently, triggered by the revelation of rigged TV quiz shows, any number of people have gotten into the act.

Thus, for example, in a recent column Walter Lippmann seems to transfer the responsibility for this rigging wholly to the shoulders of "advertisers"—not to particular advertisers, and not in any degree to those of the educator-idol whose feet of clay furnished all the drama.

Note, too, the adverbs used by Father P. P. Harbrecht, S.J., in a recent booklet issued by the Twentieth Century Fund on his excellent study, "Toward the Paraproprietal Society." Speaking of such big corporations as General Motors, du Pont, U.S. Steel, Alcoa, and General Electric, he says (italics mine): "Their research and innovations transform our lives, *quietly* with home appliances or *dramatically* with atomics and space flight; *brashly* with TV advertising or *culturally* with subsidies to education." Is all the TV advertising of all these firms done "brashly"?

Now, let me say clearly that advertising needs, is entitled to, and can profit from criticism of the most public kind. It needs it more than ever today because advertising has become one of the most potent forces in our culture —ranking as an "institution" with the church and education, according to Professor Potter of Yale, in his book "People of Plenty."

But it needs that criticism in the form that the dictionary defines as "the act of passing judgment on the merits of anything"; that is, discriminating criticism, which applauds the good and damns the bad.

No one is more concerned about the misuses of advertising than the responsible people in advertising. And, in fact, they have been trying for a very long time to do something about these misuses. If any of the shoot-from-the-hip critics of this activity would take the same trouble to understand my specialty as I was taking to understand that of Dr. Herrick, these are some of the things they would find:

First, that the technical literature of advertising is currently filled with the kind of "good-and-bad" criticism advertising needs.

Second, that advertising people have promoted and secured the adoption of "Truth in Advertising" laws in over half our states, and have supported the work of Better Business Bureaus in policing these laws.

Third, that they have supported the purposes, if not always the methods, of the Federal Trade Commission, to prevent the use of advertising in ways unfair to competition.

Fourth, that in their various trade and professional organizations advertising men have drafted any number of codes of "ethical" practices— and have been busy reactivating these lately!

Fifth, that many important advertising media refuse to accept advertising for certain classifications of products; and that the largest advertising agency in the world has never undertaken advertising for "hard" liquors— all at a considerable cost to their revenues.

All these things have, in fact, brought improvements in the use of advertising, as a recent writer noted. "In front of us," he says, "is a 1913 advertisement pointing out the advantages of Postum over Brazilian coffee. Among the ills attributed to coffee: 'Sallow Complexions; Stomach Trouble; Bad Liver; Heart Palpitations; Shattered Nerves; Caffeine, a Drug; Weakness from Drugging.' We doubt if the present owners of Postum would O.K. copy like this today. Even if they didn't own Maxwell House."

But all this is not enough, and nobody knows it better than those hardworking creators of much of our advertising, inaccurately stereotyped as "Madison Avenue."

The reason why it is not enough is that, as developed in America, the set of facilities and techniques called advertising has become the most powerful single means that the world has ever seen for informing, persuading, and inspiring a people to action. As such, it becomes vital that its potentialities for good or ill become fully recognized; that the responsibilities for its use be squarely shouldered; and that the magnificent opportunities for its use in the public service, as now amply demonstrated in the work of the Advertising Council, be fully exploited.

It is therefore my thesis that what advertising now needs is to be given, in public print, the same kind of continuing, knowing, responsible criticism as that given to the theatre, music, the arts, books, and other major aspects of our culture. It needs a "career critic," keeping a steady spotlight on both the good and the bad in the uses of advertising, and on its unexploited social potentialities.

What would be the qualifications for such a public critic of advertising—assuming the judicial temperament of the responsible man?

First, he should know that "advertising" is a set of facilities and techniques as impersonal as electricity or atomic energy, and thus equally usable for noble ends or shabby ones. Hence he will avoid the "pathetic fallacy" of animating the inanimate, into which so many critics of advertising fall. It is *advertisers* who need criticism—not advertising.

Second, he will understand clearly the economic necessities which brought advertising into existence, and still control its use. These were well stated in 1870 by Walter Bagehot in his classic work "Lombard Street." Said Bagehot:

> Our current political economy does not sufficiently take account of *time* as an element in trade operations. But as soon as the division of labour has once established itself in a community, two principles at once begin to be important, of which time is the very essence. These are—

First, that as goods are produced to be exchanged, it is good that they should be exchanged as quickly as possible.

Secondly, that as every producer is mainly occupied in producing what others want, and not what he wants himself, it is desirable that he should always be able to find, without effort, without delay, and without uncertainty, others who want what he can produce.

These words are even truer today than when Bagehot wrote them. To understand the workhorse job of advertising in a high production-consumption economy such as ours is primary for any intelligent criticism of its uses.

Third, he must understand that the methods by which advertising gets the workhorse job done in today's economy have been greatly developed since Bagehot's day; and why in these methods are to be found some of the roots of the criticisms of advertising.

. . . early in the expansion of the use of advertising it was discovered that the mere repetition of a name or trademark could produce a preference for one product over another. Remember "Gold Medal Flour—Eventually, Why Not Now?" This sort of advertising worked because mere familiarity is a *value* to the human being. It satisfies one of his deepest needs: for a sense of "at-homeness" in this world. You can check this, perhaps, by recalling when, in a crowd of strangers, you have found yourself gravitating toward one familiar face—possibly even that of a person not well liked. Familiarity is a value, and no advertising works which does not, in some form, deliver a value to somebody.

Then it was discovered that there is a function for advertising merely as a "re-minder" of something we are already "minded" to do. For example, to "Say it with flowers!" when you have a wedding anniversary coming up. A service, surely, in the cause of domestic tranquillity!

After this, as railroads made a national market possible, came a development in the *news* use of advertising. Just as the Associated Press came into being to gather and transmit general news, so the advertising agency came into being to gather and transmit commercial news, thus making possible the announcement, say, of a new model automobile on the same day everywhere.

But there is also another kind of "news," in the advertising sense. It is the kind of news you pay no attention to until you need to know it. In our long march from the cradle to the grave we pass into, and out of, many areas of experience. And as we do, our receptivity to all sorts of news changes. Thus the young woman who ignores the infant-feeding advertisement of today may become its most eager reader next year.

Then, along the way, came the discovery that advertising could be used to overcome human inertia. Hell is indeed paved with many good intentions, toward such things as making a will, taking out adequate life insurance, seeing the dentist regularly, and so on. In all such things the reward for action taken, or the punishment for action postponed, is remote and delayed. Advertising, by making more vivid such rewards or punishments, can often overcome the inertia—to the profit of the reader or listener as well as the advertiser.

Religions have always had to deal with this problem in the training of ministers, and here it seems always to have been a moot question whether portrayal of the rewards of heaven or of the punishments of hell converted more sinners.

Then, finally, came the discovery that advertising could *add a value not in the product.* And because these values were subjective ones (such as status symbols; or, say, the luxury of bathing with the same soap the movie stars use; or what Edith Wharton once called "the utility of the useless"), here advertising really got into trouble. For in this area of subjective values, one man's meat is definitely another man's poison.

In this area, too, our critic will come face to face with one of his most difficult problems. Advertising, like editing, politics, and even to some extent education, always operates within the context of the culture of its day. One irony of its present situation is that some of the people who are most vocal in their negative attitudes toward advertising may themselves have contributed to some aspects of it which they most deplore. By supporting liberal policies for the wider distribution of wealth in this country, they have helped bring into existence a mammoth class of *nouveau riche,* whose incomes have improved faster than their tastes and subjective values.

In addition to such an understanding of the ways in which advertising works, our critic must grasp some of the trends in our economy which have major impacts on the creation of advertising.

The most important of these lie in our technology. Innovation has become an industry, as Dr. Sumner Slichter pointed out. Theoretically, our accelerated rate of innovation should produce more and more advertising news about distinction in products. But counter forces produce in some considerable degree an opposite effect.

One of these counter forces is governmental pressure for the preservation of competition. This tends to force a cross-licensing of patents which rapidly spreads any given innovation throughout an industry. Thus, for instance, when one manufacturer of television sets produces a more compact tube, soon many of his major competitors have the benefit of it.

Then, too, innovation often comes, not from the end-producer of the product or service, but from the supplier of an ingredient or part, whose interest is to gain its adoption by as many end-producers as possible. See, for example, the current jet plane advertising of our airlines.

Added to these we have, in this country, a widespread "free trade" in technological ideas, through such channels as the Society of Automotive

Engineers and numerous trade and technical journals. The result is that innovating ideas get "in the air," and soon all our automobiles, for example, become more and more alike.

All these forces result in the reverse of a distinction between competitive products and services. But the advertising man is expected to present each of them as one with important differences, leading to the manufacture of mountains out of molehills in the advertising. Our critic must be knowledgeable about this problem, and about the constructive ways to deal with it.

Finally, and most importantly, our critic should be conscious of the still underdeveloped use of advertising as a social force outside the exchange of goods and services.

He must know of the remarkable results that the Advertising Council has produced over the last fifteen years for some fifty "good causes"— through the voluntary services of advertising men, and with contributions of some $180 million annually, in time and space, from advertisers and media.

And he should know, too, of the following-up of this lead in such fine corporation advertising campaigns as:

a. The striking campaign of the Standard Oil Company (N.J.) in the interest of international friendship.

b. The Weyerhaeuser Company's campaign for the preservation of our forests and for conservation through tree-farming.

c. The campaign for better schools, safer highways, forest fire prevention, and other useful purposes of the Caterpillar Tractor Co.

d. The campaign of the New York Life Insurance Company to help parents guide their children in career choices, or the notable campaign of the Metropolitan Life Insurance Company on behalf of better health.

e. The campaign for citizen responsibility of Nationwide Insurance.

An alert critic might see, too, in such uses of advertising, potentialities for our great foundations; for the use of some of their funds in the *distribution* of knowledge, through this most modern high-speed means of communication.

In all this let our critic be not only objective but specific. Let him deal, not with "advertising," but with its uses, good and bad. Let him examine:

Whether there is too much crowding of advertising in time and space—such as commercials per TV program, and billboards per scenic mile?

Whether there is too much stridency and bad manners in some advertising, now that it can project personal salesmanship into the living room?

Whether the paucity of real buying information, and the superfluity of adjectives in some advertising is, not a crime, but worse—a mistake?

Would such a critic have any real effect on the advertising scene? All I know is that the genius of advertising is reiteration, and that its prophet, Isaiah, said: "Whom shall he teach knowledge? and whom shall he make to understand doctrines? . . . For precept must be upon precept; precept upon precept; line upon line; line upon line; here a little, and there a little."

What I am looking for is a publisher or editor with the insight and courage to enter this new field of criticism—and for the competent critic to aid him. Such a publisher or editor will have to take some risks with his advertisers, yes. But he will, I believe, make a major contribution to the better and wiser use of advertising in our day; he will find himself attracting a surprising volume of mail from his readers; and, in the longer haul, profiting from the sharp attention given his publication by advertisers and advertising men.

Are there any takers in the house?

PART THREE
SEXUAL
CONDUCT

A large number of our moral problems revolve about sex. Here more than anywhere else is the area in which institutional restraints are pitted against resistant drives, where there are radical discrepancies between what we preach and what we practice,[1] and where, therefore, values are in a state of flux.

In many instances, to be sure, we know where we stand: there is no difference among us and no question concerning the immorality of obscenity, promiscuity, prostitution. Differences arise, however, concerning whether a particular book or moving picture is obscene. Prudery can be as objectionable as prurience, and in our time prudery—which is not to be confused with modesty—is regarded with as much misgiving as promiscuity. Other differences arise concerning the kind of precaution to take: shall pornography and prostitution be outlawed; or shall we avoid legal curbs and rely on the power of education and public opinion? The evil of both pornography and prostitution is acknowledged; the problem here is the recurrent one of not courting a greater evil as we endeavor to combat a lesser one.

In other instances, however, the moral problems are more acute and they grow even more so. These concern such issues as premarital and extramarital sexual experience, divorce, and birth control. Here standards have undergone drastic change as reflected in new attitudes towards the use of contraceptives, greater ease in obtaining divorce and an enormous increase in the divorce rate, and surveys indicating a significantly large proportion of women reporting extramarital sexual experience. Everywhere one encounters perplexity and a need for moral guidance. But authorities are themselves in doubt and disagreement, and the counsel we get is conflicting.

Conflicts, deep or otherwise, are best dramatized by particular events. It was only several years ago that Bertrand Russell, by common consent the world's greatest living philosopher and one of the greatest men of our age, was dismissed by the City College of New York, where he was visiting lecturer, because, in a book written many years before, he had advocated experimental marriage. That one of the most cosmopolitan and reputedly

_____

[1]It is reliably estimated, for example, that in the United States, where abortion is illegal unless the life of the mother is at stake, 5,000 women die each year at the hands of illegal, unqualified abortionists, and from 1 to 3 million abortions are performed each year. Since it is illegal to abort a woman who contracts an illness (e.g., German measles) that may result in the birth of a blind or mentally retarded child, or even to abort a victim of rape, flouting of the law is almost certain.

tolerant cities in the world suffered an agony of shame over this episode suggests the dimensions of the conflict, as does the invitation to teach at Harvard that the Harvard faculty promptly extended Lord Russell.

Topics dealing with sexual conduct fall logically into two parts. One part embraces deviant or aberrational sexuality, specifically perversion, obscenity, prudery, and prostitution. Here concern is with the psychopathic or sociopathic and with how to deal with it. The second part embraces "normal" sexuality, that is, questions concerning guidance of the sexual development of adolescents, the role of love, extramarital relationships, marriage and divorce, birth control. Here sex deviancy is irrelevant and psycho- or sociopathic behavior are only indirectly if at all involved.

Considerations of space limit the number of selected topics to two: pornography and how to control it, and extramarital sexual experience.

PORNOGRAPHY AND
ITS CONTROL

What is pornography? We have traveled a long distance since Walter Hines Page, then with Doubleday, Page and Co., refused to publish a book which contained the word "chaste" because it was too "suggestive." The Massachusetts Supreme Court would not now sustain the conviction of a publisher for selling Theodore Dreiser's *An American Tragedy* as it did in 1930. Even so, it was only yesterday that *Lady Chatterley's Lover* became available to American readers (pirated editions have been sold, of course, from the beginning); and it was only a day before yesterday that producers of the motion picture version of *A Streetcar Named Desire* were persuaded to delete the last three words from a line in the Tennessee Williams play that reads, "I would like to kiss you softly and sweetly on the mouth."

In a book he wrote in 1927 about Anthony Comstock, Heywood Broun reminded his readers that sex is not an invention of the novelists, not even the modern ones. "Both the fundamentalists and the evolutionists agree," Broun wrote, "that the scheme has at least the merit of antiquity. Anthony Comstock may have been entirely correct in his assumption that the division of living creatures into male and female was a vulgar mistake, but a conspiracy of silence about the matter will hardly alter the facts."[1]

Today, nearly all responsible people will applaud Broun's verdict, and, with motion pictures dealing in such taboo themes as Lesbianism, incest, and even child molestation, and mass-circulation periodicals using words heretofore banned in all except the most vulgar company, the day of permissiveness perhaps has dawned. Even so, the nature of obscenity and its control remains controversial.

If the canon ecclesiastical lawyers did not spell out the meaning of the word "obscene," says Father Gardiner,[2] this was because they did not con-

---

[1]*Anthony Comstock* (New York: A. & C. Boni, Inc., 1927), p. 274. Written with Margaret Leech. This, with *The Censor Marches On* by Morris L. Ernst and Alexander Lindey, is a good account of early difficulties with the censors.

[2]Harold C. Gardiner, S.J., *Catholic Viewpoint on Censorship,* Image Books edition, revised (Garden City, N.Y.: Doubleday & Company, Inc., 1961), pp. 64–65.

ceive that the word was complicated or obscure. They took it for granted, as it were, that the word was rather self-evident." But Father Gardiner concedes that "in a pluralistic society such as ours" the problem *has* arisen, and he therefore defines obscenity in a book or painting as "the intrinsic tendency or bent of the work to arouse sexual passion, or, to put it more concretely, the motions of the genital apparatus which are preparatory to the complete act of sexual union." Father Gardiner adds that "a particular work . . . may not always and in all circumstances so arouse this or that individual. It is not so much a matter of the individual's own reaction here and now as the nature of the work under consideration. . . . it must, of its nature, be such as actually to arouse in the viewer or reader such venereal pleasure."

Psychologists Eberhard Kronhausen and Phyllis Kronhausen disagree. They distinguish between erotic realism and pornography: "In pornography . . . the main purpose is to stimulate erotic response in the reader. And that is all. In erotic realism, truthful description of the basic realities of life is of the essence. . . ." And, ". . . if while writing realistically on the subject of sex the author succeeds in moving his reader, this too is erotic realism, *and it is axiomatic that the reader should respond erotically to such writing,* just as the sensitive reader will respond, perhaps by actually crying, to a sad scene . . ."[3]

Pondering such differing views of obscenity and recalling that reproductions of Goya's famous Nude (or Naked) Maja decorate an official postage stamp in Catholic Spain whereas in "pluralistic" America reproductions were banned in the mails, we have turned for enlightenment to an exchange between a distinguished Catholic prelate and the editor of one of our best monthly periodicals.

But here, as in other cases, moral perplexities are best exhibited by viewing them in a particular context. The experiences of one of our most noted writers provide such a context. Henry Miller, described by his admirers as being a "free spirit" in the tradition of Thoreau and Whitman and as having "a deep and pure sense of morality," has engaged over a long period of years in a series of self-revelations that his severer critics have denounced as exercises in scatology. Among the most notable of these are *Tropic of Cancer* and *Tropic of Capricorn,* both often described as written by a man wallowing in prurience and both banned from this country until 1961, when federal restraints were removed. Their fate in local jurisdictions, as the selections below will indicate, has been an uneven one, although some would say they are more likely—if Judge Woolsey's language in the *Ulysses* case may be borrowed—to act as an emetic than as an aphrodisiac.

---

[3]*Pornography and the Law* (New York: Ballantine Books, Inc., 1959), p. 18. With an introduction by Dr. Theodore Reik.

Miller himself, despite his animadversions about America ("Fresh from Europe, the American scene held about as much charm for me as a dead rattlesnake lying in a deep freeze"), has abandoned the Left Bank for California's Big Sur—an exile's return that has evoked mixed feelings among his countrymen. Now an aging guru dispensing controversial wisdom to a coterie of admirers, his personal trials are over—thanks to the legal trials that have brought enough notoriety to his books to introduce him to the privileges of royalties.

The two decisions below illustrate the problems involved in first defining and then controlling pornography. The first is an opinion of Judge Stephens for the majority of the U.S. Court of Appeals (Ninth Circuit). The second is an opinion of Justice Cutter for the majority of the Supreme Judicial Court of Massachusetts.[4] A third selection provides appropriate comment by John Ciardi, poetry editor of the *Saturday Review*. In contending that Miller is a serious artist, Ciardi agrees with such older *literati* as George Orwell, Lawrence Durrell, and Ezra Pound.

---

[4]Most recent action (February 1963) of the U.S. Supreme Court has been an 8 to 1 decision holding unconstitutional certain activities of the Rhode Island Commission to Encourage Morality in Youth. Between 1957 and 1960 the commission had sent some 35 notices to distributors of books and magazines; in these notices, the commission urged removal of certain publications and threatened prosecution by the state attorney general in the event of failure to comply. Copies of the titles were sent to the police, who usually called to see whether the objectionable publications had been withdrawn from sale. In his opinion for the majority of the court, Justice William J. Brennan, Jr., found that the commission "acted as an agency not to advise, but to suppress." He also observed that bold and creative artistic expression is "often separated from obscenity by a dim and uncertain line," so that judicial scrutiny of attempted suppression is especially important.

THE HARM GOOD PEOPLE DO[1]
John Fischer

John Fischer is editor-in-chief of Harper's Magazine *and succeeded Bernard De Voto as the occupant of its "Easy Chair." However upholstered the chair may be, its occupants have rarely given comfort to the smug and sanctimonious. Fischer's articles enjoy a wide circle of thoughtful and appreciative readers.*

A little band of Catholics is now conducting a shocking attack on the rights of their fellow citizens. They are engaged in an un-American activity which is as flagrant as anything the Communist party ever attempted—and

---

[1]*Harper's Magazine*, October 1956, pp. 14–20. © 1956 by Harper & Row, Publishers, Inc. Reprinted from *Harper's Magazine* by special permission.

which is, in fact, very similar to Communist tactics. They are harming their country, their Church, and the cause of freedom.

Their campaign is particularly dangerous because few people realize what they are up to. It can hurt you—indeed, it already has—without your knowing it. It is spreading rapidly but quietly; and so far no effective steps have been taken to halt it.

Even the members of this organization probably do not recognize the damage they are doing. They are well-meaning people, acting from deeply moral impulses. They are trying, in a misguided way, to cope with a real national problem, and presumably they think of themselves as patriots and servants of the Lord. Perhaps a majority of Americans, of all faiths, would sympathize with their motives—though not with their methods.

They do not, of course, speak for all Catholics. On the contrary, they are defying the warnings of some of their Church's most respected teachers and theologians. The Catholic Church as a whole certainly cannot be blamed for their actions, any more than it could be held responsible a generation ago for the political operations of Father Coughlin.

This group calls itself the National Organization for Decent Literature. Its headquarters are in Chicago; its director is the Very Reverend Monsignor Thomas Fitzgerald. Its main purpose is to make it impossible for anybody to buy books and other publications which it does not like. Among them are the works of some of the most distinguished authors now alive—for example, winners of the Nobel Prize, the Pulitzer Prize, and the National Book Award.

Its chief method is to put pressure on news dealers, drug stores, and booksellers, to force them to remove from their stocks every item on the NODL blacklist. Included on this list are reprint editions of books by Ernest Hemingway, William Faulkner, John Dos Passos, George Orwell, John O'Hara, Paul Hyde Bonner, Emile Zola, Arthur Koestler, and Joyce Cary. In some places—notably Detroit, Peoria, and the suburbs of Boston—the organization has enlisted the local police to threaten booksellers who are slow to "co-operate."

This campaign of intimidation has no legal basis. The books so listed have not been banned from the mails, and in the overwhelming majority of cases no legal charges have ever been brought against them. Indeed, it seems that the National Organization for Decent Literature deliberately prefers to ignore the established legal channels for proceedings against books which it thinks improper. Its chosen weapons are boycott and literary lynching.

For example, early last year committees of laymen from Catholic churches in the four northern counties of New Jersey—Union, Hudson, Essex, and Bergen—began to call on local merchants. These teams were armed with the NODL lists. They offered "certificates," to be renewed each month, to those storekeepers who would agree to remove from sale all of the listed publications. To enforce their demands, they warned the merchants that their parishioners would be advised to patronize only those stores displaying a certificate.

Contact, a bulletin published by the Sacred Heart Parish Societies of Orange, New Jersey, listed fourteen merchants in its March 1955 issue. "The following stores," it said, "have agreed to co-operate with the Parish Decency Committee in not displaying or selling literature disapproved by the National Organization for Decent Literature. . . . Please patronize these stores only. They may be identified by the certificate which is for one month only."

Similar tactics have been followed in scores of other communities. Even in Nevada—a state not noted for Puritanical temper—the Council of Catholic Men has asked booksellers to purge from their shelves a list of books which included such widely read novels as *Mr. Roberts* and *From Here to Eternity.* When an Associated Press reporter pointed out that millions of people already were familiar with these works, in print and on film, the state chairman of the campaign, Paul Laxalt of Carson City, replied:

"We've got to stand by the list. If we make one exception the list would be chopped up."

Such tactics are highly effective. Most news dealers, druggists, and similar merchants carry paper-bound books only as a minor side line. Moreover, they receive from the wholesalers more books than they have space for; if they remove one title from their racks, there are plenty of others to take its place. They don't want trouble. It is never good business to argue with a customer—so most of them readily comply with this form of private censorship. After all, their other customers, who might want to read a book by Faulkner or Hemingway or Zola, will never know that it has been suppressed, and when they don't find it on the shelves they probably will buy something else.

For these reasons it was possible for the Archdiocesan Council of Catholic Men in St. Louis to report recently that it had "obtained the consent of about one-third of the store owners approached in a campaign to ask merchants to submit to voluntary screening. . . ."

Something—but not much—can be said in defense of the National Organization for Decent Literature and its local campaigners. A good many tawdry and disreputable magazines, paper-bound reprints, and comic books have been offered for sale on a lot of newsstands. A few publishers unquestionably have tried to base their sales appeal on sex and violence; the pictures and text on the covers of their publications often hint that the contents are far more salacious than they are in fact. (Such misrepresentation, however, is less common now than it was a few years ago, and both the contents and the covers of most pocket-size books seem to be growing less lurid.)

It can be argued, too, that law enforcement agencies in some cities have not been vigorous in enforcing the statutes against obscene publications. Finally, the "decent literature" campaigners apparently feel that their main mission is to protect young people, whose judgment is unformed and who might be attracted to sleazy reading matter by a provocative newsstand display; they seem to take far less interest in the hard-bound editions of the same books available in libraries or regular book stores. The Detroit NODL, for example, states that its list is "not intended as a restrictive list for adults"—though it does not explain how adults could purchase the books if merchants have been persuaded not to stock them.

But the motives of these zealous people are not the issue. The real issue is whether any private group—however well-meaning—has a right to dictate what other people may read.

Clearly any church, or any sub-group within a church, has a right to advise its own members about their reading matter.

Clearly, too, anybody has a right to try to *persuade* other people to read or refrain from reading anything he sees fit.

The National Organization for Decent Literature, however, goes much further. Its campaign is not aimed at Catholics alone, and it is not attempting to *persuade* readers to follow its views. It is *compelling* readers, of all faiths, to bow to its dislikes, by denying them a free choice in what they buy.

This principle is of course unacceptable to Catholics—as it is to all Americans—if they take the trouble to think about it for a moment. How would Catholics react if, say, a group of Jewish laymen were to threaten merchants with boycott unless they banned from their shops all publications which referred to the divinity of Christ? Some religious denominations believe that gambling is immoral; most Catholics do not, and many of their parishes raise considerable sums by means of bingo games and raffles. What if some Protestant sect were to try to clean out of the stores all publications which spoke tolerantly of gambling, and to boycott every merchant who bought a raffle ticket?

The principle at stake was set forth with admirable clarity by Father John Courtney Murray, S.J., professor of moral theology at Woodstock College, Maryland, in a recent address on "Literature and Censorship." He listed four rules, which ought to command the enthusiastic support of all Americans regardless of religious belief:

(1) "Each minority group has the right to censor for its own members, if it so chooses, the contents of the various media of communication,

and to protect them, by means of its own choosing, from materials considered harmful according to its standards." (He also pointed out that in the United States "all religious groups . . . are minority groups.")

(2) "No minority group has the right to demand that government should impose a general censorship" on material "judged to be harmful according to the special standards held within one group."

(3) "Any minority group has the right to work toward the elevation of standards of public morality . . . through the use of the methods of persuasion and pacific argument."

(4) "No minority group has the right to impose its own religious or moral views on other groups, through the use of methods of force, coercion, or violence."

And Father Murray went on to warn that methods of coercion are especially imprudent for Catholic associations.

"The chief danger," he said, "is lest the Church itself be identified in the public mind as a power-association. The identification is injurious; it turns into hatred of the faith. And it has the disastrous effect of obscuring from the public view the true visage of the Church as God's kingdom of truth and freedom, justice and love."

He quoted from Jacques Leclercq "of the Catholic University of Louvain, who is no slight authority" the dictum that "no government has ever succeeded in finding a balanced policy of combating unhealthy sexual propaganda without injuring legitimate freedom or provoking other equally grave or worse disorders."

Finally, Father Murray emphasized that "censorship in the civil order must be a judicial process," carried out under the statutes and according to the due processes of law.

The conclusions which flow from Father Murray's teachings seem plain enough:

(1) *For the National Organization for Decent Literature.* It should stop immediately its campaign of threats, blacklisting, and boycott. It should then pursue its aims by the legitimate methods of persuasion, propaganda, and action through the courts. Most states have adequate laws against the publication and sale of indecent literature. In cases where the law seems inadequate, the legislature can be persuaded to amend it, by the normal means of lobbying and petition. In cases where the law is not enforced, public officials should certainly be reminded of their duty—and opposed at the polls, in the democratic way, if they fall down on their jobs.

Above all, the NODL ought to consider the possibility of guiding young readers by positive rather than negative techniques. Youngsters are not likely to read trash whenever they have good books readily available. If they are brought up in homes where good literature is a constant part of their environment—where parents read to them from infancy, and encourage them to build up their own libraries—then there is scant chance that they will be attracted by comics or two-bit horrors.

What has the NODL done to urge parents to give their children such basic moral training? Has it done all it can to foster topnotch libraries— public, school, church, and family? In how many communities has it sponsored campaigns to stimulate good reading?

(2) *For news dealers, booksellers, and other merchants.* They should muster the courage to defy any group of private citizens which tries to impose its own brand of censorship on the publications they offer for sale. And, with equal courage, they should set their own house in order; they should refuse to sell any publication which—in their own untrammeled judgment—falls below their own standards as responsible business men.

(3) *For the patriotic citizen.* He should protest against the lynching of books just as vigorously as against the lynching of people. He should go out of his way to support the merchants who resist such coercion. He should point out to the members of the National Organization for Decent Literature (and to any other self-appointed censors in his community) the immeasurable damage they are doing to the American way of life, to the very foundation of democratic government.

For the gravest harm done here is not to the Catholic Church—though, as Father Murray noted, that is dangerous enough—or to the individual who is denied the right to choose his own books. The great peril is to the fabric of orderly government. It is always injured when any group takes the law into its own hands. And whenever such a band of vigilantes succeeds in imposing its will by force, some other—and perhaps more sinister —group is encouraged to try the same thing.

Dean Joseph O'Meara of the Notre Dame Law School recently put it like this:

"Unfortunately many sincere people do not comprehend the genius of our democracy . . . such people would deny free speech to those with whom they are in fundamental disagreement. . . . They would establish a party line in America—*their* party line, of course. This is an alien concept, a totalitarian concept; it is not consonant with the American tradition; it is anti-democratic; it is, in short, subversive and it should be recognized for what it is."

Still another eminent Catholic—Senator John Kennedy of Massachusetts—summed up the case in even more prophetic terms.

"The lock on the door of the legislature, the parliament, or the assembly hall," he said, "by order of the King, the Commissar, or the Führer— has historically been followed or preceded by a lock on the door of the printer's, the publisher's, or the bookseller's."

THE BAD ARGUMENTS
INTELLIGENT PEOPLE MAKE[1]

John Courtney Murray, S.J.

Since he is one of American Catholicism's most brilliant and fluent spokesmen, it will not be regarded as disproportionate if this volume relies on John Courtney Murray, S.J., for comments on two topics instead of one. His views concerning the relation of church and state will be found on pages 270–285. Although another competent spokesman for the Catholic view on the present topic might have been found, Father Murray has been enlisted because his remarks are directly responsive to John Fischer and hence provide a clear joining of some of the basic issues involved in the current debates about pornography.

From his "Editor's Easy Chair" (*Harper's,* October 1956) John Fischer looks out and sees "immeasurable damage" being done "to the American way of life and to the very foundations of democratic government." This has become a familiar vision; many of us share it. But we frequently differ on the question, who or what is doing the damage?

In Mr. Fischer's view the damage is being done by "a little band of Catholics" who are "conducting a shocking attack on the rights of their fellow citizens" through the medium of an organization called the National Organization for Decent Literature, which undertakes to "censor" certain publications.

I take a rather broader view. I see a large band of people, of all faiths, who are conducting a shocking attack on the reason of their fellow citizens through the medium of passionately irrational argument about important public issues. I believe that nothing is more damaging to democracy than lack of rationality in public argument. The foundations of our society are indeed laid in an identifiable consensus. But they are more importantly laid in a reasonable disposition to argue our many disagreements in intelligent and temperate fashion, using restrained language, avoiding misstatements, overstatements or simplifications, and endeavoring to define issues with precision in the light of all the relevant principles and facts. I believe that whatever corrupts rational public argument corrupts democracy.

[1]Reprinted from *America, the National Catholic Weekly Review,* 920 Broadway, New York 10, N.Y. (November 3, 1956), pp. 120–123. Reprinted by permission.

It has seemed to me that censorship is one of the public issues that are being deformed by bad argument, emanating from all sides. Hence on May 4, 1956, in a talk given before the Thomas More Association in Chicago and printed in the organ of the Thomas More Book Shop, *Books on Trial,* I made an attempt at a contribution to good public argument on this difficult subject. Part of my argument consisted in stating four practical rules that should govern the action of minority groups in a pluralist society, in their legitimate efforts to improve public morality. These rules were not original. I had seen them stated in substance in a news release of a paper given at Marquette University on March 23, 1956, by Prof. Vernon J. Bourke of St. Louis University.

Mr. Fischer quotes my statement of these four procedural rules in support of certain conclusions of his own with regard to the activities of the National Organization for Decent Literature. Perhaps Mr. Bourke will undertake to say whether, and how far, Mr. Fischer's conclusions follow from the four norms of action for whose formulation, in language somewhat different from my own, he should be given the credit. . . . My own major concern is with a broader question—the quality of public argument. My question is whether Mr. Fischer has made a contribution to rational public argument on the issue of censorship. I am afraid my answer must be No.

Consider the preliminary question of language. In his opening paragraph Mr. Fischer asserts that a "little band of Catholics" is "engaged in an un-American activity which is as flagrant as anything the Communist party ever attempted—and which is in fact very similar to Communist tactics." Does one open a rational public argument by two such attacks on the reason of the reader? That tired old cuss-word, "un-American activity" —has it not gone the way of all cuss-words, into meaninglessness? And the tactic of slapping the label "Communist" on your adversary's position— have we not agreed that this is a tactic of unreason? As for the later argument by epithet (the NODL is "lynching" books), one hardly expects to find it in *Harper's,* however much it may be used on the hustings.

The more substantive question is this: has Mr. Fischer done justice to the NODL's own understanding of its purposes and methods, as these are stated in its explanatory literature?

The literature is easily obtainable from the central office. . . . On reading it, one would come, I think, to the following conclusions. The NODL is simply a "service organization," not an "action group." Its major service consists in offering to "responsible individuals and organizations an evaluation of current comic books, magazines and pocket-size books." This is the famous "NODL list." The evaluation of these types of publications (only these) is done singly from the standpoint of what is objectionable as juvenile reading. The standards of evaluation are nine in number. All of them are common-sense norms; none of them are special tenets of any type of "group morality." Methods of review vary for each type of publication. Five reviewers vote on each item. The purpose is to "encourage the publishing and distribution of good literature," as well as to discover what is unfit for adolescents.

NODL also distributes information about ways of organizing decent-literature campaigns on the community or parish levels. It is clearly stated that the list is merely an expression of a publication's nonconformity with the NODL code and that "the list is not to be used for purposes of boycott or coercion." The recommended procedures seem to rest on the suppositions that the ordinary merchant is a responsible man; that he would welcome some assistance in ridding his shop of stuff that responsible parents fairly judge to be unfit for their children; that if he accepts the assistance, he is to be commended; that if he rejects it, he is to be left alone. (NODL says: "Instruct your committee workers to leave silently if the owner, manager or clerk refuses cooperation.")

The general conclusion, on the basis of its own statements about itself, would be that the NODL looks to voluntary reform, through cooperation between parent-citizens and merchants, in an area where a special problem of public morality exists. That problem arises out of the ready accessibility to boys and girls of a rather immense amount of cheap literature that is objectionable on common-sense grounds of morality and taste.

Consider now Mr. Fischer's description of the NODL. "Its main purpose is to make it impossible for anybody to buy books and other publications which it does not like." "Its chief method is to put pressure on newsdealers, drug stores and booksellers to force them to remove from their stocks every item on the NODL blacklist." It "deliberately prefers to ignore the established legal channels for proceedings against books which it thinks improper. Its chosen weapons are boycott and literary lynching." It is embarked upon a "campaign of intimidation."

Something is wrong here. When Mr. Fischer describes the NODL he is obviously not describing the same thing that NODL describes when it describes itself. Thus you have reproduced the perfect pattern—the perfectly wretched pattern—of so much American public argument at the moment. There is really no argument at all—at least not yet. The two sides are not talking about the same thing. Hence the exchange proceeds to the customarily futile end. On the basis of his own description Mr. Fischer asserts that NODL "is *compelling* [emphasis his] readers, of all faiths, to bow to its dislikes, by denying them a free choice in what they buy." Hence he defines the issue thus: "The real issue is whether any private group—however well-meaning—has a right to dictate what other people may read."

To Mr. Fischer's charges the NODL would, I expect, reply to this effect: "But we are not compelling anybody to do or not to do anything. We are not doing any such arbitrary thing as making our own 'dislikes' the coercive standard for the reading of the general public. We are not trying to do any 'dictating.' And as for denying to readers of all faiths a free choice in what they buy—that is not the real issue at all."

Thus the argument fulfils the customary American pattern. The next step is for the contestants to retire from the field, either in sorrow or in anger or in both. Thereafter their partisans move in. Epithets are bandied; labels are exchanged; *non sequiturs* proliferate. Until finally, both sides mutter disgustedly, "So's your old man." And there is, for a time, a sullen silence.

Maybe the argument could be rescued from this dismal end, to which most arguments in America seem to be condemned. Mr. Fischer could have rescued it, ·but he didn't. The NODL could have obviated the need for rescue, but it hasn't. The point where rescue begins is, of course, a fact. Mr. Fischer notes the fact, but he abuses it to advance his own purposes. The NODL must surely recognize the fact, but it has not acted on the recognition, to the detriment of its own purposes. The fact is that in half-a-dozen or more cities and towns the police have made use of the NODL list in order to threaten, coerce or punish dealers in reading matter.

Unquestionably, officers of the law have full right to use the weapons of law, which are coercive. The point in question, however, is their use of the NODL list. This puts NODL in an ambiguous position. It cannot expect to have the thing both ways. It cannot, on the one hand, protest that "the list is not to be used for purpose of boycott or coercion," and, on the other hand, fail to protest against the use of the list by the police. It has to choose its cooperators—either the merchant or the police. It cannot choose both; for the choice is really between opposed methods of cooperation—the method of voluntary cooperation as between equal citizens, or the method of coercion as used by the police.

If NODL consents to the use of its list by the police, it creates an ambiguity that its critics may rightly seize upon, as Mr. Fischer did; what is worse, it obscures from public view its own "idea," the altogether valid idea of voluntary reform. On the other hand, if NODL does not consent to the use of its list by the police, it should say so—publicly, and on every necessary occasion. Surely part of its service must be the supervision, conducted on its own principles, of the uses to which its list is put.

There is another inappropriateness here. Officers of the law must operate under statutes which in this matter are, or ought to be, narrowly drawn. On the other hand, voluntary reform, precisely because it is voluntary, may be based on the somewhat broader categories of common-sense judgment. The latter are employed by the NODL, rightly enough. But for this very reason it is not right for the police to use NODL's judgments in enforcing the law. The law must have its own standards, minimal enough to sustain the challenge of due process.

In this connection another fact must be noted. The fact is that on

NODL lists there appear some twenty-odd works that either have received literary honors or at least have been acclaimed by serious critics. Doubtless high-school teachers could not, without absurdity, make them required reading for their students. But the police cannot, without equal absurdity, make them prohibited reading. Such stultification of the law is itself immoral.

There is a third fact of some consequence. The history of censorship has been a history of excess. The NODL has the problem of the local zealot, operating far from the central office in Chicago, and way outside the four pages of sensible procedures sent out from it. He or she "has the zeal of God indeed, but not according to understanding" (Romans 10:2). Such zealots are righteous, usually indignant, people. They have a good cause. They want results. What they lack is St. Paul's "understanding," which bears, he said, on "the *way* of justification."

I shall not labor the analogy. The point of it, in our case, is that the zealot at times fails to see how his zeal for results may betray him into the use of methods that will in turn betray his cause. Mr. Fischer, for example, in his zeal for his own cause, which is a good one, fell into a bad method of argument. Among other faults, he fails to distinguish between the "idea" of the NODL, which is the substantive issue, and the applications of the idea, which raise issues of procedure. In good "liberal" fashion he assigns the primacy to the procedural over the substantive. Contrariwise, in good "Catholic" fashion, the local zealot for the NODL cause assigns the primacy to the substantive over the procedural. He, or she, wants the newsstands "cleaned up"; and he, or she, in some instances doesn't greatly care how.

At that, Mr. Fischer is more nearly right. In this sensitive area the question of procedure is all-important. Part of the service of NODL to its own cause should be what I can only call a service of fraternal correction. It should somehow find a way of rebuking, or at least disavowing, the local zealot who violates, or goes beyond, the cooperative procedures, none of them coercive, which it officially stands for. (As for Mr. Fischer, maybe I have myself done him some service of intellectual charity?)

At this point, with all the ambiguities at least sorted out, if not cleared up, we could begin the rational public argument. The starting-point would be a fact—the existence of a "real national problem" (Mr. Fischer's words). Then the questions arise. For instance, does Mr. Fischer adequately measure the dimensions of the problem? He says:

"A good many tawdry and disreputable magazines, paperbound reprints and comic books have been offered for sale on a lot of newsstands. A few publishers unquestionably have tried to base their sales appeal on sex and violence; the pictures and text on the covers of their publications often hint that the contents are far more salacious than they are in fact."

He adds that "law-enforcement agencies in some cities have not been vigorous in enforcing the statutes against obscene publications." And that's it.

Or is it? Others would maintain that this is an astonishing understatement of the real national problem. They see the problem much more ominously large. A major issue in public morality has arisen; the morals of youth are particularly involved in it; the problem is growing. They further see a causal line between bad magazines, etc., and immorality. And they feel it imperative to "do something" about the bad literature.

When these last statements are made, they start up the current argument between sociology and common sense. The sociologist expresses professional doubt about the causal line between bad reading and immorality; he finds insufficient evidence for it. The common-sense view asserts that the causal line is sufficiently established by the nature, content, tendency, etc., of the literature itself. At least a strong presumption is thus created; and it furnishes reason for action, until—and maybe after—all the Ph.D. theses, pro and con, have been written.

The word "action" disturbs the jealous advocate of civil rights. He therefore comes up with his own causal line—between any attempt at suppressing any kind of literature and the subversion of the foundations of the Republic. The common-sense view expresses doubt about this causal line. There is, it says, insufficient evidence that any such alarming consequences will follow, if the action taken is rational and prudent.

Here the real issue begins to appear: what kinds of action, as taken by whom, are rational and prudent in the circumstances? And what promise of effectiveness do they offer?

Mr. Fischer has his own program of action, which deserves consideration. He recommends two positive courses. The first is self-regulation by newsdealers, booksellers and other merchants. They should, he says, "set their own house in order; they should refuse to sell any publication which —in their own untrammeled judgment—falls below their own standards as responsible businessmen."

A question of fact occurs here: how effective so far has the principle of self-regulation been in the solution of our real national problem? The evidence suggests a discouraging answer. Some efforts in this direction have been made, always under the pressure of public opinion; but their slim success bases little hope for the future. Second, the principle itself may be, and has been, called in question. For instance, in a report entitled *The Freedom to Read,* written for the National Book Committee, Richard McKeon, Walter Gellhorn and Robert K. Merton say this:

"The dangers of police censorship are obvious; but we are convinced that the dangers of a code of self-censorship are even greater. It provides the means by which all kinds of restrictions can be put on freedom of expression, and it places the freedom to read in the hands of a group which does not even have the accountability to the public which a chief of police has."

I don't necessarily endorse this judgment; but it may suggest that Mr. Fischer is on shaky ground.

There are other questions too. What, I might ask, is the right of a newsdealer to "untrammeled judgment"? Is his judgment, as a matter of fact, untrammeled? And whether it is or not, why should one trust it as a means of solution for our real national problem? Is he a better critic of literature, a better judge of morality, than the average parent? How is one even to know what his "standards as a responsible businessman" are? And if they could be known, is there to be no possibility of public judgment on them? On what title is this Olympian immunity claimed? One would like to know.

The second positive course is the action of law—legislative and court action. I am inclined to think that Mr. Fischer's confidence in the efficacy of legal action as a corrective in this difficult field of printed media will be astonishing to students of the law. If I mistake not, it is pretty generally admitted that the present legal picture is a muddle. It is further admitted that the difficulties encountered in trying to straighten it out are immense. There are the two sacred legal doctrines that must be protected—prior restraint and due process. Furthermore, there are certain adverse high-court decisions that seem to have reduced the law to a state of practical impotence, not least in the two crucial areas of obscenity and violence.

What is even more decisive, even if the law could be lifted to the full height of its legitimate potency, it would still be largely impotent to cope with the new problem of mass media, whose crude subtleties seem to defeat the subtle crudities of the law. The grounds for accepting the relative ineffectiveness of law in this special field, where the moral issue is not justice, are both theoretical and practical—to be found both in the art of jurisprudence and in the lessons of history.

Mr. Fischer suggests two manners of action—one private, the other public—whose possibilities ought by all means be explored and exploited. But in the course of rational public argument it would, I think, appear that his program of positive action is inadequate to the real national problem that confronts us. His negative demand is more acceptable. He wants organizations of private right to stop campaigns of coercion. So do I. Mr. Fischer's reasons are, I think, doctrinaire; further argument would have to illuminate the fact, if it is a fact. Whereas, I, as a Catholic, am not a doctrinaire.

In my Chicago lecture I said that ". . . it is not possible to prove the position, taken by some, that an action like the boycott of a moving picture is somehow 'unrightful,' or 'undemocratic' or 'unconstitutional.' No one can show that such an action lies beyond the limits of a primeval

American right to protest and object. The action may indeed be strenuous; but the American right to protest and object is permitted to run to some pretty strenuous extremes. This said against the doctrinaire, it remains true that methods of action which verge upon the coercive exhibit some incongruity when used by citizen-groups in the interests of morality in literature or on the screen. Even if they raise no issue of abstract right, they do raise the concrete issue of prudence, which, equally with justice, is one of the cardinal virtues."

I hold to this position now, against Mr. Fischer (I think), and also (I think) against the NODL in its present ambiguous situation—certainly in its representation by local zealots and by the secular arm of the police.

I further hold to my previous position that private agencies such as the NODL can perform an indispensable public function in the promotion of public morality—provided they understand what their function is. It is not to supplant the coercive function of the agencies of public law. It is to represent, soberly and honestly, the principle of voluntary reform, to be accomplished on the basis of social cooperation—that sincere cooperation which in America is always ready to be stimulated but often needs stimulation.

This principle of reform is altogether valid in itself. Its applications call for prudence—concretely, as I have previously said, for "men and women of prudence, who understand the art of procedure, and understand too that we are morally bound, by the virtue of prudence, to a concrete rightness of method in the pursuit of moral aims." For the rest, the rationality of this method of social reform will be understood, and its pitfalls will be avoided, if we can all somehow hold to high standards of public discussion. In this respect the editor of *Harper's* has failed. But his failure is less reprehensible than that of Catholics who miss their present opportunity —and duty—to perform the instant task, which is to inject the Catholic tradition of rationality into a mass democracy that is rapidly slipping its moorings in reason.

BESIG v. UNITED STATES[1]

United States Circuit Court of Appeals

Two books entitled respectively "Tropic of Cancer" and "Tropic of Capricorn," which were written by Henry Miller and were printed in Paris, were intercepted at an American port of entry and labeled . . . as obscene. The district court found them to be obscene and ordered them destroyed. Besig, the owner of the books, is here appealing upon the ground that neither of the two books, which are commonly referred to together as "The Tropics," is obscene.

The word "obscene" is not uncommon and is used in English and American speech and writings as the word symbol for indecent, smutty, lewd or salacious reference to parts of the human or animal body or to their functions or to the excrement therefrom. Each of The Tropics is written in the composite style of a novel-autobiography, and the author as a character in the book carries the reader as though he himself is living in disgrace, degradation, poverty, mean crime, and prostitution of mind and body. The vehicle of description is the unprintable word of the debased and morally bankrupt. Practically everything that the world loosely regards as sin is detailed in the vivid, lurid, salacious language of smut, prostitution, and dirt. And all of it is related without the slightest expressed idea of its abandon. Consistent with the general tenor of the books, even human excrement is dwelt upon in the dirtiest words available. The author conducts the reader through sex orgies and perversions of the sex organs, and always in the debased language of the bawdy house. Nothing has the grace of purity or goodness. These words of the language of smut, and the disgraceful scenes, are so heavily larded throughout the books that those portions which are deemed to be of literary merit do not lift the reader's mind clear of their sticky slime. And it is safe to say that the "literary merit" of the books carries the reader deeper into it. For this reason, The Tropics are far more dangerous than "Confessions of a Prostitute" which was the subject of our opinion in Burstein v. United States. . . . There, the scenes depicted are obscene because of the scene itself which in its stark ugliness might well repel many. The Tropics lure on with the cleverness of scene, skilfulness of

---

[1]Ninth Circuit, before Stephens, Orr, and Pope, San Francisco, California, October 23, 1953 (208 F.2d 142).

recital, and the use of worse than gutter words. All of this is sought to be justified through the sophistry, as the trial judge, Honorable Louis E. Goodman, put it, of "confession and avoidance." It is claimed that they truthfully describe a base status of society in the language of its own iniquities. And that, since we live in an age of realism, obscene language depicting obscenity in action ceases to be obscenity.

Whether the moral conventions should be flouted in the cause of frankness, art, or realism, we have no occasion to decide. That question is for the policy branches of the government. Nor do we understand that we have the legal power to hold that the statute authorizing the seizure of obscene books is inapplicable to books in which obscenity is an integral part of a literary work. So that obscenity, though a part of a composition of high literary merit, is not excepted from operation of the statute, whether written in the style of the realists, surrealists, or plain shock writers. The civilization of our times holds to the premise that dirt in stark nakedness is not generally and at all times acceptable. And the great mass of the people still believe there is such a thing as decency. Indecency is easily recognizable. Such is the premise of the statute. The Congress has chosen to enact a censorship which would not have been possible except for the self-styled prophets of truth who offend so grievously.

It is of course true that the ears of some may be so accustomed to words which are ordinarily regarded as obscene that they take no offense at them, but the law is not tempered to the hardened minority of society. The statute forbidding the importation of obscene books is not designed to fit the normal concept of morality of society's dregs, nor of the different concepts of morality throughout the world, nor for all time past and future, but is designed to fit the normal American concept in the age in which we live. It is no legitimate argument that because there are social groups composed of moral delinquents in this or in other countries, that their language shall be received as legal tender along with the speech of the great masses who trade ideas and information in the honest money of decency.

Adequate provision is made in the statute in the interests of classics and the technical, by the following proviso:

> "*Provided further,* That the Secretary of the Treasury may, in his discretion, admit the so-called classics or books of recognized and established literary or scientific merit, but may, in his discretion, admit such classics or books only when imported for noncommercial purposes. . . ."

It is claimed that these books (The Tropics) are not for the immature of mind, and that adults read them for their literary and informative merits, but, whether true or untrue, we cannot measure their importability by such a yardstick. The Congress probably saw the impracticability of preventing the use of the books by the young and the pure. And of course they knew that salacious print in the hands of adults, even in the hands of those whose sun is near the western horizon, may well incite to disgusting practices and to hideous crime.

We agree that the book as a book must be obscene to justify its libel and destruction, but neither the number of the "objectionable" passages nor the proportion they bear to the whole book are controlling. If an incident, integrated with the theme or story of a book, is word-painted in such lurid and smutty or pornographic language that dirt appears as the primary purpose rather than the relation of a fact or adequate description of the incident, the book itself is obscene. We are not well acquainted with Aristophanes or his times, but we know they were different from ours. We have chanced upon Chaucer and we know his times were different from ours. Boccaccio is lurid. The Bible is not free from the recounting of immoral practices. But the translators, from the languages in which The Bible was originally written, did not word-paint such practices in the lurid-Miller-morally-corrupt manner. Dirty word description of the sweet and sublime, especially of the mystery of sex and procreation, is the ultimate of obscenity. We have referred to Aristophanes, Chaucer, Boccaccio, and The Bible only because those works were taken as examples by the author of the opinion in the case of United States v. One Book Entitled Ulysses . . . a case cited by appellant to illustrate his point that " 'No work may be judged from a selection of such paragraphs alone . . . ,' " but the point is not relevant because we have adjudged each book as an integrated whole. . . .

Appellant thinks the district court committed error in deciding contrary to the great weight of opinion evidence as to the quality of Mr. Miller's writings. The point has no merit. Opinion evidence is useful, but not controlling. We have carefully read and analyzed the voluminous affidavits and exhibits contained in the record. To a large extent they are opinions of authors who resent any limitation on their writings. Their opinions are relevant and competent evidence, but their views are advisory only as to the norm of the meaning of the word "obscene." We share the general antipathy to censorship and we are aware that individual tastes and special occasions and different times and different peoples differ as to what is offensive language. Yet we risk the assertion that there is an underlying, perhaps universal, accord that there is a phase of respectable delicacy related to sex, and that those compositions which purposefully flout such delicacy in language generally regarded as indecent come under the ban of the statute. . . .

ATTORNEY GENERAL v. THE BOOK NAMED "TROPIC OF CANCER"[1]

Supreme Judicial Court of Massachusetts

We think . . . that the First Amendment protects material which has value because of ideas, news, or artistic, literary, or scientific attributes. If the appeal of material (taken as a whole) to adults is not predominantly prurient, adults cannot be denied the material. When the public risks of suppressing ideas are weighed against the risks of permitting their circulation, the guaranties of the First Amendment must be given controlling effect. The dangers of subjective judgments in the matter of censorship lead to a strong presupposition against suppression. We conclude, therefore, . . . that, with respect to material designed for general circulation, only predominantly "hard core" pornography, without redeeming social significance, is obscene in the constitutional sense.

Whether Tropic is "obscene" in the constitutional sense thus depends upon whether the appeal (if any) of Tropic (taken as a whole) to the normal adult is predominantly prurient. It is not relevant that we think that the book at many places is repulsive, vulgar, and grossly offensive in the use of four letter words, and in the detailed and coarse statement of sexual episodes. That a serious work uses four letter words and has a grossly offensive tone does not mean that the work is not entitled to constitutional protection. Much in modern art, literature, and music is likely to seem ugly and thoroughly objectionable to those who have different standards of taste. It is not the function of judges to serve as arbiters of taste or to say that an author must regard vulgarity as unnecessary to his portrayal of particular scenes or characters or to establish particular ideas. Within broad limits each writer, attempting to be a literary artist, is entitled to determine such matters for himself, even if the result is as dull, dreary, and offensive as the writer of this opinion finds almost all of Tropic.

Competent critics assert, and we conclude, that Tropic has serious purpose, even if many will find that purpose obscure. There can be no doubt that a significant segment of the literary world has long regarded the book as of literary importance. A majority of the court are of opinion that the predominant effect and purpose of the book as a whole is not prurient.

---

[1]July 17, 1962 (184 N.E.2d 328).

. . . a majority of the court are of opinion that Tropic is more likely to discourage than "to excite lustful thoughts." We think that the book must be accepted as a conscious effort to create a work of literary art and as having significance, which prevents treating it as hard core pornography.

A CRITIC'S VERDICT[1]

John Ciardi

John Ciardi has taught at Rutgers, is himself a poet and the editor of several volumes of poetry, and a winner of the Prix de Rome. His column "Manner of Speaking" is a regular feature of the Saturday Review, *of which he is poetry editor.*

The American publication last year of Henry Miller's "Tropic of Cancer," long the under-the-counter and smuggler's classic of our times, has touched off another series of court cases, all following what has become a standard pattern.

. . . books singled out by the local censors have to be defended in a seemingly endless number of jurisdictions. The publisher must take on the burden of fighting the same case over and over, with the likelihood that he will lose by exhaustion despite the merit of his legal position. I do not have all the details of the series of legal battles in which Grove Press has found itself since publication day, but I have seen it reported in the New York *Times* that Grove has been involved in over sixty cases (more than one a week) at an estimated cost of over $100,000. The multiplication of cases has become one part of the standard pattern.

As the standard pattern of the defense; Grove Press has called upon critics and other expert witnesses to testify in court or to submit sworn affidavits in support of the book. All such depositions begin with the expert identifying himself under oath and declaring that he is thoroughly familiar with the book. He then states his position in the case, lists his qualifications (degrees, publications, honors, and positions held), and proceeds to a defense of the book, beginning usually with some generalizations on the nature of artistic merit.

The standard pattern of the prosecution is to do his best to assemble a plain-as-mud jury and to dismiss all such learned experts as strange egg-

---

[1]*Saturday Review,* June 30, 1962, p. 13. Reprinted by permission.

heads who in no sense understand the "average man" whose sensibilities are supposed to have been assaulted by the book.

In countering this anti-intellectual pattern of the prosecution, the experts have developed a more or less firm pattern of defending "Tropic of Cancer" on the grounds that it is "a great work of art." It is the wisdom of such a defense that I must question.

To describe a contemporary book as "a great work of art" is a temptation to which all enthusiasm is liable. It is a temptation to which I have myself succumbed at times. But it is finally to attribute to that book qualities that only time and the judgment of succeeding periods of varying literary taste can certify. One may safely say that "The Divine Comedy" is a great work of art; one can only assert as much about "Tropic of Cancer," or about any other contemporary book. I do not mean to deny that "Tropic of Cancer" will survive the test by time. I believe it will. But I must also doubt that it will emerge as the central monument of twentieth-century writing.

Right or wrong, what service do critics perform for literature in rushing the verdict because a book is under local attack? Or in making the central defense of a book nothing less than its "greatness"? Shall there be no mercy for the less-than-great? Are serious writers to have no legal protection from the book banners simply because they happen to be minor writers?

The one defense of freedom must defend all. "Tropic of Cancer" must be defended, but not as "a great book." It must be defended as the work of a serious artist enlarged by talent and passionately engaged in giving form (and thereby meaning) to his view of life.

A prurient person could, of course, single out passages describing specific sex acts and feast his immature eroticism (whether or not disguised as puritanical repugnance) on those. A sick-minded person could as readily go through a book of art reproductions and cut out every female breast, foot, or thigh, perhaps finding some sort of queer thrill in such fetishism. But the paintings in the book he so mutilates were never intended for such abuse. Neither was "Tropic of Cancer" intended for the sick snatcher of erotic details. Read from the beginning, as published and offered for reading, the book is, if anything, boring in its detailing of filth, of ugliness, and of the various acts of generally unattractive sex. It is only as one understands and responds to the author's full intent that such itemizations of unattractive matter become charged with meaning and, therefore, interesting.

There can be no question of that intent. The book sets out to portray the rescue of the individual life-impulse of the artist (and, therefore, of any man) in his necessary revolt against a society he takes to be shabby, grasping, hypocritical, and sterile. "Tropic of Cancer" is a novel of protest. Its protest is against all that stifles the essential life-impulse. It is also a novel of praise. What it praises is the dignity of the individual who will plunge into any experience, and welcome poverty, hunger, and ostracism, so long as he may escape hypocrisy.

Miller's protest includes mockery, a great roaring laughter, and a certain violent joy in flouting all the values socially accepted as sacred. He flatly refuses to do society the honor of taking it seriously.

But the violence of that mockery is inseparable from the moral stature of the book. Only as the author scorns what he feels to be false can he praise what he feels to be true. Were he to draw back from his assault on the social sickness he sees, were he to pass himself off, even for an instant, as a man of probity and respectability, he would have offered himself to the sickness he combats. The aesthetic integrity of his affirmation would be lost at once.

The point of all this mockery, of his posturing, and even of his animal hi-jinks, is always in praise of the free soul. His cry of anguish at what society does to the individual is inseparable from the yell of animal joy with which he celebrates his escape from stultification.

"Tropic of Cancer" must be defended not as an ultimate peak of greatness, but because, whether it succeeds or fails, it is written with power and compassion, and because it is charged in every passage with the author's aesthetic devotion to his form and with his humane devotion to the joy of life. To remove such a book from the experience of mature readers on the grounds that the prurient may use it abusively is an assault upon the aesthetic experience. It is a denial of freedom on the queasy grounds that men are not fit for freedom. It is to say that the least of men shall dictate the diet of the rest.

To base a defense on the claim of greatness is to abuse good cause. What must be defended is the right of the serious artist not to succeed, but to try.

EXTRAMARITAL
SEXUAL EXPERIENCE

The mores are flexible with reference to male chastity and rigid as regards female chastity. Such a double standard in a society that frowns upon prostitution and does not, like ancient Corinth, accept hetairas (or what the French call "women of the demimonde") is, of course, contradictory. If, besides this, one reckons with the emancipation or semi-emancipation of women, the great disparity between what we preach about chastity and what we practice should come as no surprise. In the samples studied by three authoritative surveys of premarital sexual behavior (Terman, Burgess and Wallen, Kinsey) approximately 50 percent of the women among those born after 1900 had entered marriage "nonvirginal." It is reliably estimated that over 30 percent of all unmarried women between the ages of twenty-one and twenty-five have some premarital experience.

In a country such as Sweden the mores are permissive and in our country, as might be expected, very much in transition. Meanwhile we vary in our responses to these awkward revelations between titillating ourselves with the risqué and wrestling with feelings of guilt. Few rise above the level of oblique reference to examine a subject of surpassing importance in a frank and honest way. Outside of a limited circle, the causes and consequences of the disparity between precept and practice are rarely explored, even in an age which has known Havelock Ellis and Sigmund Freud, and, in its literature, no longer bans James Joyce or D. H. Lawrence. Because this whole dimly lit world of embarrassment and evasion was suddenly, if not quite accurately, revealed in the harsh glare of the Kinsey surveys, it seems appropriate to present, in addition to the views of two renowned men, samples of the extended comment evoked by the publication of *Sexual Behavior in the Human Male* and *Sexual Behavior in the Human Female.*

Not only the content of the now famous Kinsey studies of sexual behavior but also the nature of their reception affords a revealing insight into American sex mores. This is especially true of the appearance of his *Sexual Behavior in the Human Female,* easily the most heralded and pilloried sociological study of our time. Excerpts from two reviews will therefore help throw additional light on what Mr. Lippmann has called "love in the Great Society."

MARRIAGE AND MORALS[1]

Bertrand Russell

Many who read the following selection from Bertrand Russell's
Marriage and Morals *will wish that this ruthlessly frank philosopher
had limited himself to such harmless pursuits as logic, epistemology,
and metaphysics. Russell is no sexologist, of course, and not an
authority on marriage and the family. The volume from which the
following selection is taken may well be regarded as among the less
important of his works. The selection is simply offered as a sample
of what one of the most profound thinkers of our time had to say
about a delicate and still much neglected subject.* Marriage and
Morals *was published in 1929, but there is no reason to believe that
Russell would change it materially if he were writing in 1972, when
at the age of 100, he will no doubt be embarking with youthful vigor
on some new mission—provided he succeeds in his present one,
which is to alert the world to the imminence and finality of an
atomic war.*

In a rational ethic, marriage would not count as such in the absence
of children. A sterile marriage should be easily dissoluble, for it is through
children alone that sexual relations become of importance to society, and
worthy to be taken cognisance of by a legal institution. This, of course, is
not the view of the Church, which, under the influence of St. Paul, still
views marriage rather as the alternative to fornication than as the means
to the procreation of children. In recent years, however, even clergymen
have become aware that neither men nor women invariably wait for marriage before experiencing sexual intercourse. In the case of men, provided
their lapses were with prostitutes and decently concealed, they were comparatively easy to condone, but in the case of women other than professional
prostitutes, the conventional moralists find what they call immorality much
harder to put up with. Nevertheless, in America, in England, in Germany,
in Scandinavia, a great change has taken place since [World War I] . . .
many girls of respectable families have ceased to think it worth while to
preserve their "virtue," and young men, instead of finding an outlet with
prostitutes, have had affairs with girls of the kind whom, if they were richer,
they would wish to marry. It seems that this process has gone farther in the

---

[1]From *Marriage and Morals* (New York: H. Liveright, 1929), pp. 125–133.
Reprinted by permission.

United States than it has in England, owing, I think, to Prohibition and automobiles. Owing to Prohibition, it has become *de rigueur* at any cheerful party for everybody to get more or less drunk. Owing to the fact that a very large percentage of girls possess cars of their own, it has become easy for them to escape with a lover from the eyes of parents and neighbours. The resulting state of affairs is described in Judge Lindsey's books.[2] The old accuse him of exaggeration, but the young do not. As far as a casual traveller can, I took pains to test his assertions by questioning young men. I did not find them inclined to deny anything that he said as to the facts. It seems to be the case throughout America that a very large percentage of girls who subsequently marry and become of the highest respectability have sex experience, often with several lovers. And even where complete relations do not occur, there is so much "petting" and "necking" that the absence of complete intercourse can only be viewed as a perversion.

I cannot say myself that I view the present state of affairs as satisfactory. It has certain undesirable features imposed upon it by conventional moralists, and until conventional morality is changed, I do not see how these undesirable features are to disappear. Bootlegged sex is in fact as inferior to what it might be as footlegged alcohol. I do not think anybody can deny that there is enormously more drunkenness among young men, and still more among young women, in well-to-do America than there was before the introduction of Prohibition. In circumventing the law there is, of course, a certain spice and a certain pride of cleverness, and while the law about drink is being circumvented it is natural to circumvent the conventions about sex. Here, also, the sense of daring acts as an aphrodisiac. The consequence is that sex relations between young people tend to take the silliest possible form, being entered into not from affection but from bravado, and at times of intoxication. Sex, like liquor, has to be taken in forms which are concentrated and rather unpalatable, since these forms alone can escape the vigilance of the authorities. Sex relations as a dignified, rational, wholehearted activity in which the complete personality co-operates, do not often, I think, occur in America outside marriage. To this extent the moralists have been successful. They have not prevented fornication; on the contrary, if anything, their opposition, by making it spicy, has made it more common. But they have succeeded in making it almost as undesirable as they say it is, just as they have succeeded in making much of the alcohol consumed as poisonous as they assert all alcohol to be. They have compelled young people to take sex neat, divorced from daily companionship, from a common work, and from all psychological intimacy. The more timid of the young do not go so far as complete sexual relations, but content themselves with producing prolonged states of sexual excitement without satis-

---

[2]*The Revolt of Modern Youth,* 1925. *Companionate Marriage,* 1927.

faction, which are nervously debilitating, and calculated to make the full enjoyment of sex at a later date difficult or impossible. Another drawback to the type of sexual excitement which prevails among the young in America is that it involves either failure to work or loss of sleep, since it is necessarily connected with parties which continue into the small hours.

A graver matter, while official morality remains what it is, is the risk of occasional disaster. By ill luck it may happen that some one young person's doings come to the ears of some guardian of morality, who will proceed with a good conscience to a sadistic orgy of scandal. And since it is almost impossible for young people in America to acquire a sound knowledge of birth-control methods, unintended pregnancies are not infrequent. These are generally dealt with by procuring abortion, which is dangerous, painful, illegal, and by no means easy to keep secret. The complete gulf between the morals of the young and the morals of the old, which exists very commonly in present-day America, has another unfortunate result, namely that often there can be no real intimacy or friendship between parents and children, and that the parents are incapable of helping their children with advice or sympathy. When young people get into a difficulty, they cannot speak of it to their parents without producing an explosion—possibly scandal, certainly a hysterical upheaval. The relation of parent and child has thus ceased to be one performing any useful function after the child has reached adolescence. How much more civilized are the Trobriand Islanders, where a father will say to his daughter's lover: "You sleep with my child: very well, marry her."[3]

In spite of the drawbacks we have been considering, there are great advantages in the emancipation, however partial, of young people in America, as compared with their elders. They are freer from priggery, less inhibited, less enslaved to authority devoid of rational foundation. I think also that they are likely to prove less cruel, less brutal, and less violent than their seniors. For it has been characteristic of American life to take out in violence the anarchic impulses which could not find an outlet in sex. It may also be hoped that when the generation now young reaches middle age, it will not wholly forget its behaviour in youth, and will be tolerant of sexual experiments which at present are scarcely possible because of the need of secrecy.

The state of affairs in England is more or less similar to that in America, though not so developed owing to the absence of Prohibition and the paucity of motor-cars. There is also, I think, in England and certainly on the Continent, very much less of the practice of sexual excitement without ultimate satisfaction. And respectable people in England, with some honourable exceptions, are on the whole less filled with persecuting zeal

---

[3]Malinowski, *The Sexual Life of Savages,* p. 73.

than corresponding people in America. Nevertheless, the difference between the two countries is only one of degree.

Judge Ben B. Lindsey, who was for many years in charge of the juvenile court at Denver, and in that position had unrivalled opportunities for ascertaining the facts, proposed a new institution which he calls "companionate marriage." Unfortunately he has lost his official position, for when it became known that he used it rather to promote the happiness of the young than to give them a consciousness of sin, the Ku Klux Klan and the Catholics combined to oust him. Companionate marriage is the proposal of a wise conservative. It is an attempt to introduce some stability into the sexual relations of the young, in place of the present promiscuity. He points out the obvious fact that what prevents the young from marrying is lack of money, and that money is required in marriage partly on account of children, but partly also because it is not the thing for the wife to earn her own living. His view is that young people should be able to enter upon a new kind of marriage, distinguished from ordinary marriage by three characteristics. First, that there should be for the time being no intention of having children, and that accordingly the best available birth-control information should be given to the young couple. Second, that so long as there are no children and the wife is not pregnant, divorce should be possible by mutual consent. And third, that in the event of divorce, the wife should not be entitled to alimony. He holds, and I think rightly, that if such an institution were established by law, a very great many young people, for example students at universities, would enter upon comparatively permanent partnerships, involving a common life, and free from the Dionysiac characteristics of their present sex relations. He brings evidence to bear that young students who are married do better work than such as are unmarried. It is indeed obvious that work and sex are more easily combined in a quasi-permanent relation than in the scramble and excitement of parties and alcoholic stimulation. There is no reason under the sun why it should be more expensive for two young people to live together than to live separately, and therefore the economic reasons which at present lead to postponement of marriage would no longer operate. I have not the faintest doubt that Judge Lindsey's plan, if embodied in the law, would have a very beneficent influence, and that this influence would be such as all might agree to be a gain from a moral point of view.

Nevertheless, Judge Lindsey's proposals were received with a howl of horror by all middle-aged persons and all newspapers throughout the length and breadth of America. It was said that he was attacking the sanctity of the home; it was said that in tolerating marriages not intended to lead at once to children he was opening the floodgates to legalized lust; it was said that he enormously exaggerated the prevalence of extra-marital sexual relations, that he was slandering pure American womanhood, and that most business men remained cheerfully continent up to the age of thirty or thirty-five. All these things were said, and I try to think that among those who said them were some who believed them. I listened to many invectives against Judge Lindsey, but I came away with the impression that the arguments which were regarded as decisive were two. First, that Judge Lindsey's proposals would not have been approved by Christ; and second, that they were not approved by even the more liberal of American divines. The second of these arguments appeared to be considered the more weighty, and indeed rightly, since the other is purely hypothetical, and incapable of being substantiated. I never heard any person advance any argument even pretending to show that Judge Lindsey's proposal would diminish human happiness. This consideration, indeed, I was forced to conclude, is thought wholly unimportant by those who uphold traditional morality.

For my part, while I am quite convinced that companionate marriage would be a step in the right direction, and would do a great deal of good, I do not think that it goes far enough. I think that all sex relations which do not involve children should be regarded as a purely private affair, and that if a man and a woman choose to live together without having children, that should be no one's business but their own. I should not hold it desirable that either a man or a woman should enter upon the serious business of a marriage intended to lead to children without having had previous sexual experience. There is a great mass of evidence to show that the first experience of sex should be with a person who has previous knowledge. The sexual act in human beings is not instinctive, and apparently never has been since it ceased to be performed *a tergo*. And apart from this argument, it seems absurd to ask people to enter upon a relation intended to be lifelong, without any previous knowledge as to their sexual compatibility. It is just as absurd as it would be if a man intending to buy a house were not allowed to view it until he had completed the purchase. The proper course, if the biological function of marriage were adequately recognized, would be to say that no marriage should be legally binding until the wife's first pregnancy. At present a marriage is null if sexual intercourse is impossible, but children, rather than sexual intercourse, are the true purpose of marriage, which should therefore be not regarded as consummated until such time as there is a prospect of children. This view depends, at least in part, upon that separation between procreation and mere sex which has been brought about by contraceptives. Contraceptives have altered the whole aspect of sex and marriage, and have made distinctions necessary which could formerly have been ignored. People may come together for sex alone, as occurs in prostitution, or for companionship involving a sexual element, as in Judge Lindsey's companionate marriage, or, finally, for the purpose of rearing a family. These are all different, and no morality can be adequate to modern circumstances which confounds them in one indiscriminate total.

LOVE IN THE GREAT SOCIETY[1]

Walter Lippmann

Over a long period Walter Lippmann has been a brilliant political analyst and commentator. Through his syndicated column and numerous books and articles he has influenced public policy in America at least as much as any living writer. The Good Society *(1937),* The Public Philosophy *(1955),* The Communist World and Ours *(1959),* The Coming Test with Russia *(1961), and* Western Unity and the Common Market *(1962) are among his many works. Because in late years he has limited himself to questions of public policy—if, indeed, such an interest can be viewed as restricted—it is not always remembered that in an older work,* A Preface to Morals, *he wrote about the foundations of belief and conduct. Unlike behavior, which is the province of the psychologist, conduct is the concern of the humanist and moralist; and it is as such that Lippmann writes about sexual conduct. Although these comments were published in the same year as Russell's (1929), it is doubtful that Lippmann any more than Russell would find a need to change the text (except perhaps the frequency of his reference to Havelock Ellis) if he were writing it today.*

. . . In the popular mind it is immediately assumed that when morals are discussed it is sexual morals that are meant. The morals of the politician and the voter, of the shareholder and executive and employee, are only moderately interesting to the general public: thus they almost never supply the main theme of popular fiction. But the relations between boy and girl, man and woman, husband and wife, mistress and lover, parents and children, are themes which no amount of repetition makes stale. The explanation is obvious. The modern audience is composed of persons among whom only a comparatively negligible few are serenely happy in their personal lives. Popular fiction responds to their longings: to the unappeased it offers some measure of vicarious satisfaction, to the prurient an indulgence, to the worried, if not a way out, then at least the comfort of knowing that their secret despair is a common, and not a unique, experience.

Yet in spite of this immense preoccupation with sex it is extraordinarily difficult to arrive at any reliable knowledge of what actual change in human

[1]Reprinted from *A Preface to Morals* by Walter Lippmann (New York: The Macmillan Company, 1929), pp. 285–313. Copyright 1929 by The Macmillan Company; copyright 1957 by Walter Lippmann. By permission of the publisher.

behavior it reflects. This is not surprising. In fact this is the very essence of the matter. The reason it is difficult to know the actual facts about sexual behavior in modern society is that sexual behavior eludes observation and control. We know that the old conventions have lost most of their authority because we cannot know about, and therefore can no longer regulate, the sexual behavior of others. It may be that there is, as some optimists believe, a fine but candid restraint practiced among modern men and women. It may be that incredible licentiousness exists all about us, as the gloomier prophets insist. It may be that there is just about as much unconventional conduct and no more than there has always been. Nobody, I think, really knows. Nobody knows whether the conversation about sex reflects more promiscuity or less hypocrisy. But what everybody must know is that sexual conduct, whatever it may be, is regulated personally and not publicly in modern society. If there is restraint it is, in the last analysis, voluntary; if there is promiscuity, it can be quite secret.

The circumstances which have wrought this change are inherent in modern ways of living. Until quite recently the main conventions of sex were enforced first by the parents and then by the husband through their control over the life of the woman. The main conventions were: first, that she must not encourage or display any amorous inclinations except where there was practical certainty that the young man's intentions were serious; second, that when she was married to the young man she submitted to his embraces only because the Lord somehow failed to contrive a less vile method of perpetuating the species. All the minor conventions were subsidiary to these; the whole system was organized on the premise that procreation was the woman's only sanction for sexual intercourse. Such control as was exercised over the conduct of men was subordinate to this control over the conduct of women. The chastity of women before marriage was guarded; that meant that seduction was a crime, but that relations with "lost" or unchaste women was tolerated. The virtuous man, by popular standards, was one who before his marriage did not have sexual relations with a virtuous woman. There is ample testimony in the outcries of moralists that even in the olden days these conventions were not perfectly administered. But they were sufficiently well administered to remain the accepted conventions, honored even in the breach. It was possible, because of the way people lived, to administer them.

The woman lived a sheltered life. That is another way of saying that she lived under the constant inspection of her family. She lived at home. She worked at home. She met young men under the zealous chaperonage of practically the whole community. No doubt, couples slipped away occasionally and more went on than was known or acknowledged. But even then there was a very powerful deterrent against an illicit relationship. This deterrent was the fear of pregnancy. That in the end made it almost certain that if a secret affair were consummated it could not be kept secret and that terrible penalties would be exacted. In the modern world effective chaperonage has become impracticable and the fear of pregnancy has been virtually eliminated by the very general knowledge of contraceptive methods. The whole revolution in the field of sexual morals turns upon the fact that external control of the chastity of women is becoming impossible.

. . . liberal reformers have . . . been urging for the removal of prohibitory laws [on birth control] and they have built their case on two main theses. They have argued, first, that the limitation of births was sound public policy for economic and eugenic reasons; and second, that it was necessary to the happiness of families, the health of mothers, and the welfare of children. All these reasons may be unimpeachable. I think they are. But it was idle to pretend that the dissemination of this knowledge, even if legally confined to the instruction of married women by licensed physicians, could be kept from the rest of the adult population. Obviously that which all married couples are permitted to know every one is bound to know. Human curiosity will make that certain. Now this is what the Christian churches, especially the Roman Catholic, which oppose contraception on principle, instantly recognized. They were quite right. They were quite right, too, in recognizing that whether or not birth control is eugenic, hygienic, and economic, it is the most revolutionary practice in the history of sexual morals.

For when conception could be prevented, there was an end to the theory that woman submits to the embrace of the male only for the purpose of procreation. She had to be persuaded to cooperate, and no possible reason could be advanced except that the pleasure was reciprocal. She had to understand and inwardly assent to the principle that it is proper to have sexual intercourse with her husband and to prevent conception. She had, therefore, to give up the whole traditional theory which she may have only half-believed anyway, that sexual intercourse was an impure means to a noble end. She could no longer believe that procreation alone mitigated the vileness of cohabiting with a man, and so she had to change her valuation and accept it as inherently delightful. Thus by an inevitable process the practice of contraception led husbands and wives to the conviction that they need not be in the least ashamed of their desires for each other.

But this transvaluation of values within the sanctity of the marital chamber could hardly be kept a secret. What had happened was that married couples were indulging in the pleasures of sex because they had learned how to isolate them from the responsibilities of parenthood. When we talk about the unconventional theories of the younger generation we might in all honesty take this fact into account. They have had it demonstrated to them by their own parents, by those in whom the administering of the conventions is vested, that under certain circumstances it is legitimate and proper to gratify sexual desire apart from any obligation to the family or to the race. They have been taught that it is possible to do this, and that it may be proper. Therefore, the older generation could no longer argue that sexual intercourse as such was evil. It could no longer argue that it was obviously dangerous. It could only maintain that the psychological consequences are serious if sexual gratification is not made incidental to the enduring partnership of marriage and a home. That may be, in fact, I think it can be shown to be, the real wisdom of the matter. Yet if it is the wisdom of the matter, it is a kind of wisdom which men and women can acquire by experience alone. They do not have it instinctively. They cannot be compelled to adopt it. They can only learn to believe it.

That is a very different thing from submitting to a convention upheld by all human and divine authority.

With contraception established as a more or less legitimate idea in modern society, a vast discussion has ensued as to how the practice of it can be rationalized. In this discussion the pace is set by those who accept the apparent logic of contraception and are prepared boldly to revise the sexual conventions accordingly. They take as their major premise the obvious fact that by contraception it is possible to dissociate procreation from gratification, and therefore to pursue independently what Mr. Havelock Ellis calls the primary and secondary objects of the sexual impulse. They propose, therefore, to sanction two distinct sets of conventions: one designed to protect the interests of the offspring by promoting intelligent, secure, and cheerful parenthood; the other designed to permit the freest and fullest expression of the erotic personality. They propose, in other words, to distinguish between parenthood as a vocation involving public responsibility, and love as an art, pursued privately for the sake of happiness.

As a preparation for the vocation of parenthood it is proposed to educate both men and women in the care, both physical and psychological, of children. It is proposed further that mating for parenthood shall become an altogether deliberate and voluntary choice: the argument here is that the duties of parenthood cannot be successfully fulfilled except where both parents cheerfully and knowingly assume them. Therefore, it is proposed, in order to avert the dangers of love at first sight and of mating under the blind compulsion of instinct, that a period of free experimentation be allowed to precede the solemn engagement to produce and rear children. This engagement is regarded as so much a public responsibility that it is even proposed, and to some extent has been embodied in the law of certain jurisdictions, that marriage for parenthood must be sanctioned by medical authority. In order, too, that no compulsive considerations may determine what ought to be a free and intelligent choice, it is argued that women should be economically independent before and during marriage. As this may not be possible for women without property of their own during the years when they are bearing and rearing children, it is proposed in some form or other to endow motherhood. This endowment may take the form of a legal claim upon the earnings of the father, or it may mean a subsidy from the state through mothers' pensions, free medical attention, day nurseries, and kindergartens. The principle that successful parenthood must be voluntary is maintained as consistently as possible. Therefore, among those who follow the logic of their idea, it is proposed that even marriages deliberately entered into for procreation shall be dissoluble at the will of either party, the state intervening only to insure the economic security of the offspring. It is proposed, furthermore, that where women find the vocation of motherhood impracticable for one reason or another, they may be relieved of the duty of rearing their children.

Not all of the advanced reformers adopt the whole of this program, but the whole of this program is logically inherent in the conception of parenthood as a vocation deliberately undertaken, publicly pursued, and motivated solely by the parental instincts.

The separate set of conventions which it is proposed to adopt for the development of love as an art have a logic of their own. Their function is not to protect the welfare of the child but the happiness of lovers. It is very easy to misunderstand this conception. Mr. Havelock Ellis, in fact, describes it as a "divine and elusive mystery," a description which threatens to provide a rather elusive standard by which to fix a new set of sexual conventions. But baffling as this sounds, it is not wholly inscrutable, and a sufficient understanding of what is meant can be attained by clearing up the dangerous ambiguity in the phrase "love as an art."

There are two arts of love and it makes a considerable difference which one is meant. There is the art of love as Casanova, for example, practiced it. It is the art of seduction, courtship, and sexual gratification: it is an art which culminates in the sexual act. It can be repeated with the same lover and with other lovers, but it exhausts itself in the moment of ecstasy. When that moment is reached, the work of art is done, and the lover as artist "after an interval, perhaps of stupor and vital recuperation" must start all over again, until at last the rhythm is so stale it is a weariness to start at all; or the lover must find new lovers and new resistances to conquer. The aftermath of romantic love—that is, of love that is consummated in sexual ecstasy—is either tedium in middle age or the compulsive adventurousness of the libertine.

Now this is not what Mr. Ellis means when he talks about love as an art. "The act of intercourse," he says, "is only an incident, and not an essential in love." Incident to what? His answer is that it is an incident to an "exquisitely and variously and harmoniously blended" activity of "all the finer activities of the organism, physical and psychic." I take this to mean that when a man and woman are successfully in love, their whole activity is energized and victorious. They walk better, their digestion improves, they think more clearly, their secret worries drop away, the world is fresh and interesting and they can do more than they dreamed that they could do. In love of this kind sexual intimacy is not the dead end of desire as it is in romantic or promiscuous love, but periodic affirmation of the inward delight of desire pervading an active life. Love of this sort can grow; it is not, like youth itself, a moment that comes and is gone and remains only a memory of something which cannot be recovered. It can grow because it has something to grow upon and to grow with; it is not contracted and stale because it has for its object, not the mere relief of physical tension, but all the objects with which the two lovers are concerned. They desire their worlds in each other, and therefore their love is as interesting as their worlds and their worlds are as interesting as their love.

It is to promote unions of this sort that the older liberals are proposing a new set of sexual conventions. There are, however, reformers in the field who take a much less exalted view of the sexual act, who regard it, indeed, not only as without biological or social significance, but also as without any very impressive psychological significance. "The practice of birth control," says Mr. C. E. M. Joad, for example, "will profoundly modify our sexual habits. It will enable the pleasures of sex to be tasted without its penalties, and it will remove the most formidable deterrent to irregular intercourse." For birth control "offers to the young . . . the prospect of shameless, harmless, and unlimited pleasure." But whether the reformers agree with Mr. Ellis that sexual intimacy is, as he says, a sacrament signifying some great spiritual reality, or with Mr. Joad that it is a harmless pleasure, they are agreed that the sexual conventions should be revised to permit such unions without penalties and without any sense of shame.

They ask public opinion to sanction what contraception has made feasible. They point out that "a large number of the men and women of to-day form sexual relationships outside marriage—whether or not they ultimately lead to marriage—which they conceal or seek to conceal from the world." These relationships, says Mr. Ellis, differ from the extramarital manifestations of the sexual life of the past in that they do not derive from prostitution or seduction. Both of these ancient practices, he adds, are diminishing, for prostitution is becoming less attractive and, with the education of women, seduction is becoming less possible. The novelty of these new relations, the prevalence of which is conceded though it cannot be measured, lies in the fact that they are entered into voluntarily, have no obvious social consequences, and are altogether beyond the power of law or opinion to control. The argument, therefore, is that they should be approved, the chief point made being that by removing all stigma from such unions, they will become candid, wholesome, and delightful. The objection of the reformers to the existing conventions is that the sense of sin poisons the spontaneous goodness of such relationships.

The actual proposals go by a great variety of fancy names such as free love, trial marriage, companionate marriage. When these proposals are examined it is evident they all take birth control as their major premise, and then deduce from it some part or all of the logical consequences. Companionate marriage, for example, is from the point of view of the law, whatever it may be subjectively, nothing but a somewhat roundabout way of saying that childless couples may be divorced by mutual consent. It is a proposal, if not to control, then at least to register publicly, all sexual unions, the theory being that this public registration will abolish shame and furtiveness and give them a certain permanence. Companionate marriage is frankly an attempt at a compromise between marriages that are difficult to dissolve and clandestine relationships which have no sanction whatever.

The uncompromising logic of birth control has been stated more clearly, I think, by Mr. Bertrand Russell than by anyone else. Writing to Judge Lindsey during the uproar about companionate marriage, Mr. Russell said:

> I go further than you do: the things which your enemies say about you would be largely true of me. My own view is that the state and the law should take no notice of sexual relations apart from children, and that no marriage ceremony should be valid unless accompanied by a medical certificate of the woman's pregnancy. But when once there are children, I think that divorce should be avoided except for very grave cause. I should not regard physical infidelity as a very grave cause and should teach people that it is to be expected and tolerated, but should not involve the begetting of illegitimate children—not because illegitimacy is bad in itself, but because a home with two parents is best for children. I do not feel that the main thing in marriage is the feeling of the parents for each other; the main thing is cooperation in bearing children.

In this admirably clear statement there is set forth a plan for that complete separation between the primary and secondary function of sexual intercourse which contraception makes possible.

It is one thing, however, to recognize the full logic of birth control and quite another thing to say that convention ought to be determined by that logic. One might as well argue that because automobiles can be driven at a hundred miles an hour the laws should sanction driving at the rate of a hundred miles an hour. Birth control is a device like the automobile, and its inherent possibilities do not fix the best uses to be made of it.

What an understanding of the logic of birth control does is to set before us the limits of coercive control of sexual relations. The law can, for example, make divorce very difficult where there are children. It could, as Mr. Bertrand Russell suggests, refuse divorce on the ground of infidelity. On the other hand the law cannot effectively prohibit infidelity, and as a matter of fact does not do so to-day. It cannot effectively prohibit fornication though there are statutes against it. Therefore, what Mr. Russell has done is to describe accurately enough the actual limits of effective legal control.

But sexual conventions are not statutes, and it is important to define quite clearly just what they are. In the older world they were rules of conduct enforceable by the family and the community through habit, coercion, and authority. In this sense of the word, convention tends to lose force and effect in modern civilization. Yet a convention is essentially a theory of conduct and all human conduct implies some theory of conduct. Therefore, although it may be that no convention is any longer coercive, conventions remain, are adopted, revised, and debated. They embody the considered results of experience: perhaps the experience of a lonely pioneer or perhaps the collective experience of the dominant members of a community. In any event they are as necessary to a society which recognizes no authority as to one which does. For the inexperienced must be offered some kind of hypothesis when they are confronted with the necessity of making choices: they cannot be so utterly open-minded that they stand inert until something collides with them. In the modern world, therefore, the function of conventions is to declare the meaning of experience. A good convention is one which will most probably show the inexperienced the way to happy experience.

Just because the rule of sexual conduct by authority is dissolving, the need of conventions which will guide conduct is increasing. That, in fact, is the reason for the immense and urgent discussion of sex throughout the modern world. It is an attempt to attain an understanding of the bewilderingly new experiences to which few men or women know how to adjust themselves. The true business of the moralist in the midst of all this is not to denounce this and to advocate that, but to see as clearly as he can into the meaning of it, so that out of the chaos of pain and happiness and worry he may help to deliver a usable insight.

It is, I think, to the separation of parenthood as a vocation from love as an end in itself that the moralist must address himself. For this is the heart of the problem: to determine whether this separation, which birth control has made feasible and which law can no longer prevent, is in harmony with the conditions of human happiness.

Among those who hold that the separation of the primary and secondary functions of the sexual impulse is good and should constitute the major premise of modern sexual conventions, there are, as I have already pointed out, two schools of thought. There are the transcendentalists who believe with Mr. Havelock Ellis that "sexual pleasure, wisely used and not abused, may prove the stimulus and liberator of our finest and most exalted activities," and there are the unpretentious hedonists who believe that sexual pleasure is pleasure and not the stimulus or liberator of anything important. Both are, as we say, emancipated: neither recognizes the legitimacy of objective control unless a child is born, and both reject as an evil the traditional subjective control exercised by the sense of sin. Where they differ is in their valuation of love.

Hedonism as an attitude toward life is, of course, not a new thing in the world, but it has never before been tested out under such favorable conditions. . . . There is now a generation in the world which is approaching middle age. They have exercised the privileges which were won by the iconoclasts who attacked what was usually called the Puritan or Victorian tradition. They have exercised the privileges without external restraint and without inhibition. Their conclusions are reported in the latest works of fiction. Do they report that they have found happiness in their freedom? Well, hardly. Instead of the gladness which they were promised, they seem . . . to have found the wasteland. . . .

If you start with the belief that love is the pleasure of a moment, is it really surprising that it yields only a momentary pleasure? For it is the most ironical of all illusions to suppose that one is free of illusions in contracting any human desire to its primary physiological satisfaction. Does a man dine well because he ingests the requisite number of calories? Is he freer from illusions about his appetite than the man who creates an interesting dinner party out of the underlying fact that his guests and he have the need to fill their stomachs? Would it really be a mark of enlightenment if each of them filled his stomach in the solitary and solemn conviction that good conversation and pleasant companionship are one thing and nutrition is another?

This much the transcendentalists understand well enough. They do not wish to isolate the satisfaction of desire from our "finest and most exalted activities." They would make it "the stimulus and the liberator" of these activities. They would use it to arouse to "wholesome activity all the complex and interrelated systems of the organism." But what are these finest and most exalted activities which are to be stimulated and liberated? The discovery of truth, the making of works of art, meditation and insight? Mr. Ellis does not specify. If these are the activities that are meant, then the discussion applies to a very few of the men and women on earth. For the activities of most of them are necessarily concerned with earning a living and managing a household and rearing children and finding recreation. If the art of love is to stimulate and liberate activities, it is these prosaic activities which it must stimulate and liberate. But if you idealize the logic of birth control, make parenthood a separate vocation, isolate love from work and the hard realities of living, and say that it must be spontaneous and carefree, what have you done? You have separated it from all the important activities which it might stimulate and liberate. You have made love spontaneous but empty, and you have made home-building and parenthood efficient, responsible, and dull.

What has happened, I believe, is what so often happens in the first enthusiasm for a revolutionary invention. Its possibilities are so dazzling that men forget that inventions belong to man and not man to his inventions. In the discussion which has ensued since birth control became generally feasible, the central confusion has been that the reformers have tried to fix their sexual ideals in accordance with the logic of birth control instead of the logic of human nature. Birth control does make feasible this dissociation of interests which were once organically united. There are undoubtedly the best of reasons for dissociating them up to a point. But how completely it is wise to dissociate them is a matter to be determined not by saying how completely it is possible to dissociate them, but how much it is desirable to dissociate them.

All the varieties of the modern doctrine that man is a collection of separate impulses, each of which can attain its private satisfaction, are in fundamental contradiction not only with the traditional body of human wisdom but with the modern conception of the human character. Thus in one breath it is said in advanced circles that love is a series of casual episodes, and in the next it transpires that the speaker is in process of having himself elaborately psychoanalyzed in order to disengage his soul from the effects of apparently trivial episodes in his childhood. On the one hand it is asserted that sex pervades everything and on the other that sexual behavior is inconsequential. It is taught that experience is cumulative, that we are what our past has made us and shall be what we are making of ourselves now, and then with bland indifference to the significance of this we are told that all experiences are free, equal, and independent.

It is not hard to see why those who are concerned in revising sexual conventions should have taken the logic of birth control rather than knowledge of human nature as their major premise. Birth control is an immensely beneficent invention which can and does relieve men and women of some of the most tragic sorrows which afflict them: the tragedies of the unwanted child, the tragedies of insupportable economic burdens, the tragedies of excessive child-bearing and the destruction of youth and the necessity of living in an unrelenting series of pregnancies. It offers them freedom from intolerable mismating, from sterile virtue, from withering denials of happiness. These are the facts which the reformers saw, and in birth control they saw the instrument by which such freedom could be obtained.

The sexual conventions which they have proposed are really designed to cure notorious evils. They do not define the good life in sex; they point out ways of escape from the bad life. Thus companionate marriage is proposed by Judge Lindsey not as a type of union which is inherently desirable, but as an avenue of escape from corrupt marriages on the one hand and furtive promiscuity on the other. The movement for free divorce comes down to this: it is necessary because so many marriages are a failure. The whole theory that love is separate from parenthood and home-building is supported by the evidence in those cases where married couples are not lovers. It is the pathology of sexual relations which inspires the reformers of sexual conventions.

There is no need to quarrel with them because they insist upon remedies for manifest evils. Deep confusion results when they forget that these remedies are only remedies, and go on to institute them as ideals. It is better, without any doubt, that incompatible couples should be divorced and that each should then be free to find a mate who is compatible. But the frequency with which men and women have to resort to divorce because they are incompatible will be greatly influenced by the notions they have before and during marriage of what compatibility is, and what it involves. The remedies for failure are important. But what is central is the conception of sexual relations by which they expect to live successfully.

They cannot—I am, of course, speaking broadly—expect to live successfully by the conception that the primary and secondary functions of sex are in separate compartments of the soul. I have indicated why this conception is self-defeating and why, since human nature is organic and experience cumulative, our activities must, so to speak, engage and imply each other. Mates who are not lovers will not really cooperate, as Mr. Bertrand Russell thinks they should, in bearing children; they will be distracted, insufficient, and worst of all they will be merely dutiful. Lovers who have nothing to do but love each other are not really to be envied; love and nothing else very soon is nothing else. The emotion of love, in spite of the romantics, is not self-sustaining; it endures only when the lovers love many things together, and not merely each other. It is this understanding that love cannot successfully be isolated from the business of living which is the enduring wisdom of the institution of marriage. Let the law be what it may be as to what constitutes a marriage contract and how and when it may be dissolved. Let public opinion be as tolerant as it can be toward any and every kind of irregular and experimental relationship. When all the criticisms have been made, when all supernatural sanctions have been discarded, all subjective inhibitions erased, all compulsions abolished, the convention of marriage still remains to be considered as an interpretation of human experience. It is by the test of how genuinely it interprets human experience that the convention of marriage will ultimately be judged.

The wisdom of marriage rests upon an extremely unsentimental view of lovers and their passions. Its assumptions, when they are frankly exposed, are horrifying to those who have been brought up in the popular romantic tradition of the Nineteenth Century. These assumptions are that, given an initial attraction, a common social background, common responsibilities, and the conviction that the relationship is permanent, compatibility in marriage can normally be achieved. It is precisely this that the prevailing sentimentality about love denies. It assumes that marriages are made in heaven, that compatibility is instinctive, a mere coincidence, that happy unions are, in the last analysis, lucky accidents in which two people who happen to suit each other happen to have met. The convention of marriage rests on an interpretation of human nature which does not confuse the subjective feeling of the lovers that their passion is unique, with the brutal but objective fact that, had they never met, each of them would in all probability have found a lover who was just as unique. . . .

This is the reason why the popular conception of romantic love as the meeting of two affinities produces so much unhappiness. The mysterious glow of passion is accepted as a sign that the great coincidence has occurred; there is a wedding and soon, as the glow of passion cools, it is discovered that no instinctive and preordained affinity is present. At this point the wisdom of popular romantic marriage is exhausted. For it proceeds on the assumption that love is a mysterious visitation. There is nothing left, then, but to grin and bear a miserably dull and nagging fate, or to break off and try again. The deep fallacy of the conception is in the failure to realize that compatibility is a process and not an accident, that it depends upon the maturing of instinctive desire by adaptation to the whole nature of the other person and to the common concerns of the pair of lovers.

The romantic theory of affinities rests upon an immature theory of desire. It springs from an infantile belief that the success of love is in the satisfactions which the other person provides. What this really means is that in child-like fashion the lover expects his mistress to supply him with happiness. But in the adult world that expectation is false. Because nine-tenths of the cause, as Mr. Santayana says, are in the lover for one-tenth that may be in the object, it is what the lover does about that nine-tenths which is decisive for his happiness. It is the claim, therefore, of those who uphold the ideal of marriage as a full partnership, and reject the ideal which would separate love as an art from parenthood as a vocation, that in the home made by a couple who propose to see it through, there are provided the essential conditions under which the passions of men and women are most likely to become mature, and therefore harmonious and disinterested.

They need not deny, indeed it would be foolish as well as cruel for them to underestimate, the enormous difficulty of achieving successful marriages under modern conditions. For with the dissolution of authority and compulsion, a successful marriage depends wholly upon the capacity of the man and the woman to make it successful. They have to accomplish wholly by understanding and sympathy and disinterestedness of purpose what was once in a very large measure achieved by habit, necessity, and the absence of any practicable alternative. It takes two persons to make a successful marriage in the modern world, and that fact more than doubles its difficulty. For these reasons alone the modern state ought to do what it would none the less be compelled to do: it ought to provide decent ways of retreat in case of failure.

But if it is the truth that the convention of marriage correctly interprets human experience, whereas the separatist conventions are self-defeating, then the convention of marriage will prove to be the conclusion which emerges out of all this immense experimenting. It will survive not as a rule of law imposed by force, for that is now, I think, become impossible. It will not survive as a moral commandment with which the elderly can threaten the young. They will not listen. It will survive as the dominant insight into the reality of love and happiness, or it will not survive at all. That does not mean that all persons will live under the convention of marriage. As a matter of fact in civilized ages all persons never have. It means that the convention of marriage, when it is clarified by insight into reality, is likely to be the hypothesis upon which men and women will ordinarily proceed. There will be no compulsion behind it except the compulsion in each man and woman to reach a true adjustment of his life.

It is in this necessity of clarifying their love for those who are closest to them that the normal problems of the new age come to a personal issue. It is in the realm of sexual relations that mankind is being schooled amidst pain and worry for the novel conditions which modernity imposes. It is there, rather than in politics, business, or even in religion, that the issues are urgent, vivid, and inescapable. It is there that they touch most poignantly and most radically the organic roots of human personality. And it is there, in the ordering of their personal attachments, that for most men the process of salvation must necessarily begin.

For disinterestedness in all things, as Dean Inge says, is a mountain track which the many are likely in the future as in the past to find cold, bleak, and bare: that is why "the road of ascent is by personal affection for man." By the happy ordering of their personal affections they may establish the type and the quality and the direction of their desires for all things. It is in the hidden issues between lovers, more than anywhere else, that modern men and women are compelled, by personal anguish rather than by laws and preachments or even by the persuasions of abstract philosophy, to transcend naive desire and to reach out towards a mature and disinterested partnership with their world.

HULLABALOO ON K-DAY[1]

Bruce Bliven

Bruce Bliven has been a member of The New Republic *editorial board, New York correspondent for the* Manchester Guardian, *and is at present a lecturer at Stanford University.*

The year 1953 might go down in history in various ways and one of them, certainly, would be as the year of the great Kinsey hullabaloo. If any other book has ever had so much attention from the press as the long-awaited study of the sex life of the human female, I can't recall it. Newspapers and magazines were alerted by Dr. Kinsey far in advance, and an arbitrary release date for press material was chosen, several weeks ahead of the theoretical publication of the book itself. Some magazines actually changed their time of printing so that their September issues could conform to this deadline.

When K-Day arrived, newspapers across the country printed several columns of carefully prepared press association reports, done by topnotch writers with, I am sure, prayerful consultation with executives as to what could and could not be said to an audience of a hundred million or so. Despite the heavy pressure that was undoubtedly applied, the stories were surprisingly candid, using words and describing activities that could not possibly have appeared in print even twenty years ago.

When one reads the big new book, it is at first glance a little hard to see what all the uproar is about. First, the volume itself is full of qualifications and disclaimers, nearly all of which of course tend to disappear when you try to cram the information into three or four thousand words for a magazine. It is based on interviews with only about 8,000 women, of which fewer than 6,000 were really complete. Even of the 6,000, a substantial proportion are partly invalid because the Kinsey interrogators changed some of their questions in the middle of the interviewing. The authors carefully point out that the sample doesn't by any means accurately report on American womanhood. It overrepresents, among others, those with college educations, youngish women, Protestants or those without formal religion, city dwellers, those living in the Northeast, Florida and California, and of course (and this is important) those interested in a study of this type and willing to Tell All. Even more significant is the fact that it virtually ignores attitudes toward sex now prevalent in Europe, Asia and Africa, as well as those of extinct civilizations. Dr. Kinsey would, I am sure, be the first to admit that there is no such thing as a sexual pattern distinct from the culture-matrix in which you grew up.

And beyond all this, there is little news in this volume that was not present or implicit five years ago in *Sexual Behavior in the Human Male*. Women—or at least, many of the women among this 8,000—seem to mature sexually somewhat later than do men, and may continue sexually vigorous after the potency of their husbands has begun to fade. Half the married women in his sample had had intercourse before marriage, but half of these, again, had had relations only with the man they subsequently married, an experience all but universal in the rural populations of some European countries until about one hundred years ago, and undoubtedly still very common today.

Adultery is twice as frequent among married men as among married women but four percent more common among women born after 1900 than before that date. On the other hand, premarital relations are about twice as common among women born since 1900, which seems to suggest that the common notions about the influence of birth control, the automobile, and so on, are correct. In this sample, about 40 percent of the husbands involved know of the wife's adultery and condone it, and only 20 percent are ignorant (or pretend to be, like Napoleon in Shaw's sardonic little play). Active homosexuality is nearly twice as common among the men Kinsey has interviewed as among the women (37 percent as against 20).

Yet the superficial impression that the Kinsey uproar is unjustified is false. In a deep sense, it represents one phase of a wide struggle against our monumental public hypocrisy. We will pay lip service to a Puritan idea of monogamy and chastity that probably never existed except in a highly neurotic minority and certainly does not exist today. This dichotomy between what most Americans do and what they say appears in many forms. We tell our young children things about sex which, when they grow up, they find to be false and, as one adult to another, we at last sheepishly admit they are false. Irregular sexual relationships involving noted public figures are condoned and chuckled over as long as they are loosely kept secrets; but when "what everybody knows" is printed—usually after it has become a basis for court action—the career of the public figure, whether he be Hollywood movie star, banker, politician or whatever, is put into grave jeopardy.

As a nation we are unwilling to surrender our hypocrisy, but we feel guilty about it. Like a suspected criminal taking a lie detector test, we jump when the truth is mentioned; and that jump accounts for the clamor over Kinsey. When he tells us that chastity may actually be psychologically harmful, that premarital relations, even with a number of partners, may conduce to a satisfactory sex relation in marriage, and that virtue may be less the expression of morality than of a weak sex impulse, we cluck our tongues because we are not sure he isn't right (even though, on a basis of the evidence here offered, we can't be sure he isn't wrong). For those whose Puritan load of guilt is extra heavy, Kinsey's two books taken together offer a sort of ready-made self-psychoanalysis: your wickedness is not unique as you thought but has been shared by 71 percent of the sample. . . .

MORALS AND MAJORITIES[1]

W. E. Garrison

W. E. Garrison, former literary editor of the Christian Century, *is now a professor at the University of Chicago.*

The factual core of the [Kinsey] book seems to be that 5,940 women, when interviewed by the author or one of his associates, gave reports of their sexual experiences which, which summarized, indicated that about half of them had been incontinent before marriage and one-fourth of them (if married) had been unfaithful thereafter. Many other data are reported, with such ramifications and refinements as would suggest themselves to the mind of any competent statistician. For the present purpose, these can be ignored. What it boils down to is that there is vastly more illicit sexual indulgence among women than anybody supposed, though not quite as much as the previous Kinsey book showed there is among men.

---

[1]*Christian Century,* September 17, 1952, p. 1053. Copyright 1952 Christian Century Foundation. Reprinted by permission from The Christian Century.

This, if true, is a sociological fact of importance. To the director of this research, this is doubtless the aspect which makes it interesting, but it would be incredibly naive to suppose that the furor of prepublication journalistic excitement reflected a sudden surge of nationwide interest in sociology as such. The popular appeal is not to scientific interest. It would seem that a good sociologist—especially one who knows so much about sex—would have known that in advance.

Three questions seem to arise: (1) Did the 5,940 women who were interviewed all tell the truth about themselves? (2) Supposing they did, are they a sufficient sample on which to build a sound generalization regarding the other 50 or 60 million women in the country? (3) Supposing they are (though I think they are not), what conclusion will this generalization inevitably suggest to the wavering and immature—including mentally and morally immature adults—in regard to the conduct of their own lives?

First, then, did the women tell the truth? I doubt it. They were all volunteers. Volunteers for interviews on this subject would inevitably include a large proportion of virtual exhibitionists, more concerned to tell an exciting story than to tell a true one. In a conversation on a subject somewhat related to this, though not involving "immorality," one of the most distinguished physiologists in the country answered a question by saying: "We don't know a thing about it. Old men are such liars about it that we can't get any reliable data." The chances are that a lot of the ladies lied.

Second, can a trustworthy generalization be drawn from a random sampling in the ratio of approximately one out of 10,000? I am no statistician but I have taught logic and it is my opinion that the inductive process gives very unreliable results when it rests upon a base that is relatively so small. The wider the diversification of the individuals in the total group, the less reliable the generalization is. Dr. Kinsey of course knows this perfectly well, and knows also that it is all the worse because his samples were not very satisfactorily distributed among the various classes in the total group, and therefore he has been very careful (so it is reported) not to say that the percentages in his tables represent anything except what he learned about his volunteers. It is therefore unjust to say that he has "insulted American womanhood." Nevertheless, the wider inference is the one that would inevitably be drawn by the public. It is hard to believe that he did not expect and intend that this wider inference should be drawn. Otherwise what was the point in the whole study? It would scarcely be sociological research at all if its findings had no application beyond the individuals studied.

It may be added, as casting further doubt upon the representative character of the "samples," that the call for volunteers would almost certainly bring a response from a great many persons who, having actually done what they later confessed doing, were suffering from the tensions of concealment and felt that they could ease their consciences and "cleanse the stuffed bosom of the perilous stuff" by sharing the secret with the interviewer, and at the same time mitigate the offense by raising the percentage of those who were guilty of it. On such a shaky basis of observation as the 5,940 volunteers, no stable conclusion can be erected.

Third, if the generalization is true, what then? "Why, nothing," says the sociologist; "I'm through. My business is just to find out the facts." The public can take it from there. And so the public does. Here is where the thing gets dangerous—and, I still think, dangerous without any intention on the part of the sociologist that it should be so.

Where does the general public get its ideas of morality? From the mores, or customs, or behavior patterns of contemporary society. Obviously there is a vicious circle in that reasoning: the public gets its rules of conduct from the public! What this means is that individuals tend to substitute conformity with the behavior patterns of the majority for any sort of critical judgment as to what is right and what is wrong, and to feel that they have a right to do anything that is rather generally done.

So long as the imitation of the majority takes the place of ethical principles as the determiner of conduct for the morally unstable and immature, and so long as there are so many of these, it is impossible for any professedly scientific description of human behavior not to be, in effect, more than that. If, whether by assertion or by implication, it gives the impression of presenting the hitherto hidden facts about the behavior of a majority of the people—including, naturally, a great many respectable people and doubtless a good many "men [and women] of distinction"— the cold statistical tables and sociological data will be regarded as equivalent to a license to go and do likewise.

I am too much opposed to the hush-hush attitude toward embarrassing social problems to have much sympathy with the heated denunciations of Dr. Kinsey for writing a "licentious book" and "insulting womanhood," and none whatever with the proposal to bar it from the mails. Yet it is perfectly clear that, whatever its intent, the book lends itself to base uses as well as to sensational exploitation. The only antidotes I can think of for such poison as it may contain are these two: first, to make it clear that the boasted "facts" pertain to exactly 5,940 women, not to 50 million, and therefore throw no perceptible light on the behavior of "the human female" in general as comprehensively claimed in the title; and second, to get it into the minds of as many people as possible as quickly as possible that matters of right and wrong are not decided by majority vote.

PART FOUR

THE CHURCH
AND
SOCIETY

CHURCH AND STATE

Our churches face many problems with significant moral implications that must go unexplored here. Among such problems are the confusion of superstition, which Thomas Aquinas once called the vice of excess in religion, with religion itself; the polarity between religious fundamentalism and liberalism; the disparity between what one observer has called passion in the pulpit and apathy in the pew, and with this the weakness of the religious commitment in a secular society; the limits and possibilities of the ecumenical movement; the strengths and weaknesses of evangelical Christianity. The selections are limited to two topics, both of great interest to most thoughtful people.

The first of these concerns the relation of church and state. Since America is without an established church, and most American Catholics are reconciled to religious pluralism, the problem is not as acute with us as with some European countries. Nevertheless, persistent controversies remind us that the problem is far from solved. The fate of federal aid to education hinges on the support of Catholics, and the Catholic hierarchy, in opposition to our first Catholic President, withholds approval so long as private schools are declared ineligible for public aid. The issues range from this central one to somewhat less urgent matters such as Massachusetts' and Connecticut's use of police power to proscribe the use of contraceptives in order to enforce religious scruples not shared by all their citizens.

Beyond such specific issues and important to their understanding are certain more general and more fundamental differences. Article I of the Constitution declares that "Congress shall make no law respecting an establishment of religion, or prohibiting the free exercise thereof. . . ." Although the latter provision establishes pluralism as the foundation of our religious life, interpretations of pluralism continue to vary not only in applying it to particular cases but in understanding its essential meaning. Even the first provision of the article suddenly erupts into controversy as when the U.S. Supreme Court rules (6 to 1) against official prayers in the public schools. The Court, citing the First Amendment, has declared that "it is no part of the business of government to compose official prayers for any group of American people to recite as part of a religious program carried on by the government." The ensuing repercussions[1] suggest that the accommodation of church and state is not yet stable. The first two selections in this part deal with this basic problem. They are supplemented by what might be called a case study.

A second topic is equally important. It concerns the role organized religion and its spokesmen should play and have played in correcting the great social abuses to which most men have been heir. At issue is the very meaning of the religious experience.

Some urge that the church must concern itself with inner rectitude and man's relation to God. If the first is cultivated and the second properly ordered, this is all that matters. Thereupon individuals will pursue the good, and social justice will ensue as a matter of course. It is then with individual vice and virtue that the church must concern itself. There are many variations on this theme—ranging all the way from a naive, simplistic treatment of problems of personal morality by the evangelists to the more wordly dependence of the Buchmanites on suddenly converted moral "heroes."

Others argue that this is sheer religiosity, a desirable escape when men are powerless to remedy the evils of the world in which they live, but irrelevant to our time and place. It is urged that preoccupation with goodness and evil in the abstract is simply an opportunist evasion of responsibility for attacking specific social abuses. When the church shuns the great moral issues—racial segregation, poverty in the midst of opulence, greed and hypocrisy in high places——its role degenerates into an apology for the existing order and a diversionary excoriation of minor, imagined, or harmless vices. The Hebrew prophets and Christian martyrs denounced social abuses. Where are their modern counterparts? Certainly in many places, including Czarist Russia, religion *was* the "opiate of the masses." If too many people have turned to the secular religion of which Karl Marx, who coined that phrase, is the prophet, is this not because the church has abdicated its proper role? This, with variations, has been the argument

---

[1]Cardinal Spellman was "shocked and frightened" by the decision, adding that "it strikes at the very heart of the Godly tradition in which America's children have so long been raised." Protestant Dwight Eisenhower said, "I always thought this nation was essentially a religious one" and Herbert Hoover saw in the decision a "disintegration of one of the most sacred of American heritages." None of them remembered that Founding Father James Madison believed even tax exemption for churches to be unconstitutional. Perhaps Father Murray had Madison as well as the Supreme Court in mind when, encountering Justice Douglas at the Center for the Study of Democratic Institutions, he observed that he had been formulating a new school prayer that might be acceptable to the Court. The prayer would start, "To whom it may concern. . . ."

not only of those who remain outside the church because they find insufficient moral outlet through it, but of the Social Gospel Movement that through the years has imparted significant momentum to the cause of social reform.

A third position is taken by those who argue that, although the Christian ethic provides a basis on which to criticize the social order, attempts to derive a program for the reconstruction of society from the teachings of Jesus are futile. The discussions that follow will reflect some of these standpoints.

CIVIL UNITY AND RELIGIOUS INTEGRITY[1]

John Courtney Murray, S.J.

John Courtney Murray's distinction as a theologian has already been noted.[2] Here, in an eloquent and scholarly statement, he explains why he believes that Catholics can in good conscience and without reservation respect the First Amendment.

As it arose in America, the problem of pluralism was unique in the modern world, chiefly because pluralism was the native condition of American society. It was not, as in Europe and in England, the result of a disruption or decay of a previously existent religious unity. This fact created the possibility of a new solution; indeed, it created a demand for a new solution. The possibility was exploited and the demand was met by the American Constitution.

The question here concerns the position of the Catholic conscience in the face of the new American solution to a problem that for centuries has troubled, and still continues to trouble, various nations and societies. A new problem has been put to the universal Church by the fact of America—by the uniqueness of our social situation, by the genius of our newly conceived constitutional system, by the lessons of our singular national history, which has molded in a special way the consciousness and

[1]From *We Hold These Truths: Catholic Reflections on the American Proposition* by Rev. John Courtney Murray, S.J. (New York: Sheed & Ward, Inc., 1960), pp. 45–78. © Sheed & Ward, Inc. 1960. Reprinted by permission.
[2]Cf. above, p. 228.

temper of the American people, within whose midst the Catholic stands, sharing with his fellow citizens the same national heritage. The Catholic community faces the task of making itself intellectually aware of the conditions of its own coexistence within the American pluralistic scene. We have behind us a lengthy historical tradition of acceptance of the special situation of the Church in America, in all its differences from the situations in which the Church elsewhere finds herself. But it is a question here of pursuing the subject, not in the horizontal dimension of history but in the vertical dimension of theory.

The argument readily falls into two parts. The first part is an analysis of the American Proposition with regard to political unity.

The unity asserted in the American device, "E pluribus unum" . . . is a unity of a limited order. It . . . must not hinder the various religious communities in American society in the maintenance of their own distinct identities. Similarly, the public consensus, on which civil unity is ultimately based, must permit to the differing communities the full integrity of their own religious convictions. The one civil society contains within its own unity the communities that are divided among themselves; but it does not seek to reduce to its own unity the differences that divide them. In a word, the pluralism remains as real as the unity. Neither may undertake to destroy the other. Each subsists in its own order. And the two orders, the religious and the civil, remain distinct, however much they are, and need to be, related. All this, I take it, is integral to the meaning attached in America to the doctrine of religious freedom and to its instrumental companion-doctrine called (not felicitously) separation of church and state. I use the word "doctrine" as lawyers or political philosophers, not theologians, use it.

We come therefore to the second question. It concerns the American solution to the problem put by the plurality of conflicting religions within the one body politic. In its legal form (there are other forms, as I shall later say) the solution is deposited in the First Amendment to the Federal Constitution: "Congress shall make no law respecting an establishment of religion or prohibiting the free exercise thereof. . . ." What then is the Catholic view of this constitutional proviso?

The American Catholic is entirely prepared to accept our constitutional concept of freedom of religion and the policy of no establishment as the first of our prejudices. He is also prepared to admit that other prejudices may obtain elsewhere—in England, in Sweden, in Spain. Their validity in their own context and against the background of the history that generated them does not disturb him in his conviction that his own prejudice, within his own context and against the background of his own history, has its own validity.

American Catholics would even go as far as to say of the provisions of the First Amendment what Burke, in his *Reflections,* said of the English Church Establishment, that they consider it as "essential to their state; not as a thing heterogeneous and separable, something added from accommodation, what they may either keep up or lay aside, according to their temporary ideas of convenience. They consider it as the foundation of their whole Constitution, with which, and with every part of which, it holds an indissoluble union." The prejudice formulated in the First Amendment is but the most striking aspect of the more fundamental prejudice that was the living root of our constitutional system—the prejudice in favor of the method of freedom in society and therefore the prejudice in favor of a government of limited powers, whose limitations are determined by the consent of the people. The American people exempted from their grant of power to government any power to establish religion or to prohibit the free exercise thereof. The Catholic community, in common with the rest of the American people, has historically consented to this political and legal solution to the problem created by the plurality of religious beliefs in American society. They agree that the First Amendment is by no means destitute of reason; that it involves profound and extensive wisdom; that its wisdom has been amply substantiated by history. Consequently, they share the general prejudice which it states; often enough both in action and in utterances they have made this fact plain. And that should be the end of the matter.

THEOLOGIES OF THE FIRST AMENDMENT

But, as it happens, one is not permitted thus simply to end the matter. I leave aside the practical issues that have arisen concerning the application of the First Amendment. The question here is one of theory, the theory of the First Amendment in itself and in its relation to Catholic theories of freedom of religion and the church-state relation. It is customary to put to Catholics what is supposed to be an embarrassing question: Do you really believe in the first two provisions of the First Amendment? The question calls to mind one of the more famous among the multitudinous queries put by Boswell to Dr. Johnson, "whether it is necessary to believe all the Thirty-Nine Articles." And the Doctor's answer has an applicable point: "Why, sir, that is a question which has been much agitated. Some have held it necessary that all be believed. Others have considered them to be only articles of peace, that is to say, you are not to preach against them."

An analogous difference of interpretation seems to exist with regard to the first two articles of the First Amendment.

On the one hand, there are those who read into them certain ultimate beliefs, certain specifically sectarian tenets with regard to the nature of religion, religious truth, the church, faith, conscience, divine revelation, human freedom, etc. In this view these articles are invested with a genuine sanctity that derives from their supposed religious content. They are dogmas, norms of orthodoxy, to which one must conform on pain of some manner of excommunication. They are true articles of faith. Hence it is necessary to believe them, to give them a religiously motivated assent.

On the other hand, there are those who see in these articles only a law, not a dogma. These constitutional clauses have no religious content. They answer none of the eternal human questions with regard to the nature of truth and freedom or the manner in which the spiritual order of man's life is to be organized or not organized. Therefore they are not invested with the sanctity that attaches to dogma, but only with the rationality that attaches to law. Rationality is the highest value of law. In further consequence, it is not necessary to give them a religious assent but only a rational civil obedience. In a word, they are not articles of faith but articles of peace, that is to say, you may not act against them, because they are law and good law. . . .

What is in question is the meaning and the content of the first of our American prejudices, not its genesis. Do these clauses assert or imply that the nature of the church is such that it inherently demands the most absolute separation from the state? Do they assert or imply that the institutional church is simply a voluntary association of like-minded men; that its origins are only in the will of men to associate freely for purposes of religion and worship; that all churches, since their several origins are in equally valid religious inspirations, stand on a footing of equality in the face of the divine and evangelical law; that all ought by the same token to stand on an equal footing in the face of civil law? In a word, does separation of church and state in the American sense assert or imply a particular sectarian concept of the church?

Further, does the free-exercise clause assert or imply that the individual conscience is the ultimate norm of religious belief in such wise that an external religious authority is inimical to Christian freedom? Does it hold that religion is a purely private matter in such wise that an ecclesiastical religion is inherently a corruption of the Christian Gospel? Does it maintain that true religion is religion-in-general, and that the various sects in their dividedness are as repugnant religiously as they are politically dangerous? Does it pronounce religious truth to be simply a matter of personal experience, and religious faith to be simply a matter of subjective impulse, not related to any objective order of truth or to any structural economy of salvation whose consistence is not dependent on the human will?

The questions could be multiplied, but they all reduce themselves to two. Is the no-establishment clause a piece of ecclesiology, and is the free-exercise clause a piece of religious philosophy? The general Protestant tendency, visible at its extreme in the free-church tradition, especially among the Baptists, is to answer affirmatively to these questions. Freedom of religion and separation of church and state are to be, in the customary phrase, "rooted in religion itself." Their substance is to be conceived in terms of sectarian Protestant doctrine. They are therefore articles of faith; not to give them a religious assent is to fall into heterodoxy.

The secularist dissents from the Protestant theological and philosophical exegesis of the first of our prejudices. But it is to him likewise an article of faith (he might prefer to discard the word, "faith," and speak rather of ultimate presuppositions). Within this group also there are differences of opinion. Perhaps the most sharpened view is taken by those who in their pursuit of truth reject not only the traditional methods of Christian illumination, both Protestant and Catholic, but also the reflective methods of metaphysical inquiry.

These men commit themselves singly to the method of scientific empiricism. There is therefore no eternal order of truth and justice; there are no universal verities that require man's assent, no universal moral law that commands his obedience. Such an order of universals is not empirically demonstrable. Truth therefore is to be understood in a positivistic sense; its criteria are either those of science or those of practical life, i.e., the success of an opinion in getting itself accepted in the market place. With this view of truth there goes a corresponding view of freedom. The essence of freedom is "non-committalism." I take the word from Gordon Keith Chalmers. He calls it a "sin," but in the school of thought in question it is the highest virtue. To be uncommitted is to be in the state of grace; for a prohibition of commitment is inherent in the very notion of freedom. The mind or will that is committed, absolutely and finally, is by definition not free. It has fallen from grace by violating its own free nature. In the intellectual enterprise the search for truth, not truth itself or its possession, is the highest value. In the order of morals the norm for man is never reached by knowledge. It is only approximated by inspired guesses or by tentative practical rules that are the precipitate of experience, substantiated only by their utility.

This school of thought, which is of relatively recent growth in America, thrusts into the First Amendment its own ultimate views of truth, freedom, and religion. Religion itself is not a value, except insofar as its ambiguous reassurances may have the emotional effect of conveying reassurance. Roman Catholicism is a disvalue. Nevertheless, religious freedom, as a form of freedom, is a value. It has at least the negative value of an added emancipation, another sheer release. It may also have the positive value of another blow struck at the principle of authority in any of its forms; for in this school authority is regarded as absolutely antinomous to freedom.

Furthermore, this school usually reads into the First Amendment a more or less articulated political theory. Civil society is the highest societal form of human life; even the values that are called spiritual and moral are values by reason of their reference to society. Civil law is the highest form of law and it is not subject to judgment by prior ethical canons. Civil rights are the highest form of rights; for the dignity of the person, which grounds these rights, is only his civil dignity. The state is purely the instrument of the popular will, than which there is no higher sovereignty. Government is to the citizen what the cab-driver is to the passenger (to use Yves Simon's descriptive metaphor). And since the rule of the majority is the method whereby the popular will expresses itself, it is the highest governing principle of statecraft, from which there is no appeal. Finally, the ultimate value within society and state does not consist in any substantive ends that these social forms may pursue; rather it consists in the process of their pursuit. That is to say, the ultimate value resides in the forms of the democratic process itself, because these forms embody the most ultimate of all values, freedom. There are those who pursue this theory to paradoxical lengths—perhaps more exactly, to the lengths of logical absurdity—by maintaining that if the forms of democracy perish through the use of them by men intent on their destruction, well then, so be it.

Given this political theory, the churches are inevitably englobed within the state, as private associations organized for particular purposes. They possess their title to existence from positive law. Their right to freedom is a civil right, and it is respected as long as it is not understood to include any claim to independently sovereign authority. Such a claim must be disallowed on grounds of the final and indivisible sovereignty of the democratic process over all the associational aspects of human life. The notion that any church should acquire status in public life as a society in its own right is per se absurd; for there is only one society, civil society, which may so exist. In this view, separation of church and state, as ultimately implying a subordination of church to state, follows from the very nature of the state and its law; just as religious freedom follows from the very nature of freedom and of truth.

The foregoing is a sort of anatomical description of two interpretations of the religion clauses of the First Amendment. The description is made anatomical in order to point the issue. If these clauses are made articles of faith in either of the described senses, there are immediately in this country some 35,000,000 dissenters, the Catholic community. Not being either a Protestant or a secularist, the Catholic rejects the religious position of Protestants with regard to the nature of the church, the meaning of faith, the absolute primacy of conscience, etc.; just as he rejects secularist views with regard to the nature of truth, freedom, and civil society as man's last end. He rejects these positions as demonstrably erroneous in themselves. What is more to the point here, he rejects the notion that any of these sectarian theses enter into the content or implications of the First Amendment in such wise as to demand the assent of all American citizens. If this were the case the very article that bars any establishment of religion would somehow establish one. . . .

If it be true that the First Amendment is to be given a theological interpretation and that therefore it must be "believed," made an object of religious faith, it would follow that a religious test has been thrust into the Constitution. The Federal Republic has suddenly become a voluntary fellowship of believers either in some sort of free-church Protestantism or in the tenets of a naturalistic humanism. The notion is preposterous. The United States is a good place to live in; many have found it even a sort of secular sanctuary. But it is not a church, whether high, low, or broad. It is simply a civil community, whose unity is purely political, consisting in "agreement on the good of man at the level of performance without the necessity of agreement on ultimates" (to adopt a phrase from the 1945 Harvard Report on General Education in a Free Society). As regards important points of ultimate religious belief, the United States is pluralist. Any attempt at reducing this pluralism by law, through a process of reading certain sectarian tenets into the fundamental law of the land, is prima facie illegitimate and absurd.

The truth of history happens to be more prosaic than the fancies of the secular liberals. In seeking an understanding of the first of our prejudices we have to abandon the poetry of those who would make a religion out of freedom of religion and a dogma out of separation of church and state. We have to talk prose, the prose of the Constitution itself, which is an ordinary legal prose having nothing to do with doctrinaire theories.

ARTICLES OF PEACE

From the standpoint both of history and of contemporary social reality the only tenable position is that the first two articles of the First Amendment are not articles of faith but articles of peace. Like the rest of the Constitution these provisions are the work of lawyers, not of theologians or even of political theorists. They are not true dogma but only good law. That is praise enough. This, I take it, is the Catholic view. But in thus qualifying it I am not marking it out as just another "sectarian" view. It is in fact the only view that a citizen with both historical sense and common sense can take.

That curiously clairvoyant statesman, John C. Calhoun, once observed that "this admirable federal constitution of ours is superior to the wisdom of any or all the men by whose agency it was made. The force of circumstances and not foresight or wisdom induced them to adopt many of its wisest provisions." The observation is particularly pertinent to the religion clauses of the First Amendment. If history makes one thing clear it is that these clauses were the twin children of social necessity, the necessity of creating a social environment, protected by law, in which men of differing religious faiths might live together in peace. . . . This mark of inevitability is an index of goodness. And it is perhaps nowhere more strikingly manifest than in the institutions which govern the relation of government to religion. These institutions seem to have been preformed in the peculiar conditions of American society. It did indeed take some little time before the special American solution to the problem of religious pluralism worked itself out; but it is almost inconceivable that it should not have worked itself out as it did. One suspects that this would have been true even if there had been no Williamses and Penns, no Calverts and Madisons and Jeffersons. The theories of these men, whatever their merits, would probably have made only literature, not history, had it not been for the special social context into which they were projected. Similarly, the theories of these men, whatever their defects, actually made history because they exerted their pressure, such as it was, in the direction in which historical factors were already moving the new American society.

To say this is not of course to embrace a theory of historical or social determinism. It is only to say that the artisans of the American Republic and its Constitution were not radical theorists intent on constructing a society in accord with the a priori demands of a doctrinaire blueprint, under disregard for what was actually "given" in history. Fortunately they were, as I said, for the most part lawyers. And they had a strong sense of that primary criterion of good law which is its necessity or utility for the preservation of the public peace, under a given set of conditions. All law looks to the common good, which is normative for all law. And social peace, assured by equal justice in dealing with conflicting groups, is the highest integrating element of the common good. This legal criterion is the first and most solid ground on which the validity of the First Amendment rests. . . .

The demands of social necessity were overwhelming. It remains only to insist that in regarding the religion clauses of the First Amendment as articles of peace and in placing the case for them on the primary grounds of their social necessity, one is not taking low ground. Such a case does not appeal to mean-spirited expediency nor does it imply a reluctant concession to *force majeure*. In the science of law and the art of jurisprudence the appeal to social peace is an appeal to a high moral value. Behind the will to social peace there stands a divine and Christian imperative. This is the classic and Christian tradition. . . .

The First Amendment . . . does not say that there is no distinction between true and false religion, good and bad morality. But it does say that in American circumstances the conscience of the community, aware of its moral obligations to the peace of the community, and speaking therefore as the voice of God, does not give government any mandate, does not impose upon it any duty, and does not even communicate to it the right to repress religious opinions or practices, even though they are erroneous and false.

On these grounds it is easy to see why the Catholic conscience has always consented to the religion clauses of the Constitution. They conform to the highest criterion for all legal rulings in this delicate matter. The criterion is moral; therefore the law that meets it is good, because it is for the common good. Therefore the consent given to the law is given on grounds of moral principle. To speak of expediency here is altogether to misunderstand the moral nature of the community and its collective moral obligation toward its own common good. The origins of our fundamental law are in moral principle; the obligations it imposes are moral obligations, binding in conscience. One may not, without moral fault, act against these articles of peace.

THE DISTINCTION OF CHURCH AND STATE

If the demands of social necessity account for the emergence in America of religious freedom as a fact, they hardly account for certain peculiarities of the first of our prejudices and for the depth of feeling that it evokes. Another powerful historical force must be considered, namely, the dominant impulse toward self-government, government by the people in the most earnest sense of the word. Above all else the early Americans wanted political freedom. And the force of this impulse necessarily acted as a corrosive upon the illegitimate "unions" of church and state which the post-Reformation era had brought forth. The establishments of the time were, by and large, either theocratic, wherein the state was absorbed in the church, or Erastian, wherein the church was absorbed in the state. In both cases the result was some limitation upon freedom, either in the form of civil disabilities imposed in the name of the established religion, or in the form of religious disabilities imposed in the name of the civil law of the covenanted community. The drive toward popular freedom would with a certain inevitability sweep away such establishments. Men might share the fear of Roger Williams, that the state would corrupt the church, or the fear of Thomas Jefferson, that the church would corrupt the state. In either case their thought converged to the one important conclusion, that an end had to be put to the current confusions of the religious and political orders. The ancient distinction between church and state had to be newly reaffirmed in a manner adapted to the American scene. Calvinist theocracy, Anglican Erastianism, Gallican absolutism—all were vitiated by the same taint: they violated in one way or another this traditional distinction. . . .

. . . the distinction of church and state, one of the central assertions of this tradition, found its way into the Constitution. There it received a special embodiment, adapted to the peculiar genius of American government and to the concrete conditions of American society.

How this happened need not concern us here. Certainly it was in part because the artisans of the Constitution had a clear grasp of the distinction between state and society, which had been the historical product of the distinction between church and state, inasmuch as the latter distinction asserted the existence of a whole wide area of human concerns which were remote from the competence of government. Calhoun's "force of circumstances" also had a great deal of influence; here again it was a matter of the Fathers building better than they knew. Their major concern was sharply to circumscribe the powers of government. The area of state—that is, legal—concern was limited to the pursuit of certain enumerated secular purposes (to say that the purposes are secular is not to deny that many of them are also moral; so for instance the establishment of justice and peace, the promotion of the general welfare, etc.). Thus made autonomous in its own sphere, government was denied all competence in the field of religion. In this field freedom was to be the rule and method; government was powerless to legislate respecting an establishment of religion and likewise powerless to prohibit the free exercise of religion. Its single office was to take legal or judicial steps necessary on given occasions to make effective the general guarantee of freedom.

The concrete applications of this, in itself quite simple, solution have presented great historical and legal difficulties. This has been inevitable, given the intimacy with which religion is woven into the whole social fabric, and given, too, the evolution of government from John Adams' "plain, simple, intelligible thing, quite comprehensible by common sense," to the enormously complicated and sprawling thing which now organizes a great part of our lives, handles almost all education, and much social welfare. In particular, we have not yet found an answer to the question whether government can make effective the primary intention of the First Amendment, the guarantee of freedom of religion, simply by attempting to make more and more "impregnable" what is called, in Roger Williams' fateful metaphor, the "wall of separation" between church and state. However, what concerns us here is the root of the matter, the fact that the American Constitution embodies in a special way the traditional principle of the distinction between church and state.

For Catholics this fact is of great and providential importance for one major reason. It serves sharply to set off our constitutional system from the system against which the Church waged its long-drawn-out fight in the nineteenth century, namely, Jacobinism, or (in Carlton Hayes's term) sectarian Liberalism, or (in the more definitive term used today) totalitarian democracy.

It is now coming to be recognized that the Church opposed the "separation of church and state" of the sectarian Liberals because in theory and in fact it did not mean separation at all but perhaps the most drastic unification of church and state which history had known. The Jacobin "free state" was as regalist as the *ancien régime,* and even more so. Writing as a historian, de Tocqueville long ago made this plain. And the detailed descriptions which Leo XIII, writing as a theologian and political moralist, gave of the Church's "enemy" make the fact even more plain. Within this "free state" the so-called "free church" was subject to a political control more complete than the Tudor or Stuart or Bourbon monarchies dreamed of. The evidence stretches all the way from the Civil Constitution of the Clergy in 1790 to the Law of Separation in 1905.

In the system sponsored by the sectarian Liberals, as has been well said, "The state pretends to ignore the Church; in reality it never took more cognizance of her." In the law of 1905, the climactic development, the Church was arrogantly assigned a juridical statute articulated in forty-four articles, whereby almost every aspect of her organization and action was minutely regulated. Moreover, this was done on principle—the principle of the primacy of the political, the principle of "everything within the state, nothing above the state." This was the cardinal thesis of sectarian Liberalism, whose full historical development is now being witnessed in the totalitarian "people's democracies" behind the Iron Curtain. As the Syllabus and its explicatory documents—as well as the multitudinous writings of Leo XIII—make entirely clear, it was this thesis of the juridical omnipotence and omnicompetence of the state which was the central object of the Church's condemnation of the Jacobin development. It was because freedom of religion and separation of church and state were predicated on this thesis that the Church refused to accept them as a thesis.

This thesis was utterly rejected by the founders of the American Republic. The rejection was as warranted as it was providential, because this thesis is not only theologically heterodox, as denying the reality of the Church; it is also politically revolutionary, as denying the substance of the liberal tradition. The American thesis is that government is not juridically omnipotent. Its powers are limited, and one of the principles of limitation is the distinction between state and church, in their purposes, methods, and manner of organization. The Jacobin thesis was basically philosophical; it derived from a sectarian concept of the autonomy of reason. It was also theological, as implying a sectarian concept of religion and of the church. In contrast, the American thesis is simply political. It asserts the theory of a free people under a limited government, a theory that is recognizably part of the Christian political tradition, and altogether defensible in the manner of its realization under American circumstances.

It may indeed be said that the American constitutional system exaggerates the distinction between church and state by its self-denying ordinances. However, it must also be said that government rarely appears to better advantage than when passing self-denying ordinances. In any event, it is one thing to exaggerate a traditional distinction along the lines of its inherent tendency; it is quite another thing to abolish the distinction. In the latter case the result is a vicious monistic society; in the former, a faultily dualistic one. The vice in the Jacobin system could only be condemned by the Church, not in any way condoned. The fault in the American system can be recognized as such, without condemnation. There are times and circumstances, Chesterton jocosely said, when it is necessary to exaggerate in order to tell the truth. There are also times and circumstances, one may more seriously say, when some exaggeration of the restrictions placed on government is necessary in order to insure freedom. These circumstances of social necessity were and are present in America.

THE FREEDOM OF THE CHURCH

Here then is the second leading reason why the American solution to the problem of religious pluralism commends itself to the Catholic conscience. . . . In contrast to the Jacobin system in all its forms, the American Constitution does not presume to define the Church or in any way to supervise her exercise of authority in pursuit of her own distinct ends. The Church is entirely free to define herself and to exercise to the full her spiritual jurisdiction. It is legally recognized that there is an area which lies outside the competence of government. This area coincides with the area of the divine mission of the Church, and within this area the Church is fully independent, immune from interference by political authority.

The juridical result of the American limitation of governmental powers is the guarantee to the Church of a stable condition of freedom as a matter of law and right. It should be added that this guarantee is made not only to the individual Catholic but to the Church as an organized society with its own law and jurisdiction. The reason is that the American state is not erected on the principle of the unity and indivisibility of sovereignty which was the post-Renaissance European development. Nowhere in the American structure is there accumulated the plenitude of legal sovereignty possessed in England by the Queen in Parliament. In fact, the term "legal sovereignty" makes no sense in America, where sovereignty (if the alien term must be used) is purely political. The United States has a government, or better a structure of government operating on different levels. The American state has no sovereignty in the classic Continental sense. Within society, as distinct from the state, there is room for the independent exercise of an authority which is not that of the state. This principle has more than once been affirmed by American courts, most recently by the Supreme

Court in the *Kedroff* case. The validity of this principle strengthens the stability of the Church's condition at law. . . .

THE AMERICAN EXPERIENCE

One final ground for affirming the validity of the religion clauses of the First Amendment as good law must be briefly touched on. Holmes's famous dictum, "The life of the law is not logic but experience," has more truth in it than many other Holmesian dicta. When a law ceases to be supported by a continued experience of its goodness, it becomes a dead letter, an empty legal form. Although pure pragmatism cannot be made the philosophy of law, nonetheless the value of any given law is importantly pragmatic. The First Amendment surely passes this test of good law. In support of it one can adduce an American experience. One might well call it *the* American experience in the sense that it has been central in American history and also unique in the history of the world.

This experience has three facets, all interrelated.

First, America has proved by experience that political unity and stability are possible without uniformity of religious belief and practice, without the necessity of any governmental restrictions on any religion. . . .

For a century and a half the United States has displayed to the world the fact that political unity and stability are not necessarily dependent on the common sharing of one religious faith.

The reach of this demonstration is, of course, limited. Granted that the unity of the commonwealth can be achieved in the absence of a consensus with regard to the theological truths that govern the total life and destiny of man, it does not follow that this necessary civic unity can endure in the absence of a consensus more narrow in its scope, operative on the level of political life, with regard to the rational truths and moral precepts that govern the structure of the constitutional state, specify the substance of the common weal, and determine the ends of public policy. Nor has experience yet shown how, if at all, this moral consensus can survive amid all the ruptures of religious division, whose tendency is inherently disintegrative of all consensus and community. But this is a further question, for the future to answer. . . .

The second American experience was that stable political unity, which means perduring agreement on the common good of man at the level of performance, can be strengthened by the exclusion of religious differences from the area of concern allotted to government. In America we have been rescued from the disaster of ideological parties. They are a disaster because, where such parties exist, power becomes a special kind of prize. The struggle for power is a partisan struggle for the means whereby the opposing ideology may be destroyed. It has been remarked that only in a disintegrating society does politics become a controversy over ends; it should be simply a controversy over means to ends already agreed on with sufficient unanimity. The Latin countries of Europe have displayed this spectacle of ideological politics, a struggle between a host of "isms," all of which pretend to a final view of man and society, with the twin results of governmental paralysis and seemingly irremediable social division. In contrast, the American experience of political unity has been striking. (Even the Civil War does not refute this view; it was not an ideological conflict but simply, in the more descriptive Southern phrase, a war between the states, a conflict of interests.) To this experience of political unity the First Amendment has made a unique contribution; and in doing so it has qualified as good law.

The third and most striking aspect of the American experience consists in the fact that religion itself, and not least the Catholic Church, has benefited by our free institutions, by the maintenance, even in exaggerated form, of the distinction between church and state. Within the same span of history the experience of the Church elsewhere, especially in the Latin lands, has been alternately an experience of privilege or persecution. The reason lay in a particular concept of government. It was alternatively the determination of government to ally itself either with the purposes of the Church or with the purposes of some sect or other (sectarian Liberalism, for instance) which made a similar, however erroneous, claim to possess the full and final truth. The dominant conviction, whose origins are really in pagan antiquity, was that government should represent transcendent truth and by its legal power make this truth prevail. However, in the absence of social agreement as to what the truth really was, the result was to involve the Catholic truth in the vicissitudes of power. It would be difficult to say which experience, privilege or persecution, proved in the end to be the more damaging or gainful to the Church.

In contrast, American government has not undertaken to represent transcendental truth in any of the versions of it current in American society. It does indeed represent the commonly shared moral values of the community. It also represents the supreme religious truth expressed in the motto on American coins: "In God we trust." The motto expresses the two truths without which, as the Letter to the Hebrews says, "nobody reaches God's presence," namely, "to believe that God exists and that he rewards those who try to find him" (Hebrews 11:6). For the rest, government represents the truth of society as it actually is; and the truth is that American society is religiously pluralist. The truth is lamentable; it is nonetheless true. Many of the beliefs entertained within society ought not to be believed, because they are false; nonetheless men believe them. It is not the function of government to resolve the dispute between conflicting truths, all of which claim the final validity of transcendence. As representative of a pluralist society, wherein religious faith is—as it must be—free, government undertakes to represent the principle of freedom.

In taking this course American government would seem to be on the course set by Pius XII for the religiously pluralist international community, of which America offers, as it were, a pattern in miniature. . . .

In consequence of this American concept of the representative function of government the experience of the Church in America, like the general American experience itself, has proved to be satisfactory when one scans it from the viewpoint of the value upon which the Church sets primary importance, namely, her freedom in the fulfillment of her spiritual mission to communicate divine truth and grace to the souls of men, and her equally spiritual mission of social justice and peace. The Church has not enjoyed a privileged status in public life; at the same time she has not had to pay the price of this privilege. A whole book could be written on the price of such legal privilege. Another book could be written on the value of freedom without privilege. In fact, both books have been written, on the metaphorical pages of history. And looking over his own continually unrolling historical manuscript the American Catholic is inclined to conclude that his is a valid book.

It does not develop a doctrinal thesis, but it does prove a practical point. The point is that the goodness of the First Amendment as constitutional law is manifested not only by political but also by religious experience. By and large (for no historical record is without blots) it has been good for religion, for Catholicism, to have had simply the right of freedom. This right is at the same time the highest of privileges, and it too has its price. But the price has not been envy and enmity, the coinage in which the Church paid for privilege. It has only been the price of sacrifice, labor, added responsibilities; and these things are redemptive.

CONCLUSION

In the final analysis any validation of the First Amendment as good law—no matter by whom undertaken, be he Protestant, Catholic, Jew, or secularist—must make appeal to the three arguments developed above—the demands of social necessity, the rightfulness within our own circumstances of the American manner of asserting the distinction between church and state, and the lessons of experience. Perhaps the last argument is the most powerful. It is also, I may add, the argument which best harmonizes with the general tone which arguments for our institutions are accustomed to adopt.

In a curiously controlling way the tone was set by the *Federalist* papers. These essays were not political treatises after the manner of Hobbes and Hegel, Rousseau and Comte, or even John Locke. It has been remarked that in America no treatises of this kind have been produced; and it is probably just as well. The authors of the *Federalist* papers were not engaged in broaching a political theory universal in scope and application, a plan for an Ideal Republic of Truth and Virtue. They were arguing for a particular

Constitution, a special kind of governmental structure, a limited ensemble of concrete laws, all designed for application within a given society. They were in the tradition of the Revolutionary thinkers who led a colonial rebellion, not in the name of a set of flamboyant abstractions, but in the name of the sober laws of the British Constitution which they felt were being violated in their regard. It has been pointed out that the only real slogan the Revolution produced was: "No taxation without representation." It has not the ring of a trumpet; its sound is more like the dry rustle of a lawyer's sheaf of parchment.

It is in the tone of this tradition of American political writing that one should argue for the First Amendment. The arguments will tend to be convincing in proportion as their key of utterance approaches a dry rustle and not a wild ring. The arguments here presented are surely dry enough. Perhaps they will not satisfy the American doctrinaire, the theologizer. But they do, I think, show that the first of our prejudices is "not a prejudice destitute of reason, but involving in it profound and extensive wisdom." This is all that need be shown; it is likewise all that can be shown.

The Catholic Church in America is committed to this prejudice by the totality of her experience in American history. As far as I know, the only ones who doubt the firmness, the depth, the principled nature of this commitment are not Catholics. They speak without knowledge and without authority; the credence they command has its origins in emotion. If perhaps what troubles them is the fact that the commitment is limited, in the sense that it is not to the truth and sanctity of a dogma but only to the rationality and goodness of a law, they might recall the story of Pompey. After the capture of Jerusalem in 63 B.C. he went to the Temple and forced his way into the Holy of Holies. To his intense astonishment he found it empty. He should not have been astonished; for the emptiness was the symbol of the absence of idolatry. It symbolized the essential truth of Judaism, that One is the Lord. Professor Boorstin, who recounts the tale, adds: "Perhaps the same surprise awaits the student of American culture [or, I add, the American Constitution] if he finally manages to penetrate the arcanum of our belief. And for a similar reason. Far from being disappointed, we should be inspired that in an era of idolatry, when so many nations have filled their sanctuaries with ideological idols, we have had the courage to refuse to do so."

The American Catholic is on good ground when he refuses to make an ideological idol out of religious freedom and separation of church and state, when he refuses to "believe" in them as articles of faith. He takes the highest ground available in this matter of the relations between religion and government when he asserts that his commitment to the religion clauses of the Constitution is a moral commitment to them as articles of peace in a pluralist society.

TWO VIEWS OF PLURALISM[1]

Frederick A. Olafson

Frederick A. Olafson is a member of the Department of Philos-
ophy at Johns Hopkins University and editor of Society, Law and
Morality *(1961).* *The following selection is his critical commentary*
on the views propounded by Father Murray in We Hold These
Truths. *Although his concern is with the American Catholic position*
on the relation of church and state, Professor Olafson's excellent
statement is helpful in understanding the doctrine of natural law
that, although primarily associated with the Catholic tradition, has
lately attracted many non-Catholics in quest of an escape from
moral relativism.[2]

Since much of Professor Olafson's argument concerning na-
tural law is based on views of Father Murray that are not set forth
in the preceding selection, it may be well to summarize these views
here. Father Murray's central premise is that the consensus reflected
in our constitution whereby we acquire our identity as a people and
whereby our society "is endowed with its vital form, its entelechy,
its sense of purpose as a collectivity organized for action in history"
is no rationalization of an economic interest, no "set of working
hypotheses whose value is pragmatic," but an "ensemble of substan-
tive truths . . . an order of elementary affirmations that reflect reali-
ties inherent in the order of existence."[3] It is, he says, an "intuitional
a priori," and as such it implies not only that there are certain basic
truths we hold in common but also that there is "a natural law that
makes known to all of us the structure of the moral universe in such
wise that all of us are bound by it in a common obedience."[4] It was
this tradition of natural law, Father Murray urges, that prevailed
with the "Fathers of the Republic" as with the "Fathers of the
Church." In its political implications this tradition means "that gov-
ernment has a moral basis; that the universal moral law is the foun-
dation of society; that the legal order of society—that is, the state—
is subject to judgment by a law that is not statistical but inherent
in the nature of man; that the eternal reason of God is the ultimate
origin of the law; that this nation in all its aspects—as a society, a
state, an ordered and free relationship between governors and
governed—is under God."[5] It is from such a concept of natural law
and the implications it involves that Professor Olafson dissents.

[1]*Yale Review,* Summer 1962, pp. 519–531. Copyright 1962 Yale University Press.
Reprinted by permission.
[2]Cf. below, pp. 367 ff.
[3]*We Hold These Truths* (New York: Sheed & Ward, Inc., 1960), p. 9.
[4]*We Hold These Truths,* p. 40.
[5]*We Hold These Truths,* p. 42.

To the many earlier attempts to define the public philosophy of the American political enterprise, two years ago there was added a closely argued interpretation of our political tradition by the well-known Jesuit theologian, Father John Courtney Murray (*We Hold These Truths,* Sheed and Ward). There can be little doubt that Father Murray's "reflections on the American proposition" constitute the most considerable effort yet made by an American Catholic to provide a rationale for the American political system that remains consistent with the assumptions of the older tradition of Catholic social thought. To many, the principal interest of these reflections will lie in the support they give to the view that American Catholics can in good conscience accept American constitutional arrangements and, in particular, the religious pluralism of American society and the religious neutrality of our political institutions.

One would be doing less than full justice to Father Murray's position, however, if on the strength of these conclusions one were simply to docket him as a "liberal Catholic," without really understanding the reasoning on which his assessment of our political tradition rests. There is a real danger that in the easy euphoria of unaccustomed agreement, much that is important and distinctive in Father Murray's thought will be elided and its conclusions finally misunderstood because of a failure to set them firmly in the context of the wider social philosophy by which they are inspired. This would be all the more unfortunate because one principal merit of these essays is that they enable us to locate, with considerable precision, certain radical differences that still separate Catholic and non-Catholic views of the subjects with which they deal.

In the past these differences have never been more apparent than in just this matter of pluralism that occupies so central a place in Father Murray's thought. While I do not think it was any part of his intention to offer his acceptance of pluralism as an olive branch to liberal opinion in this country, espousals of religious pluralism by Catholic thinkers tend to be wishfully interpreted by American liberals; and there is already some evidence that these essays by Father Murray are, through no lack of clarity on his part, being read in a way that I believe to be quite mistaken. There is, I think, no good reason why liberal opinion should not be as clearly aware of the differences between its conception of pluralism and this Catholic version as Father Murray himself is. This essay is intended to make these differences clear.

Father Murray's statement of what he takes to be the central elements of the American philosophy of government turns on a contrast with what he calls the Jacobin tradition of "totalitarian democracy." This is the view, rather clearly prefigured in Rousseau's political thought, that concentrates the whole moral business of a society in its political institutions and, in its extreme form, refuses to recognize the need for any independent moral appraisal of the political order. By contrast, the Founding Fathers explicitly recognized, so Father Murray tells us, that government is limited and not co-extensive with society; that its acts are not self-validating but must conform to an antecedent moral standard; and that free political institutions that permit the participation of the people in the making of law and the formulation of policy are the indispensable guarantee that government will be responsive to moral opinion. This conception of the role of government is, of course, in sharp contrast both with the ancient Roman unification of *sacerdotium* and *imperium* in the person of the emperor and with the modern totalitarian tendency to attribute an automatic normative significance to the deliverances of the popular will.

The heart of the American political tradition, as Father Murray interprets it, is a rejection of all such forms of social monism and an emphatic assertion that the moral order is independent of and superordinate to political and legal institutions. To use a phrase to which Father Murray later gives a somewhat more controversial sense, one may say that the "American proposition" is that there shall be "not one but two"—not a juridical order but a moral order as well—and that the proper ordering of their relationship to one another is the central problem of good government.

Although this statement of principles is cast in a philosophical vocabulary that is perhaps not widely used by non-Catholic political thinkers in this country, there is probably little in it that would not meet with general acceptance. Broadly speaking, Americans seem to believe that law is an agency designed to serve moral ends and that it is rightly held responsible to moral standards. Indeed, if one may believe certain highly qualified observers of our public life, such as Mr. George Kennan, this conviction has assumed the exaggerated and potentially dangerous form in this country to which the name of "moralism" properly applies.

But when Father Murray goes on to argue that only the doctrine of natural law construes the nature of man and society in a way that does justice to the moral responsibilities of the state, and that it is on the natural-law theory of society that the American polity therefore rests, he is arguing for a position that has been and still is hotly contested. Historically, it is of course true that belief in a "higher law" held an important place in the political philosophy of the Founding Fathers. By the time it reached them, however, the "natural law" of the eighteenth century had been heavily diluted by infusions of a Lockian doctrine of natural rights, which Father Murray declares to be an individualistic corruption of the authentic doctrine of St. Thomas. So his thesis is not likely to be well served by historical arguments. What is much more to the point is Father Murray's contention that the hope of bringing moral considerations to bear upon our thinking about political affairs is dependent on the restoration to a place of honor in our intellectual world of the doctrine of natural law.

What are the merits of natural law theory that justify such an ambitious claim in its behalf? Father Murray's answer is that the morality of natural law alone provides a set of rational procedures by which universally valid and authoritative answers can be given to moral and social questions. The moral imperatives of natural law issue from a rational insight into the nature of man and are therefore entirely free of the taint of voluntarism and subjectivism which Father Murray discovers in a wide range of modern conceptions of morality. The doctrine of natural law, resting as it does on a human nature that is common to all men, is not, according to Father Murray, in any sense distinctively Catholic. It represents, instead, the indispensable minimum of rationally grounded consensus without which even a pluralistic society cannot survive. At this point Father Murray's argument takes on, as he admits, a surprisingly pragmatic cast. He says, in effect, that a return to the abandoned tradition of natural law is a necessary condition of our survival as a civil society.

In the foregoing summary I have been unfaithful to Father Murray's line of thought to the extent that in characterizing the sphere of morality I have spoken of moral "opinion" and not of moral "truth." It is very emphatically the latter that he is interested in and the existence of which he believes to be pre-supposed by the "American proposition." The importance of natural law to his argument can indeed be explained by the fact that it alone is supposed to enable us to make this crucial distinction between opinion and truth in the moral sphere. Now if this were the fundamental option of the moral life it would clearly be perverse to come down on the side of opinion. It is equally apparent, however, that if Father Murray's somewhat simplistic conception of moral truth is adopted, the case for pluralism, by becoming a case for allowing people to persist in error, would take on a very different aspect. What I wish to suggest here is that the concept of moral truth on which the natural law theory depends is seriously defective and that its repercussions on Father Murray's pluralism are both extensive and disquieting.

It is one thing to adopt an intellectualistic vocabulary for talking about moral deliberation, and quite another to provide solutions to moral problems that command rational assent. Admittedly, many minds find a sort of comfort in the elaborate paraphernalia of rationality with which natural law theory has always surrounded itself, but the real issue has to do with the logical power of that theory as manifested by the justification it is able to provide for the specific directives for conduct which it is supposed to produce. There is unfortunately, in the writings of natural law theorists, and in these essays by Father Murray as well, a kind of abstract and rhetorical intellectualism that runs well ahead of any demonstrated capability to construct justificatory arguments whose validity cannot be challenged.

Consider, for example, those first principles of the practical order from which all moral reasoning is supposed to begin: "the good is to be done and

promoted and evil is to be avoided." St. Thomas says that these are necessary truths of reason. From them, by way of a process that Father Murray
calls "particularization," moral argument descends to practical conclusions.
Unfortunately, these primal truths impose themselves so irresistibly only
because they are not the kind of assertion that anyone, no matter what his
moral views, would feel obliged to deny. No one except a Satanist goes
around preaching that good is to be avoided and evil sought after. Real
moral disagreement, on the other hand, cannot be explained by saying that
one person apprehends these truths and another does not. Indeed, both
parties to a moral conflict could in fact accept these resounding truisms in
good faith and yet differ in the way they "particularize" the good, i.e. in
the criteria by which they identify good things or right actions.

In order to make out a convincing case for the compelling intellectual
authority of natural law, it would have to be shown that some ways of parti-
cularizing the good are self-contradictory or invalid in some other sense.
It is a pity that Father Murray does not cast any new light on this crucially
important process. Like many other natural law theorists, he manages to
suggest that once the primary truths are accepted, there becomes operative
a set of rational controls that guides the well-disposed reasoner to the right
answer; but he never gives any indication of what the sequence of the argument is. As a result, the rigorously rational character that he repeatedly
attributes to the "moral order" of which he speaks remains unsubstantiated
by evidence. It suggests itself that the voluntaristic character of much
modern moral philosophy which Father Murray so deplores is due to a
recognition that the claims of moral intellectualism cannot in fact be made
good and that at crucial points in the process of moral deliberation it is more
appropriate to speak of "choice" and "decision" than of "particularizations"
and "deductions" that prove on inspection to be disguised choices.

But if "true" answers to substantive moral questions do not follow from
first principles without the intervention of more subjective factors, what are
we to make of Father Murray's confident assertion that "moral reality" is
"permeable to human reason"? Is he just wrong, or is there more to his
argument than at first appears? I think the latter is more likely and that at
least a partial explanation is to be found in a tacit assumption that Father
Murray evidently makes, but the full significance of which for his argument
is not developed. This is the assumption that there is an institution that is
uniquely qualified to interpret the "moral a priori." That institution is of
course the Roman Catholic Church, whose authority in matters of morals
can be usefully compared to the authority that in a political society is dele-
gated to judges, whose decisions—or interpretations of statute law—are
thereby made the authoritative reading of the law. A judicial decision is
binding not because it is possible even in principle to retrace the deductions
by which the judge moved from the statute to the decision but because the

decision was made by the person or persons whose decision by law counts as the authoritative one. In spite of the great and important differences between straightforward deduction and practical conclusions whose validity rests on a procedural convention of this sort, I would suggest that Father Murray does not clearly distinguish them. Because he fails to do so, he is able to impute a rational necessity to the set of conclusions that the Catholic tradition of social thought has extracted from a "moral a priori" that is in fact logically sterile. The illusion of a seamless logical continuity in moral deliberation that could hardly have been produced by logical operations upon such vacuous "principles" as those noted above is made possible by the covert assumption of a uniquely empowered interpretative agency. Unfortunately the effect of this added premise is to make it quite impossible for Father Murray to argue, as he does, that there is nothing peculiarly Catholic about the theory of natural law and that it is thus well suited to acceptance as the public philosophy of American society.

The role of the Church as a moral arbiter raises another point that has an important bearing on Father Murray's general thesis. He has argued —rightly, as I believe—that the state must recognize that the moral personality of its citizens is not exhausted by their civic and political functions and that the private associations and the various forms of expression and communication through which moral opinions are formed and revised must not only not be impeded by the state but, wherever possible, encouraged. This view yields the previously noted contrast between the formalized political sphere and the wider and looser sphere of private moral opinion. The traditional American understanding of this contrast, as Father Murray very candidly states, has been that the sphere of moral opinion should never be forced into a single institutional framework. It is par excellence the domain of private associations, no one of which has any privilege or official connection with the political order. The mediating link between "morality," conceived of as sets of opinions held by the members of these groups, and the state is just the individual person who, of course, lives in both spheres and is free to attempt by legal means to translate his moral views into law and public policy. But if Father Murray clearly sees that this moral individualism is basic to the "American proposition," it becomes equally clear to the reader that he does not subscribe to it. The point is a central one and bears close examination.

The traditional Catholic view has been that the individual conscience will inevitably buckle under the weight of the moral responsibility assigned to it by liberalism and that it is foolish to expect a just and stable social order to emerge out of the competition of moral pressure groups, no matter how scrupulously the procedural rules governing this competition are observed. Catholic thought has therefore assumed the necessity of some authoritative direction of moral opinion, and it is clear that the institution that assumes the responsibility becomes, in so doing, more than just a private voluntary association. *Both* the political and the moral sphere must, on this view, have a formalized institutional expression. Furthermore, since the general relationship between the two institutions so created is itself to be determined in accordance with the directives of natural law of which the Church is the final interpreter, it is evident that the Church is the superior member of this "dyarchy." It may of course make certain spheres of action the independent responsibility of the state, just as it may tolerate the existence of other churches. The essential point, however, is that the Church has the right to define its relationship to the state as well as to its direct competitors in the moral-religious sphere.

It is the relation in which Father Murray stands to this tradition of thought that needs clarifying. In the form of rhetorical questions, he seems plainly to indicate his convictions that the liberal faith in the individual conscience is misplaced, but he does not explicitly draw the conclusion— which he as a Catholic can hardly resist—that the mediating function of which he speaks must be performed by the Church and not just by individuals. He does, however, speak of something he calls the "freedom of the Church," which he feels has been sadly neglected in favor of the freedom of individual conscience. He can scarcely mean by the "freedom of the Church" the freedom that the Church enjoys as a private voluntary association, since he recognizes that *that* freedom is complete, at least in this country. One can only suppose, therefore, that in demanding the "freedom of the Church" he is proposing a new and more extensive role for the Church than is permitted by its status as a voluntary association. How such a recognition of the "freedom of the Church" would differ from arrangements in countries where the Church enjoys, by law, a privileged position, Father Murray does not explain.

That Father Murray is dissatisfied with the Church's present status as a voluntary private association is made abundantly clear by his attack on the social "monism" which he believes to be implicit in the doctrine of sovereignty. In this connection, it is to be regretted that Father Murray never gives a neutral statement of what the doctrine of sovereignty really comes to and that, as a result, it functions in these essays as a sort of all-purpose bugaboo. Stripped of its adventitious associations with the various forms of government that have used it for their own purposes, this doctrine emerges as the essentially formal and morally innocuous requirement that the legal order form a self-contained system in the sense that there be a defined procedure available for resolving all questions that come before the body politic. In this sense the United States is as fully sovereign as any European monarchy has ever been. Nothing is implied by this doctrine as to what this juridically complete system will do or what laws it will make.

A state that severely limits freedom of expression or the rights of its citizens to participate in the process of government is not a whit more sovereign than the liberal society that recognizes and protects the most extensive political rights for its citizens.

It is surprising and a little disheartening that so judicious a writer as Father Murray should repeat the absurd charge that the Communist state is the logical outcome of the modern doctrine of sovereignty. What is true is that the Communist state does not recognize the desirability of a parallel activity of discussion and deliberation in voluntary associations or otherwise and that it has suppressed the free institutions which, according to the American proposition as stated by Father Murray, are the guarantee of the responsiveness of the state to moral pressures. Through the agency of the one uniquely authorized party, the Communists have regimented opinion and effectively destroyed the fruitful contrast between the political and the moral spheres. In so doing, the Communist state has not made itself more sovereign; it has only made itself illiberal and tyrannical. It is a striking paradox that Father Murray should propose by implication an institutionalization of the moral sphere and thereby place himself in opposition to the liberal tradition and on the side of the totalitarians.

As a result of Father Murray's failure to make these vital distinctions, the morally neutral and the aggressively illiberal forms of "sovereignty" are connected in such a way that, to avoid the latter, one has to reject the former as well. Indeed, it becomes difficult to see how Father Murray could be satisfied with anything short of an explicit recognition by the state that it is not master of its own house. If it claims that it is, it has on his reasoning taken the road that leads to totalitarianism. But if the state is not master of its own house, who is? Not the moral consciousness of its citizens, as expressed through the political process itself, for it is precisely in this role that Father Murray believes that individual conscience has failed; and in any case the supremacy of the moral consciousness is already recognized by the establishment of free institutions that permit the individual citizen to participate in government.

The only sure antidote to the pernicious social disease of "sovereignty," in Father Murray's peculiar use of that term, would inevitably be some form of recognition by the state of an independent institution enjoying at least coordinate status with itself and endowed with special authority in matters of morals, i.e. a church. The precise juridical character of the relationship between these two elements of the "dyarchy" of which Father Murray speaks would no doubt allow for a good deal of slack. The tendency of all such arrangements is, however, as evident as it is, in the light of Father Murray's distaste for "monism," ironical. It would merely transfer sovereignty from the secular state to a new corporate entity—the state-cum-church (or church-cum-state, depending on whether the predominance of power was held by the secular or the spiritual bureaucracy). In either case, society as a whole would be finally contained in a single institutional carapace which would be all the more confining because, unlike the state, a hierarchical church charged with the direction of consciences can hardly allow itself to be judged by an independent moral standard. One could wish that Father Murray, who is markedly sensitive to the temptations of power that are the inseparable accompaniment of political integration, had indicated a corresponding awareness of the even more insidious temptations to which such a church in its "freedom" would be exposed.

These considerations must inevitably qualify any initial enthusiasm that may have been felt over Father Murray's apparent acceptance of religious pluralism. Indeed, the terms in which that acceptance is formulated are in themselves sufficient to inspire some doubts. A great deal of the supporting argument is devoted to the point that American religious pluralism is not a universally valid article of faith, but a sagacious political arrangement that has to be justified by reference to the historical circumstances under which the American polity came into being. To this it might be replied that it matters little what these "articles of peace" are called, so long as the commitment to them of all groups in American society is a firm one and is not based on a tactical situation which is subject to change. Unfortunately when Father Murray carries a qualifying reference to the "given circumstances" over into his assertion that the American government "has neither the mandate nor the duty nor the right to legislate in favor of or against any of the religious confessions existent in American society," one does not have to be a secularist fanatic to be made somewhat uneasy. Elsewhere, Father Murray explicitly declares that it is a "lamentable" truth that American society is religiously pluralistic. It is surely not unreasonable, therefore, to ask what these "given circumstances" are in which the American government does not have this right, and to want to know in what circumstances it would, on the Catholic view, acquire that right. The American proposition, as widely understood, holds that no change in given circumstances would justify the establishment of a confessional state in this country. To speak bluntly, many Americans believe that the leadership of the Roman Catholic Church in this country accepts the religious neutrality of the state only provisionally and lives in expectation of the demographic shifts that will make other more congenial arrangements politically feasible. If this is a false belief, as Father Murray would apparently have us think, then the qualifying phrase, "in the given circumstances," must be elucidated in some other way. It is to be regretted that Father Murray has not performed this much-needed service. Because he has not done so, his acceptance of pluralism retains the very flavor of reluctance and conditionality which he seems to have wished to avoid.

These doubts extend to the very conception of pluralism that Father Murray is at least provisionally defending. At bottom, the question is one that has to do with the various roles or identities that the members of a society sustain by virtue of their membership in various sub-societies, and of the proper relation between these identities. Pluralism in the American tradition is not just a "lamentable" fact that has to be lived with; it is only one aspect of a wider social ideal. This ideal of pluralism is that a society should comprise a variety of institutions that maintain a meaningful degree of independence of one another, and that no individual's identity should be exhausted by his affiliation with any one of them. The one identity that all members of the society share is political: the status of citizens; and the state provides the indispensable legal framework within which limited private associations find their place. When properly understood, this comprehensiveness that is peculiar to the political order has nothing in the least sinister about it; and the liberal pluralist view is that the tendency to elephantiasis, which seems to be latent in every institutional affiliation, must be resisted when it is our identity as citizens that tends to blot out all other identities, as it must in all other cases. Which identity—civic, religious, professional— needs to be strengthened and which needs to be contained within limits is a judgment that will be made differently in the light of tendencies that may be paramount in a given society at a given time.

This at least is the liberal understanding of pluralism as a social philosophy. I do not think that it is Father Murray's. His great fear is that our secular identity as citizens will absorb or distort all our other identities and that it is therefore the most important of these—our religious identity— which requires special attention and solicitude. Here I cannot agree. My own feeling is that our sense of civic identity and of membership and participation in the American political enterprise is not as strong as it might be and that it needs strengthening. I think there is a real danger that our civic identity may be squeezed flat by the expanding demands of other institutional loyalties. But if pluralism is to mean something more than a progressive compartmentalization of our society, steps will have to be taken to give to our public and political life an ideal meaning that it can hardly be said to have for most of us at the present time. Specifically, unless there are occasions on which Americans come together simply as citizens and not as delegates of the religious institutions with which they are affiliated, it is fairly certain that our political institutions will in fact become the "servile and secondary thing" that less careful Catholic apologists have declared them to be.

The case for such a reinforcement of our public identity becomes even stronger when one recalls, as Father Murray does, that in this country a sense of civic participation has never carried with it the kind of aggressively antireligious spirit that has marked the evolution of secular political institutions in Europe. Why then does Father Murray persist in the sterile animosity toward the state that is evident on virtually every page of this book and which seems to have been inspired, in good part, by the experiences of the Church under the Third Republic in France? In the absence of provocation, this competitive and suspicious·attitude looks remarkably like a case of projection, in which an unsatisfied aspiration to dominance on the part ʼof the Church is imputed to a secular political institution which does not, at least in this country, make any claim that is really comparable. In particular, the disproportionate emphasis that Father Murray gives to the limited character of government suggests to me not so much any fear that the specific freedoms by which that limitation is realized may be in danger as a generalized suspicion of all forms of secular idealism and particularly of those that find their expression in political activity.

It is this deep hostility to a secular conception of political life that robs Father Murray's acceptance of religious pluralism of any real relevance to the American political situation. One may agree with him that a pluralistic society, like any other, rests on a consensus—a body of shared beliefs—and that these are not just procedural in character (the "democratic method") but in part directly moral as well. Such a society will, however, always come up against the question of the language in which this consensus is to be formulated. Now, if each religious community within the larger society states these principles in a way that makes them dependent on assumptions peculiar to its own religious faith, certain results may be expected. It will almost certainly be more difficult for the members of any given religious community to recognize that they share these principles with other groups, and the distinction between their beliefs as members of a restricted religious community and those they hold as members of a wider political society will be blurred. But just this public awareness that there *is* a body of shared religiously neutral beliefs, whether moral or "procedural," is of vital importance to a pluralistic society which must, after all, recognize itself for what it is. In the absence of such an awareness, the social strategy of religious communities that lack a sense of being part of a larger society with principles of its own will inevitably be absorptive and eventually totalitarian.

Father Murray makes the claim that the theory of natural law can provide the common vocabulary that our pluralistic society needs. I have tried to show why I think he is mistaken. I would argue, against his claim, that if competing religious groups are not going to destroy such social unity as we actually enjoy by futile attempts to pull the "American proposition" into their own orbits of belief, there must be an explicit recognition that our "consensus" is secular in character. By "secular" I do not mean to imply that individuals or groups may not continue to find additional reasons for preferring free institutions in their religious beliefs. What is meant is simply that the public or shared formulation of the principles of a free society must not be one that stands and falls with the special assumptions of particular religious groups about the metaphysical status of moral truth or the nature of human reason. At bottom, these "principles" are very general ways of acting and of comporting oneself in relation to other human beings; and the working out of their precise nature is the task of secular political and social philosophy. There is, I think, every reason to suppose that this enterprise is of central importance to our society and that our public life will in the end be better served by a clear delineation of the "logic" of a free society than by the search for metaphysical underpinnings.

If there is one thing that disfigures these essays by Father Murray, it is the extraordinary and ill-informed animus that he displays toward the whole tradition of secular political philosophy. It is next to impossible to discover in the caricatured versions of Hobbes and Locke and Bentham that he offers us the thinkers who, whatever their failures, really tried to devise a rationale of human society that would be genuinely independent, as Father Murray's is not, of special assumptions of a religious nature. To me there is a strangeness bordering on outright paradox in a procedure that violently rejects virtually the whole intellectual heritage of liberalism but accepts the open and pluralistic society that it has produced. No doubt it is possible to provide a new set of foundations for an older set of political institutions; but in this case I can only think that a pluralistic society that tries to make its unifying political and moral principles religious in any nontrivial sense is in for trouble; and that Father Murray's attempt to organize the public consciousness and the public area of concern around the idea of natural law is most unlikely to allow them the degree of separate identity that will insure effective social unity. By recognizing that public consciousness only when it is willing to express itself in the special moral-political vocabulary of his faith, he has really avoided the problem that he ostensibly set himself: how does one live together in a civil society with those whose religious beliefs one does not share?

EVERSON v. EWING TOWNSHIP BOARD OF EDUCATION[1]

Supreme Court of the United States

As always, a particular case, even a minor one, helps to throw the larger conflict of principles into dramatic highlight, especially if it occasions vigorous differences among justices of the U.S. Supreme Court. The fact that Justice Hugo Black, speaking for the majority, and Justice Robert Jackson, dissenting, are usually on the same side of most of the issues dividing the Supreme Court makes their difference in the present instance all the more interesting. The case concerns a township's provision of bus fares for parochial-school pupils. The decision is significant in that, while assenting, the Court for the first time explicitly elaborated the doctrine of separation of church and state as embodied in the First Amendment and invoked the Jeffersonian dictum that the amendment (along with the Fourteenth Amendment, which made it applicable to the states) erected "a wall of separation between Church and State."

Mr. Justice Black delivered the opinion of the Court: A New Jersey statute authorizes its local school districts to make rules and contracts for the transportation of children to and from schools. The appellee, a township board of education, acting pursuant to this statute, authorized reimbursement to parents of money expended by them for the bus transportation of their children on regular busses operated by the public transportation system. Part of this money was for the payment of transportation of some children in the community to Catholic parochial schools. These church schools give their students, in addition to secular education, regular religious instruction conforming to the religious tenets and modes of worship of the Catholic faith. The superintendent of these schools is a Catholic priest.

The appellant, in his capacity as a district taxpayer, filed suit in a State court challenging the right of the Board of Education to reimburse parents of parochial school students. . . .

The only contention here is that the State statute and the resolution, insofar as they authorized reimbursement to parents of children attending parochial schools, violates the Federal Constitution. . . .

The New Jersey statute is challenged as a "law respecting the establishment of religion.". . .

---

[1]330 US1, 1947.

The meaning and scope of the First Amendment, preventing establishment of religion or prohibiting the free exercise thereof, in the light of its history and the evils it was designed forever to suppress, have been several times elaborated by the decisions of this Court prior to the application of the First Amendment to the states by the Fourteenth. The broad meaning given the Amendment by these earlier cases has been accepted by this Court in its decisions concerning an individual's religious freedom rendered since the Fourteenth Amendment was interpreted to make the prohibitions of the First applicable to state action abridging religious freedom. There is every reason to give the same application and broad interpretation to the "establishment of religion" clause. . . .

The "establishment of religion" clause of the First Amendment means at least this: Neither a state nor the Federal Government can set up a church. Neither can pass laws which aid one religion, aid all religions, or prefer one religion over another. Neither can force nor influence a person to go to or to remain away from church against his will or force him to profess a belief or disbelief in any religion. No person can be punished for entertaining or professing religious beliefs or disbeliefs, for church attendance or non-attendance. No tax in any amount, large or small, can be levied to support any religious activities or institutions, whatever they may be called, or whatever form they may adopt to teach or practice religion. Neither a state nor the Federal Government can, openly or secretly, participate in the affairs of any religious organizations or groups and vice versa. In the words of Jefferson, the clause against establishment of religion by law was intended to erect "a wall of separation between Church and State." . . .

We must consider the New Jersey statute in accordance with the foregoing limitations imposed by the First Amendment. But we must not strike that state statute down if it is within the State's constitutional power even though it approaches the verge of that power. . . . New Jersey cannot consistently with the "establishment of religion" clause of the First Amendment contribute tax-raised funds to the support of an institution which teaches the tenets and faith of any church. On the other hand, other language of the amendment commands that New Jersey cannot hamper its citizens in the free exercise of their own religion. Consequently, it cannot exclude individual Catholics, Lutherans, Mohammedans, Baptists, Jews, Methodists, Non-believers, Presbyterians, or the members of any other faith, *because of their faith, or lack of it,* from receiving the benefits of public welfare legislation. While we do not mean to intimate that a state could not provide transportation only to children attending public schools, we must be careful, in protecting the citizens of New Jersey against state-established churches, to be sure that we do not inadvertently prohibit New Jersey from extending its general state law benefits to all its citizens without regard to their religious belief.

Measured by these standards, we cannot say that the First Amendment prohibits New Jersey from spending tax-raised funds to pay the bus fares of parochial school pupils as a part of a general program under which it pays the fares of pupils attending public and other schools. It is undoubtedly true that children are helped to get to church schools. There is even a possibility that some of the children might not be sent to the church schools if the parents were compelled to pay [for] their children going to and from church [schools out of their own] pockets when transportation to a public school would have been paid for by the State. The same possibility exists where the state requires a local transit company to provide reduced fares to school children including those attending parochial schools, or where a municipally owned transportation system undertakes to carry all school children free of charge. Moreover, state-paid policemen, detailed to protect children going to and from church schools from the very real hazards of traffic, would serve much the same purpose and accomplish much the same result as state provisions intended to guarantee free transportation of a kind which the state deems to be best for the school children's welfare. And parents might refuse to risk their children to the serious danger of traffic accidents going to and from parochial schools, the approaches to which were not protected by policemen. Similarly, parents might be reluctant to permit their children to attend schools which the state had cut off from such general government services as ordinary police and fire protection, connections for sewage disposal, public highways and sidewalks. Of course, cutting off church schools from these services, so separate and so indisputably marked off from the religious function, would make it far more difficult for the schools to operate. But such is obviously not the purpose of the First Amendment. That Amendment requires the state to be a neutral in its relations with groups of religious believers and non-believers; it does not require the state to be their adversary. State power is no more to be used so as to handicap religions than it is to favor them.

This Court has said that parents may, in the discharge of their duty under state compulsory education laws, send their children to a religious rather than a public school if the school meets the secular educational requirements which the state has power to impose. . . . It appears that these parochial schools meet New Jersey's requirements. The State contributes no money to the schools. It does not support them. Its legislation, as applied, does no more than provide a general program to help parents get their children, regardless of their religion, safely and expeditiously to and from accredited schools.

The First Amendment has erected a wall between church and state. That wall must be kept high and impregnable. We could not approve the slightest breach. New Jersey has not breached it here.

Affirmed.

Mr. Justice Jackson, dissenting. I find myself, contrary to first impressions, unable to join in this decision. I have a sympathy, though it is not ideological, with Catholic citizens who are compelled by law to pay taxes for public schools, and also feel constrained by conscience and discipline to support other schools for their own children. Such relief to them as this case involves is not in itself a serious burden to taxpayers and I have assumed it to be as little serious in principle. Study of this case convinces me otherwise. The Court's opinion marshals every argument in favor of state aid and puts the case in its most favorable light, but much of its reasoning confirms my conclusions that there are no good grounds upon which to support the present legislation. In fact, the undertones of the opinion, advocating complete and uncompromising separation of Church from State, seem utterly discordant with its conclusion yielding support to their commingling in educational matters. The case which irresistibly comes to mind as the most fitting precedent is that of Julia who, according to Byron's reports, "whispering 'I will ne'er consent,'—consented."

The Township of Ewing is not furnishing transportation to the children in any form; it is not operating school busses itself or contracting for their operation; and it is not performing any public service of any kind with this taxpayer's money. All school children are left to ride as ordinary paying passengers on the regular busses operated by the public transportation system. What the Township does, and what the taxpayer complains of, is at stated intervals to reimburse parents for the fares paid, provided the children attend either public schools or Catholic Church schools. This expenditure of tax funds has no possible effect on the child's safety or expedition in transit. As passengers on the public busses they travel as fast and no faster, and are as safe and no safer, since their parents are reimbursed as before. . . .

Whether the taxpayer constitutionally can be made to contribute aid to parents of students because of their attendance at parochial schools depends upon the nature of those schools and their relation to the Church. The Constitution says nothing of education. It lays no obligation on the states to provide schools and does not undertake to regulate state systems of education if they see fit to maintain them. But they cannot, through school policy any more than through other means, invade rights secured to citizens by the Constitution of the United States. . . . One of our basic rights is to be free of taxation to support a transgression of the constitutional command that the authorities "shall make no law respecting an establishment of religion, or prohibiting the free exercise thereof." . . .

The function of the Church school is a subject on which this record is meager. It shows only that the schools are under superintendence of a priest and that "religion is taught as part of the curriculum." But we know that such schools are parochial only in name—they, in fact, represent a world-wide and age-old policy of the Roman Catholic Church. Under the rubric "Catholic Schools," the Canon Law of the Church, by which all Catholics are bound, provides:

> 1215. Catholic children are to be educated in schools where not only nothing contrary to Catholic faith and morals is taught, but rather in schools where religious and moral training occupy the first place. . . .
> 1216. In every elementary school the children must, according to their age, be instructed in Christian doctrine.
> The young people who attend the higher schools are to receive a deeper religious knowledge, and the bishops shall appoint priests qualified for such work by their learning and piety. . . .
> 1224. The religious teaching of youth in any school is subject to the authority and inspection of the Church. . . .

It is no exaggeration to say that the whole historic conflict in temporal policy between the Catholic Church and non-Catholics comes to a focus in their respective school policies. The Roman Catholic Church, counseled by experience in many ages and many lands and with all sorts and conditions of men, takes what, from the viewpoint of its own progress and the success of its mission, is a wise estimate of the importance of education to religion. It does not leave the individual to pick up religion by chance. It relies on early and indelible indoctrination in the faith and order of the Church by the word and example of persons consecrated to the task.

Our public school, if not a product of Protestantism, at least is more consistent with it than with the Catholic culture and scheme of values. It is a relatively recent development dating from about 1840. It is organized on the premises that secular education can be isolated from all religious teachings so that the school can inculcate all needed temporal knowledge and also maintain a strict and lofty neutrality as to religion. The assumption is that after the individual has been instructed in worldly wisdom he will be better fitted to choose his religion. Whether such a disjunction is possible, and if possible whether it is wise, are questions I need not try to answer.

I should be surprised if any Catholic would deny that the parochial school is a vital, if not the most vital, part of the Roman Catholic Church. If put to the choice, that venerable institution, I should expect, would forego its whole service for mature persons before it would give up education of the young, and it would be a wise choice. Its growth and cohesion, discipline and loyalty, spring from its schools. Catholic education is the rock on which the whole structure rests, and to render tax aid to its Church school is indistinguishable to me from rendering the same aid to the Church itself.

It is of no importance in this situation whether the beneficiary of this expenditure of tax-raised funds is primarily the parochial school and incidentally the pupil, or whether the aid is directly bestowed on the pupil with indirect benefits to the school. The state cannot maintain a Church and it can no more tax its citizens to furnish free carriage to those who attend a Church. The prohibition against establishment of religion cannot be circumvented by a subsidy, bonus or reimbursement of expense to individuals for receiving religious instruction and indoctrination.

The Court, however, compares this to other subsidies and loans to individuals and says, "Nor does it follow that a law has a private rather than a public purpose because it provides that tax-raised funds will be paid to reimburse individuals on account of money spent by them in a way which furthers a public program. . . ." Of course, the state may pay out tax-raised funds to relieve pauperism, but it may not under our Constitution do so to induce or reward piety. It may spend funds to secure old age against want, but it may not spend funds to secure religion against skepticism. It may compensate individuals for loss of employment, but it cannot compensate them for adherence to a creed.

It seems to me that the basic fallacy in the Court's reasoning, which accounts for its failure to apply the principles it avows, is in ignoring the essentially religious test by which beneficiaries of this expenditure are selected. A policeman protects a Catholic, of course—but not because he is a Catholic; it is because he is a man and a member of our society. The fireman protects the Church school—but not because it is a Church school; it is because it is property, part of the assets of our society. Neither the fireman nor the policeman has to ask before he renders aid "Is this man or building identified with the Catholic Church?" But before these school authorities draw a check to reimburse for a student's fare they must ask just that question, and if the school is a Catholic one they may render aid because it is such, while if it is of any other faith or is run for profit, the help must be withheld. To consider the converse of the Court's reasoning will best disclose its fallacy. That there is no parallel between police and fire protection and this plan of reimbursement is apparent from the incongruity of the limitation of this Act if applied to police and fire service. Could we sustain an Act that said the police shall protect pupils on the way to or from public schools and Catholic schools but not while going to and coming from other schools, and firemen shall extinguish a blaze in public or Catholic school buildings but shall not put out a blaze in Protestant Church schools or private schools operated for profit? That is the true analogy to the case we have before us and I should think it pretty plain that such a scheme would not be valid. . . .

There is no answer to the proposition, more fully expounded by Mr. Justice Rutledge, that the effect of the religious freedom Amendment to our Constitution was to take every form of propaganda of religion out of the realm of things which could directly or indirectly be made public business and thereby be supported in whole or in part at taxpayers' expense. That is a difference which the Constitution sets up between religion and almost every other subject matter of legislation, a difference which goes to the very root of religious freedom and which the Court is overlooking today. This freedom was first in the Bill of Rights because it was first in the forefathers' minds; it was set forth in absolute terms, and its strength is its rigidity. It was intended not only to keep the state's hands out of religion, but to keep religion's hands off the state, and, above all, to keep bitter religious controversy out of public life by denying to every denomination any advantage from getting control of public policy or the public purse. Those great ends I cannot but think are immeasurably compromised by today's decision.

This policy of our Federal Constitution has never been wholly pleasing to most religious groups. They all are quick to invoke its protections; they all are irked when they feel its restraints. . . .

THE CHURCH AND
SOCIAL REFORM

In the second decade of this century, when Protestant churches were preoccupied with problems of personal morality, especially with temperance and sex, an obscure seminary professor achieved fame almost overnight by calling upon the church to address itself to rampant social abuses. Henry Emerson Fosdick has described Walter Rauschenbusch as "the voice of his generation's Christian protest against the evils of an industrial society." It will be heard in the pages that follow.

Reinhold Niebuhr is likewise a militantly liberal social reformer. And yet, as a conservative and pessimist in theology, he has engaged in prolonged polemics against theological liberals, including—as the selection below indicates—those who have been influenced by Rauschenbusch. (Needless to say, he has been at least as severe with fundamentalists.)

The answer to this paradox is to be found in the fact that, although Niebuhr believes that man is capable of love and realizes himself most completely through love, man is also finite and sinful. Hence, like Christ, perfect love although eternally relevant to human affairs is doomed in actual history, he tells us, to frustration, i.e., to crucifixion. Niebuhr's acute awareness of man's imperfections—man's "sin"—enables him not to ask or expect too much of man, and hence to eschew sentimental optimism and escape the disappointments to which such optimism is foredoomed. "All have sinned and fall short of the glory of God." (Rom. 3:23)

A parallel position prompts Niebuhr to warn that such moral heights as the individual is capable of scaling are not for groups of men. Thus, he argues that we must distinguish sharply "between the moral and social behavior of individuals and of social groups, national, racial and economic; and that this distinction justifies and necessitates political policies which a purely individualistic ethic must always find embarrassing."[1]

---

[1]*Moral Man and Immoral Society* (New York: Charles Scribner's Sons, 1932), p. xi.

None of this means that Niebuhr is a defeatist preaching the futility of effort. On the contrary his aim is to define the conditions of moral action which, he believes, can be effective only if we are aware of *both* its limitations and potentialities. That is why he takes issue, in the selections cited below, with his brother Richard's defense of an ethic of disinterestedness.

The issue is joined here by two distinguished theologians in a remarkable fraternal debate. In fairness to Richard Niebuhr it must be said that his counsel of inactivity implies no beatification of the status quo. Much quietist teaching—that is, that the spirit of God is within and that the social problem is not the church's problem, etc.—has been of this nature. Much of the church's inactivity still reflects a contentment with things as they are, if not on the part of clergymen then on the part of vocal members of their congregations, who, in the end, determine much church policy. However, few if any responsible clergymen or theologians would today take such a position, and Richard Niebuhr's creed of inactivity is clearly not intended as an apology for the existing order. Even so, many, including his brother, would contend that, like the teaching of Luther,[2] it may serve the same purpose.

---

[2]Cf. above, p. 24 .

CHRISTIANITY AND THE SOCIAL CRISIS[1]

Walter Rauschenbusch

(1861–1918)

Walter Rauschenbusch began as a minister in Hell's Kitchen where he had a chance to observe slum life at its worst. That experience embarked him on a lifelong mission, which he pursued with prophetic zeal to ally the church with the forces of social reform. More than anyone else he is responsible for a major reorientation in American Protestantism. Among his most influential writings are Christianizing the Social Order (1912), A Theology for the Social Gospel (1917), *and* Christianity and the Social Crisis. *Many of the*

---

[1]New York: The Macmillan Company, 1907. Reprinted in *A Rauschenbusch Reader,* compiled by B. Y. Landis (New York: Harper & Row, Inc., 1957), pp. 6–22. Copyright 1957 by Harper & Row, Publishers, Incorporated. Reprinted by permission.

abuses he castigated have been corrected, an outcome to which he surely contributed by his tireless insistence that the words of the Lord's Prayer be taken seriously: "Thy Kingdom come, thy will be done, on earth as it is in heaven."

The prophets . . . are the beating heart of the Old Testament. A comprehension of the essential purpose and spirit of the prophets is necessary for a comprehension of the purpose and spirit of Jesus and of genuine Christianity. The real meaning of his life and the real direction of his purposes can be understood only in that historical connection.

The fundamental conviction of the prophets which distinguished them from the ordinary religious life of their day, was the conviction that God demands righteousness and demands nothing but righteousness.

The prophets were public men and their interest was in public affairs. Some of them were statesmen of the highest type. All of them interpreted past history, shaped present history, and foretold future history on the basis of the conviction that God rules with righteousness in the affairs of nations, and that only what is just, and not what is expedient and profitable, shall endure. . . .

The prophets demanded right moral conduct as the sole test and fruit of religion, and . . . the morality which they had in mind was not the private morality of detached pious souls but the social morality of the nation. This they preached, and they backed their preaching by active participation in public action and discussion. . . .

Here then we have a succession of men perhaps unique in religious history for their moral heroism and spiritual insight. They were the moving spirits in the religious progress of their nation; the creators, directly or indirectly, of its law, its historical and poetical literature, and its piety; the men to whose personality and teaching Jesus felt most kinship; the men who still kindle modern religious enthusiasm. Most of us believe that their insight was divinely given and that the course they steered was set for them by the Captain of history.

These men were almost indifferent, if not contemptuous, about the ceremonial side of customary religion, but turned with passionate enthusiasm to moral righteousness as the true domain of religion. Where would their interest lie if they lived today?

Their religious concern was not restricted to private religion and morality, but dealt pre-eminently with the social and political life of their nation. Would they limit its range today?

Their sympathy was wholly and passionately with the poor and oppressed. If they lived today, would they place the chief blame for poverty on the poor and give their admiration to the strong? . . .

Is it likely that the same attitude of mind which enlarged and purified the religion of the Hebrew leaders would deteriorate and endanger the religion of Christian leaders? . . . If anyone holds that religion is essentially ritual and sacramental; or that it is purely personal; or that God is on the side of the rich; or that social interest is likely to lead preachers astray; he must prove his case with his eye on the Hebrew prophets, and the burden of proof is with him. . . .

There was a revolutionary consciousness in Jesus; not, of course, in the common use of the word "revolutionary," which connects it with violence and bloodshed. But Jesus knew that he had come to kindle a fire on earth. Much as he loved peace, he knew that the actual result of his work would be not peace but the sword. His mother in her song had recognized in her own experience the settled custom of God to "put down the proud and exalt them of low degree," to "fill the hungry with good things and to send the rich empty away." King Robert of Sicily recognized the revolutionary ring in those phrases, and thought it well that the Magnificat was sung only in Latin. The son of Mary expected a great reversal of values. The first would be last and the last would be first. He saw that what was exalted among man was an abomination before God, and therefore these exalted things had no glamour for his eye. This revolutionary note runs even through the Beatitudes where we should least expect it. The point of them is that henceforth those were to be blessed whom the world had not blessed, for the Kingdom of God would reverse their relative standing. Now the poor and the hungry and sad were to be satisfied and comforted; the meek who had been shouldered aside by the ruthless would get their chance to inherit the earth, and conflict and persecution would be inevitable in the process. . . .

That was the faith of Jesus. Have his followers shared it? We shall see later what changes and limitations the original purpose and spirit of Christianity suffered in the course of history. But the Church has never been able to get entirely away from the revolutionary spirit of Jesus. It is an essential doctrine of Christianity that the world is fundamentally good and practically bad, for it was made by God, but is now controlled by sin. If a man wants to be a Christian, he must stand over against things as they are and condemn them in the name of that higher conception of life which Jesus revealed. If a man is satisfied with things as they are, he belongs to the other side. For many centuries the Church felt so deeply that the Christian conception of life and the actual social life are incompatible, that anyone who wanted to live the genuine Christian life, had to leave the world and live in a monastic community. Protestantism has abandoned the monastic life and settled down to live in the world. If that implies that it accepts the present condition as good and final, it means a silencing of its Christian protest and its surrender to "the world." There is another alternative. Ascetic Christianity called the world evil and left it. Humanity is waiting for a revolutionary Christianity which will call the world evil and change it. We do not want "to blow all our existing institutions to atoms," but we do want to remold every one of them. A tank of gasoline can blow a car sky-high in a single explosion, or push it to the top of a hill in a perpetual succession of little explosions. We need a combination between the faith of Jesus in the need and the possibility of the Kingdom of God, and the modern comprehension of the organic development of human society.

Jesus was not a mere social reformer. Religion was the heart of his life, and all that he said on social relations was said from the religious point of view. He has been called the first socialist. He was more; he was the first real man, the inaugurator of a new humanity. But as such he bore within him the germs of a new social and political order. He was too great to be the Saviour of a fractional part of human life. His redemption extends to all human needs and powers and relations. Theologians have felt no hesitation in founding a system of speculative thought on the teachings of Jesus, and yet Jesus was never an inhabitant of the realm of speculative thought. He has been made the founder and organizer of a great ecclesiastical machine, which derives authority for its offices and institutions from him, and yet "hardly any problem of exegesis is more difficult than to discover in the gospels an administrative or organizing or ecclesiastical Christ." There is at least as much justification in invoking his name today as the champion of a great movement for a more righteous social life. He was neither a theologian, nor an ecclesiastic, nor a socialist. But if we were forced to classify him either with the great theologians who elaborated the fine distinctions of scholasticism; or with the mighty popes and princes of the Church who built up their power in his name; or with the men who are giving their heart and life to the propaganda of a new social system—where should we place him? . . .

The demoralization of society ought to appeal most powerfully to the Church, for the Church is to be the incarnation of the Christ-spirit on earth, the organized conscience of Christendom. It should be swiftest to awaken to every undeserved suffering, bravest to speak against every wrong, and strongest to rally the moral forces of the community against everything that threatens the better life among men.

The gospel, to have full power over an age, must be the highest expression of the moral and religious truths held by that age. If it lags behind and deals in outgrown conceptions of life and duty, it will lose power over the ablest minds and the young men first, and gradually over all. In our thought today the social problems irresistibly take the lead. If the Church has no live and bold thought on this dominant question of modern life, its teaching authority on all other questions will dwindle and be despised. It cannot afford to have young men sniff the air as in a stuffy room when they enter the sphere of religious thought. When the world is in travail with a higher ideal of justice, the Church dare not ignore it if it would retain its moral leadership. On the other hand, if the Church does incorporate the new social terms in its synthesis of truth, they are certain to throw new light on all the older elements of its teaching. The conception of race sin and race salvation become comprehensible once more to those who have made the idea of social solidarity in good and evil a part of their thought. The law of sacrifice loses its arbitrary and mechanical aspect when we understand the vital union of all humanity. Individualistic Christianity has almost lost sight of the great idea of the Kingdom of God, which was the inspiration and center of the thought of Jesus. Social Christianity would once more enable us to understand the purpose and thought of Jesus and take the veil from our eyes when we read the synoptic gospels.

The social crisis offers a great opportunity for the infusion of new life and power into the religious thought of the church. It also offers the chance for progress in its life. When the broader social outlook widens the purpose of a Christian man beyond the increase of his church, he lifts up his eyes and sees that there are others who are at work for humanity besides his denomination. Common work for social welfare is the best common ground for the various religious bodies and the best training school for practical Christian unity. The strong movement for Christian union in our country has been largely prompted by the realization of social needs, and is led by men who have felt the attraction of the Kingdom of God as something greater than any denomination and as the common object of all. Thus the divisions which were caused in the past by differences in dogma and church polity may perhaps be healed by unity of interest in social salvation.

As we have seen, the industrial and commercial life today is dominated by principles antagonistic to the fundamental principles of Christianity, and it is so difficult to live a Christian life in the midst of it that few men even try. If production could be organized on a basis of co-operative fraternity; if distribution could at least approximately be determined by justice; if all men could be conscious that their labor contributed to the welfare of all and that their personal well-being was dependent on the prosperity of the Commonwealth; if predatory business and parasitic wealth ceased and all men lived only by their labor; if the luxury of unearned wealth no longer made us all feverish with covetousness and a simpler life became the fashion; if our time and strength were not used up either in getting bare living or in amassing unusable wealth and we had more leisure for the higher pursuits of the mind and the soul—then there might be a chance to live such a life of gentleness and brotherly kindness and tranquillity of heart as Jesus desired for men. It may be that the co-operative Commonwealth would give us the first chance in history to live a really Christian life without retiring from the world, and would make the Sermon on the Mount a philosophy of life feasible for all who care to try.

This is the stake of the Church in the social crisis. If society continues to disintegrate and decay, the Church will be carried down with it. If the Church can rally such moral forces that injustice will be overcome and fresh red blood will course in a sounder social organism, it will itself rise to higher liberty and life. Doing the will of God it will have new visions of God. With a new message will come a new authority. If the salt lose its saltness, it will be trodden under foot. If the Church fulfills its prophetic functions, it may bear the prophet's reproach for a time, but it will have the prophet's vindication thereafter.

The conviction has always been embedded in the heart of the Church that "the world"—society as it is—is evil and some time is to make way for a true human society in which the spirit of Jesus Christ shall rule. For fifteen hundred years those who desired to live a truly Christian life withdrew from the evil world to live a life apart. But the principle of such an ascetic departure from the world is dead in modern life. There are only two other possibilities. The Church must either condemn the world and seek to change it, or tolerate the world and conform to it. In the latter case it surrenders its holiness and its mission. The other possibility has never yet been tried with full faith on a large scale. All the leadings of God in contemporary history and all the promptings of Christ's spirit in our hearts urge us to make the trial. On this choice is staked the future of the church.

THE ETHIC OF JESUS AND THE SOCIAL PROBLEM[1]

Reinhold Niebuhr

Reinhold Niebuhr is American Protestantism's most distinguished theologian. His work is as respected by professional philosophers as it is by those responsible for guiding public policy.

He has written multitudinous articles in addition to his three best-known works: Moral Man and Immoral Society (1932); *the* Gifford Lectures, published as The Nature and Destiny of Man (1943); *and* The Children of Light and the Children of Darkness (1944).

The selection below was written during a period of more militant social protest than our own and reflects the point of view of a

[1]*Religion in Life,* Spring 1932. Copyright renewed 1960 by Abingdon Press. Reprinted in *Love and Justice,* edited by D. B. Robertson (Philadelphia: The Westminster Press, 1957), pp. 29–40. Used by permission.

vigorous critic of social abuses who rejects both *the opportunism of the church and the Christian Gospel Movement as represented by Rauschenbusch.*

Since Walter Rauschenbusch aroused the American church to the urgency of the social problem and its relation to the ethical ideals of the gospel, it has been rather generally assumed that it is possible to abstract an adequate social ethic for the reconstruction of society from the social teachings of Jesus. Dozens of books have been written to prove that Jesus' ideals of brotherhood represented an outline of the ideal society, that his law of service offered an alternative to the competitive impulse in modern society, that guidance for the adjustment of every political and economic problem could be found in his words, and that nothing but a little logic would serve to draw out the "social implications" of his teachings.

Most of this energy has been vainly spent and has served to create as much confusion as light. There is indeed a very rigorous ethical ideal in the gospel of Jesus, but there is no social ethic in the ordinary sense of the word in it, precisely because the ethical ideal is too rigorous and perfect to lend itself to application in the economic and political problems of our day. This does not mean that the ethic of Jesus has no light to give to a modern Christian who faces the perplexing economic and political issues of a technological civilization. It means only that confusion will be avoided if a rigorous distinction is made between a perfectionist and absolute ethic and the necessities of a social situation.

The ethic of Jesus was, to begin with, a personal ethic. It was not individual in the sense that he believed in individual perfection abstracted from a social situation. He saw that wealth tempted to covetousness and that poverty prompted the virtue of humility. He spoke of the Kingdom and not of salvation, and the Kingdom meant an ideal social relationship, even though he might emphasize that it proceeded from internal spiritual forces. His ethic was an ethic of love, and it therefore implied social relationships. But it was an individual ethic in the sense that his chief interest was in the quality of life of an individual. He regarded as a temptation the suggestion that he become a political leader or that he develop the political implications of the Messianic idea, and he resisted the effort to make him king. He was not particularly interested in the Jewish people's aspirations toward freedom from Rome, and skillfully evaded the effort to make him take sides in that political problem. He accepted monarchy on the one hand and slavery on the other, though he called attention to the difference between the ideal of his Kingdom, which measured greatness by service, and the kind of greatness which the "kings of the Gentiles" attained.

His lack of concern for social and political issues is, however, not as important from the perspective of this problem as the kind of ethical ideal which he actually developed. In terms of individual life his ethical ideal was one of complete disinterestedness, religiously motivated. No one was to seek his own. The man who asked him to persuade his brother to divide an inheritance with him was rudely rebuked. Evil was not to be resisted, the borrower was to be given more than he asked for without hope of return. A special premium was placed upon actions which could not be rewarded. In other words, the prudential motive was treated with utmost severity. There are, of course, words in the teachings of Jesus which are not as rigorous as this. He promised rewards. Some of these words belong to a humanist strain in his teachings in which he merely makes a shrewd analysis of the effect of certain actions. The severe judge will be judged severely. The proud man will be abased and the humble man exalted. Here the social rewards of social attitudes are recognized. Other offers of reward occur, but with one or two exceptions they can be placed in the category of ultimate rewards—"in the resurrection of the just," "treasures in heaven," favor with God. On the whole, they do not seriously qualify his main position that moral action must be motivated purely by obedience to God, emulation of God's attributes, and gratitude for the forgiving grace of God. An ulterior motive (desire for social approval, for instance) for a worthy action would destroy the virtue of the action and would result only in the attainment of the object of the ulterior motive—"verily, they have their reward."

Jesus did not deny that disinterested action would result in rewards; "all these things" would be added, and the man who forgot himself completely would find himself most truly. Here is the recognition of the basic ethical paradox that the highest result of an action can never be its desired result. It must be a by-product. If it is desired, the purity of the action is destroyed. If I love to be loved or to be socially approved, I will not be loved or approved in the same way as if my fellow men caught in me a glimpse of pure disinterestedness. Obviously the only way to achieve such pure disinterestedness is to have actions motivated purely by religious motives. But this very emphasis upon religious motives lifts the ethic of Jesus above the area of social ethics. We are asked to love our enemies, not because the social consequences of such love will be to make friends of the enemies, but because God loves with that kind of impartiality. We are demanded to forgive those who have wronged us, not because a forgiving spirit will prove redemptive in the lives of the fallen, but because God forgives our sins. Here we have an ethic, in other words, which we can neither disavow nor perfectly achieve. We cannot disavow it because it is a fact that the prudential motive destroys the purity of every ethical action. We have a right to view the social and personal consequences of an action in retrospect, but if we view it in prospect we have something less than the best. So powerful is the drive of self-interest in life, however, that this ideal is as difficult to achieve as it is to disavow. It remains, therefore, as an ideal which convicts every moral achievement of imperfection, but it is always a little beyond the realm of actual human history.

Though Jesus was as indifferent to the social consequences of pure disinterestedness as he was critical of concern for the personal consequences, it is not difficult to draw conclusions in regard to the social ideal implied by such disinterestedness. In practical terms it means a combination of anarchism and communism dominated by the spirit of love. Such perfect love as he demands would obviate the necessity of coercion on the one hand because men would refrain from transgressing upon their neighbor's rights, and on the other hand because such transgression would be accepted and forgiven if it did occur. This is anarchism, in other words. It would mean communism because the privileges of each would be potentially the privileges of all. Where love is perfect the distinctions between mine and thine disappear. The social ideal of Jesus is as perfect and as impossible of attainment as is his personal ideal. But again it is an ideal that cannot be renounced completely. Whatever justice men attain in the society in which they live is always an imperfect justice. The careful limitation and definition of rights which Stoicism gave to the world as a social ideal always develop into injustice in actual life because every person views rights not from an absolute but from a biased perspective. The result is a society in which the perspective of the strong dictates the conceptions of justice by which the total community operates and necessitates social conflict through the assertion of the rights of the weak before the injustice is corrected. Justice, in other words, that is only justice is less than justice. Only imaginative justice, that is, love that begins by espousing the rights of the other rather than self, can achieve a modicum of fairness.

Whether we view the ethical teachings of Jesus from the perspective of the individual or of society we discover an unattainable ideal, but a very useful one. It is an ideal never attained in history or in life, but one that gives us an absolute standard by which to judge both personal and social righteousness. It is a standard by comparison with which all human attainments fall short, and it may offer us the explanation of Jesus' words, "Why callest thou me good? no one is good save God." Perhaps it ought to be added that an attempt to follow this ideal in a world that is, particularly in its group relationships, hardly human and certainly not divine, will inevitably lead us to where it led Jesus, to the cross.

Valuable as this kind of perfectionism is, it certainly offers no basis for a social ethic that deals responsibly with a growing society. Those of us who believe in the complete reorganization of modern society are not wrong in using the ideal of Jesus as a vantage point from which to condemn the present social order, but I think we are in error when we try to draw from the teachings of Jesus any warrant for the social policies which we find necessary to attain to any modicum of justice. We may be right in believing that we are striving for a justice which approximates the Christian ideal more closely than the present social order, but we are wrong when we talk about achieving a "Christian social order." The Barthians are quite right, I think, in protesting against the easy identification of the Kingdom of God with every movement of social reform and social radicalism that has prevailed in American Christianity in particular and in liberal Protestantism in general. Those of us who dissociate ourselves from the easy optimism of modern liberalism and who believe that a just society is not going to be built by a little more education and a few more sermons on love have particular reason to reorient our thinking in this matter so that we will not come forward with a social ethic involving the use of force and coercion and political pressure of every kind and claim the authority of Jesus for it.

Our confusion is, of course, no worse than that of the conventional teachers of Christian ethics and theology who have a rather complacent attitude toward the present economic society and criticize us for violating the ethic of Jesus in our espousal of the class struggle, for instance. Our confusion is, in fact, not quite as bad as theirs. They have used every kind of exegetical device to prove that the teachings of Jesus are not incompatible with participation in nationalistic wars or, if they have been a little more clearheaded, they have found ethical justification for their actions by proving that the ethic of Jesus does not provide for the responsibilities of politics and economics, and therefore leaves them free to choose a political strategy that is most consonant with their conception of the moral good will which they believe Jesus to idealize. The critics of the former type have no ground to stand upon at all when they accuse radical Christians of violating the ethic of Jesus; for participation in a nonviolent strike action, to choose an obvious example, is certainly not more incompatible with the ethic of Jesus than participation in an international conflict. Critics of the latter type have cut the ground for criticism from under their own feet. They admit that any responsible relationship to political and economic affairs involves compromise, and they ought to have a difficult time proving that the assertion of national interest or the protection of national rights is more compatible with the perfectionist ideal of pure disinterestedness than the assertion of class interests and the protection of class rights.

But the confusion of our critics does not absolve us of the necessity of clear thought for ourselves. The struggle for social justice in the present economic order involves the assertion of rights, the rights of the disinherited, and the use of coercion. Both are incompatible with the pure love ethic found in the Gospels. How, then, do we justify the strategy of the "class struggle"? We simply cannot do so in purely Christian terms. There is in the absolute sense no such thing as "Christian socialism." We must justify ourselves by considerations of the social situation that we face and the human resources that are available for its solution. What we discover in the social situation is that human life in its group interests moves pretty much upon the basis of the economic interests of various groups. We realize that intelligence and spiritual and moral idealism may qualify economic interest, but they do not destroy it. Whatever may be possible for individuals, we see no possibility of a group voluntarily divesting itself of its special privileges in society. Nor do we see a possibility of pure disinterestedness and the spirit of forgiveness on the part of an underprivileged group shaming a dominant group into an attitude of social justice. Such a strategy might possibly work in intimate personal relationships but it does not work in the larger group relations. The Negro has been forgiving in his subordinate position in society for a long time, but he has not persuaded the white man to grant him larger privileges in society. Whatever place the industrial worker has won in society has been won by the assertion of his rights through his trade-union organizations. Even the most imaginative urban dwellers lack the imagination to envisage the needs of the farmer. The farmer has been forced to exert political pressure for the attainment of even such minimum justice as he is granted in the present economic organization of our country. No one who looks realistically at the social scene can fail to discover that economic, racial, and national groups stand on a moral level considerably lower than that of the most sensitive individuals. They are not easily persuaded to a voluntary sacrifice of privileges, and an attitude of pure nonresistance on the part of those who suffer from their exactions does not produce the spirit of repentance among them. Intelligence, which may create a spirit of justice among individuals by persuading them to grant to their fellows what they claim for themselves, is generally not acute enough to function in similar fashion in group relations. More frequently it does no more than to create rational sanctifications for special group interests. Only rarely does intellectual force rise high enough to create a perspective from which group prejudices and biases have been banished. The relations between groups are so indirect that the consequences of our actions in the life of another group are not easily discerned, and we therefore continue in unethical conduct without the restraint upon our conscience that intimate personal relations create. Very few white men have any conception of the havoc that is wrought in the souls and upon the bodies of Negroes by prevailing race prejudices; and there is not one American in a million who knows what our reparations policy means for starving workers of Germany. This unhappy group seems under the necessity of asserting its interests, not only against the rest of the world, but against the more comfortable middle classes of their own country.

The social struggle involves a violation of a pure ethic of love, not only in the assertion of rights, but in the inevitable use of coercion. Here again one need but state the obvious; but the obvious is usually not recognized by academic moralists. No society can exist without the use of coercion, though every intelligent society will try to reduce coercion to a minimum and rely upon the factor of mutual consent to give stability to its institutions. Yet it can never trust all of its citizens to accept necessary social arrangements voluntarily. It will use police force against recalcitrant and antisocial minorities, and it will use the threat of political force against a complacent and indifferent group of citizens which could never be relied upon to initiate adequate social policies upon its own accord. No government can wait upon voluntary action on the part of the privileged members of a community for an adequate inheritance or income tax. It will use political force created by the votes of the disinherited and less privileged to initiate and enforce taxation policies, designed to equalize privileges. Privileged groups may accept such legislation without violent revolt, but they will probably argue against its justice until the day of their death. An intelligent society will constantly strive toward the goal of a more equal justice by initiating a more rigorous policy just as soon as a previous and more tentative one has been accepted and absorbed into the social standards of the community. If this is not done by gradual process, with the unrealized goal of essential equality beckoning each generation to surpass the approximations of justice achieved in the past, the inequalities of the social order, always increasing through natural process, are bound to grow until an outraged sense of justice (probably spurred by actual physical want on the part of the least privileged members of a community) will produce a violent revolt. In such nations as Germany, for instance, it is really an open question whether any political measures can achieve the desired end of social justice quickly enough to prevent violent revolution.

The necessity of this kind of coercion, based upon the assertion of interest on the part of the less privileged, is such a clear lesson of history that one hesitates to belabor the point and would refrain from doing so were it not for the fact that half of the academic treatises on social ethics and Christian ethics were written as if no such necessity existed. In this respect secular moralists are frequently as naïve as religious ones. In the one case it is expected that a change in educational technique will eliminate the drive of self-interest which determines economic life and in the other case there is a naïve confidence in the possibility of changing human nature by religious conversion or religious inspiration. It is the thesis of the radical wing of Christian social theorists, whether in England, Germany, or America, that nothing accomplished by either education or religious suasion will be able to abolish the social struggle. We believe that such hopes are corrupted by the sentimentalities of the comfortable classes and are caused by their lack of understanding of the realities of an industrial civilization. In what sense, then, may we call ourselves Christian, or how do we hope to insinuate Christian and ethical values into the social struggle? The simplest answer is that we believe that the highest ethical and spiritual insight may mitigate the social struggle on the one hand and may transcend it on the other.

We believe that it makes some difference whether a privileged group makes a stubborn and uncompromising defense of its special privileges or whether it has some degree of social imagination and tries to view its privileges in the light of the total situation of a community. Education ought to create some of that social imagination, and in so far as it does, it will mitigate the class struggle or the social struggle between races. The religious contribution to the same end may consist of various elements. Real religion produces the spirit of humility and repentance. It destroys moral conceit. Moral conceit is precisely what makes privileged groups so stubborn in the defense of their privileges. The human animal is just moral enough to be unable to act immorally with vigor if he cannot find a moral justification for his actions. If the Christian church used the ethical ideal of Jesus, the ideal of pure disinterestedness, more rigorously, and if the modern pulpit made a more astute analysis of human motives in the light of this ideal, many of the rationalizations that now support the antisocial policies and attitudes of privileged and powerful people would be destroyed. At least they might be qualified. One of the most unfortunate facts about our contemporary moral situation is that the church has ceased to convict men of selfishness at the precise moment in history when human greed is more obvious and more dangerous than at any previous time. Nowhere has the liberal church played more false to its generation than in its optimistic and romantic interpretation of human nature, just when an industrial civilization revealed the drive of self-interest in all its antisocial power. The part of the Christian church that has tried to convict the generation of sin knows too little about the problems of modern life to convict men of their significant sins. Thus religion has on the whole produced moral complacency rather than the spirit of repentance. The number of men who are sufficiently sensitized by religion actually to renounce their privileges must always remain small. But it ought not to be impossible for the church to create enough contrition and consciousness of human selfishness to prompt men to a more willing acceptance of and less stubborn resistance against social policies that aim at the restriction of power and privilege. If we dealt realistically with the facts of human nature, we might be able to create an attitude of complacency toward increasing social restraint, based upon the realization that few, if any, of us are wise enough to restrain our expansive desires voluntarily in a degree sufficient for the needs of our highly interdependent society. If there were a better understanding of human nature in the church today, an understanding that we could acquire by the study of psychology and economics but which we might appropriate just as easily from the insights of great religion, there would be fewer Christian captains of industry who lived under the illusion that they were good enough and wise enough to hold irresponsible power and exercise it for the good of the community. They would know that the very possession of irresponsible power tempts to its selfish use and that the benevolent pretensions of despotism rest either on unconscious self-deception or conscious hypocrisy.

True religion could mitigate the cruelties of the social struggle by its creation of the spirit of love as well as the spirit of repentance. The love ideal which Jesus incarnates may be too pure to be realized in life, but it offers us nevertheless an ideal toward which the religious spirit may strive. All rational idealism creates a conflict between the mind and the impulses, as in Stoicism and Kantian morality. The mind conceives ideals of justice which it tries to force upon recalcitrant selfish impulses. Real religion transmutes the social impulses until they transcend the limits set them by nature (family, race, group, etc.) and include the whole human community. Real religious imagination is able, furthermore, to create an attitude of trust and faith toward human beings, in which the potentialities rather than the immediate realities are emphasized. Through such imagination the needs of the social foe are appreciated, his inadequacies are understood in the light of his situation, and his possibilities for higher and more moral action are recognized. Only the religious spirit which surveys the human scene from the perspective of its presuppositions about the character of life is thus able to disregard present facts and appeal to ultimate possibilities. The fact that in Jesus the spirit of love flowed out in emulation of God's love, without regard to social consequences, cannot blind the eye to the social consequences of a religiously inspired love. If modern religion were really producing it, it would mitigate the evils of the social struggle. It would, to emphasize the obvious once more, not abolish the social struggle, because it would not approximate perfection in sufficiently numerous instances. The fight for justice in society will always be a fight. But wherever the spirit of justice grows imaginative and is transmuted into love, a love in which the interests of the other are espoused, the struggle is transcended by just that much.

It is the fashion among many Christian idealists to criticize the political movements of the disinherited for the spirit of hatred which they generate. The church, so it is said, would espouse their cause much more readily if the spirit of love were manifest in it. What the church fails to realize is that its responsibility is chiefly for the moral and spiritual attitudes of the privileged rather than the disinherited; for it is the former who makes professions of Christian idealism. If the church wants to insinuate the spirit of love into the social struggle, it ought to begin with the privileged groups, not only because it has greater responsibility for them, but because those who hold entrenched positions in the social struggle are obviously under the greater obligation to be imaginative in gauging the needs and discounting the limitations of those who suffer from social injustice. The perfectionist ethic of Jesus allows for no such distinctions; for it demands that love be poured forth whether or not we suffer from injustice. But no one can avow such an ethic from the vantage point of privilege and security. If the portion of society that benefits from social inequality and which is endangered by a rising tide of social discontent attempts to counsel love, forgiveness, and patience to the discontented, it will convict itself of hypocrisy, except it is able first of all to reveal fruits of the Spirit, which it commends, in its own life. Even if it were to reveal some fruits, but too meager to justify a more trusting and a less vehement attitude on the part of the underprivileged, its moral ideals would be regarded as pretensions. The race situation in the South offers interesting commentary upon this point. The fine work which the interracial commission has done has failed to preserve the respect of the more eager young Negroes for it, because they feel that through its efforts of conciliation white men have yielded only inconsequential social advantages in order that they may hold to their major ones. The most perfect love may not ask for social justification, but any love within the capacity of ordinary men and groups does. The disinherited will have their spirits corrupted by hatred and their policies tinctured with violence except they are able to detect some genuinely ethical elements in the policies of the privileged and entrenched social groups. If the spirit of love is to qualify and mitigate the social struggle, the groups that profess to believe in the efficacy of love and who, at the same time, have favored positions in society are clearly under obligation to introduce this Christian element in society. They may be quite sure that any solid ethical achievement among them would result in practically immediate ethical reactions of trust and faith among those who are trying to advance socially. Only the faith and trust of the advancing group will not and ought not ever rise to the point where purely voluntary action toward equality is expected. A degree of ethical insight on the part of the whole community will not abolish the necessity of social conflict, but it may prevent violence and reduce the hatred that must inevitably arise when the disinherited are faced, not only with the stubborn greed of the powerful and comfortable social classes, but also with the protection of their privileges by the covert use of force and their hypocritical pretension of virtue.

A Christian ethical idealism that espouses the cause of proletarian groups and identifies itself with their political movements is, in short, as pure as any Christian movement that assumes a responsible attitude toward society. The compromises that it makes with the pure Christian ethic are inevitable compromises which everyone must make who deals with the social problem from the perspective of society rather than that of the individual. It might claim, in addition, to appropriate the Christian ethical ideal more closely than a type of thought that fears contamination in the social struggle. For the social struggle is a reality in society and we will be contaminated by it except we get out of society. The ascetic may possibly have a vantage point from which to criticize the ethical purity of Christian socialism or Christian radicalism. Those who stay in society have not. If our critics were less confused about the moral and social realities of modern society, they would know that neutrality in a social struggle between entrenched and advancing social classes really means alliance with the entrenched position. In the social struggle we are either on the side of privilege or need. No ethical perfectionism can save us from that choice.

THE GRACE OF DOING NOTHING[1]

H. Richard Niebuhr

In the following selection Richard Niebuhr defends an ethic of disinterestedness—contending that the true Christian will, qua Christian, be inactive in the presence of social injustice. His brother responds in the article that follows. That the disagreement was provoked by events which seem in these troubled times to have occurred a thousand years ago—Japan's pre-war aggressions in China—makes no difference. Today, Red China or Russia could be substituted for the Japan of 1932. The terms in which the issue is explored are timeless. At the time this debate took place both brothers were professors of Christian ethics, H. Richard at Yale and Reinhold at Union Theological Seminary. Richard Niebuhr has written The Social Source of Denomination *(1929),* The Kingdom of God in America *(1937), and* The Purpose of the Church and Its Ministry *(1956).*

It may be that the greatest moral problems of the individual or of a society arise when there is nothing to be done. When we have begun a certain line of action or engaged in a conflict we cannot pause too long to decide which of various possible courses we ought to choose for the sake of the worthier result. Time rushes on and we must choose as best we can, entrusting the issue to the future. It is when we stand aside from the conflict, before we know what our relations to it really are, when we seem to be condemned to doing nothing, that our moral problems become greatest. How shall we do nothing?

[1]*The Christian Century,* March 23, 1932, pp. 378–380. Copyright 1932 Christian Century Foundation. Reprinted by permission from *The Christian Century.*

The issue is brought home to us by the fighting in the East. We are chafing at the bit, we are eager to do something constructive; but there is nothing constructive, it seems, that we can do. We pass resolutions, aware that we are doing nothing; we summon up righteous indignation and still do nothing; we write letters to congressmen and secretaries, asking others to act while we do nothing. Yet is it really true that we are doing nothing? There are, after all, various ways of being inactive, and some kinds of inactivity, if not all, may be highly productive. It is not really possible to stand aside, to sit by the fire in this world of moving times; even Peter was doing something in the courtyard of the high-priest's house—if it was only something he was doing to himself. When we do nothing we are also affecting the course of history. The problem we face is often that of choice between various kinds of inactivity rather than of choice between action and inaction.

Our inactivity may be that of the pessimist who watches a world go to pieces. It is a meaningful inactivity for himself and for the world. His world, at all events, will go to pieces the more rapidly because of that inactivity. Or it may be the inactivity of the conservative believer in things as they are. He does nothing in the international crisis because he believes that the way of Japan is the way of all nations, that self-interest is the first and only law of life, and that out of the clash of national, as out of that of individual, self-interests the .greater good will result. His inactivity is one of watchful waiting for the opportunity when, in precisely similar manner, though with less loss of life and fortune, if possible, he may rush to the protection of his own interests or promote them by taking advantage of the situation created by the strife of his competitors. This way of doing nothing is not unproductive. It encourages the self-asserters and it fills them with fear of the moment when the new competition will begin. It may be that they have been driven into their present conflict by the knowledge or suspicion that the watchful waiter is looking for his opportunity, perhaps unconsciously, and that they must be prepared for him.

The inactivity of frustration and moral indignation is of another order. It is the way of those who have renounced all violent methods of settling conflicts and have no other means at hand by which to deal with the situation. It is an angry inactivity like that of a man who is watching a neighborhood fight and is waiting for the police to arrive—for police who never come. He has renounced for himself the method of forcible interference, which would only increase the flow of blood and the hatred, but he knows of nothing else that he can do. He is forced to remain content on the sidelines, but with mounting anger he regards the bully who is beating the neighbor, and his wrath issues in words of exasperation and condemnation. Having tied his own hands he fights with his tongue and believes that he is not fighting because he inflicts only mental wounds. The bully is for him an outlaw, a person not to be trusted, unfair, selfish, one who cannot be redeemed save by restraint. The righteous indignation mounts and mounts, and must issue at last—as the police fail to arrive—either in his own forcible entry into the conflict, despite his scruples, or in apoplexy.

The diatribes against Japan which are appearing in the secular and religious press today have a distressing similarity to the righteously indignant utterances which preceded our conflicts with Spain and with Germany. China is Cuba and Belgium over again; it is the Negro race beaten by Simon Legree. And the pacifists who have no other program than that of abstention from the unrighteousness of war are likely to be placed in the same quandary in which their fellows were placed in 1860, 1898 and 1915, and —unless human attitudes have been regenerated in the interim—they are likely to share the same fate, which was not usually incarceration. Here is a situation which they did not foresee when they made their vow; may it not be necessary to have one more war to end all war? Righteous indignation not allowed to issue in action is a dangerous thing—as dangerous as any great emotion nurtured and repressed at the same time. It is the source of sudden explosions or the ground of long, bitter and ugly hatreds.

If this way of doing nothing must be rejected the Communists' way offers more hope. Theirs is the inactivity of those who see that there is indeed nothing constructive to be done in the present situation, but that, rightly understood, this situation is after all preliminary to a radical change which will eliminate the conditions of which the conflict is a product. It is the inactivity of a cynicism which expects no good from the present, evil world of capitalism, but also the inactivity of a boundless faith in the future. The Communists know that war and revolution are closely akin, that war breeds discontent and misery, and that out of misery and discontent new worlds may be born. This is an opportunity, then, not for direct entrance into the conflict, not for the watchful waiting of those who seek their self-interest, but for the slow laborious process of building up within the fighting groups those cells of communism which will be ready to inherit the new world and be able to build a classless international commonwealth on the ruins of capitalism and nationalism. Here is inactivity with a long vision, a steadfast hope and a realistic program of non-interfering action.

But there is yet another way of doing nothing. It appears to be highly impracticable because it rests on the well-nigh obsolete faith that there is a God—a real God. Those who follow this way share with communism the belief that the fact that men can do nothing constructive is no indication of the fact that nothing constructive is being done. Like the Communists they are assured that the actual processes of history will inevitably and really bring a different kind of world with lasting peace. They do not rely on human aspirations after ideals to accomplish this end, but on forces which often seem very impersonal—as impersonal as those which eliminated slavery in spite of abolitionists. The forces may be as impersonal and as actual as machine production, rapid transportation, the physical mixtures of races, etc., but as parts of the real world they are as much a part of the total divine process as are human thoughts and prayers.

From this point of view, naïvely affirming the meaningfulness of reality, the history of the world is the judgment of the world and also its redemption, and a conflict like the present one is—again as in communism—only the prelude both to greater judgment and to a new era. The world being what it is, these results are brought forth when the seeds of national or individual self-interest are planted; the actual structure of things is such that our wishes for a different result do not in the least affect the outcome. As a man soweth so shall he reap. This God of things as they are is inevitable and quite merciless. His mercy lies beyond, not this side of, judgment. This inactive Christianity shares with communism also the belief in the inevitably good outcome of the mundane process and the realistic insight that that good cannot be achieved by the slow accretion of better habits alone but more in consequence of a revolutionary change which will involve considerable destruction. While it does nothing it knows that something is being done, something which is divine both in its threat and in its promise.

This inactivity is like that of the early Christians whose millenarian mythology it replaces with the contemporary mythology of social forces. (Mythology is after all not fiction but a deep philosophy.) Like early Christianity and like communism today radical Christianity knows that nothing constructive can be done by interference, but that something very constructive can be done in preparation for the future. It also can build cells of those within each nation who, divorcing themselves from the program of nationalism and of capitalism, unite in a higher loyalty which transcends national and class lines of division and prepare for the future. There is no such Christian international today because radical Christianity has not arrived as yet at a program and a philosophy of history, but such little cells are forming. The First Christian international of Rome has had its day; the Second Christian international of Stockholm is likely to go the way of the Second Socialist international. There is need and opportunity for a Third Christian international.

While the similarities of a radically Christian program with the Communist program are striking, there are also great dissimilarities. There is a new element in the inactivity of radical Christianity which is lacking in communism. The Christian reflects upon the fact that his inability to do anything constructive in the crisis is the inability of one whose own faults are so apparent and so similar to those of the offender that any action on his part is not only likely to be misinterpreted but is also likely—in the nature of the case—to be really less than disinterested. He is like a father who, feeling a righteous indignation against a misbehaving child, remembers that that misbehavior is his fault as much as the child's and that indignation is the least helpful, the most dangerous of attitudes to take; it will solve nothing, though it may repress.

So the American Christian realizes that Japan is following the example of his own country and that it has little real ground for believing America to be a disinterested nation. He may see that his country, for which he bears his own responsibility as a citizen, is really not disinterested and that its righteous indignation is not wholly righteous. An inactivity then is demanded which will be profoundly active in rigid self-analysis. Such analysis is likely to reveal that there is an approach to the situation, indirect but far more effective than direct interference, for it is able to create the conditions under which a real reconstruction of habits is possible. It is the opposite approach from that of the irate father who believes that every false reaction on the part of his child may be cured by a verbal, physical or economic spanking.

This way of doing nothing the old Christians called repentance, but the word has become so reminiscent of emotional debauches in the feeling of guilt that it may be better to abandon it for a while. What is suggested is that the only effective approach to the problem of China and Japan lies in the sphere of an American self-analysis which is likely to result in some surprising discoveries as to the amount of renunciation of self-interest necessary on the part of this country and of individual Christians before anything effective can be done in the East.

The inactivity of radical Christianity is not the inactivity of those who call evil good; it is the inaction of those who do not judge their neighbors because they cannot fool themselves into a sense of superior righteousness. It is not the inactivity of a resigned patience, but of a patience that is full of hope and is based on faith. It is not the inactivity of the noncombatant, for it knows that there are no noncombatants, that everyone is involved, that China is being crucified (though the term is very inaccurate) by our sins and those of the whole world. It is not the inactivity of the merciless, for works of mercy must be performed though they are only palliatives to ease present pain while the process of healing depends on deeper, more actual and urgent forces.

But if there is no God, or if God is up in heaven and not in time itself, it is a very foolish inactivity.

MUST WE DO NOTHING?[1]

Reinhold Niebuhr

Having expressed his misgivings about the gospel of social commitment espoused by liberal Christianity,[2] Reinhold Niebuhr here takes issue with his brother's opposite counsel of disinterestedness. His comments are followed by Richard's rejoinder.

There is much in my brother's article, "The Grace of Doing Nothing," with which I agree. Except for the invitation of the editors of The Christian Century I would have preferred to defer voicing any disagreement with some of his final conclusions to some future occasion; for a casual article on a specific problem created by the contemporary international situation hardly does justice to his general position. I believe the problem upon which he is working—the problem of dissociating a rigorous gospel ethic of disinterestedness and love from the sentimental dilutions of that ethic which are current in liberal Christianity—is a tremendously important one. I owe so much to the penetrating thought which he has been giving this subject that I may be able to do some justice to his general position even though I do not share his conviction that a pure love ethic can ever be made the basis of a civilization.

He could not have done better than to choose the Sino-Japanese conflict, and the reactions of the world to it, in order to prove the difficulty, if not the futility, of dealing redemptively with a sinful nation or individual if we cannot exorcise the same sin from our own hearts. It is true that pacifists are in danger of stirring up hatred against Japan in their effort to stem the tide of Japanese imperialism. It is true that the very impotence of an individual who deals with a social situation which goes beyond his own powers tempts him to hide his sense of futility behind a display of violent emotion. It is true that we have helped to create the Japan which expresses itself in terms of materialistic imperialism. The insult we offered her in our immigration laws was a sin of spiritual aggression. The white world has not only taught her the ways of imperialism, but has pre-empted enough of the yellow man's side of the world to justify Japan's imperialism as a vent for pent-up national energies.

---

[1]*The Christian Century,* March 30, 1932, pp. 415–417. Copyright 1932 Christian Century Foundation. Reprinted by permission from *The Christian Century.*
[2]Cf. above, p. 312 ff.

It is also true that American concern over Japanese aggression is not wholly disinterested. It is national interest which inspires us to desire stronger action against Japan than France and England are willing to take. It is true, in other words, that every social sin is, at least partially, the fruit and consequence of the sins of those who judge and condemn it, and that the effort to eliminate it involves the critics and judges in new social sin, the assertion of self-interest and the expression of moral conceit and hypocrisy. If anyone would raise the objection to such an analysis that it finds every social action falling short only because it measures the action against an impossible ideal of disinterestedness, my brother could answer that while the ideal may seem to be impossible the actual social situation proves it to be necessary. It is literally true that every recalcitrant nation, like every antisocial individual, is created by the society which condemns it, and that redemptive efforts which betray strong ulterior motives are always bound to be less than fully redemptive.

My brother draws the conclusion from this logic that it is better not to act at all than to act from motives which are less than pure, and with the use of methods which are less than critical (coercion). He believes in taking literally the words of Jesus, "Let him who is without sin cast the first stone." He believes, of course, that this kind of inaction would not really be inaction; it would be, rather, the action of repentance. It would give every one involved in social sin the chance to recognize how much he is involved in it and how necessary it is to restrain his own greed, pride, hatred and lust for power before the social sin is eliminated.

This is an important emphasis particularly for modern Christianity with its lack of appreciation of the tragic character of life and with its easy assumption that the world will be saved by a little more adequate educational technique. Hypocrisy is an inevitable by-product of moral aspiration, and it is the business of true religion to destroy man's moral conceit, a task which modern religion has not been performing in any large degree. Its sentimentalities have tended to increase rather than to diminish moral conceit. A truly religious man ought to distinguish himself from the moral man by recognizing the fact that he is not moral, that he remains a sinner to the end. The sense of sin is more central to religion than is any other attitude.

All this does not prove, however, that we ought to apply the words of Jesus, "Let him who is without sin cast the first stone," literally. If we do we will never be able to act. There will never be a wholly disinterested nation. Pure disinterestedness is an ideal which even individuals cannot fully achieve, and human groups are bound always to express themselves in lower ethical forms than individuals. It follows that no nation can ever be good enough to save another nation purely by the power of love. The relation of nations and of economic groups can never be brought into terms of pure love. Justice is probably the highest ideal toward which human groups can aspire. And justice, with its goal of adjustment of right to right, inevitably involves the assertion of right against right and interest against interest until some kind of harmony is achieved. If a measure of humility and of love does not enter this conflict of interest it will of course degenerate into violence. A national society will be able to develop a measure of the kind of imagination which knows how to appreciate the virtues of an opponent's position and the weakness in one's own. But the ethical and spiritual note of love and repentance can do no more than qualify the social struggle in history. It will never abolish it.

The hope of attaining an ethical goal for society by purely ethical means, that is, without coercion, and without the assertion of the interests of the underprivileged against the interests of the privileged, is an illusion which was spread chiefly among the comfortable classes of the past century. My brother does not make the mistake of assuming that this is possible in social terms. He is acutely aware of the fact that it is not possible to get a sufficient degree of pure disinterestedness and love among privileged classes and powerful nations to resolve the conflicts of history in that way. He understands the stubborn inertia which the ethical ideal meets in history. At this point his realistic interpretation of the facts of history comes in full conflict with his insistence upon a pure gospel ethic, upon a religiously inspired moral perfectionism, and he resolves the conflict by leaving the field of social theory entirely and resorting to eschatology. The Christian will try to achieve humility and disinterestedness not because enough Christians will be able to do so to change the course of history, but because this kind of spiritual attitude is a prayer to God for the coming of his kingdom.

I will not quarrel with this apocalyptic note, as such, though I suspect many Christian Century readers will. I believe that a proper eschatology is necessary to a vigorous ethic, and that the simple idea of progress is inimical to the highest ethic. The compound of pessimism and optimism which a vigorous ethical attitude requires can be expressed only in terms of religious eschatology. What makes my brother's eschatology impossible for me is that he identifies everything that is occurring in history (the drift toward disaster, another world war and possibly a revolution) with the counsels of God, and then suddenly, by a leap of faith, comes to the conclusion that the same God who uses brutalities and forces, against which man must maintain conscientious scruples, will finally establish an ideal society in which pure love will reign.

I have more than one difficulty with such a faith. I do not see how a revolution in which the disinterested express their anger and resentment, and assert their interests, can be an instrument of God, and yet at the same time an instrument which religious scruples forbid a man to use. I should think that it would be better to come to ethical terms with the forces of nature in history, and try to use ethically directed coercion in order that violence may be avoided. The hope that a kingdom of pure love will emerge out of the catastrophes of history is even less plausible than the Communist faith that an equalitarian society will eventually emerge from them. There is some warrant in history for the latter assumption, but very little for the former.

I find it impossible to envisage a society of pure love as long as man remains man. His natural limitations of reason and imagination will prevent him, even should he achieve a purely disinterested motive, from fully envisaging the needs of his fellow men or from determining his actions upon the basis of their interests. Inevitably these limitations of individuals will achieve cumulative effect in the life and actions of national, racial and economic groups. It is possible to envisage a more ethical society than we now have. It is possible to believe that such a society will be achieved partly by evolutionary process and partly by catastrophe in which an old order, which offers a too stubborn resistance to new forces, is finally destroyed.

It is plausible also to interpret both the evolutionary and the catastrophic elements in history in religious terms and to see the counsels of God in them. But it is hardly plausible to expect divine intervention to introduce something into history which is irrelevant to anything we find in history now. We may envisage a society in which human co-operation is possible with a minimum amount of coercion, but we cannot imagine one in which there is no coercion at all—unless, of course, human beings become quite different from what they now are. We may hope for a society in which self-interest is qualified by rigorous self-analysis and a stronger social impulse, but we cannot imagine a society totally without the assertion of self-interest and therefore without the conflict of opposing interests.

I realize quite well that my brother's position both in its ethical perfectionism and in its apocalyptic note is closer to the gospel than mine. In confessing that, I am forced to admit that I am unable to construct an adequate social ethic out of a pure love ethic. I cannot abandon the pure love ideal because anything which falls short of it is less than the ideal. But I cannot use it fully if I want to assume a responsible attitude toward the problems of society. Religious perfectionism drives either to asceticism or apocalypticism. In the one case the problem of society is given up entirely; in the other individual perfection is regarded as the force which will release the redemptive powers of God for society. I think the second alternative is better than the first, and that both have elements which must be retained for any adequate social ethic, lest it become lost in the relativities of expediency. But as long as the world of man remains a place where nature and God, the real and the ideal, meet, human progress will depend upon the judicious use of the forces of nature in the service of the ideal.

In practical, specific and contemporary terms, this means that we must try to dissuade Japan from her military venture, but must use coercion to frustrate her designs if necessary, must reduce coercion to a minimum and prevent it from issuing in violence, must engage in constant self-analysis in order to reduce the moral conceit of Japan's critics and judges to a minimum, and must try in every social situation to maximize the ethical forces and yet not sacrifice the possibility of achieving an ethical goal because we are afraid to use any but purely ethical means.

To say all this is really to confess that the history of mankind is a personal tragedy; for the highest ideals which the individual may project are ideals which he can never realize in social and collective terms. If there is a law in our members which wars against the law that is in our minds as individuals, this is even more true when we think of society. Individuals set the goal for society but society itself must achieve the goal, and society is and will always remain sub-human. The goal which a sensitive individual sets for society must therefore always be something which is a little outside and beyond history. Love may qualify the social struggle of history but it will never abolish it, and those who make the attempt to bring society under the dominion of perfect love will die on the cross. And those who behold the cross are quite right in seeing it as a revelation of the divine, of what man ought to be and cannot be, at least not so long as he is enmeshed in the processes of history.

Perhaps that is why it is inevitable that religious imagination should set goals beyond history. "Man's reach is beyond his grasp, or what's a heaven for." My brother does not like these goals above and beyond history. He wants religion and social idealism to deal with history. In that case he must not state his goal in absolute terms. There can be nothing absolute in history, no matter how frequently God may intervene in it. Man cannot live without a sense of the absolute, but neither can he achieve the absolute. He may resolve the tragic character of that fact by religious faith, by the experience of grace in which the unattainable is experienced in anticipatory terms, but he can never resolve in purely ethical terms the conflict between what is and what ought to be.

THE ONLY WAY INTO THE
KINGDOM OF GOD[1]

H. Richard Niebuhr

Editor The Christian Century
Sir: Since you have given me leave to fire one more shot in the fraternal
war between my brother and me over the question of pacifism, I shall attempt to place it as well as I can, not for the purpose of demolishing my
opponent's position—which our thirty years have shown me to be impossible—but for the sake of pointing as accurately as I can to the exact locus
of the issue between us. It does not lie in the question of activity or inactivity, to which my too journalistic approach to the problem directed attention; we are speaking after all of two kinds of activity. The fundamental
question seems to me to be whether "the history of mankind is a perennial
tragedy" which can derive meaning only from a goal which lies beyond
history, as my brother maintains, or whether the "eschatological" faith, to
which I seek to adhere, is justifiable. In that faith tragedy is only the prelude
to fulfilment, and a prelude which is necessary because of human nature;
the kingdom of God comes inevitably, though whether we shall see it or
not depends on our recognition of its presence and our acceptance of the
only kind of life which will enable us to enter it, the life of repentance and
forgiveness.

For my brother God is outside the historical processes, so much so
that he charges me with faith in a miracle-working deity which interferes
occasionally, sometimes brutally, sometimes redemptively, in this history.
But God, I believe, is always in history; he is the structure in things, the
course of all meaning, the "I am that I am," that which is that it is. He is
the rock against which we beat in vain, that which bruises and overwhelms
us when we seek to impose our wishes, contrary to his, upon him. That
structure of the universe, that creative will, can no more be said to interfere
brutally in history than the violated laws of my organism can be said to
interfere brutally with my life if they make me pay the cost of my violation.
That structure of the universe, that will of God, does bring war and depression upon us when we bring it upon ourselves, for we live in the kind of

---

[1]*The Christian Century*, April 6, 1932, p. 447. Copyright 1932 Christian Century
Foundation. Reprinted by permission from *The Christian Century*.

world which visits our iniquities upon us and our children, no matter how much we pray and desire that it be otherwise.

Self-interest acts destructively in this world; it calls forth counter-assertion; nationalism breeds nationalism; class assertion summons up counter-assertion on the part of exploited classes. The result is war, economic, military, verbal; and it is judgment. But this same structure in things which is our enemy is our redeemer; "it means intensely and it means good"—not the good which we desire, but the good which we would desire if we were good and really wise. History is not a perennial tragedy but a road to fulfil-ment and that fulfilment requires the tragic outcome of every self-assertion, for it is fulfilment which can only be designated as "love." It has created fel-lowship in atoms and organisms, at bitter cost to electrons and cells; and it is creating something better than human selfhood but at bitter cost to that selfhood. This is not a faith in progress, for evil grows as well as good, and every self-assertion must be eliminated somewhere and somehow—by inno-cence suffering for guilt, it seems.

If, however, history is no more than tragedy, if there is no fulfilment in it, then my brother is right. Then we must rest content with the clash of self-interested individuals, personal or social. But in that case I see no rea-son why we should qualify the clash of competition with a homeopathic dose of Christian "love."

The only harmony which can possibly result from the clash of interests is the harmony imposed by the rule of the strong or a parallelogram of social forces, whether we think of the interclass structure or the international world. To import any pacifism into this struggle is only to weaken the weaker self-asserters (India, China or the proletariat) or to provide the strong with a façade of "service" behind which they can operate with a salved conscience. (Pacifism, on the other hand, as a method of self-asser-tion is not pacifism at all but a different kind of war.)

The method which my brother recommends, that of qualifying the social struggle by means of some Christian love, seems to me to be only the old method of making Christian love an ambulance driver in the wars of interested and clashing parties. If it is more than that, it is a weakening of the forces whose success we think necessary for a juster social order. For me the question is one of "either-or"; either the Christian method, which is not the method of love but of repentance and forgiveness, or the method of self-assertion; either nationalism or Christianity, either capitalism-com-munism or Christianity. The attempt to qualify the one method by the other is hopeless compromise.

I think that to apply the terms "Christian perfectionism" or "Christian ideal" to my approach is rather misleading. I rather think that Dewey is quite right in his war on ideals; they always seem irrelevant to our situation and betray us into a dualistic morality. The society of love is an impossible human ideal, as the fellowship of the organism is an impossible ideal for the cell. It is not an ideal toward which we can strive, but an "emergent," a potentiality in our situation which remains unrealized so long as we try to impose our pattern, our wishes upon the divine creative process.

Man's task is not that of building utopias, but that of eliminating weeds and tilling the soil so that the kingdom of God can grow. His method is not one of striving for perfection or of acting perfectly, but of clearing the road by repentance and forgiveness. That this approach is valid for societies as well as for individuals and that the opposite approach will always involve us in the same one ceaseless cycle of assertion and counter-assertion is what I am concerned to emphasize.

PART FIVE

DISCRIMINATION
AND THE NEGRO

December 5, 1946, is a significant date in the recent history of the struggle for civil rights. On that day President Truman, by executive order, created a Committee on Civil Rights. The now famous report of the Committee, entitled "To Secure These Rights," was issued in 1947.

Since the recommendations of the Committee have often been denounced as "Communist inspired" and even the "neutral" *Congressional Digest* refers to the civil-rights program as "weighted down by the unqualified and violent support of extreme left-wing, radical, and Communist organizations," it may be well to list some of its members. The chairman of the Committee was Charles E. Wilson, then head of General Electric; and it included, among others, Catholic Bishop Frank J. Haas of Michigan; Francis P. Matthews, who was an Omaha, Nebraska, lawyer and utility director, later appointed Secretary of the Navy; Episcopalian Bishop Henry Knox Sherrall of Boston; John S. Dickey, president of Dartmouth College; Charles Luckman, then president of Lever Brothers; Frank P. Graham, then president of the University of North Carolina and later a U.S. Senator; and James B. Carey, who spearheaded the anti-Communist drive in the C.I.O.

The Committee's report provided the basis for President Truman's "civil-rights" message to Congress in February 1948, in which he urged legislation creating a National Fair Employment Practices Commission and passage of federal laws prohibiting lynching, racial segregation, and the poll tax. Civil-rights legislation was one of the major issues in the presidential election that followed. Both major parties included a "civil-rights" plank in their platform. Despite major defections in the South (not to mention Wallace's abortive third-party movement in the North) Truman scored the now historical upset victory over Dewey. It appeared that a new era might be opening for the victims of race prejudice.

However, we are still far from solving what Myrdal called the "American Dilemma." We have made progress, but racial prejudice remains now, as before, an affront to the American conscience. Progress always seems more rapid to those who act to correct an abuse than to those who suffer from it. Members of the majority group may be impressed by how far we have traveled since the Supreme Court's desegregation decision. To the Negro the rate of progress must seem painfully slow.

More than a decade separates the statements by Milton R. Konvitz and Donald Richberg cited below, a period marked by the Supreme

Court's unanimous decision outlawing segregation in the schools, the Montgomery bus boycott, the sending of federal troops to Little Rock, the slow acquiescence of the border states in integration, the stubborn resistance of the Deep South—climaxed as this is written by armed intervention in Mississippi, and, above all, the emergence of a new generation of Negroes in the South committed to a policy of nonviolent resistance. Perhaps fewer responsible Southerners would voice Mr. Richberg's views today.

Even so, the racial ghettos of our cities, Northern as well as Southern, although in part economic in origin, testify eloquently to the presence of patterns of racial segregation that have a long chain of consequences including *de facto* racial segregation in the public schools. Differences of opinion as to how to achieve integration of the schools, as reflected in the last two selections, illustrate some of the painful ambivalences in which the North is involved.

FREEDOM OF ASSOCIATION[1]

Donald R. Richberg

(1881–1960)

Donald R. Richberg, a constitutional lawyer, was co-author of the Railway Labor Act of 1926, general counsel and later chairman of the National Recovery Administration (1933–35), Executive Director of the National Emergency Council (1934–35), and Special Assistant to the Attorney General of the United States.

People are pleased to be told they have a "right" to do what they want to do. They applaud the politician who assures them that they have a "right" to enjoy the things they desire.

It is much more comforting to be assured that you have a right to obtain a good job from some one, than to be informed that you have a duty to do a good job for some one. But, let's not forget, that no right can be enforced for one person without compelling another to fulfill a duty. In the language of the courts: "When a right is invaded a duty is violated." "There is no right where there is no remedy."

---

[1]*Washington Star,* January 4, 1949. Reprinted by permission from the Washington, D.C., *Star.*

Even the basic right of my individual liberty cannot be enforced except by imposing restraints on your individual liberty. The claim of a right is worthless against more and more domestic conflicts, less and less internal peace.

Long ago a great philosopher pointed out that "the right of all to all things" means "the war of all against all." The surest way to destroy the fundamental freedoms of American life would be to build up a vast legal structure of social, economic and political rights, all of them creating corresponding duties, and all of them enforced by governmental restraints upon individual freedom.

Communists and their dupes complain that a "hysteria" of anti-communism is causing the suppression of civil rights in the United States. So now they are diligently fomenting a "counter-hysteria" for expanding civil rights until the basic rights of life, liberty and property will be completely lost in a maze of petty rights and duties and regulations which only a communistic dictatorship could possibly enforce.

The horrible and outstanding example of this civil rights hysteria is the recent report of the President's Committee on Civil Rights, which is probably the most mischievous document that has been published since Marx and Engels produced the Communist Manifesto 100 years ago.

In the name of "liberty" this report proposes to compel American men, women and children to live and work in a social and economic system created and regulated by Government, a system in which their most profound emotions and ambitions are to be suppressed at the will of political monitors.

Here are the two most fundamental recommendations of the committee, in its own language:

"The elimination of segregation, based on race, color, creed or national origin, from American life."

"The enactment of a Federal Fair Employment Practices Act, prohibiting all forms of discrimination in private employment, based on race, color, creed or national origin."

Please note that segregation is to be eliminated—not only from Government operations, but everywhere "from American life." That is precisely the aim of the committee, which announces, with the voice of omnipotent omniscience: "We can tolerate no restrictions upon the individual which depend upon irrelevant factors such as his race, his color, his religion or the social position to which he was born."

Hundreds of millions of Protestants, Catholics, Jews, Mohammedans, Buddhists and Hindus have believed and taught for centuries the One Way of Living, or the One Road to Salvation, was divinely ordained and revealed in the articles of their particular faith. Any one's religion is necessarily a restriction on him and, if he is to be free in the exercise of his religion (a freedom expressly guaranteed in our Constitution), then he must be free to restrict his associations with others in accordance with his feelings and his convictions as to what is necessary and desirable. Yet the committee would have a man forced by law into associations which may be repulsive to him—not because of any narrow prejudice but because of his profound religious convictions.

Race and color may seem "irrelevant" to the committee. Yet differences of race and color have divided mankind for centuries. They may fade in the coming centuries. But they cannot be wiped out by a state or federal law; and every such foolish effort only intensifies prejudice and intolerance, creates disrespect for law, and is itself an intolerant violation of individual liberty.

Curiously enough the committee observed that an essential part of our freedom is that we "are free to be different." Evidently the committee is willing to have us differ in our taste for cigarettes, but not in our taste for companions. But, in another breath, the committee says: "In a democracy, each individual must have freedom to choose his friends and to control the pattern of his personal and family life." Nevertheless in order to eliminate "segregation" and to prevent "discrimination," the committee insists that this "free" American shall be compelled to spend his working life with undesirable associates, and to send his children to schools, to eat in restaurants, to live in hotels and enjoy all public amusements, in the company of those whose company he would not voluntarily choose.

The logic of the report is very difficult to follow. But, as the King said in Alice in Wonderland, "If there's no meaning in it that saves a world of trouble, you know, as we needn't try to find any."

Let us assume, however, that every like or dislike based on race, color or religion is unreasonable and unfair, and that such prejudices ought to be eliminated from human thinking. Nevertheless, is it proper or even possible for the Government of a free people to attempt to prevent men and women in business or social life from acting in accord with their prejudices? Now this is an entirely different question from asking whether the Government itself should deny equality of opportunity to some of its citizens.

Political equality, in the right to vote, in the administration of justice and in the rendering of public services, is due to all citizens. But unless Government is to destroy an economic system of competitive freedom and a social system of free association, it cannot undertake to level down the inequalities that result from differing abilities and opportunities, or to interfere with the voluntary selection of one's associates in work or play.

No one would dare to propose that an employer be given the right by law to compel a man to work for him. That would be "involuntary servitude"—slavery. Yet it is solemnly proposed that an employer shall be forbidden to refuse to employ a "qualified" man because of his race or religion.

This means, in practical effect, that if a Government regulator says that a man is "qualified" and rules that he has been denied employment because of race, color or religion, then he must be employed.

We know from experience under the Wagner Act that the employer would be presumed to be wrong. "Sentence first, verdict afterwards" is the conventional procedure. It seems to be forgotten that an employer works for his employes, just as they do for him. He is obligated by law to do a great many things for his employe. So the proposed law would force an employer into involuntary servitude to men who are under no obligation to work for him.

Superficially, it may seem to be a noble project for government to insure to all citizens an equality of opportunity to earn a livelihood and "to enjoy the benefits of society." But, no government can insure equality of opportunity to human beings who differ so widely in natural capacity and who, because of parental variances in ability and fortune, are so differently nurtured. It should also be pointed out that the benefits of a democratic, free society are not gathered by an omnipotent government into one treasure house for distribution to a dependent population. On the contrary, individuals in a host of big and little enterprises, work and produce things and seek to gain out of their cooperation with others the benefits and satisfactions which they desire and for which they are willing to work and sacrifice.

The concept of a society in which all are working for the common good and obtain only their proportionate share of the total product is the idealism of communism. Now that the world has had a good look at communism in actual operation, it has become quite clear that only a ruthless despotism can compel human beings to live and work in such a regimented society. Furthermore, it has been demonstrated up to date that the productivity of free men and women, working primarily for their own gain and reaping individual rewards, is far, far greater than the productivity of a people working ostensibly for equalitarian progress. Indeed the reward of individual merit has been reluctantly adopted in Russia as a drastic compromise of communistic theory which was necessary to prevent economic disaster.

It is most significant that the shrill slogan of all those fomenting the civil rights hysteria is "equality," although the great declared purpose of the Constitution was, not to achieve an impossible equality among unequal human beings, but to "secure the blessings of liberty" so that men could be free to be different and to realize their differing ambitions with their differing abilities. Every law which seeks to give a man a right to something which as a free man he cannot gain for himself, must impose burdens and restraints on the freedom of other men.

We may, reasonably, tax the fortunate to give aid to the less fortunate. We may, reasonably, prevent the abuse of freedom by those who heedlessly or ruthlessly injure others in the pursuit of selfish gain. We may, reasonably, enact laws to protect the right of every citizen to an equal participation in government and to equal treatment in all government operations. But, let us be watchful against every effort to create by law a "right" in one man to compel others to associate with him or to accept obligations to him in the domain of private enterprise or private life. Let us realize, not only that it is a part of our heritage that "a man's house is his castle," but also that freedom of association in work or play is the most precious of all our liberties.

STAND OUT OF MY SUNSHINE[1]

Milton R. Konvitz

Milton R. Konvitz, author of numerous works on civil rights and civil liberties, is Professor of Industrial and Labor Relations and Professor of Law at Cornell University. He has also been a member of the faculty of the Institute for Advanced Study and the Salzburg Seminar in American Studies. He directed the project that prepared the Code of Laws for the Republic of Liberia and has worked in close association with the National Association for the Advancement of Colored People and the American Civil Liberties Union.

In the six years immediately following *Brown* v. *Topeka* [U.S. Supreme Court desegregation decision], President Eisenhower, by his statements and by the things he left unsaid, reflected the views and sentiments of large sections of the American people who were inclined to question the efficacy of law as an instrument of social control and advancement in the field of race relations. Persons with this point of view tended to condemn both those who resorted to legal measures to vindicate and implement the desegregation decision and those who resorted to force, demagoguery, and knavery to defeat that decision. To Eisenhower, both parties were "extremists." He urged "moderation," waiting for an inner change, a change within the heart that would bear fruit in peaceful and constructive actions— on the eve of the centenary of the Civil War.

At a news conference in 1959 Eisenhower declared racial segregation

---

[1]*A Century of Civil Rights* (New York: Columbia University Press, 1961), pp. 255–272. Reprinted by permission.

morally wrong when it stands in the way of equality of opportunity in *economic* and *political* fields. By failing to mention, in the context, equality of opportunity in *education,* the statement implied that desegregation of the schools was not a moral imperative. He took this line in his solemn Christmas message of 1960, in which he said:

> Too often we discern an apathy towards violations of laws and standards of public and private integrity. When, through bitter prejudice and because of differences in skin pigmentation, individuals cannot enjoy equality of political and economic opportunity we see another of these imperfections, one that is equally plain to those living beyond our borders.

The omission of any reference to equality of educational opportunity could not but suggest that "he who is silent is understood to consent."

In the same Christmas message Eisenhower again made the point that law will be ineffective if it is more advanced than morals. On this occasion he stated the argument as follows:

> Though we boast that ours is a government of laws, completeness in this work [of living by our national ideals] cannot be achieved by laws alone, necessary though these be. Law, to be truly effective, must command the respect and earnest support of public opinion, both generally and locally. And each of us helps form public opinion.

. . . Eisenhower also expressed a theory of federal-state relations that was reminiscent of the views of Andrew Johnson. His statements suggested that perhaps the "Southern manifesto," issued in 1956 by fifteen United States Senators and eighty-one members of the House of Representatives, was not altogether unwarranted when it called the Supreme Court decision "a clear abuse of judicial power" and an encroachment upon states' rights, and when it blamed the Court for "destroying the amicable relations between the white and Negro races."

Let us examine some of these propositions. . . .

Opposition to *Brown* v. *Topeka* often takes the form of an assertion that racial adjustments must be left to voluntary conduct. They must flow from the heart or conviction. Any attempt to coerce adjustments in the direction of wider equality, it is said, is bound to fail.

Often, however, a distinction is made between equality in some relations and equality in other relations. President Eisenhower, as we have noted, believed that the law may be used to achieve for the Negro political and economic equality, but he refused to assert that the law may also be used to achieve desegregation in the schools—although if the question concerned "separate but equal" schools, it may be assumed that he would have said that the law may be used to compel the states to provide "equal" schools for the Negro race.

In his widely reprinted public letter to the President, Carleton Putnam made the following distinction:

> I would emphatically support improvement of education in Negro schools, if and where it is inferior. Equality of opportunity and equality before the law, when not strained to cover other situations, are acceptable ideals because they provide the chance to earn and to progress—and consequently should be enforced by legal fiat as far as is humanly possible. But equality of association, which desegregation in Southern schools involves, pre-supposes a status which in the South the average Negro has not earned. To force it upon the Southern white will, I think, meet with as much opposition as the prohibition amendment encountered in the wet states.

Most white Southerners would not even concede that equality of economic and political opportunity may be implemented by legal process. The Southern states have not adopted fair employment practices acts, and they have consistently opposed any bill in Congress that would outlaw racial discrimination in employment. The votes in Congress on the Civil Rights Acts of 1957 and 1960—acts that have a bearing on the right of suffrage—clearly showed Southern opposition to legal guarantees of political equality. When it comes to equality of educational opportunity, the record of cases in the courts before 1954 shows that the South had interpreted the "separate but equal" doctrine as permission to deny to the Negro the educational equality that the Constitution commands.

It is difficult to see by virtue of what principle it is possible to distinguish legal coercion in favor of economic and political equality from legal coercion in favor of educational equality, for their interdependence is obvious. In the absence of educational equality, it is hard to see how the Negro can hope to achieve equality in economic and political life. "Today," as Chief Justice Warren said for the unanimous Court,

> education is perhaps the most important function of state and local governments. Compulsory school attendance laws and the great expenditures for education both demonstrate our recognition of the importance of education to our democratic society. It is required in the performance of our most basic responsibilities, even service in the armed forces. It is the very foundation of good citizenship. Today it is a principal instrument in awakening the child to cultural values, in preparing him for later professional training, and in helping him to adjust normally to his environment. In these days, it is doubtful that any child may reasonably be expected to succeed in life if he is denied the opportunity to an education. Such an opportunity, where the state has undertaken to provide it, is a right which must be made available to all on equal terms.

Segregation, said the Court, denotes the inferiority of the Negro race, and a sense of inferiority affects the motivation to learn, retards the development of the Negro children, and deprives them of benefits they would receive in a nonsegregated school.

This deprivation must carry over to later economic and political opportunities. . . .

One may safely say, then, that at the time the Court announced its unanimous decision in *Brown* v. *Topeka,* outside of the states where school segregation was enforced by state laws, the official policies of the federal government, and of the governments of states in which some two-thirds of the American people lived, were against racial segregation or other forms of discrimination.

The letter of Carleton Putnam drew an analogy between opposition to school desegregation and opposition to the Prohibition Amendment, and Senator Fulbright, when he told the Senate that "legislation to regulate men's mores is doomed to failure," also referred to the American experience with prohibition as a precedent. But the analogy disregards crucial differences. At the time when the states were taking action on the Eighteenth Amendment, saloons were illegal in approximately 90 percent of the area of the nation and nearly two-thirds of the population were living in dry territory. When the amendment was ratified, thirty of the forty-eight states had prohibition statutes or constitutional amendments. By 1933, when prohibition was repealed, the overwhelming majority of the people had changed their position. The reasons for this reversal of public opinion are many but not relevant here, except that one point may be made: neither Congress nor the states provided adequate machinery for the enforcement of prohibition, and the local police forces "were either indifferent to the prohibition law or became the allies and protectors of the [racketeering liquor] industry."

With respect to *Brown* v. *Topeka,* on the other hand, the opposition is not national but regional. The American people in general have not found the experiment with equality unsatisfactory. There is no national movement for the repeal of the Fourteenth Amendment. Even in the Deep South— witness Little Rock and St. Louis—school desegregation would have a good chance of success if the demagogic politicians would give the citizens an opportunity to try it. But the rabble-rousing politicians would sooner see their states become a Congolese-like battleground, where law and order were subverted and neighbor lifted sword against neighbor, than let school desegregation be tried even at a snail's pace.

It is odd, to say the least, to hear Southerners argue in favor of "voluntarism." For the record is clear that the people in the South have not practiced voluntarism in race relations. They have always used the full power of the law to compel all persons, without regard to their own thoughts or feelings, to practice racial segregation. They have not left the matter of race relations to education, discussion, and similar methods that are used to reach the mind or heart of a person. They have relied on the power of the law to achieve their ends.

Let us consider an incident that may be taken as typifying the Southern record of action.

In 1855, through the efforts of John G. Fee, a Kentucky abolitionist minister who was disinherited by his slave-holding parents for his anti-slavery views, Berea College was founded as a coeducational, nonsectarian institution of practical and liberal education. Work was suspended in 1859 and resumed in 1865. Berea was located in Kentucky for the benefit mainly of the people of the mountains of the eastern part of the state, and was the only college in Kentucky that admitted both white and Negro students.

In 1904 Berea College had an enrollment of 174 Negro and 753 white students. In that year the Kentucky legislature enacted a statute that made it unlawful to maintain any college or school "where persons of the white and Negro races are both received as pupils for instruction." The penalty for maintaining such a college or school was a fine of $1,000, and an additional fine of $500 for each day the institution was operated after conviction. Any white or Negro student attending such school was subject to a fine of $50 for each day he attended. The law provided that a college could operate a branch for the other race "in a different locality, not less than twenty-five miles distant."

The officers and trustees of Berea College—the only institution affected by the law—protested, but to no avail. When the college opened for the academic year 1904–1905, the Negroes were not admitted but placed by the administration in Negro colleges. . . .

The racism of the South left little to the free will of the citizens. Segregation was required by law at circuses and tent shows; at theaters and public halls; in parks, playgrounds, and at beaches; at race tracks; in billiard and pool rooms. Members of the two races were prohibited from forming fraternal benefit associations together. A Negro minister could not perform the marriage ceremony for a white couple. There were scores of laws that made it *impossible* for persons to use their own judgment as to whether to associate or not associate with members of the other race.

But all this is conveniently forgotten when a court issues a desegregation decree or when Congress considers a civil rights law, for then the cry is heard that Americans are losing their liberty, that the government is invading the private lives of its citizens. Were the Black Codes and the Jim Crow laws attempts at implementing the Declaration of Independence? . . .

Another example of Southern dedication to the philosophy of voluntarism and to freedom of association—which are at the heart of Carleton Putnam's protest against the desegregation decree—may be seen in the all-out attack on the National Association for the Advancement of Colored

People (N.A.A.C.P.) in some of the Southern states. In a society in which citizens and public officials are zealously devoted to the maximization of personal freedom, people have the right to join associations for educational, charitable, mutual aid, civil liberties, and other purposes. But Southern practices contradict Southern protestations. Let us examine briefly several Supreme Court decisions in which the Southern practice stands out in total nakedness.

In *N.A.A.C.P.* v. *Alabama,* decided in 1958, the attorney general of Alabama sought an injunction in the state courts to oust the association from the state. He ordered the association to produce records and papers, including names and addresses of all of the association's members and agents in the state. The association produced all the records except the membership lists. As to those lists, the association contended that the state could not compel disclosure without violation of freedom of association.

Unanimously reversing the state courts that had upheld the action of the attorney general of Alabama, the United States Supreme Court, in an opinion by Justice Harlan, said that the association had the right to protect its membership lists on behalf of the right of the members to associate freely with others in the pursuit of their private interests. This right of the members—citizens of the state of Alabama—is protected by the constitutional liberty to engage in association for the advancement of beliefs and ideas pertaining to political, economic, religious, or cultural matters. The attorney general's order to produce the membership lists, supported by the coercive power of the state courts, must be regarded, said Justice Harlan,

> as entailing the likelihood of a substantial restraint upon the exercise by petitioner's members of their right to freedom of association. Petitioner has made an uncontroverted showing that on past occasions revelation of the identity of its rank-and-file members has exposed these members to economic reprisals, loss of employment, threat of physical coercion and other manifestations of public hostility. . . .
>
> We hold that the immunity from state scrutiny of membership lists which the Association claims on behalf of its members is here so related to the right of the members to pursue their lawful private interests privately and to associate freely with others in so doing as to come within the protection of the Fourteenth Amendment.

In another case, in which two Arkansas cities sought from the N.A.A.C.P. its list of members and contributors, the Supreme Court said:

> On this record it sufficiently appears that compulsory disclosure of the membership lists of the local branches of the National Association for the Advancement of Colored People would work a significant interference with the freedom of association of their members.

There was substantial uncontroverted evidence that public identification of persons in the community as members of the organization had been followed by harassment and threats of bodily harm. There was also evidence that fear of community hostility and economic reprisals that would follow public disclosure of the membership lists had discouraged new members from joining the organizations and induced former members to withdraw. This repressive effect, while in part the result of private attitudes and pressures, was brought to bear only after the exercise of governmental power had threatened to force disclosure of the members' names. . . . Thus, the threat of substantial government encroachment upon important and traditional aspects of individual freedom is neither speculative nor remote.

Before the Civil War the South was willing to repress and stifle the civil rights and liberties of all citizens in order to maintain slavery; today, much of the same antilibertarian atmosphere persists in an effort to maintain "freedom of association," by which is meant, of course, compulsory segregation of the races. The Aesopian language of the South and its protagonists often tends to create the impression that the South is, in fact, fighting for the fundamental liberties of Americans to live as they please, to associate as they please, that the struggle is to give effect to the ideal of "Live and let live!", although the record of the Southern states shows that, when it has been a question of race relations, they have not been willing to let this question be decided by each person for himself. Instead, the force of the states has interposed itself between man and man, just as today some of the Southern states attempt to interpose themselves between the citizen and the Constitution.

A statement against civil rights laws and fair employment practices acts concludes on the following deep and pious note:

When one's fellow men interpose force and compulsion between him and the Source of his being—whether by the device of government or otherwise—it amounts to interrupting his self-improvement, in conflict with what seems to be the Divine design. Man must be left free to discriminate and to exercise his freedom of choice. This freedom is a virtue and not a vice. And freedom of choice sows the seeds of peace rather than of conflict.

No mention is made of the Jim Crow laws and customs, of the Black Codes, of the private reprisals, of the economic sanctions that the South has used to deny "freedom of choice."

Nor does the South see that by encouraging flouting of the Constitution in the name of voluntarism, freedom of association, and freedom to discriminate, it is sowing the dragon's teeth of criminality and anarchy; for when children see that their parents have no respect for fundamental law, they cannot help but draw the inference that man lives by might and not

by right, that an ounce of force may be worth more than a pound of constitutional law. Enforcement of law in itself is an instrument that aids voluntarism, for when it is certain that "every one who breaks the law will be
dealt with by the law, the less will the power of coercion be felt. The more
that resistance is seen to be hopeless, the more can the use of force remain
latent."

Often, when these arguments are made against the South, the point is
made that there is also racial discrimination in the North, and the inference
is drawn that the struggle is not really over civil rights but is rather a sectional feud. Of course there is discrimination in the North, but the orders
of magnitude are altogether different. While in the North one needs to look
for discrimination—and if one looks for it, he will find it—in the South
one needs to look for instances of nondiscrimination—and if one looks for
such instances, he will find them. . . .

The American people—through Congress, through the Supreme
Court, through states' civil rights and fair employment practices acts, through
executive action affecting the military and civilian population, and through
a Civil War that was the bloodiest and costliest war in American history—
have rejected the slavery arguments for the inherent inferiority of the Negro
race. With the ending of slavery, a hundred years ago, there should have
come an end to the incidents and badges of slavery, concretized in racial
segregation enforced by state law and custom. For these badges and incidents of slavery were based on an immoral opinion of what human nature
is. Now Americans must still teach one another what it means to be a
human being. The choice is not between law as a means and education as
a means; for the law is itself a teaching device and education is itself an
enforcing device. The disagreements are only superficially over the means.
The real disagreements are over the ends—the inclusion of the Negro race
in the community of citizens and in the communion of human beings. But
in this instance, end and means are inextricably intertwined; for the Constitution, which is a law, demands that the school shall itself be a means
and an end: that it be a demonstration of the ideal of equality, and that it
contribute to the establishment of a society in which equality is a working
ideal. The question that *Ecclesiasticus* asks about one's self can be asked
also of a nation: "Who will justify him that sinneth against his own soul?
and who will glorify him that dishonoreth his own life?" As the Negro struggles for freedom from dishonor and freedom from indignity, he struggles,
too, to free America from dishonor and from indignity. The demand that
the Negro makes today is as reasonable as that which Diogenes made of
Alexander: "Stand out of my sunshine!"

THE SOUTH MUST BE LEFT ALONE[1]

James Fulbright

*

Senator James Fulbright is the distinguished chairman of the Senate Foreign Relations Committee. He was a Rhodes Scholar and, before entering Congress, served as president of the University of Arkansas. He is generally regarded by Northerners as the ablest Southerner in Congress. The brief comments below are excerpted from statements he made on the floor of the Senate in connection with pending civil-rights legislation. The typical Southerner will regard them as sincere. Northerners will see them as an example of the moral predicament in which enlightened Southern office holders find themselves and of the desperate devices to which they have recourse.

. . . racial relations in the South, at which this proposed [civil rights] legislation is directed, will be sacrificed again on the altar of political expediency. Before the Supreme Court desegregation decision of 1954, we were making real progress in creating better racial relations in the South. The lines of communication were open between the races, and real progress was being made in bringing about better economic and social conditions for the colored people. These accomplishments were made sometimes at the expense of similar treatment for the white people. For example, in my State, since 1945, 60 percent of our school construction money has been devoted to building modern educational facilities for the Negro schoolchildren. I realize that this emphasis was necessary to live up to the spirit of the "separate but equal" doctrine laid down in Plessy against Ferguson. The spirit of improvement which prevailed in the South before the 1954 Supreme Court decision has been badly trampled and abused by that decision and the subsequent agitation from groups outside the South. The dangerous atmosphere of resentment and distrust between the North and the South and the Negro and the white races cannot be cleared by enactment of additional sectional and class legislation. The split between the races created by the current political approach to racial problems may take generations to heal. It will never heal unless we accept the fact that progress in this area can be achieved only through good will, education, and mutual respect, which cannot be achieved through legislation or judicial orders. The South must be

---

[1]*Congressional Record,* Vol. 106, Pt. 3, 3992–3993.

left alone, to handle the problem as any human relationship problem must be resolved; by patience, understanding, and, above all, education. The continued treatment of our section as a conquered territory will create more fear, distrust, and turmoil and set back racial relations even further. Throughout the civil rights controversy over the last few years there has been a tragic misunderstanding of human instincts and impulses. The citizens of the South are prisoners of their environment. When sudden change is attempted to be imposed upon attitudes or principles deeply imbedded within them by inheritance, tradition, or environment they, as any other similar group, are likely to react almost as by involuntary reflex, and often violently. This is the basic factor which all proponents of this coercive legislation overlook, or refuse to recognize. It is a basic sociological truism that no law can be effective which does not take into consideration the conditions and attitudes in the community for which it is designed. Certainly the conditions and attitude of the South have not been considered or recognized in the present proposals. . . .

AN EPITAPH FOR DIXIE[1]

Harry Ashmore

Harry Ashmore, editor-in-chief of the Encyclopaedia Britannica, *came to national attention as editor of the Little Rock* Gazette *during the crisis that caused President Eisenhower to send federal troops to Little Rock. Ashmore was awarded a Pulitzer prize for distinguished service in the Little Rock integration controversy, as was the newspaper of which he was editor—the first double award in Pulitzer-prize history.*

The former editor of Arkansas's leading newspaper views the travail of the South in a different light than does its distinguished senator.

. . . In the private places of their minds many white Southerners would agree with Albert Dent, the Negro president of Dillard University, who has said that in retrospect they would one day look upon the Supreme Court's segregation decisions as the beginning of their own emancipation—the dawn of the day when they may at last put down the spiritual burden that

---

[1](New York: W. W. Norton & Company, Inc., 1957), pp. 20–25. Copyright 1957, 1958 by Harry S. Ashmore. Reprinted by permission.

comes with being on the wrong side of a moral issue. But at the moment the South faces the practical problem of creating a new social order to replace a system already eroded to the point where effective communication between the races no longer exists.

The void is not unique to the South. In the new Negro ghettoes that have mushroomed in all the great industrial centers of the nation, colored people still live apart, behind barriers of extralegal segregation. For the mass the migration of the last generation has been horizontal; only the outstanding few have begun vertical ascent in the social structure. But there is a fundamental difference. The non-South, newly confronted with large concentrations of Negroes, has found their accommodation on terms of full equality a problem, but insists that it can and will be solved; the South so far has simply refused to face it.

So, outwardly, the old tragic pattern repeats itself. In 1958, as in 1860, the region finds itself standing alone in naked defiance of the nation's declared public policy. Now, as then, the border states have fallen away to go with the Union; the roll call of states that voluntarily abandoned segregation in the wake of the 1954 Supreme Court decision has a historic ring: Delaware, Maryland, the District of Columbia, West Virginia, Kentucky, Missouri, and Oklahoma.

Briefly the Upper South wavered, but in the end its leaders bowed to the Deep South. Now Byrd of Virginia marches with Talmadge of Georgia, Fulbright of Arkansas with Eastland of Mississippi; the moderate voices are stilled and the hotspurs are in the saddle. Once again a solid political front extends from the Potomac to the Rio Grande.

But behind the front the South is far from solid. A great deal, of course, depends upon where you are. In the nature of the distribution of population, and the local political situation, a man is likely to be more excited in Louisiana than in Tennessee, in Alabama than in North Carolina. Out on the fringes the new Southern cause has generated considerable passion; in the rural places the hot-eyed orators once again holler nigger and conjure up their evil visions. But the cold atavistic wind of fear has produced more bewilderment than anger. The prevailing mood is escapist; actuality is not yet at hand, and most Southerners still hope that somehow it will go away.

This time around even those who have mounted the barricades know, and privately concede, that the cause was lost before it was launched; there is no glory here, only bitterness. The battlecry is not "On to victory" but "Not in this generation." This rearguard action has been aptly described by Ralph McGill of the *Atlanta Constitution* as guerrilla fighting among the ruins of the old segregated society; it can be brutal, and it can delay the orderly process of transition, but it cannot turn back the forces that are reshaping the Southern region in the nation's image.

The primary battleground will be in the courts, the legislatures, and the Congress; and a generation of litigation is in prospect. But no people can live forever with an impasse and—sooner in the Upper South than the Deep—the effort will be resumed to find a rational means of adjusting the attitude of the prevailing white majority, which is not yet willing to accept the Negro as an equal, to that of the colored minority, which is no longer willing to accept anything less.

The task, as I have suggested, is complicated by the breakdown of communication between the races—the drawing apart which began when the Negro rejected those social conventions that carry with them a connotation of inferiority. But bridges have been erected, and despite the alarums and excursions of the moment, they still stand and there is traffic across them. At the top level of the educational structure, in the graduate schools of most Southern universities, Negroes and whites have been studying together for almost a decade. On the political front, the emergence of the Negro as a voting citizen has given him new leverage on the machinery of government; Negroes have not yet achieved public office in significant number, but they have found their place in the private places where campaign strategy is plotted. The court decisions have served to give the moral issue of segregation a new focus, and there is great ferment in the churches. The Southern denominations, Protestant and Catholic, including those that split off from their parent bodies in the Civil War, have now taken the occasion to affirm their belief that forced racial segregation is contrary to the Christian ethic.

There are those who profess a willingness to guard the approaches to these bridges with their lives, but they are a comparatively small minority; their support among the rank and file is passive, and it takes more than acquiescence to maintain a crusade. Once there were only two American attitudes toward the Negro: the passionate conviction that he must forthwith be admitted at every level of society as a matter of moral right, and the equally passionate conviction that survival of the white race required that he be barred forever from social intercourse with his masters. Today there is a third attitude: indifference. It may be seen in the Southern generation that fought the Second World War. Few of its members share their fathers' deep emotional concern with the crumbling of the peculiar institutions; if they cannot be aroused to battle for the rights of the downtrodden blacks, neither are they willing to pay the price of blind opposition to the Negro's effort to gain a higher place in the social scale. The view from the picture window of a suburban ranch house may be no clearer than that framed by the pillars of a porticoed veranda, but it is different—and as the older generation surrenders the places of power this is the view that increasingly will prevail.

So it does not seem to me premature to begin the preparation of an

epitaph for Dixie. Will the New South be a better place than the Old? Materially, almost certainly. Spiritually, perhaps. Behind the façade of harsh
words and extremist laws there is already emerging the pattern in which the
South will finally accommodate its dwindling Negro population as it moves
from second- to first-class citizenship; it will be imperfect but reasonably
effective, and in the end it will be far easier to achieve than the accommodation produced by trial and error in the bloodshot aftermath of Reconstruction. But the transition can be accomplished only at the expense of the
qualities that made the South distinctive, and cast it in the remarkable role
it has played in the history of the Republic. Perhaps, a generation from now
when the last shovelful of earth is patted down on the grave, we shall be
able to see the vanishing age more clearly, to examine its virtues without
being distracted by its faults. . . .

DE FACTO SEGREGATION[1]

James B. Conant

*Dr. James B. Conant, one-time president of Harvard Univer-
sity, distinguished scientist, and former ambassador to the German
Federal Republic, has in recent years turned his attention to public
education.*

His The American High School Today, The Child, the Parent,
and the State, *and* Education in the Junior High School Years *are
already classics.* Slums and Suburbs, *from which the following
selection is taken, is a commentary on metropolitan-area schools.*

. . . I should like to turn to a thorny subject of great concern to those
interested in improving Negro education. This is the question of whether or
not *de facto* segregation, as some like to call it, is detrimental to the education of the Negro. Closely related is a second question, namely, should the
school authorities endeavor to move Negro children into purely white
schools in order to have as many mixed schools as possible? The issue is a
very real one, and in a sense it is primarily political. At this point I must
make reference to the Supreme Court decisions of 1954 and 1955 because
of a tendency to regard them not only as the law of the land but as a sacred
text on education. Clearly even a unanimous opinion of the Supreme Court

[1]*Slums and Suburbs* (New York: McGraw-Hill Book Company, 1961), pp. 27–
32. Reprinted by permission.

fails to determine educational policy except within the framework set by the issues before the Court—in this case, the "segregation of children in public schools solely on the basis of race." It is necessary to point out this obvious fact, for I have heard the statement made that because the Supreme Court expressed the opinion that "Separate educational facilities are inherently unequal," all completely Negro schools are morally wrong and that there is essentially no difference between *de jure* segregation still found in almost all Southern communities and what some call *de facto* segregation in portions of the large Northern cities. The point is important and deserves discussion.

If one turns to the Supreme Court decision in the case of *Brown et al. v. Board of Education of Topeka* [347 U.S. 483 (1954], one finds the sentence I have just quoted about separate educational facilities. Taken out of context, the conclusion might be drawn that the justices declared separate educational facilities *for whatever reason provided* are morally wrong and if supported by tax funds are illegal. Yet on reading carefully the whole opinion, I think the key sentence is the question defined by the Court: "Does segregation of children in public schools *solely* on the basis of race, even though the physical facilities and other 'tangible' factors may be equal, deprive the children of the minority group of equal educational opportunities? We believe that it does." I have italicized the word "solely," as I presume to think it is the essential word. The justices appear to have expressed no view as to whether the pupils in a completely Negro school are deprived of equal educational opportunity if they are not assigned solely because of their race. In short, if one group of children is separated from another group because of the neighborhood in which they live, the fact of this separation is, of and by itself, no evidence of an inequality in education. Whether in fact the facilities and instruction are equal in a 100 per cent white school, a mixed school, and a 100 per cent Negro school in a large city is to be determined by examining the schools, not by appeal to phrases such as *de facto* segregation with the implication that it is to be condemned by all right-thinking people who condemn *de jure* segregation.

In some cities, political leaders have attempted to put pressure on the school authorities to have Negro children attend essentially white schools. In my judgment the cities in which the authorities have yielded to this pressure are on the wrong track. Those which have not done so, like Chicago, are more likely to make progress in improving Negro education. It is my belief that satisfactory education can be provided in an all-Negro school through the expenditure of more money for needed staff and facilities. Moreover, I believe that any sense of inferiority among the pupils caused by the absence of white children can be largely if not wholly eliminated in two ways: first, in all cities there will be at least some schools that are in fact mixed because of the nature of the neighborhood they serve;

second, throughout the city there ought to be an integrated staff of white and Negro teachers and administrators.

To insist that such solutions cannot be acceptable and to assume instead that the schooling of Negroes can be satisfactory only if in each schoolroom there are present some white children is to take an extremely defeatist view of Negro education in the large cities. The proposal to move any appreciable number of white children by bus into what are now Negro schools or to move all the Negro children in a Negro neighborhood into what are now white schools presents a transportation problem that is quite insoluble. An examination of the geography of the Negro and white sections of the large cities makes this evident. If some children are to be transported, the question arises which children and how many. I am not discussing here what seems to me to be a separate question; namely, the crossing of school attendance lines when waves of population movement create overcrowded conditions in one attendance area and vacancies in another. Nor am I justifying the gerrymandering of attendance lines; such a procedure amounts to separating pupils *solely* on the basis of race.

At the elementary school level the issue seems clear. To send young children day after day to distant schools by bus seems out of the question. It must be remembered that unless by the accident of population migration there are empty seats in the predominantly white schools, white children would have to be transported to Negro areas in order to free the necessary space. Clearly a complicated arrangement for moving large groups of young children around a city for the sake of mixing all the elementary schools is hardly worth discussing. At the high school level, the youth are certainly old enough to commute; one complication present in the elementary schools has disappeared. Still, a great network of transportation would have to be provided in a number of cities if the goal were to have every high school a mixed school. I have already noted the problem of determining the proper degree of admixture of white and Negro children. The more one considers the matter, the more one is convinced that children should not be manipulated for the purpose of seating Negro children in white schools or vice versa. To my mind, the city school superintendent is right who said he was in the education business and should not become involved in attempts to correct the consequences of voluntary segregated housing.

I know the argument is being made that crossing attendance lines should be permissive and without cost to the city and that the refusal of this right is a psychological blow to the pride of the members of the Negro race. But the reason for demanding such a privilege is the allegation that education in an all-Negro school to which pupils are not assigned *solely* on account of race is inherently inferior. Once this allegation is granted, the foundation for improving Negro education in the large cities is undermined. Since I believe the evidence indicates that it is the socio-economic situation, not the color of the children, which makes the Negro slum schools so difficult, the real issue is not racial integration but socio-economic integration.

Put another way, if there is no inherent difference in potential ability, and if educational opportunity is equal, the poor achievement of the children in both the Negro and white slums which I described earlier may be ascribed to their depressing cultural and socio-economic backgrounds. One might argue, therefore, that *all* slum schools ought to be integrated with schools in economically favored areas. If the body politic through its school board once sets out on a course of neighborhood desegregation, a good case can be made for transporting *white* children from slum schools to schools in high-income residential districts and vice versa.

Much as I admire the comprehensive high school in the town with one high school and see it as an instrument of democracy, it seems impossible for school authorities in a large city to create artificially a series of such schools. If a policy were to be adopted that, as an ideal, every neighborhood school should have a widely heterogeneous school population represented by all socio-economic backgrounds, school administrators would be forced to move children about as though they were pawns on a chessboard.

If good schools can exist only with a heterogeneous student population, one could argue just as logically that state authorities should adjust all school district lines so that the high-income suburban high school would include students from a neighboring depressed area. Another impossible proposal. Antithetical to our free society as I believe *de jure* segregation to be, I think it would be far better for those who are agitating for the deliberate mixing of children to accept *de facto* segregated schools as a consequence of a present housing situation and to work for the improvement of slum schools whether Negro or white. The problems in these schools are far more difficult to solve than in other schools, larger and better staffs should be available, more money is required. It is my firm belief that actions based on the premises I have outlined are in the best interests of the Negro and of the nation. Through the existence of at least some mixed schools, integrated teaching staffs, and increased expenditures in slum schools, I suggest that the education of Negroes in Northern cities can be made satisfactory and their status improved.

ON ENDING DE FACTO SEGREGATION[1]

Dan Dodson

Dan Dodson is a Texan by birth. He is director of the Center of Human Relations and Community Studies of New York University and a member of the faculty of the School of Education of that university. He has contributed to numerous community studies intended to reduce racial concentration in the schools. The following selection is from a statement presented to the United States Commission on Civil Rights.

. . . There is very little preparation made ordinarily for desegregation unless and until a community is brought to confrontation with the issue. Most of the time this involves conflict in some degree. It is illogical to assume that people who are comfortable in their dominant power role in the community will relinquish the community structure which they have created and on which their status depends without resistance. Confrontation is produced through legal decisions, community pressure, political pressure, or other such designs.

Professional school leadership is rarely instrumental in determining the policy of who is going to school with whom. This is largely a political science matter. It is usually settled by lawyers, judges, politicians, or non-school community leadership. Power, rather than educational merit, usually determines the outcome. Educators may be put through the paces doing studies or otherwise interpreting policies, but they are rarely the decision makers. Some have gotten great credit for what has been done once it is accomplished, but such accolades have frequently been because our press felt a great need to advertise our successes, rather than because of a front-line role played by the professional educators.

Because the initial stages of desegregation involve power groups which do not include the professional staff, it is highly important that there be a clear concise statement of policy on desegregation, and that it be rooted firmly in the authority of the community. In other words, there is the need for educators to feel the support of the authority of the community, and to feel secure that the authority is legitimate. It is not an accident that segregationists both in the South and the North try to attack the legitimacy of the

---

[1]Statement, Conference before the United States Commission on Civil Rights, Washington, D.C., May 4, 1962, pp. 138–141.

court's decisions. In a like manner there is need to feel that political leadership is not being pushed by organized pressure groups, rather than operating on their own initiative.

If groups who oppose desegregation feel that by "hollering" they will get a hearing, they are going to "holler." Implementers of public policy must move from clearly defined policy, and with mandates which are unequivocal. Sometimes these are from State departments of education. Other times they are from the courts. At others, the policy must be wrought out of the white heat of community controversy.

Although professional educators are usually not key persons so far as responsibility for decision making is concerned, their responsibility for interpretation of educational matters to power figures is important. In this role they could help enormously if they were clear about what they believe good education to be. Some places where they are ambivalent include:

a. The merit of a desegregated educational experience for all children—not just Negro children. A good case could be made that the major thing we are teaching our children in today's world is how to hide. We are hiding in lily-white suburbs, we are hiding in large-scale homogeneous redevelopment projects. We are hiding in our churches, according to many observers of the American scene. While there has been a great return to the church since the war, there is little indication that it represents a return to the Lord. Now, all of a sudden, the neighborhood school has become sacred. It might be added that the nearer Negroes get to it the more sacred it becomes. The concept was borrowed from the idea of the community school. The community school, however, never was intended to be a "turf" which shut out life. Its strength was because of the very opposite connotation. It was that all the community's children would go to school together.

b. The real issue before us is how to lead *all* the community's children to meaningful encounters with each other to the end that they develop the skills of citizenship commensurate with the demands of the times in which they live. Do educators really cherish this value as a part of the growth and development of all children? If they do, what weight are they prepared to give it in relation to other weights which enter into the decision as to where children shall attend school? For the most part, professional educational leadership has been remiss, in my judgment, in its leadership at this level. For the most part, permissive zoning, open enrollment, or transfer have been the concessions made to pressure from the community that desegregation be accomplished. This has meant that a few concerned parents of Negro background have had to take the responsibility for arranging these encounters for their children as a civil right, rather than that the school system arranged the encounters for all the children as a part of an educational experience. Only a few communities have resorted to open enrollment, redesignation of school plants—such as the Princeton plan, and use of urban renewal and other city planning resources to bring about desegregation as a school's responsibility for good education for all children.

c. A third thing about which there is confusion is the import of the de facto segregated school. Conant in *Slums and Suburbs* draws a clear distinction between de facto and de jure segregation, and indicates his belief that there is nothing wrong with segregated schools, provided they reflect the neighborhood; are not the result of assignment because of race; and provided they offer as high quality of education as do the other schools which are not segregated. On the other hand, there is little, if any, evidence to indicate that a de facto segregated school can be made equal in its educational program. If the entire culture conceives a "Jim Crow" school as inferior, does this in fact make it so? If it does, does not the requirement that a youth attend it violate his civil rights? I believe it does. The all-Negro schools tend to be older. The staff tend to be those marginal to the system—the novitiates and the superannuates. Academic standards fall as the school approaches all-Negro proportions. Morale which makes a climate conducive to learning is lost. The evidence is growing that segregation which is de facto is inherently inferior, the same as that which is by law. To this point, however, it seems easier for judges to see these limitations of racially segregated experiences than it is for educators. It would help if educators possessed more clarity about these basic factors of growth and development.

d. It would help if educators knew more of the skills of group leadership so that grouping practices within the school buildings did not frustrate the policy goals even where desegregation is accomplished. Some school systems capitalize on the disadvantage of the Negro youth because of his traumas of the past, and group on so-called ability bases, and provide a high degree of segregation. Sometimes one is led to think it is only coracial education in the same building. Homogeneous grouping is still another device to help us hide respectably in too many instances.

In summary, perhaps the major problem relates to how educators see their role in leading children in the growth and development process. Piaget has written perceptively of the art of matching up the maturation phases of youth's growth with experiences appropriate to each phase. Not the least important of this process is the development of self-other. It is important for youth to learn himself as against other-selves. It is equally important, however, that the ranges of "ourselves" be increasingly widened.

For us all there is the growing sense of alienation which leaves us with the feeling that a considerable part of us is not really "ourselves." Some have referred to this as "the stranger within us." I would submit that it is impossible to come to confrontation with this "stranger," which is the part of us, without coming to grips with the issue of the stranger among us. In other words, neither the minority nor the majority can psychologically cope with the alienation of his soul successfully without successfully facing the confrontation of "self-other" that is implied in race relations. Perhaps if educators could see this and be able to interpret it to the communities with whom they are planning, this would be the most important contribution of all. . . .

PART SIX
CONCLUSION

Running like a connecting thread through all these discussions is a vocabulary that includes the following: conscience, obligation, duty, responsibility, justice, virtue, commitment, the moral order, welfare, value and disvalue, good and evil, right and wrong. Clearly, men of intelligence and good will differ vigorously over the interpretation and application of these basic concepts. Many readers will ponder man's contentiousness and be content to let the case rest here. Of these, some will have found their own views reinforced and will defend them with renewed confidence. Others will have been changed by new and persuasive arguments. Still others who have had no position on certain critical issues may now find themselves with strong convictions. And here many will close the book.

However, some readers—the most thoughtful—will feel forced by the specific differences explored above to move beyond them and raise more fundamental questions. What is the basis of moral judgment? What are the sources of value? What are the criteria by reference to which good and bad, right and wrong may be distinguished? They will be thrust back, that is to say, upon ethics—philosophy.

Joseph Wood Krutch, whose comments conclude this collection, is not a professional philosopher. Although he is philosophical in interest and orientation, as is anyone who is interested in (and troubled about) the quality of American life and the criteria by means of which quality may be assessed, it is just as well that he ignores the technical and more recondite problems in which professional philosophers too often become lost.

Mr. Krutch may or may not have indicated the direction in which an answer to the questions posed above is to be sought. If, after reading him, we are still unsure of where the answer lies, a large literature is available to the more diligent. The rest will derive some comfort from having had the problem clearly formulated. They may console themselves with the words of Socrates—who likewise lacked answers: "In this respect only I believe myself to differ from men in general, and may perhaps claim to be wiser than they are—that whereas I know but little of the world below, I do not suppose that I know." At least such readers will have escaped what Socrates called "that ignorance of a disgraceful sort, the ignorance which is the conceit that a man knows what he does not know."

LIFE, LIBERTY AND THE
PURSUIT OF WELFARE[1]

Joseph Wood Krutch

*Before his retirement Joseph Wood Krutch was Professor of
Dramatic Literature at Columbia University and drama critic for
The Nation. He continues a long and productive life as a writer and
acute observer of the human scene by contributing a regular column
to The American Scholar. He has written* The Modern Temper
(1929), Samuel Johnson (1944), Thoreau (1948), The Measure
of Man (1954), *and* The Great Chain of Life (1956).

. . . What is the ultimate definition of welfare—in what does it consist, and who decides what it is? Or, to put the question in a simpler form:
Does the promotion of welfare mean giving people what they want or seem
to want or think they want, or does it consist in giving them what they ought
to have?

The answer implied in various specific welfare proposals is sometimes
the one and sometimes the other. But few have ever dared to put the question boldly and to give a positive answer one way or another. If welfare
means that people get what they want, then which wants of which people
come first? If welfare means giving them what they ought to have, then who
decides what they ought to have, and on the basis of what criteria is the
decision made?

This last is a very tough question indeed for an age which has rejected
absolutes and enthusiastically embraced both cultural and moral relativism.
One of the few bold answers I have ever encountered was given by David
Thompson, a lecturer in history at Cambridge University. "The welfare
state," said he, "exists to promote whatever the community regards as
beneficial and good. If the community regards automobiles, TV sets and
football pools as of greater value than better schools, more generous care
for old people, and creative use of leisure, then the democratic state will
provide more automobiles, TV sets and football pools."

In the course of the article Mr. Thompson gives the impression that
he has preferences of his own and that they are not what he believes to be

---

[1]*Saturday Evening Post,* July 15, 1961, pp. 19 ff. © 1961, The Curtis Publishing
Company. Reprinted by permission.

those of most people. But he does not appear to have his tongue in his cheek when he yields to the only definition of democracy and the only definition of welfare which his relativistic philosophy will permit. Like most of our contemporaries, he is unwilling to consider the possibility that what the community regards as valuable is not the only possible standard by which values may be judged. Nor, as a matter of fact, can anyone escape such a conviction unless he is willing to assume what most today refuse to assume, namely, that some basis for calling one thing intrinsically and absolutely better or righter or higher than another can be found somewhere: In nature, in reason or in the law of God—all of which are independent of either custom or majority opinion.

Refuse, as most sociologists, psychologists and anthropologists do refuse, to make such an assumption, and you are driven to the conclusion which Mr. Thompson accepts: That nothing is better or more desirable than anything else except insofar as more people want it. Thus he comes to defend democracy not because of any conviction that its decisions are wiser by some independent standards than those arrived at by other forms of government, but simply because any decision which has majority sanction is wise and right by the only possible definition of those terms.

If, as most people seem to assume, the normal is merely the average, if the good life is whatever the majority thinks or has been persuaded to think it is, if what men should do is whatever they do do, then it must follow that the desirable is whatever is most widely desired, and that democracy means that what the majority admires is necessarily to be called excellent. Mr. Thompson himself may prefer what he calls "the creative use of leisure" to TV sets and football pools, but he is too broad-minded—as we now call it—to suppose that such a preference is anything more than just another one of those tastes about which there is no disputing.

Laissez faire is generally supposed to describe the social theory diametrically opposed to that of the welfare state, but here one sort of *laissez faire* is exchanged for another. Though the economy is to be planned, society is to be allowed to drift intellectually and culturally with whatever economic, technological or other currents may vary in this direction or that.

Under democracy of the older sort the most fundamental right of the citizen was assumed to be the pursuit of happiness. The welfare state substitutes welfare—usually defined in material terms—for happiness. But by way of compensation it assures the citizen that his right is not merely to pursue happiness but to attain welfare; and under this arrangement we lose something as well as, perhaps, gain something. Though we may pursue whatever kind of happiness seems to us most worth pursuing, the welfare which is going to be assured us must be mass-produced, whether it is defined, under a dictatorship, as what the dictator thinks we ought to have, or, as in our society, by what the majority wants or has been persuaded to want.

If I object that to define welfare as whatever most people seem to want tends to mean more things and fewer ideas and, in general, tends toward the vulgarest possible conception of what constitutes the good life, I will be told that the answer is education—that, given enough schools, and schools that are good enough, the community will want what is truly most desirable; and that, if properly educated, it will provide for itself and ultimately reach a truly acceptable definition of welfare.

But despite all the schooling which Americans get, many of them do not seem to be very effectively learning any ideals or cultivating any interests other than those which seem to prevail among the uneducated. High-school graduates and college graduates also very frequently prefer television and shinier automobiles to any of the more intellectual and less material forms of welfare.

This fact brings us again up against the unanswered question and it suggests that education is failing to help people to achieve an acceptable definition of welfare for the same reason that the ideal of welfare itself is failing—because, in other words, we are unable to give any definition of education except the same kind of definition we give of welfare.

If students do not want classical literature, philosophy or science, if they do want sports, courses in movie appreciation and in the accepted social conventions, then, just as the other things constitute welfare, so these things must constitute education. Once the school, like the church, tended to embody a protest, or at least a countervailing influence, against what the other forces in society tended to make of that society and of man himself. The church held that man undisciplined by religion was wicked. The school held that unless he was educated, he would be ignorant and crass. But both the church and the school seem now to have fallen in love with the world as it is. They talk more and more about adjustment—and by that to mean "adjustment to things as they are."

The church halfheartedly, the school with real enthusiasm, gives up the attempt to direct society and is content to follow it, like the political leader who watches where the mob is going, puts himself at the head of it and says, "Follow me." Educators so-called have said, "Don't teach literary English; teach acceptable English." If, as a New York commission recently has proposed, children are not interested in the classics, don't waste time trying to arouse their interests; give them something they are interested in— teach them how to drive automobiles, how lipstick is best applied or, and this is part of one actual course in a Midwestern institution of learning, how to order groceries over the telephone.

These are the things many of the students will be doing; this is what their lives will be made up of. And if the business of education is to prepare for life, then these are the things that they ought to be taught. But the statement so commonly made, that education should be a preparation for life, is meaningless unless the kind of life it is supposed to prepare for is specified. If education is properly defined as hardly more than what anthropologists call "acculturation," then it is worth taking account of the fact that most children get much more of their education in this sense from advertisements, moving pictures, television, popular songs and so on, than they do from school. Preparation for life as the schools are tending to define it is much better accomplished by those institutions outside the school system than by those within it.

It would, of course, be inaccurate as well as unfair to leave the impression that there is no protest against the ideals and practices of the schools as typified by the examples just given. During the past few years such protests have grown from a whisper to an outcry. Various organizations, notably the Council for Basic Education, have been formed to combat the prevailing tendencies. The latter especially has conducted a vigorous campaign of propaganda, buttressed by news bulletins, which report both outrageous examples of denatured education and reforms in the directions of which it approves. . . .

Even more important perhaps is the fact that many parents have expressed their dissatisfaction and called for reform. The National Education Association, a very powerful and well entrenched group, has bitterly resented most such criticisms, but if the tide has not actually turned, it looks as though it might be on the point of turning.

Nevertheless, it is not enough merely to ridicule current extravagances, to call for a return to the three R's and to insist that education does not consist in miscellaneous instruction in such varied specific subjects as safety rules for automobilists, the use of consumer credit and the current conventions governing "dating." Neither is it enough to say only that schools should be concerned primarily with the intellect and that those who talk about "educating the whole child" seem to forget that his head is part of him. Any rational theory must be based upon some conviction that the man of whom the child is the father ought to be in mind, in taste and in conviction something more than what he will be if he is allowed to follow only his simplest inclinations and whatever happens to be the current conventions of his group. In other words, what is necessary is a standard of values. Education is simply not changing people as much as it should.

Many critics of our society have said that we lack standards. This has been said so often by preachers and by the makers of commencement addresses that we have almost stopped asking what, if anything, it means to say that our society "lacks standards." But that we do lack standards for welfare and standards for education is obvious. Welfare turns into vulgar materialism because we have no standard by which to measure it. Education fails because it also refuses to face the responsibility of saying in what education consists. Both tend to become merely what people seem to want.

To any such complaint most sociologists, psychologists and educators will shrug and say, "Perhaps. But where can you find standards other than those which are set by society itself? Who is arrogant enough to set them up? Where can the authority for such standards be found?"

Most periods of human history have believed that they could be found somewhere outside mere custom. They have usually been sought in one or all of three places: (1) In the revealed will of God; (2) in the operation of right reason, supposedly capable of defining good and evil; (3) in something permanent in human nature itself.

If I say this to the modern relativist, he replies that none of these things will any longer do. (1) God no longer exists. (2) Though man is capable of thinking instrumentally—that is to say, capable of scheming to get what he wants—there is no such thing as pure reason capable of reaching an absolute; and whenever men have thought they were doing so, they were, in fact, only rationalizing their desires or the customs of their particular country. (3) What we call "human nature" is merely the result of the conditioning of the individual, either by the society in which he lives or by the peculiar experiences which have happened to be his. Since neither God nor pure reason exists, and since human nature is infinitely variable, it is evident that morals are merely mores, or custom; that right reason is merely a rationalization of the prejudices of the individual or his society; and that human nature is merely what social circumstances have made it.

If all these characteristic modern convictions—or lack of convictions —are sound, then we must agree that whatever most people want is welfare, and that whatever pupils think they would least dislike doing in school is education. It is then useless to ask whether society is going in the right direction or whether men today are leading a good life. Nothing is absolutely better than anything else; things are what they are and will be what they will be, and we cannot control or direct. We must follow where events may lead us.

Before accepting this counsel of despair once and for all, it would be worth while to ask again if it really is certain that all three of the conceivable bases upon which some standard might be founded really are merely illusory. Each of them might be taken up in turn. One might ask again does God exist; one might ask again is right reason a mere figment of the imagination? Does human nature exist?

I here raise only what is perhaps the least difficult of all these questions—the last one. Granted that man may be conditioned in various ways, is it nevertheless true that there are limits to the extent to which he can be conditioned? Is it true that human nature tends to return to some norm, that it is not limitlessly conditionable? And is it possible that to some extent one thing is better or higher or more valuable than another because human nature tends persistently to think that it is? Or, to put the question in its most general form, is there a good life which might be loosely defined as "that which is in accord with the most fundamental and persistent wants, desires and needs of human nature"?

If ours is the richest and most powerful civilization that has ever existed, but if it is also the most anxious and ill at ease, is that in part because human nature needs something more than the wealth and power it has acquired? Is it possibly because human nature needs to believe just what modern thought has forbidden it to believe—that is, that morals are more than mores and that value judgments are more than merely rationalized prejudices? Once you insist that human nature as such does not exist, all the relativisms of our time—cultural, moral and social—inevitably follow. So, almost in desperation, let us ask again, "How good is the evidence that there is no such thing as human nature, that it is nothing but what experience or culture has made it?"

We must begin by remembering that the theory that human nature is nothing in itself is not actually new. In that enormously influential seventeenth-century book, *Leviathan* by Thomas Hobbes, the theory is already implicit. Hobbes attempts to account for all the phenomena of human life by assuming that there is nothing innate in man except the ability to receive stimuli, the ability to react to them and the desire to experience pleasure. There is, accordingly, nothing in the mind which has not been first in the senses. There are no such things as innate ideas or desires other than the simple desire to experience pleasure or to exercise power, which latter is said to be the same thing. Hence man becomes whatever experience makes him and, to use the phrase which became popular later, he is born with a blank slate upon which anything may be written.

We have enormously complicated this theory. We have drawn from it many deductions. But we have added little if anything essentially new. The whole of modern relativism seems to follow logically from Hobbes. If the human mind begins as a blank slate upon which anything may be written, then morals are only mores, our ideas of what is good or evil, just or unjust, beautiful or ugly, seemly or unseemly, are simply learned from the society in which we grow up. Nothing is eternally or inherently better than anything else—cultures vary from time to time and from place to place, but there is no external standard by which one may be judged as better than another. Incidentally, this complete abandonment of the right to judge we now commonly call "getting rid of our prejudices."

Contemporary anthropologists are fond of pointing out that what was considered right and desirable in one society was not so considered in another. Already by the end of the nineteenth century the historian Lecky could assert in his *History of European Morals* that there is no act which has not at one time or place been commanded as a duty and at another time or place forbidden as a sin—which is to say again that morals are only mores. Or, as a contemporary college textbook on psychology, written by a professor at the University of Southern California, puts it in a very short chapter on morals, "We call a man moral when he acts in accord with the laws and customs of his society"—by which definition, no doubt, a Nazi who took part in the persecution of the Jews would be a moral man, and one who did not would be an immoral one.

In a world which has so definitely rejected transcendental sanctions for either codes of morals or standards of value, the question whether human nature itself might supply them becomes enormously important. Is the usual negative answer really justifiable? Shall we one day swing again in a different direction and discover evidence now neglected that human nature is something in itself and does provide certain absolutes, valid at least within the human realm?

Have the anthropologists, for instance, been so preoccupied with the collection of materials to demonstrate the enormous differences between cultures that they have overlooked some things which are common to all? Have the experimental psychologists been so busy conditioning both men and animals that they have paid little attention to the resistance to conditioning which both can put up?

One little breeze in psychological doctrine might seem to point in this direction. Some skeptical psychologists have begun to wonder whether instinct on the one hand and the conditioned reflex on the other really can account for all of the behavior of living organisms. Certain sufficiently obvious facts have recently been re-emphasized.

Consider three of them which seem ludicrously simple. (1) Birds know by instinct how to fly and do not have to be taught, though mother birds sometimes seem to be teaching them. This is an example of instinct. (2) Seals do not instinctively know how to swim, but they learn very easily how to swim when they are taught by their parents. (3) You would have a very hard time indeed teaching most songbirds to swim. In other words, there are not just two classes of animal behavior—that which is inborn and that which is learned. There is also a third and possibly an enormously important one—namely, that behavior which is not inborn, though the ability to learn it easily is.

Considering such facts, some have begun to wonder whether the same might be true not only of skills but throughout the whole psychic realm of beliefs, tastes, motives, desires and needs. The thesis of the moral relativist is—to take an extreme case—that since no one is born with an innate idea that dishonesty and treachery are evil, then the conviction that they are evil can be nothing but the result of social education, and the opposite could just as easily have been taught, since value judgments are merely the rationalized prejudices of a given culture. May it not be true on the contrary that certain ideas are much more easily learned than others, and that what the eighteenth century called natural law, natural taste and the rest, is real —consisting in those beliefs and tastes which are most readily learned and most productive of health and happiness?

Perhaps you can condition an individual or a society to think and behave unnaturally just as you might possibly teach a robin to swim, but men who have been conditioned to think or behave unnaturally are unhappy—as unhappy and as inefficient as swimming robins. Perhaps Hobbes was right to the extent that no ideas are innate; but if the capacity to entertain readily some ideas and not others is innate, then it comes down to much the same thing. As Alexander Pope wrote nearly two and a half centuries ago, "Nature affords at least a glimmering light; the lines, though touched but faintly, are drawn right"—which is to say that the faint lines on the not quite blank slate constitute the reality behind the idea of a normal human being.

What Pope thought of as a metaphor may be an accurate biological statement. On the not quite blank slate the lines are touched too faintly to constitute an automatic instinct—they may even be destroyed by resolute conditioning and education—but they are rather like a latent image on a photographic plate, imperceptible until developed, though development will reveal only what already exists. If this is true, then there is such a thing as human nature. What we are born with is not a blank slate, but a film bearing already a latent image.

No doubt, as Pope himself said elsewhere, as experimental psychologists prove in the laboratory and as dictators as well as educators have too often demonstrated, the lines may be overlaid, and the unnatural may cease to seem a creature of hideous mien. But the conditioners have to work hard. Men, I suspect, believe much more readily in the reality of good and evil than they accept cultural relativism. Perhaps that means that belief in the reality of good and evil is according to nature and the modern tendency to dismiss them as mere prejudices of culture is fundamentally unnatural.

Such an assumption is at least one which no valid science forbids, and if we make even such a minimum assumption, we can be saved from the nihilism of the present-day social, cultural and moral relativism. We have again some point of reference now lacking in every inquiry which sets out to determine what kind of society or education or culture would be best for us. One thing is no longer as good as another provided only it can be shown or made to exist. We would no longer need to talk only about what can be done to men or what we might possibly be able to make them into, for we would be able to talk again about what men are in themselves.

We would have the beginning of a basis for a definition of welfare and a definition of education such as we now totally lack. We could say, for example, that welfare is not merely what people at a given moment believe they want, but that which experience has proved to be conducive to health and happiness.

We could say that education is not whatever a pupil thinks he wants in school, but that it is that which experience has shown will lead to a true understanding of his own nature, his own needs and his own wants. We could say the ideal of education is not conformity, not acculturation, but the full development of human nature's potentialities.

We could say that the normal is not the same as the average, but rather that the normal is normative—that is to say, that by which a thing is to be judged. And we could add that the normal human being is not the average human being, but the thing to which human nature aspires.

To attempt to determine what is part of permanent human nature is to undertake no easy task. To distinguish between what is truly natural and what is merely conditioned is extremely difficult. But to conclude that the question is actually a meaningful one is already to have concluded something vastly important. We talk much today about the extent to which we can control nature and our destiny, of how we have taken the future of the human race into our hands. But control implies some idea of the direction in which you want to go. We have the power, perhaps, but what good is the power unless we know what we want to do with it? "Give me a fulcrum for my lever, and I will move the world," said Archimedes. But a fulcrum for a lever is exactly what we lack. It implies a point of support which is necessary if you are going to move the world. We are trying to lever society without having any fulcrum on which to rest the lever, and, in the absence of any other, we might possibly find it in some understanding of fundamental human nature.

However much there may be still to learn about human nature, certain of its characteristics seem to me obvious enough to suggest some of the ways in which our society has been going wrong.

The first of these permanent characteristics seems to me to be that man is inveterately a maker of value judgments. His idea of what constitutes right and wrong conduct, of what is just or unjust, has been—perhaps will continue to be—extremely diverse. But he has nearly always believed that good and evil, justice and injustice, are realities which it is of the first importance to define and to cherish, while moral and cultural relativism—the idea that morals are nothing but mores and that one society is not absolutely better than another—is so profoundly unnatural a conviction that it has seldom been entertained for long and is destructive of human welfare when it is.

Closely related to the value judgment is the idea of justice. Men have varied enormously, irreconcilably, over the question of what constitutes justice. But they have nearly always believed that there is some such thing and that they should adhere to it. Part of that feeling is, I believe, the conviction that acts should have consequences, and that the way you are treated should be in some degree affected by the way in which you behave. A spoiled child, one who never pays any penalty for his follies or misdeeds, one who is given what some of the modern educators call "uncritical love," is usually an unhappy child because something fundamental in his human nature tells him that acts should have consequences and makes him profoundly uneasy in a world where they do not.

Similarly I believe that a society is unhappy if it holds—as so many sociologists now profess to hold—that no man should be held responsible for his imprudences or his crimes. He may be glad to escape those consequences, but he is finding himself in a world without justice, in a world where the way in which you act has no effect upon the way in which you are treated. And I believe that, like the spoiled child, he is profoundly uneasy in that unnatural situation.

I believe that it is also in accord with fundamental human nature to want some goods other than the material, that a society which defines the good life as merely a high standard of living and then defines the high standard of living in terms of material things alone is one which, in that respect, is denying expression to a fundamental characteristic of man. Few societies, whether primitive or not, have ever accepted the belief that welfare thus narrowly defined is the one and only supreme good. Men have sought all sorts of other things—they have sought God, they have sought beauty, they have sought truth or they have sought glory, militarily or otherwise. They have sought adventure; they have even—so anthropologists tell us—sometimes believed that a large collection of dried human heads was the thing in all the world most worth having. But seldom if ever, so it seems to me, have they confessedly sought only what is now called "welfare."

This is a mere beginning. You may dispute, if you like, even the few general statements I have made about permanent human nature. But if you admit that some things are and some things are not in accord with human nature, then you have grasped an instrument capable of doing something which few men today seem able to do, namely, attempt a rational criticism of things as they are.